PALANPUR: the Economy of an Indian Village

by C. J. Bliss and N. H. Stern

CLARENDON PRESS · OXFORD · 1982

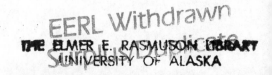

Oxford University Press, Walton Street, Oxford OX2 6DP
London Glasgow New York Toronto
Delhi Bombay Calcutta Madras Karachi
Kuala Lumpur Singapore Hong Kong Tokyo
Nairobi Dar es Salaam Cape Town
Melbourne Auckland

and associates in
Beirut Berlin Ibadan Mexico City Nicosia

Published in the United States by
Oxford University Press, New York

British Library Cataloguing in Publication Data
Bliss, Christopher J.,
Palanpur
1. Palanpur, India (Uttar Pradesh)-
Economic conditions
1. Title   II. Stern, Nicholas Herbert
330.9'54'2   HC438.P/   80-4040T
ISBN 0-19-828419-5

Typesetting by India Offset Press, New Delhi
and printed in Great Britain
at the University Press, Oxford
by Eric Buckley
Printer to the University

For
S.S. Tyagi, Jr.
and V.K. Singh

Preface

This book is concerned with the study of an Indian village, particularly its agriculture, from the point of view of theories of economic development. Such a brief summary of its intent leaves much to be explained but it already indicates that we may expect a diverse audience and that some of our readers will know things which we shall have to explain for the benefit of others. With this in mind we have endeavoured to signpost the reader's way through the book so that he will know what to expect at each point. The chapters are divided into sections and at the start of a chapter a short introduction is provided in which is detailed what each section will contain. In Chapter 1 there is a plan of the book in which the subject matters of the various chapters are similarly described.

We shall not assume very much prior knowledge of India or of agriculture but we shall be assuming that our readers know something of economic theory. Generally, however, the demands on that knowledge will be moderate. The exceptions are to be found in Chapter 3, where some harder theory will be discussed and where we shall make use of mathematics. However, we doubt that the non-economist will be prohibited from understanding what we have to say by the difficulty of those passages. They may be skipped or scanned without losing hold of the argument, and the conclusions are readily intelligible whether or not the reader chooses to follow the argument in detail. A more continuous demand will be for an understanding of the basics of single-equation econometrics. As we make great use of that approach, it would be difficult to comprehend and assess our findings without a grasp of that method. We have taken care to help the reader with references to relevant readings on the economic theory and on some particular points concerning the econometrics. Despite there being some technical material in the volume, a large part of it will be readily comprehensible to any reader with a general interest in economics, including all of Chapters 1, 2, 4, and 10, and not a little of the other chapters.

Tables, figures, mathematical equations, and chapter sections are each numbered sequentially through a chapter. References to equations are within the chapter unless otherwise indicated. We shall sometimes refer to individual households by code numbers, for example 307. The first digit indicates the caste (see Table 2.1, p.12) and the second two digits the serial number within the caste.

A Glossary gives the meaning of technical terms and abbreviations, including Hindi words. We have generally preferred English to Hindi but have not avoided the use of Hindi words where they are frequently employed in the literature or where translations are not straightforward. Thus, for example, we refer to the main crop seasons as the *rabi* and the *kharif*, as do most writers on Indian agriculture, although 'winter season' and 'summer season' would be adequate English renderings. It would be difficult, on the other hand, to find a short translation of *zamindars* which carried with it a sense of the particular features of the institution which those men represented. Similarly, *dhobi* could be translated as 'washerman', but only at the cost of introducing misleading overtones.

Where we have referred to villagers by name we have made use of suitable aliases. By this means we have attempted to leave our respondents with some anonymity while lending an appropriate colour to our account of the village by the use of local names.

We have frequently employed the present tense in describing the village but strictly all such references, unless the context makes it clear that something else is intended, are to the position in the winter of 1974-5, and in the case of family data and land ownership, to the November of that winter.

As a very rough guide to the values of sums of money to which we shall refer, we note that during the time of our residence in the village one pound sterling was worth at the official exchange rate about 18.5 rupees (R18.5). The average income per household for the agricultural year 1974-5 was about 7000 rupees.

Our first application for support for our proposed project was made in the autumn of 1973. We arrived in Palanpur to establish ourselves and begin the collection of data at the end of September 1974. In the interim we examined some previous studies and talked to individuals with relevant knowledge and experience. Of particular help at that stage were members of UNRISD in Geneva and the IDS in Sussex. We visited UNRISD in April 1974 to discuss, with its organizer Andrew Pearse, the results of the UNDP Global 2 project on 'The Social and Economic Implications of the Large-Scale Introduction of High-Yielding Varieties of Food Grain'. As a part of the Global 2 project Dr. Roshan Singh of RBS College, Agra, carried out a valuable study (Roshan Singh, 1973) of wheat in Muzaffarnagar District of West U.P. The villages at which he looked were some of the candidates in our selection of a village for our own work.

We paid several visits to the IDS in Sussex where many individuals and the library facilities were very helpful. At this time we also spoke to Brian Farmer of the Centre for South Asian Studies at Cambridge University which was organizing a study of agricultural change in South India and Sri Lanka. He provided us with a number a useful suggestions, as did J.A. Allan of the Geography Department at SOAS, who had recently been working on Bulandshahr District of West U.P.

A preliminary journey was made to Delhi and Muzaffarnagar District of West U.P. in July 1974 to visit some villages which had emerged as possible candidates from Roshan Singh's work[1] and to look for research assistance. We went to India again in September 1974 and after considering and visiting several more villages we decided on Palanpur. The criteria on the basis of which we selected the village are described in Chapter 1. During this last period we concentrated on villages which had been studied previously by the AERC in Delhi University.

[1] We eventually abandoned Muzaffarnagar District because of the dominant role of sugar in the local agriculture.

Our two research investigators S. S. Tyagi Jr. and V. K. Singh were affiliated to the AERC (Delhi) and RBS College (Agra) respectively. S. S. Tyagi Jr. was from Bulandshahr District of West U.P. and was at the time residing in Delhi. He had an M.A. in economics from the University of Agra and considerable experience in the collection of data from villages. Dr. H. Laxminarayan, the Acting Director of the AERC, was kind enough to release him from his duties to accompany us on our visits to various villages in September 1974 and then to work with us during the study in Palanpur. V. K. Singh was from Mainpuri District in West U.P. and had an M.Sc. in agriculture from the RBS College in Agra. He also had experience in collection of agricultural statistics and had been actively involved in the management of the family farm.

From September to June S. S. Tyagi Jr. and V. K. Singh spent most of their time in residence in the village and we lived there for the majority of our time until we returned to England at the end of April 1975.

Sowing for the *rabi* season was from October to December [2]. When we arrived at the end of September, the *kharif* harvest was nearly completed and the *rabi* ploughing had begun. When we left at the end of April, much of the *rabi* harvest was already in. The harvest remained to be completed and post-harvest activities included threshing, winnowing, and marketing. The research investigators collected data up to the completion of these activities in June 1975. The life in the village is described in Chapters 1 and 2. Our living arrangements are outlined in § 1.1, and the details of the data we collected are given in § 1.2.

The coding and analysis of our data and the writing of this book were lengthy processes, which were spread over the following three years. We returned to Delhi and to Palanpur in August 1977 to present some results to seminars and to visit the village. This visit is described in Chapter 10.

From the very beginning of the idea of this study, through the collection and analysis of the data, to the eventual completion of the manuscript of this book, five years have passed. Looking back it seems to us that we have been continuously accumulating debts throughout those years; debts to the many people who have helped us with advice, encouragement, financial support, research assistance, and criticism (almost without exception sympathetic and constructive) of seminar presentations and drafts of chapters. At the start we were feeling our way and were sometimes very ill-informed. Yet we nearly always met with kindness, generosity in the sharing of knowledge, and warm encouragement. Because our debts are so many, we cannot mention all the individuals and institutions who helped us but we should like to record our thanks to the following.

The British Academy provided us with financial support under its Overseas Visiting Fellowship Programme to pay for travel to and from India and for the employment of our research assistants in India. The coding and analysis of our data were assisted by a grant from the SSRC under grant No. HR4141. Support for our work was forthcoming at various times from the Universities of Essex

[2] A description of the agricultural year is given in § 2.5.

and Warwick, from St. Catherine's College, Oxford, Nuffield College, Oxford, and the Ecole Polytechnique. Bliss was granted sabbatical leave from the University of Essex and Stern from St. Catherine's College, Oxford and from the University of Oxford. St. Catherine's College generously provided a term of additional leave. The libraries and personnel of the UNRISD, Geneva, and the IDS of the University of Sussex were invaluable at various times. The ISI, Delhi, played host to us during our stay in India and gave us the pleasure of talking about economics and lecturing on cost-benefit analysis to its graduate students during our visits to the capital. The AERC in the University of Delhi and its Acting Director, Dr. H. Laxminarayan, helped us by providing access to the numerous studies of villages carried out under its auspices, thus assisting us in the choice of a village.

Without our research assistants in India, S. S. Tyagi Jr. and V. K. Singh, being regularly able to do more than anyone could reasonaly expect of them our study would never have been completed. They more than justified the confidence that we placed in them; indeed we underestimated what they could achieve, and with the benefit of hindsight, there is little doubt that they could have achieved more even than the large demands made of them.

Our research assistants in England, David Deans and Jay Kynch, were highly resourceful and thorough in their work during a whole year. Without their energies and skill we might have become disheartened by the amount of work involved in the coding and analysis of our data. We also benefited greatly from the assistance of Rachel Britton, Monica Dowley, Padmini Kurukurartchy, Clive Payne, and Kumah Tambyraja.

Our friends in India who were generous with their help and hospitality include Mrinal Datta-Chaudhuri, S. D. Gupta, BDO Chandausi, Sri Kumar of IFFCO, Moradabad, Dharma Kumar, Lovraj Kumar, Rosaleen Mulji, and Sudhir Mulji. Advice and encouragement were freely given by J. A. Allan, Ritu Anand, Sudhir Anand, Veena Das, Brian Farmer, Roy Laishley, Michael Lipton, Michael Moore, Andrew Pearse, A. K. Sen, and Roshan Singh.

We circulated rough drafts of chapters and benefited greatly from detailed and constructive comments from A. B. Atkinson, P. K. Bardhan, Meghnad Desai, Peter Diamond, Gordon Hughes, John Knight, Sudhir Mulji, David Newbery, and G. Saini. Clive Bell and T. N. Srinivasan provided advice and encouragement from the conception of the project until its end and we owe them a special debt.

The manuscript has been ably typed through many drafts by Kerrie Beale, Jean Brotherhood, Audrey Hiscock, Vera Kastner, Phyllis Pattenden, Shirley Patterson, Ann Sampson, Yvonne Slater, and Penny Sylvester and greatly improved by the able sub-editing of Lindley Lloyd.

Finally we thank the villagers of Palanpur who greeted us and our enquiries with good humour and warm friendliness.

Contents

1

Introduction

§ 1.0 The Study

The analysis of rural markets and the behaviour of those involved in them should be at the centre of the study of the economies of poor countries. This book is about such markets and our main purpose is to examine and develop theories relating to them in the context of an Indian village. At the same time we wish to employ these theories and the experience of a particular village to analyse some of the many contradictory and grand assertions about the nature and consequences of the 'Green Revolution'.

Confining the study to a single village had several attractions. It allowed, through our residence in the village, a close involvement with the households which formed the village and with the village institutions; the detailed knowledge that flowed from this involvement will be repeatedly reflected in the analysis to follow. We also wished to be closely involved in the day-to-day collection of the data. It was indeed very helpful in the analysis of the numbers which emerged to know in detail how they were assembled. These advantages went with the pleasure which we hoped would come from settling in one place and getting to know the people well.

The major disadvantage of studying a single village is that it is not easy to know whether what one observes holds for other villages. We did what we could to form a judgement of the seriousness of this problem by visiting other villages and regions and by looking at other studies.

Given our decision to study one village, the two objectives which we have described led us to look for a certain kind of village. The criteria which needed satisfying were as follows. There should be a good survey of the village from the late 1950s or early 1960s to provide us with background information on the village as it had been in the past and to allow us to make inferences concerning trends and changes. The village should not be notably odd—there are villages characterized by some peculiar feature, such as the dominance of an unusual craft or crop, which sets them apart from other villages. On the other hand, there is no such thing as the representative U.P. village and we were not looking for it. The village should be large enough to encompass a certain amount of variety but not too large to permit a detailed study including all its households. The cropping pattern was important; since the development and application of the new varieties of seed in India is especially associated with wheat, we wanted wheat to be a major crop and to be produced both for the market and for home consumption. For our convenience (we were lecturing from time to time at the Indian Statistical Institute in Delhi) we wanted the village to be accessible from Delhi but at the same time not so close to the capital, or to any other major centres of population, as to have its economy importantly influenced by the city. We hoped that tenancy would be common since, as a topic of much theoretical investigation, that subject was one of our main interests. We had to be able to make suitable arrangements for the accommodation of a team of four people and we took the view that the ideal would be independent living arrangements so that we should not be seen by the villagers as guests and associates of one particular household, of one caste, or of the richer farmers. Naturally we hoped for a hospitable village where we would be generally welcomed, where we would not become involved in feuds within the village, and where we would pass our time enjoyably. It transpired that Palanpur met these criteria admirably, as described below.

§1.1 General Description

Palanpur lies in the Moradabad District of West U.P., thirteen kilometres north of the town Chandausi, at the point 78°46′E 28°33′N. The city of Moradabad is thirty-one kilometres to the north. A railway line connects Moradabad to Chandausi and one of the small stations on this line serves a much larger village than Palanpur, called Jargaon, four kilometres to the west of the railway line. Palanpur is beside the railway line at Jargaon station.

For Palanpur the railway serves the function which for most villages would be provided by a nearby road. The nearest metalled road to Palanpur is three kilometres away and is little used by the villagers. Because the railway is the means of access to towns and to some other villages most of those who work outside the village use it as a means of transport. At the time of our survey thirty-three workers were recorded as in employment outside the village, but some of this employment was intermittent, and it was in several towns and villages, mostly within ten kilometres of Palanpur. Such distances are regularly covered by commuting workers in India who do not have the benefit of a railway so in this regard the railway is not especially significant. However four workers from Palanpur commuted daily to Moradabad, and without the railway or a bus service this would of course have been impossible. Whilst it is important as a link and provides a few jobs, the railway does not exert an influence very different from that which would be associated with a road.

By rail from Delhi, a distance of 196 kilometres, it takes at least seven hours to reach Palanpur and the journey is an inconvenient one because Jargaon Station is not a stopping point for long-distance trains. Delhi then is a very long way away and hardly any villagers have been there. Moradabad, a major city with a population of over 200,000, is only about one hour away and will have been visited at one time or another by several villagers, if only because the Collector (see Glossary) has his office and residence there. Chandausi is of more importance to Palanpur than is Moradabad and its market is the major location for both buying and selling for the farmers of Palanpur.

In November 1974 there were in Palanpur 112 agricultural households, defined as those owning or cultivating land or selling agricultural labour, comprising 762 persons including children. These are the households[1] covered by our

---

[1] One household sold its (small) landholding and left the village in November 1974. Thus we have details of family composition for 112 households but details concerning agricultural activities for

household survey (see § 1.2). The number of households was small enough to allow for checks on the accuracy of the information, and we found considerable variations between households with regard to every feature examined.

In the north and west of India, the main cereal crop is wheat which is grown in the *rabi* season. It does not follow, however, that wheat will be found to be the main crop in any particular village in U.P. The cultivation of sugar cane is of substantial importance in the region and where conditions are favourable, which means where there is plentiful irrigation and a mill is close by, the tendency is for wheat to be displaced by sugar as the main crop. In Palanpur, however, the main crop is wheat.

Our living arrangements in the village were just what we had hoped to achieve. A Co-operative Union Seed Store, hereafter referred to as the Seed Store, serving several local villages including Palanpur, stands on the edge of the village close to the railway line. It is a large concrete building mostly given over to storage rooms and an office. On top of this building is a balcony, two small rooms, and a little kitchen. These were intended to provide a residence for the manager of the Seed Store who, however, prefers to live in Chandausi and thus the rooms were empty. With the permission of the Block Development Officer and the Seed Store manager himself we were allowed to reside above the Seed Store. There we made ourselves comfortable, living simply but lacking nothing essential. We were fortunate to obtain the services of a cook from the village who had at one time worked in a hotel in Chandausi. His caste was *Dhimar* (for an explanation of the castes see the appendix to Chapter 2, and the Glossary). As well as preparing food for us and maintaining a good standard of hygiene he also served as a go-between and messenger. He was very well-liked by all the villagers and we could not have wished for a better ambassador. Thus we were able to achieve our aim of living in the village and in close contact with its life without becoming an appendage to a village family.

Just as we were fortunate in our living arrangements so we were fortunate in the welcome that the villagers of Palanpur extended to us. No doubt our presence provided a certain diversion, at least for a short while. It would have been possible for the villagers to see us as a threat. Our motives in coming to live in a poor village were for many not easy to understand. When we explained that we had come to do research and that we were interested in their agricultural practices, this not unnaturally struck some of them as rather peculiar. There were fanciful theories in circulation to explain our presence. One farmer, for example, told our research investigators (apparently in seriousness) that the British were coming back and we were an advance party. Regardless of what they believed concerning our motives it was obviously important that we should be able to reassure them that we would not make any report to the government on, for example, illegal land-leasing arrangements. We believe that in most cases we were able eventually to dispel the fears. Most of the villagers did not shrink, even at the outset, from revealing to us possibly damaging information

111. Throughout this chapter our population of households will have 112 members, subsequently it will have 111.

and even those who were more cautious and waited until they knew us better never showed any resentment to us personally for prying into their lives. In general we were given a warm welcome and nothing that could be done for us was too much trouble.

Some U.P. villages are feud-ridden and crime is very common. The Moradabad District has a bad reputation for serious crime, and Palanpur has had its feuds in the past and has witnessed criminal acts. But for the most part quarrels have stopped short of violence and while we were in the village it was harmonious and peaceful, even though the after-effects of some past feuds were still in evidence (for examples see the appendix to Chapter 2).

Theories of development economics should have the power to explain what one finds in a village such as Palanpur. It is not a rich village but it is not poor in comparison with other villages in the area. It is not a village of 'progressive farmers' but there are some farmers whose agricultural practices are quite good[2] and many others whose agricultural practices are moderate or poor by the standards of published recommendations. The caste composition of the village is not unusual for West U.P. except for the presence of one caste, the *Passis*, who migrated to Palanpur in the 1920s and 1930s. There are no *Brahmins* in the village but this is not uncommon. When the need is felt for a *Brahmin* to perform a religious ceremony he comes in from a nearby village. In the matters of education, health, and awareness of the outside world Palanpur might strike a European or an urban middle-class Indian as backward but the same would be said of most other villages in the region. It is interesting that the local officials told us that Palanpur was one of the worst villages under their care and tried to discourage us from making it the subject of our study. Later on it was not clear to us why they had such a low opinion of the village; perhaps they would have preferred us to look at a 'progressive' village and Palanpur is certainly not that. However, having failed to discourage us they remained both co-operative and helpful.

We came to know of Palanpur from a study of the village that was conducted by the Agricultural Economic Research Centre (AERC) of the University of Delhi (see Ansari, 1964). This study covered the agricultural year 1957–8 and we shall refer to it as the 1957–8 study. There was a follow-up study for the year 1962–3 but this never came to fruition in a published report. However we were fortunate to gain access to some of the data gathered for that study and while recognizing that it is not complete we have found it useful as a check on our impressions. We shall refer to this as the 1962–3 survey. The survey of Palanpur for 1957–8 is a very thorough piece of work and as our knowledge of the village grew we were impressed by how much the investigators had discovered in three months. In our own study we were to ask different questions, to adopt different approaches, and to pursue different ideas from those which feature in the AERC study. But without an authoritative survey of the village in the past we would often have been at a loss in assessing our own observations. We offer a

---

[2] We are using the term 'good' in connection with agricultural practice loosely here. Later we shall discuss how it can be made more precise (see § 7.3).

comparison between our own findings and those from the 1957−8 study in § 2.6 and discuss the changes which occurred in the intervening seventeen years. There was a connection between the team that carried out the 1957−8 study and our own team in that one of our investigators, S. S. Tyagi Jr., is the brother of the man who collected the data for the original study.

§ 1.2 The Collection of the Data

The two major calls on the research time of the team whilst in the village were the collection of data on activities on our sample of wheat plots, and the household survey. Information was collected, however, in a number of additional ways. We had lengthy discussions with the cultivators of the sample wheat plots concerning the circumstances and motivations relating to their input decisions. These discussion sessions are described in § 4.7 and § 8.5. We visited several local villages with a list of fairly general questions on caste composition and cultivation practices. These visits are described in § 2.A.5. And on our return to the village in August 1977 we had a number of detailed questions arising from our analysis which we asked to a selection of villagers. These discussions are described in Chapter 10.

Our sample of forty-seven plots of land growing wheat was selected randomly from a map. We recorded activities on these plots in considerable detail throughout the *rabi* season. The selection of these plots and the method of data collection are described in § 7.2.

The second major undertaking whilst in the village in 1974 − 5 was the household survey. We collected a great deal of information on each of those households which were involved in agriculture in any of the following sense: it owned land, cultivated land, or provided agricultural labour. This definition included 112 of the 118 households of the village in November 1974. For the remaining six we have data only on the number and characteristics of family members. The heads of the six non-agricultural households comprised two shopkeepers, a barber, a carpenter, a railway gangman, and a sweeper.

We collected data in the household survey on the following: (i) name and caste of head of household; (ii) detail of family members including relation to head, age, sex, marital status, education, and nature of occupation; (iii) detail of land owned in *rabi* 1974−5 including map references, irrigation facilities, and type of soil, together with cropping pattern including type of seed; (iv) same detail for land cultivated in *rabi* 1974−5 and in addition whether it was leased-in, if so from whom, and details of the tenancy agreement; (v) similar information as for (iii) and (iv) for *kharif* 1974; (vi) we asked also for the same information for seasons prior to *kharif* 1974, but whilst some farmers could recall several years back many were unable to remember; (vii) farm assets including draught and other animals; (viii) ownership of water resources—wells, pumping sets, and so on; (ix) labour hired out and in, total days month-by-month, and payments for agricultural and non-agricultural work separately (household services bought and sold were not included); (x) use of fertilizer and purchased irrigation (and costs) on individual plots; (xi) yield of individual plots; (xii) production of milk in kilogrammes month-by-month together with purchased feed; (xiii) ownership of consumer durables; (xiv) indebtedness.

These data were assembled gradually during the full course of our stay in the village. The family data were all completed by the end of November 1974, while the data on yields for the 1974–5 *rabi* had to wait until the end. The data were collected during visits to the households, during encounters while the householders were at work in the fields, and when they called on us in our own accommodation. Different parts of the data required different approaches to collection. Some, such as the family data, were collected at one go whilst the labour data, for example, required regular monitoring. Tenancy was a major feature of our study and we took great care with the accuracy of our data concerning it. This demanded alertness, cross-checking, and continual observation of what was going on. We always obtained information both from the landlord and from the tenant, and often from friends and relatives, and we in turn observed directly who was cultivating particular plots. Collection of these data was a sensitive matter and we had to proceed carefully and slowly. For further discussion of this problem, and its delicacy, see § 2.4.

We left the collection from households of data on indebtedness[3] until the final stages. We knew that these questions might cause embarrassment and we wanted to wait until we were as well-known and trusted as possible.

In addition to the formal questions described above we conversed regularly with the villagers, observed day-to-day happenings, and took notes of what we learnt. All our questionnaires contained space for notes and remarks on peculiarities and points of special interest concerning plot or cultivator. This non-systematic information was very useful and it is drawn on frequently in the pages that follow.

The information collected in the village is used to examine various theories and issues commonly discussed by students of economic development, as well as in the formation of some of our own ideas. We were particularly interested in tenancy and were fortunate that it proved possible to assemble a lot of accurate information on this subject. Other important concerns were with theories of the detailed functioning of labour markets,[4] and in general with knowledge, objectives, and decision-making by households under conditions of uncertainty.

We came to the village with certain theories in mind which we tried to put to empirical test. On the other hand, we also wanted to see how well we could do, using theories and ideas that existed or that might develop, at explaining things that we should discover in the village.

[3] The Seed Store manager gave us data on loans from the Co-operative to Palanpur households. See § 4.4.

[4] One theory that had interested us very much was the theory of 'efficiency wages' (see § 3.3). Palanpur turned out not to be a very fruitful place for testing this theory. However, we talked about it while we were there and have set out our ideas and findings on this subject elsewhere (see Bliss and Stern, 1978).

Our major theoretical interests were with decisions concerning outputs and inputs, and with tenancy. In our discussions of the farmer we shall pay attention to the objectives, constraints, and awareness of the individual decision-maker and shall examine especially choice under uncertainty. On tenancy we shall be particularly concerned with the choice of how much land to rent in or out, the terms of tenancy, and the difference in output levels on tenanted and untenanted plots. Our special interest in wheat was generated both by its importance in production and consumption and in its prominent role in the controversial 'Green Revolution'.

§ 1.3 Plan of the Book

In the next chapter we describe the village, its history, and its institutions. Chapter 3 is concerned with those theories of rural economies which were examined in our empirical work or which were of assistance in understanding what we found. In addition we provide a brief review of certain issues which commonly occur in discussions of Indian agriculture and on which we can comment in the light of our experience in Palanpur. The markets for factors in Palanpur are discussed in some detail in Chapter 4.

The following four chapters provide a statistical analysis of our data: on tenancy, Chapter 5; on outputs and inputs, Chapter 6; and on the sample wheat plots, Chapters 7 and 8. Chapter 9 contains our reflections on theory following upon our empirical investigations. Chapter 10 deals with various matters concerning the village after 1975, including a report on our visit in August 1977, and brings the book to a close.

2

The Village

§ 2.0 Introduction

The setting of our study is one village, Palanpur. We give in this chapter a description of the broad features of the life and economy of Palanpur. The purpose of this description is to provide essential background to the formal studies of later chapters. For example, much of the analysis of those chapters will use the household as the basic unit of observation and it is important to understand what that unit comprises. And our comments on past changes and future developments will be based in part on comparisons with previous studies of the village; thus the reader will want to know something of those studies. We have included in the main body of the chapter those aspects to which frequent reference will be made, reserving for the appendix to this chapter those to which reference is only occasional. Some of the material included in the appendix may be of particular interest to students of Indian agriculture who require more detail concerning certain features than other readers will want. Some important aspects of the village economy which are examined in detail in later chapters, in particular Chapter 4, are passed over here. Examples are credit (§ 4.3), the labour market (§ 4.1), and water sources (§ 4.4).

The contents of the sections are summarized as follows:
§ 2.1 General description of the village
§ 2.2 The structure of the population and households
§ 2.3 Land-ownership
§ 2.4 Tenancy
§ 2.5 Cropping patterns
§ 2.6 Comparison with previous studies
§ 2.7 Concluding remarks
Appendix to Chapter 2.

§ 2.1 General description of the village

On arrival at Jargaon Station, Palanpur looks much like other villages one would have passed on the way. It is quite an attractive village and there are many trees on its railway side (see map Fig. 2.1). The village is very compact (approximately 1 × ½ km). Most houses are constructed from dried mud but a few of the larger houses are made mainly from brick. Typically there are no windows looking outwards: living areas open onto a courtyard. Cooking often takes place in these courtyards and animals are kept there. The courtyards vary from the tiny to the quite spacious, varying even more than the houses in size. Access to the courtyard is always by one door which often can be securely barred and the richer houses run to a small reception area immediately behind the door.

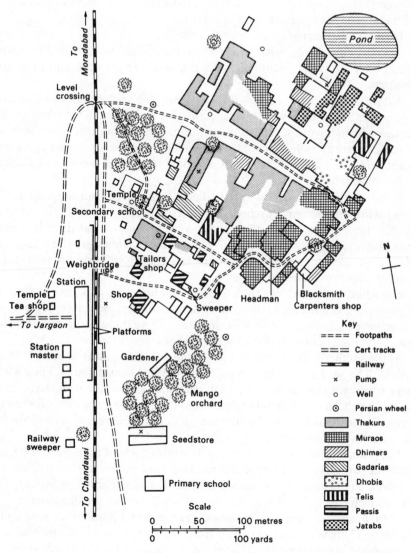

To Moradabad

Level crossing

Temple

Secondary school

Weighbridge

Station

Temple □
Tea shop □

← To Jargaon

Station master □
□
□
□

Railway sweeper □

To Chandausi

Tailors shop

Shop

Platforms

Gardener

Mango orchard

× Seedstore

Primary school

Sweeper

Headman

Blacksmith
Carpenters shop

N

Key

====	Footpaths
===	Cart tracks
▬▬	Railway
×	Pump
o	Well
⊙	Persian wheel
▒	Thakurs
▦	Muraos
▨	Dhimars
▧	Gadarias
░	Dhobis
▥	Telis
▬	Passis
▨	Jatabs

Pond

Scale

0	50	100 metres
0		100 yards

(This map was prepared by Susan Stern)

Fig. 2.1

This arrangement allows great privacy to the women of the household who do not need to be seen at all, even by visitors. This is important because the general custom in the village is that married women should not be seen by strangers. They seldom leave the house and keep their faces covered when they do so. The lower-caste women do not observe this practice so carefully and some of them not at all. It is particularly young married women who hide themselves and as girls approach the age of marriage they begin to adopt the practice of keeping themselves out of sight. The visit of our wives made villagers rather more relaxed with regard to women being seen by us; and some of the women were very anxious to meet them.

Higher-caste women do not work in the fields. Those few women who do help contribute only by getting fodder and harvesting. Inside their homes they prepare food (a time-consuming activity), tend the animals, and look after children.

Although the village is small, it takes some time to find one's way around. The houses are built close up against each other and the lanes between them are narrow with many turns, some of them abrupt. During and after the rains some of the lanes are knee-deep in mud which has been churned up by cattle. Where it is not muddy it is dusty. Finally, it is very dark at night, as there is no electricity in the village.

There is no obvious centre to the village where people can congregate. The area between the secondary school and the temple plays something of this role, as does the area by the pond near the *Murao* houses. And there is a small musical gathering each Monday by a tree near the weighbridge. The village temple is a low circular domed building only large enough to hold a few people. It is painted white and surrounded by trees.

The village is divided into caste quarters, though these abut, and without investigation it is not easy to determine the boundaries. Moreover, some of the castes have more than one distinct quarter. The wells are in the caste quarters but there is also some sharing of wells amongst certain castes.

At the southerly end of the village are the Seed Store and the Basic Primary School. The Seed Store, above which we lived, is a substantial building with a large courtyard surrounded by a high wall and on one side is the large grove marked on the map. Most of the time a colony of monkeys inhabited the mango grove. These monkeys would sometimes go into the village, sit on rooftops and set the dogs barking.

The primary school is a very simple structure, made of unfinished brick and open on two sides. However it did not house the school as the teaching was nearly all in the open. The same was true for the Secondary High School. This was a much superior building, one end of which housed the dispensary.

The tea house is intended for railway travellers and is not much used by the villagers. There is a small temple by the shop for the use of the customers.

The wooded area between the level crossing and the secondary school is used for grazing, as are one or two small areas elsewhere in the village, but for the most part animals are fed in the courtyards.

Fields are quite small (a plot of one acre would be a big one) and are not fenced. There are a few small dust tracks, leading from the village into the fields, along which a bullock cart can pass. Many farmers, however, have to drive their bullocks across the land of others to reach their fields. One would often see bullocks in the fields being driven around and around Persian wheels, raising water for irrigation (for a description of irrigation methods see § 4.4). The land is generally very flat but falls away slightly from west to east towards the river. The land is all within three kilometres of the village, so no-one has to travel very far to get to his field. Many farmers, however, cultivate plots at various different places. Further discussion and maps of the fields to illustrate this point are provided in § 5.4.

The river, which runs along the boundaries of the village land on two sides, is quite a small stream although too large to jump across. In the sugar milling season it runs brown from the effluent discharged by the mill, stinks, and is a breeding ground for mosquitoes.

In Fig. 2.2 is displayed the location of land owned by different castes in the village. It can be seen that there is some tendency for caste holdings to be

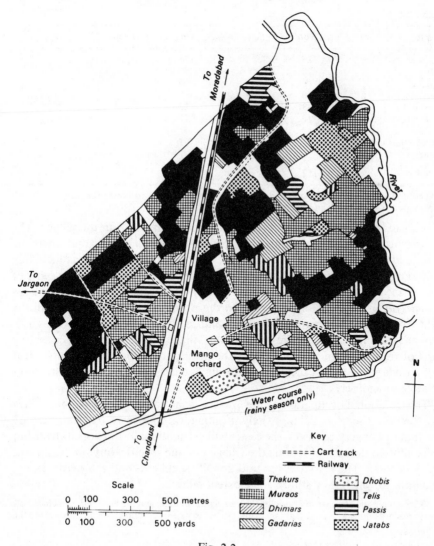

Fig. 2.2

grouped together in largish blocks. More detail on the location of owned and cultivated plots is provided in § 5.4.

Caste[1] is central to the life of Palanpur as it is in most Indian villages. Since we describe the caste system of Palanpur in § 2.A.1 in some detail, the following account deals only with essentials. Through much of this chapter we have divided households by caste, for example, in the presentation of statistics on the village. This can sometimes conceal considerable variation within a caste; thus we also consider, both here and in later chapters, some size distributions.

The castes of Palanpur with the numbers of households and numbers of persons are set out in Table 2.1.

Table 2.1

Caste	Number of households	Number of persons
Thakur	25	174
Murao	28	183
Dhimar	8	59
Gadaria	10	68
Dhobi	3	22
Teli	12	71
Passi	8	61
Jatab (Harijan)	14	97
Others*	4	27
Total	112	762

*These consist of one *Purabi*, one *Bhathagar* household (both of which are other kinds of *Passi*), one carpenter household, and one sweeper household.

The castes have been listed in approximate order of status in the village. The precise order is necessarily somewhat arbitrary except at the top and where the *Jatabs* are concerned. But note that the ranking should be seen as including some large gaps or jumps in status. The *Thakurs* are a caste in the strict sense of the term; in the traditional Hindu four-part arrangement they rank as *Kshatriyas* or warriors, second only to the *Brahmins*. In that ranking all the other inhabitants of Palanpur are either *Sudras* or without caste (see Glossary). An outstanding feature of life in an Indian village is separateness of castes, by area of residence[2], in eating, and for the most part in social intercourse. It is not always easy to say, except where the gap is a large one, how one caste ranks relative to another.

The traditional occupation of the *Muraos* is the growing of vegetables. They are *Sudras* rather than being, strictly speaking, without caste. The *Dhimars* are the first of our service castes, the castes which traditionally did not cultivate but were allotted the task of serving the village in some specific duty, in this case as water carriers. The *Gadarias* are traditionally shepherds and goatherds, an occupation to which they still to some extent adhere.

[1] Throughout the book we shall employ the term 'caste' loosely, as it is often used, to include both categories of Hindus who are strictly speaking without caste, and Muslims. See the appendix to this chapter.

[2] See the map of the village (Fig. 2.1) showing areas of residence.

The *Dhobis* are Muslims. They are traditionally washermen and as such, were they Hindus, would be the highest of the untouchables, the group below the *Sudras*. The *Telis*, also Muslims, are traditionally oil-pressers.

The *Passis*[3] are a special case. They are migrants who arrived in the 1920s and 1930s from East U.P., where they were *Harijans*. Most of the Palanpur *Harijans* or untouchables were *Chamars* (leather workers) but they call themselves *Jatabs* and we shall follow this usage.

Notwithstanding their traditional occupations members of all the castes of Palanpur are involved in agriculture as farmers. Many from the lower castes work as agricultural labourers.

Table 2.2 gives the land holdings of the various castes in *bighas*.[4] Since not every household cultivates land, land owned per household has been expressed for each caste both as *bighas* per household and also as land owned per cultivating household.

Table 2.2

Caste	Number of households	Number of households cultivating	Land owned (bighas)	Per cent of village land	Land owned per household (bighas)	Land owned per cultivating household (bighas)
Thakur	25	21	760	30.4	30.4	36.2
Murao	28	24	1006	40.3	35.9	41.9
Dhimar	8	7	85	3.4	10.6	12.1
Gadaria	10	9	177	7.1	17.7	19.7
*Dhobi**	3	3	58	2.3	19.3	19.3
Teli	12	9	89	3.6	7.4	9.9
Passi	8	4	105	4.2	13.1	26.3
Jatab	14	13	201	8.0	14.4	15.5
Others	4	1	18	0.7	4.5	18.0
Totals	112	91	2499	100.0	—	—

*Of the three *Dhobi* households only one owns any land.

Notice that the *Thakurs* and the *Muraos* between them account for 47 per cent of the village population, and own 71 per cent of the land area. However one should bear in mind that the distribution of land within each caste is extremely uneven so that membership of a caste well-endowed with land, such as the *Muraos*, is no guarantee that an individual household of that caste will be well-endowed. This point is demonstrated in Table 2.3 which shows the distribution of land by size of holding within the *Murao* caste.

[3] Not to be confused with the *Parsees*, an elite group of Persian extraction.
[4] The unit of land area in this table is the *bigha*, a local unit of area. There are 6.4 *bighas* in an acre. The actual size of the area designated by 1 *bigha* varies from region to region. Both the previous studies have worked in *bighas* and we shall follow that practice up to and including Chapter 6. In Chapters 7 and 8, where we shall report scientific studies in comparison with our own findings, it is more natural to work in acres and that is what we will do.

Table 2.3 Distribution of land among *Murao* households

Size of holding (*bighas*)			Number of households
		0	1
	<	2.5	—
2.5–	<	5	1
5–	<	7.5	—
7.5–	<	10	—
10–	<	12.5	2
12.5–	<	15	—
15–	<	20	2
20–	<	25	4
25–	<	30	7
30–	<	40	2
40–	<	50	1
50–	<	75	5
75–	<	100	3
	≥	100	—

We turn next to the question of the relations between castes. These are relatively cordial, if distant, subject to a certain contempt of high for lower and the debasement of low caste before superior caste. What is absent from Palanpur but is to be found in other villages is active and violent confrontations between castes. The main feuds that have taken place in Palanpur in recent years have been intra-caste rather than inter-caste. Like other Indian villages, Palanpur is divided into separate living areas for different castes, so that it is in principle possible to determine the caste of a household from its location. That task would not always be easy for the casual observer because the houses of the village are often packed closely together and the dividing lines between the houses of different castes not infrequently take the form of shared clay walls of houses. Nearly all aspects of life involve the complete separation of one caste from another. Each family prepares and eats its meals on its own. The women of the *Thakur* and *Murao* households very seldom leave the privacy of the family courtyard. Marriages, which are invariably arranged, are always within the caste and the spouse from another village. The woman joins her husband's household. Within the village (see Fig. 2.1) there are wells designated for the use of certain castes and from which those permitted take their drinking water. Four wells are in the *Thakur* section of the village, one of them inside a house; there are two in the *Murao* section; there is one well for the exclusive use of the *Jatabs* which no other caste would wish to use. The *Passis* use a well in a mango grove close to where they live, which is rather on the edge of the village. The Sweepers are not allowed to use a well which anyone else uses but there is a well inside one of their houses. Apart from the prohibition on *Jatabs* and the Sweepers from the use of any but their own exclusive wells, the rules governing the use of wells are not very rigid. Thus the *Thakurs* and the *Muraos* in fact use each other's wells, which same wells are used by the *Dhimars*, *Gadarias*, *Dhobis*, and *Telis*. One sometimes hears of the *Harijans* or Muslims being denied the use of any well but this is not the case in Palanpur.

§ 2.2 Population

The households of Palanpur vary considerably in size. To some extent this reflects differences in reproduction and death rates but there is another factor operating as well, namely, the tendency of some castes to live in large extended households while others more usually live in nuclear families.

Since agricultural management is a central interest of this study we have throughout made this the test for whether a particular family should be treated as a single household or part of a larger household. Thus two families were counted as one household if their cultivation decisions were taken jointly, so that the land with which they were involved was managed essentially as one unit. On the other hand, two brothers living together do not constitute one household if they are managing separate land holdings independently. Our criterion was not always easy to apply: for example, brothers who are in principle separate cultivators may consult together and arrive at the same decisions.

Table 2.4 Shows the size distribution of household numbers.

Number of members in the household	Number of households
1– 3	9
4– 6	53
7– 9	34
10–12	12
13–15	3
16+	1
	112

The household with more than sixteen members had twenty-seven members. This was a case of several brothers and their families living together and cultivating jointly. All but six of the village households were involved in agriculture (making 118 households in total) but in some cases agriculture was not the only, or even the main, source of income. As might be expected with a rapid rate of population growth there is a large number of children in the village. Of the members of our 112 households in November 1974, in all 762 persons,[5] 213 were men, 187 women, and 362 were children aged fifteen or less.

The age distribution of the villagers is given in Table 2.5.

It is interesting to note that at the present time there is a considerable recorded surplus of males over females among children, particularly in the age range 11—15, that is, just prior to the age for legal marriage (note however that marriage, particularly for girls, often occurs below the minimum age). From 16 the two sexes more or less balance. It is, we were told, quite common for people to lie about the ages of girls in the range 11–15 or even to conceal their existence. For babies and very young children the numbers are, as it happens, exactly equal. However, bear in mind that the age distribution is in part an historical record of the survival rates for males and females in the past. This is the case for

[5] The other six households provided 10 men, 9 women, and 14 children.

Table 2.5

Age range	Males	Females	Total
0– 5	78 (10.2)	78 (10.2)	156 (20.5)
6–10	68 (8.9)	57 (7.5)	125 (16.4)
11–15	52 (6.8)	29 (3.8)	81 (10.6)
16–20	37 (4.9)	36 (4.7)	73 (9.6)
21–30	65 (8.5)	63 (8.3)	128 (16.8)
31–40	48 (6.3)	35 (4.6)	83 (10.9)
41–50	32 (4.2)	27 (3.5)	59 (7.7)
51–60	21 (2.8)	21 (2.8)	42 (5.5)
61 +	10 (1.3)	5 (0.7)	15 (1.9)
Total	411	351	762

The figures in brackets denote percentages of the total population of 762 persons

the age brackets up to the early teens, while above the age of marriage girls are leaving the village and coming in as a result of marriages. Hence one cannot say with confidence whether the current generation of girl babies has a notably lower chance of survival to maturity (at least until child-bearing commences) than the corresponding generation of boy babies.

The remarkable difference between the number of males and females aged between 11 and 15 is unlikely to have occurred by chance. There are a number of possible reasons. We offer just two. There may have been dishonesty over the ages reported for females;[6] alternatively, the ages might be accurate and the figures may reflect mortality due to general ill-health at earlier ages where more males survived, because better tended.

Something that struck us when we conducted the household survey was the spacing between children. Given the rapid rate of population growth (see § 2.6) one might expect that one child would follow close on the heels of another. To a considerable extent this is indeed what happens but there are nevertheless quite large gaps between the ages of children in many cases. We calculated for each family for whom it was possible to observe directly age-gaps between surviving children (where two or more members under fifteen are still in residence), the minimum gap between children in that family and the average gap between children in that family. The frequency distributions of families with different gaps are given in Table 2.6.

Naturally it must be borne in mind that the age-gaps that we observed were only those between adjacent surviving children and that our measures of age were not very accurate, mostly to the nearest year. We did not attempt to obtain information on infant or child mortality in the past and we have no firm knowledge of its incidence today. In 1957–8 the rate of infant mortality measured by the proportion of children dying within the first five years was estimated as one-third. We are not sure that it is higher today but it may well be not very much lower.

---

[6] Reported ages might be biased downwards for unmarried girls and biased upwards for young married women.

Table 2.6 Spacing of children

Age-gap in years between surviving children of same parents	Number of instances in which the minimum gap falls in stated range	Number of instances in which the average gap falls in stated range.
1–1.9	8	4
2–2.9	54	36
3–3.9	30	32
4–4.9	5	20
5–4.9	4	6
6–6.9	2	4
7 +	2	3
Total	105	105

Population growth, while high (see § 2.6), is, we suppose, well below the biological maximum, even allowing for infant mortality, and one is led to conclude that some kinds of checks on conception must be operating. The reason is not likely to be the use of contraceptives. These are in principle available through the area's Development Officer but according to him no request for them has ever been received from a resident of Palanpur. This is not to say that the farmers are ignorant of the existence of contraception. Once a Muslim villager asked our advice on how to limit his family. However the request was somewhat casually put and we were left wondering how serious was his desire actually to do something about it. More likely there is some primitive form of contraception in use. As is generally the case in village India, Palanpur mothers nurse their babies for a very long time and the reduced fertility of lactating women may form a part of the explanation. And there may be taboos on intercourse for a certain time after the birth of a child. We did not investigate such questions.

§ 2.3 Land-ownership

The land-owning households of Palanpur mostly acquired their land as a result of the operation of the *zamindari* abolition legislation. Since that time there have been some transactions in land but the distribution of land within the village still largely reflects the distribution of land holdings leased from the *zamindars*.

The origins of the *zamindars* are unclear, but they were probably the leaders of conquering groups in pre-British times. They became responsible for collecting revenue and administering rural areas under the Moghuls, and the British took over this convenient devolution of responsibility, using the *zamindars* as intermediaries between themselves and the actual cultivators of the soil. This is not the place to enter into the question of the sense in which the *zamindars* owned the land for the administration of which they were responsible. The interested reader should consult Baden-Powell (1892) and Neale (1962). The question is difficult because traditional Indian concepts of land-ownership do not tally exactly with the British legal concepts that were applied in the nineteenth century. The purpose of *zamindari* abolition was as much a movement to free cultivators of the burden of rent as to confer on them ownership of the land which many of them cultivated as hereditary tenants by virtue of the legislation of the 1920s and 1930s. Another motive was the desire to break the power of the *zamindars* and to take wealth away from them.

In West U.P. the *zamindars* were in general smaller land-owners than in East U.P. and Bengal, and were usually not 'absentees'. They were not universally disliked; the Palanpur *zamindars*, one in particular, were felt to have been benevolent. The immediate effect of the abolition legislation was to make the cultivators tenants of the state and some of them disliked the substitution of remote officials for the *zamindar* whom they knew and who knew them. One complaint was that, while the *zamindar* was always willing to forgo the payment of rent in times of hardship, government officials had their rule books to comply with and were less amenable to pleas for time to pay.

The *Zamindari* Abolition Act was passed on the second anniversary of the independence of India and was put into force in 1952. Under the Act, former *zamindars* and tenants who had the right to transfer land by sale were given *bhumidhar* tenure. This meant that they became owners of the land with the right to sell or mortgage should they so wish, subject only to the requirement that they pay the assessed land revenue. However, there were limitations on the acquisition of land by the effect of this section. In particular, no transfers were to take place to those who would then hold more than thirty acres (192 *bighas*); a mortgagee was not to take possession; and the transfer should not create a leasehold interest. There was an important clause in the act prohibiting a holding of more than thirty acres and implying that all but the smallest ex-*zamindars* were prohibited from continuing in possession of all their land. In this and in other respects, however, the act was not generally enforced. *Zamindars* were compensated with payments amounting to about eight times the rental plus a rehabilitation grant which favoured the smaller *zamindars*; but this was paid in government bonds which lost value rapidly in the ensuing inflation.

The tenants of the *zamindars* in Palanpur did not qualify for *bhumidhari* status because they had no right to sell or mortgage their land; as protected and hereditary tenants they became *sirdars*. They had to pay their former rents to the government as land revenue, use the land for agricultural activities, and not sell or mortgage the land or lease it out. *Sirdari* land reverts to the village if these conditions are not met. A *sirdar* can become a *bhumidhar* on payment of ten times the rent, whereupon his land revenue payments become one half his former rent and he can sell or mortgage the land as he wishes.[7] In Palanpur some farmers have acquired *bhumidhari* status but very many have not bothered. Until a farmer wishes to sell or mortgage there is no great point, as the lower land revenue is not sufficient to make it a worthwhile investment.

An assessment of the achievements of the *zamindari* abolition land reform is beyond the scope of this study but some points are obvious. First, there was a very considerable transfer of land from some ˜amindars, particularly large

---

[7] He can also lease out his land in the special circumstances under which leasing is permitted, see .§ 2.4.

ones. Second, the transfer of land-ownership was not designed to produce an equal distribution of land holding, except between some *zamindars* and their tenants. Those who gained land as a result of the reform were those who already cultivated land but under lease. Those who cultivated large holdings gained large areas of land, while those who cultivated only small holdings gained only small amounts of land. The service castes and agricultural labourers who did not cultivate at all gained nothing. Both points are illustrated in the experience of Palanpur. The three Palanpur *zamindars* lost control of the land of the village which passed to the cultivators, although two of the *zamindars* are still large and prosperous farmers in the neighbouring villages. The land-ownership distribution that resulted from the reform in Palanpur was unequal and strongly favoured the higher castes. Moreover it left some households completely landless.

Throughout this book we shall refer to 'owners' of land, or land 'ownership', whenever *bhumidhari* or *sirdari* status is involved, without making a distinction between the two cases. This approach merely reflects the realities of the situation because a *sirdar* is always a potential *bhumidhar* who has not yet chosen to exercise his right to transfer to the latter category (and the sums involved are not very large—see below).

In addition to land revenue, larger landholders are supposed to pay a land development tax. It is difficult from official records to relate land revenue and land development tax to individual households. These payments are listed against groups of names and one cannot work out a single household's revenue as, even if weighted shares by area were taken, this would leave out of account soil type and other such variables which are supposed to affect the liability. Payments are owed by dead fathers, young children, and brothers living out of the village. *Thakurs* and *Muraos* are the only castes where young relatives' names are involved. This is probably a precaution against future imposition of land ceilings stricter than those presently in operation.

For Palanpur the records show 105 land-owners (remember that in this reckoning one household may contain more than one land-owner) and 98 households paying land revenue. The total collected is R2170, which is R22.1 per household or R0.84 per *bigha*. The payment per *bigha* varies greatly from caste to caste. The *Passis* pay most, R2.24 per *bigha* owned, while the *Dhobis* and the *Jatabs* pay only about R0.31 per *bigha*. The difference may reflect the quality of land owned but note anyway that these are small sums of money. The same can be said of Land Development Tax. Here only 43 households pay together R1855, that is, R43.1 per contributing household. The figures may be compared with the outputs per *bigha* of approximately R200 per annum obtained by Palanpur farmers (see Chapter 6).

What one can say about these chaotically collected land revenues and taxes is that they are not very high. The total of these payments collected from the village comes out as R35.8 per household and R1.6 per *bigha*, both per annum.

We now turn to statistics on the distribution of land owned and land cultivated in Palanpur. We find it natural and convenient to present the current position alongside the equivalent statistics from the 1957–8 survey and the 1962–3 survey. We are thus enabled to assess the current position against an historical background.

The 1957–8 survey found the total area owned by the households of Palanpur to be 2778 *bighas* (434 acres). In our survey we found the same total to be 2499 *bighas* (390 acres). The difference is mainly accounted for by the fact that some land outside Palanpur is owned by households of Palanpur, while at the same time some Palanpur land is owned by outsiders. *Thakurs* in particular have sold land to outsiders. There are no doubt some measurement errors involved as well: we took some care to get estimates of land areas right but there are limits to how accurate one can be without surveying equipment.

The recorded land holdings of the various castes in *bighas* are given below in Table 2.7, where the figures in brackets are the number of households in the respective caste at that date.

Table 2.7 Land owned by caste at various dates *(bighas)*

Agricultural year	1957–8		1962–3		1974–5	
Caste						
Thakur	908	(18)	857	(20)	760	(25)
Murao	1016	(21)	1018	(25)	1006	(28)
Dhimar	103	(10)	97	(9)	85	(8)
Gadaria	186	(9)	201	(9)	177	(10)
Dhobi	70	(2)	40	(1)	58	(3)
Teli	87	(8)	87	(9)	89	(12)
Passi	116	(12)	129	(16)	105	(8)
Jatab	241	(16)	242	(14)	201	(14)
Others	51	(9)	57	(7)	18	(4)
Totals	2778	(105)	2727	(110)	2499	(112)

Taking the castes as groups, without looking at the histories of individual households, a striking feature is the slow but steady decline in the land held by the *Thakurs*. This accords with casual hearsay evidence from the village, which relates that *Thakurs* have been selling land including sales outside the village. This is not because they have been migrating to any great extent, indeed their numbers have increased rapidly. In fact they now have only half the land per head of men, women, and children that they had in 1957–8, as Table 2.8 shows. There are various reasons for these changes: some *Thakurs* with large land holdings may have been discouraged from land-ownership by ceiling legislation; some *Thakurs* have found employment outside agriculture; in other cases the loss of land is simply the consequence of dissipated living. The *Jatabs* have also lost heavily in terms of land area owned but less than the *Thakurs* in terms of land per capita.

Table 2.9 shows the size distribution of land holdings for all three survey years. The area cultivated and the area owned are not necessarily equal because a household may take land on lease to augment its holding or it may lease-out

Table 2.8 Land owned (*bighas* per capita including children) by caste (numbers in brackets are number of people)

Agricultural year	1957–8	1962–3	1974–5
Caste			
Thakur	8.64 (105)	6.59 (130)	4.37 (174)
Murao	8.68 (117)	7.12 (132)	5.50 (183)
Dhimar	1.84 (56)	1.83 (53)	1.44 (59)
Gadaria	4.32 (43)	4.46 (45)	2.53 (68)
*Dhobi**	11.58 (6)	20.00 (2)	2.64 (22)
Teli	1.85 (47)	1.53 (57)	1.25 (71)
Passi	2.04 (57)	2.02 (64)	1.72 (61)
Jatab	3.39 (71)	3.56 (68)	2.08 (97)
Others	1.31 (34)	1.63 (32)	0.67 (27)
Totals	(536)	(583)	(762)

*There were only two households for the *Dhobis* in 1957–8 and one in 1962–3. The *Dhobis* who moved were almost landless.

part of its holding and cultivate less than the area it owns. Tenancy is, and has been throughout the years spanned by the surveys, important and it is interesting therefore to compare the size distributions of cultivated areas with those of owned areas. The former are displayed in Table 2.10. In the *rabi* season of 1974–5 and the *kharif* season of 1974, 22.8 per cent of the land cultivated by the households of Palanpur was under tenancy.

It should be remembered in examining Tables 2.9 and 2.10 that the size intervals in the left-hand column are not equal. We have given smaller intervals where the quantity of land involved is smaller. A second point which should be noted is that there are six households which are landless which were not included in our household questionnaire in 1974–5 since they had no involvement in agriculture. Thus in comparing columns for different years one should add six to the landless in Table 2.9 and to the non-cultivating in Table 2.10 for 1974–5, or subtract a corresponding number for 1957–8 or 1962–3. The question of whether such households which are not involved in agriculture should be included or excluded is not an easy one. On the one hand it might be held that it is fortuitous that, for example, a railway gangman who owns no land resides in Palanpur. On the other hand it could be the case that people have left agriculture because they are landless. Further discussions of the history of land-ownership in the village are provided in § 2.6 and the appendix.

Looking now at the situation as we found it in 1974–5 we can see that the land distribution is far from equal. There are eleven households involved in agriculture who own no land at all whereas the top fifteen of such households all own more than 50 *bighas*; and in fact these fifteen account for 39 per cent of the land owned by Palanpur households (this last figure is not displayed in the table). The inequality as measured by the Gini coefficient is discussed in § 2.6.

Comparing the distributions for land-ownership the most striking feature is the disappearance of households owning more than 100 *bighas*. In this as in most other respects the figure for 1962–3 lies between those for 1957–8 and

Table 2.9 Size Distributions of land holdings (*bighas*)

Area	Number of house-holds owning 1957–8		Number of house-holds owning 1962–3		Number of house-holds owning 1974–5	
100 and over		4 (3.8)		3 (2.7)		—
75–100	14 (13.3)	4 (3.8)	14 (12.7)	4 (3.6)	15 (13.4)	3 (2.7)
50– 75		6 (5.7)		7 (6.4)		12 (10.7)
40–50		6 (5.7)		7 (6.4)		4 (3.6)
30–40	17 (16.2)	11 (10.5)	17 (15.5)	10 (9.1)	9 (8.0)	5 (4.5)
25–30		9 (8.6)		7 (6.4)		11 (9.8)
20–25	26 (24.8)	12 (11.4)	32 (29.1)	18 (16.4)	41 (36.6)	20 (17.9)
15–20		5 (4.8)		7 (6.4)		10 (8.9)
12.5–15		5 (4.8)		4 (3.6)		4 (3.6)
10 –12.5		10 (9.5)		10 (9.1)		11 (9.8)
7.5–10	31 (29.5)	2 (1.9)	29 (26.4)	3 (2.7)	32 (28.6)	7 (6.3)
5 –7.5		13 (12.4)		10 (9.1)		2 (1.8)
2.5–5		1 (1.0)		2 (1.8)		8 (7.1)
Less than 2.5		1 (1.0)		2 (1.8)		4 (3.6)
Landless	17 (16.2)	16 (15.2)	18 (16.4)	16 (14.5)	15 (13.4)*	11 (9.8)
Total		105 (100)		110 (100)		112* (100)
Maximum Holding		235		180		99
Minimum Holding (non-zero)		2		1		1
Average Holding		26		25		22
Gini Coefficient		0.551		0.524		0.500*

Numbers in parentheses are percentages of column totals.
Left hand entries in each box refer to the sum of ranges included in the box.
*In comparing columns one should include 6 further landless households (see text for discussion of this procedure). We have included these six households in calculating the Gini coefficient: see Table 2.15.

1974–5. This is not simply due to the division of a large holding amongst sons (see the appendix). There is also a clear increase in the numbers of households owning from 15 to 30 *bighas* accompanied by a decrease in the numbers owning 30–50 *bighas*. This is probably associated with the sale of land from holdings previously in the higher category.

An inspection of Table 2.9 shows that there seems to have been a small movement in the direction of equality[8] both from 1957–8 to 1962–3 and in the longer period between 1962–3 and 1974–5. However, the number of landless households has increased slightly.

A comparison of the distribution of land owned and land cultivated (Tables 2.9 and 2.10) for 1957–8 indicates that the largest land-owners were cultivating

[8] There has been a decrease in the dispersion as measured by Gini coefficient from 1957–8 to 1962–3 and from 1962–3 to 1974–5—see Table 2.15.

Table 2.10 Size Distributions of Cultivated Areas (*bighas*)

Area	Number of households cultivating 1957–8		Number of households cultivating 1962–3		Number of households cultivating 1974–5	
100 and over		4 (3.8)		3 (2.7)		—
75–100	15 (14.3)	3 (2.9)	16 (14.6)	4 (3.6)	9 (8.0)	1 (0.9)
50– 75		8 (7.6)		9 (8.2)		8 (7.1)
40–50		9 (8.6)		5 (4.5)		4 (3.6)
30–40	18 (17.1)	9 (8.6)	18 (16.4)	13 (11.8)	20 (17.9)	16 (14.3)
25–30		10 (9.5)		7 (6.4)		19 (17.0)
20–25	28 (26.7)	12 (11.4)	37 (33.6)	16 (14.5)	43 (38.4)	16 (14.3)
15–20		6 (5.7)		14 (12.7)		8 (7.1)
12.5–15		7 (6.7)		4 (3.6)		2 (1.8)
10 –12.5		7 (6.7)		6 (5.5)		4 (3.6)
7.5–10	26 (24.8)	3 (2.9)	17 (15.5)	2 (1.8)	19 (17.0)	5 (4.5)
5 –7.5		8 (7.6)		5 (4.5)		4 (3.6)
2.5–5		1 (1.0)		0		4 (3.6)
Less than 2.5		1 (1.0)		0		2 (1.8)
not cultivating	18 (17.1)	17 (16.2)	22 (20.0)	22 (20.0)	21 (18.8)	19 (17.0)
Total		105 (100)		110 (100)		112(100)
Maximum		226		160		84
Minimum positive		2		6		2
Average (including those not cultivating)		28		25		22

their holdings rather than leasing part of them out and that some households owning fairly small amounts of land (2.5–15.0 *bighas*) were leasing-in land to bring their cultivated area above 15 *bighas*. A similar picture appears from the figures for 1962–3.

As far as leasing goes the figures for 1974–5 look very different. Households owning more than 50 *bighas* seemed to be heavily involved in leasing-out. The drop from Table 2.9 to 2.10 in the number of households in the range 2.5 to 15 *bighas* is similar to that of the previous years. It is possible that the extra leasing in the last year is the reflection of more accurate data. It would be rather surprising if not one of the seven largest land-owners leased-out any land in 1962–3. Alternatively, if the data are correct it may be that the large land-owners in the early years cultivated in a rather dilatory fashion and that extra pressure of population and demand for land induced them to lease-out what before they would have cultivated half-heartedly.

In all the years the shift away from the cultivated holdings in the range 2.5–12.5 *bighas* may reflect the view that such small amounts of cultivated land are 'uneconomic'. Thus leasing is not only in the direction of large land-owners to small land-owners or the landless. We shall have more to say on tenancy in the next section and the subject is studied intensively in Chapter 5.

§ 2.4 Tenancy

The extent of tenancy is striking in view of the fact that politicians and legislators have tried to discourage it. The attempt to discourage tenancy should be understood in terms of the history of land reform in India, the *zamindari* abolition movement, and the force of the political ideal of 'land to the tiller'. In describing the *zamindari* abolition legislation we noted that the *sirdars* were prohibited from leasing out their land, a practice which was seen as negating the intention of the legislation. In fact there have been various bills passed in the U.P. Assembly imposing prohibitions on tenancy whether by *sirdars* or *bhumidhars*. The effect of this legislation is that land illegally leased-out is liable to confiscation. A tenant may approach the authorities and ask for his claim to be the established tenant on a certain piece of land to be registered: should he succeed in his plea, he will then acquire *sirdari* rights to the land. The owner who was illegally leasing-out will have been dispossessed. There are certain exceptions to the general prohibition on tenancy in the form of a list of certain categories of persons who may own land and lease it out by virtue of their inability to cultivate it themselves. Included in the list are minors and those on military service. In considering the influence of legislation on tenancy one has to bear in mind not only legislation already on the statute book but also the possibility of future retroactive legislation. At the time of our study a tenant for a single season would have found it difficult to establish his claims to *sirdari* rights, at least so it seemed. It is hard to be more definite since we know of no case in which the law was invoked for Palanpur. However there was always the possibility in the back of people's minds that a new law might decree that anyone who could show himself to have been a tenant even for one season would by virtue of that fact become the *sirdar*. It would be reasonable to suppose that such legislation would quite likely specifically favour the Scheduled Castes. No-one in Palanpur seemed to know what the law actually was but there was a very widespread feeling that the leasing-out of land put the owner's title at risk.

It is not surprising that tenants do not try to become owners of the land they are leasing-in. For if an attempt were made the tenant would surely never be leased land again. Further, he would incur the odium of both landlords and tenants, of the former for threatening the ownership of land and of the latter for putting at risk in the village the availability of land for cultivation under tenancy. The tenant may also stand in physical fear of the landlord but such is not always the case since sometimes the tenant is a more powerful figure than the landlord.

Tenancy in Palanpur usually takes the form of share-cropping. The legislation may have had some influence in encouraging this form of tenancy; on this and the form that the agreements take, see below § 5.2.

There is no particular tendency for lettings to be confined to the same caste for both landlord and tenant. The most notable feature of the pattern of lettings by castes is the one that would be expected given the distribution of land between the castes, namely that there are more lettings from higher to lower castes than conversely. Table 2.11 shows the pattern of lettings for the *rabi* 1974–5 by caste of landlord and tenant.

Table 2.11 Lettings in the *rabi* 1974–5 (both parties in Palanpur only)

		FROM Caste								
		Thakur	Murao	Dhimar	Gadaria	Dhobi	Teli	Passi	Jatab	Other	Total
TO *Caste*	Thakur	6	5	0	0	0	0	0	2	0	13
	Murao	1	2	1	0	0	0	0	0	0	4
	Dhimar	3	2	0	0	1	0	0	0	0	6
	Gadaria	1	0	0	3	0	0	1	0	1	6
	Dhobi	0	2	0	1	0	0	0	1	1	5
	Teli	1	5	0	0	1	0	1	0	1	9
	Passi	0	0	0	1	0	0	4	1	1	7
	Jatab	2	10	0	0	0	1	1	3	0	17
	Other	0	0	0	0	0	0	0	0	0	0
	Total	14	26	1	5	2	1	7	7	4	67

Note: A letting is defined as the lease of land from one household in the village to another. Where more than one plot was leased we have counted it as one letting only.

Out of sixty-seven lettings eighteen, that is, 27 per cent, were intra-caste. The *kharif* shows a very similar pattern. Intra-caste lettings are no more important when the area involved is taken into account. Table 2.12 shows the number of *bighas* let.

We noted above (§ 2.3) that 22.8 per cent of the land of Palanpur is under tenancy. Forty households lease-in land (see Chapter 5). It is interesting to compare these numbers with those found by the National Sample Survey Organization for Western U.P. in the twenty-sixth round (1971–2). This reports 13.7 per cent of households leasing-in land and one can calculate from the figures given that 14.2 per cent of land is under tenancy (see Table 4, p. 120 of Vol. 2 of the tables on land holdings).

Table 2.12 Number of *bighas* leased in *rabi* 1974–5 (both parties in Palanpur only)

		FROM Caste								
		Thakur	Murao	Dhimar	Gadaria	Dhobi	Teli	Passi	Jatab	Other	Total
TO *Caste*	Thakur	55.5	19	0	0	0	0	0	11.5	0	86
	Murao	5	25	6	0	0	0	0	0	0	36
	Dhimar	45.5	13	0	0	14	0	0	0	0	72.5
	Gadaria	4	0	0	20.5	0	0	0	0	3	27.5
	Dhobi	0	3.75	0	1.5	0	0	0	7	2.25	14.5
	Teli	0	101.75	0	0	10.5	0	4	0	2.25	118.5
	Passi	0	0	0	0	0	0	13.5	0	14	27.5
	Jatab	16	75.5	0	0	0	5	13	13	0	122.5
	Other	0	0	0	0	0	0	0	0	0	0
	Total	126	238	6	22	24.5	5	30.5	31.5	21.5	505

Of the area leased-out as shown in the above table, 25.2 per cent was intra-caste.

§ 2.5 Cropping Patterns

The agricultural seasons are as follows. The months of May and June are dry and exceedingly hot, with long periods over 100° F, and are followed by the monsoon rains in July and August. The rains bring the temperature down although it is still very hot and now extremely humid. The temperature drops steadily from September to November and it becomes dry. By December and January the nights are cold and frost is not unknown. Some light winter rains often fall at this time of year. From January the temperature rises steadily and the nights become hot by April. The monsoon rains account for most of the annual precipitation and their effect is still reflected during the winter in the moisture content of the soil. They are variable. Table 2.13 gives annual rainfalls for the eight calendar years from 1967 to 1974 for Chandausi.

Table 2.13 Annual rainfall in inches in Chandausi, U.P.

1967	1968	1969	1970	1971	1972	1973	1974
46.1	22.0	31.4	17.3	40.9	22.8	39.0	22.8

The harvest for most of the crops grown in the *rabi* season is in April and May, and for the *kharif* is in September and October. The preparation of the land for the subsequent season begins soon after the harvest. *Rabi* crops are usually sown in October and November, and *kharif* crops in June or July. Most farmers in Palanpur wait for the arrival of the rains before sowing their *kharif* crops although this is not necessary if the land is irrigated before sowing. Most crops are grown in either the *rabi* season or the *kharif* season but sugar cane is the notable exception as it requires ten months to reach maturity. It is typically harvested around the turn of the year. Another ten-month crop which was grown in Palanpur is *arher*.

The main crops grown in Palanpur and the areas on which they were grown are set out in Table 2.14. As is obvious from the fact that little land is fallow, most land is double-cropped.[9] It might be wondered why any land is left fallow given that it could apparently be leased out. But land can be left fallow for a number of reasons. Unirrigated land may not be worth double-cropping. The owner may simply be disorganized, or he or his bullocks may fall ill. Finally he may wish to include a fallow period in his rotation.

As was explained above, one of the determining factors in our choice of a village was that the predominant crop for the *rabi* season should be wheat. Palanpur satisfies that condition but even so, wheat accounts for only 42 per cent of the *rabi* acreage.

[9] Triple-cropping, under which an irrigated crop is fitted in between the *rabi* harvest and the sowing of the *kharif*, is possible in North India but none of the Palanpur farmers follow this practice.

Table 2.14 Village-wide cropping pattern (in *bighas*)

Crop	*Rabi* Owned and cultivated	Leased-in	(% crop total)	Total	(% column total)
Wheat	740	285	(28)	1025	(42)
Barley	71	27	(28)	97	(4)
Pea	124	19	(13)	144	(6)
Gram	79	33	(30)	112	(5)
Arher	89	30	(25)	118	(5)
Sugar	374	94	(20)	468	(19)
Fallow	143	38	(21)	181	(8)
Other	237	35	(13)	272	(11)
Total	1857	560	(23)	2417	(100)

Crop	*Kharif* Owned and cultivated	Leased-in	(% crop total)	Total	(% column total)
Paddy	100	19	(16)	119	(5)
Maize	186	36	(16)	222	(9)
Jowar	102	19	(16)	121	(5)
Bajra	454	154	(25)	609	(26)
Ground-nut	89	33	(27)	122	(5)
Urd	46	10	(18)	56	(2)
Sugar	372	100	(21)	472	(20)
Fallow	283	103	(27)	386	(16)
Other	187	57	(23)	244	(10)
Total	1819	531	(23)	2350	(100)

§ 2.6 Comparison with Previous Studies

In this section we shall compare some of our observations of the village in 1974–5 with comparable observations for the year 1957–8 (reported in Ansari, 1964) and for the year 1962–3 (data made available by the AERC, Delhi). The latter data cover only household numbers and land-ownership. However the 1957–8 survey as written up gives a great deal of information and allows a number of comparisons with our own observations.

In § 2.3 we have already provided summary data of the distribution of land areas owned and cultivated. There we suggested that the ownership of land seemed to have become somewhat more equal between 1957–8 and 1974–5. Here we pursue that question further by displaying Lorenz curves for the three distributions of land area owned and by computing Gini coefficients for each of the distributions.

Figure 2.3 shows the Lorenz curves for the years 1957–8 and 1974–5. It will be seen that there is broadly a movement towards equality. The curve for 1962–3 lies between those for the other two years. Table 2.15 gives the Gini coefficients for the three years.

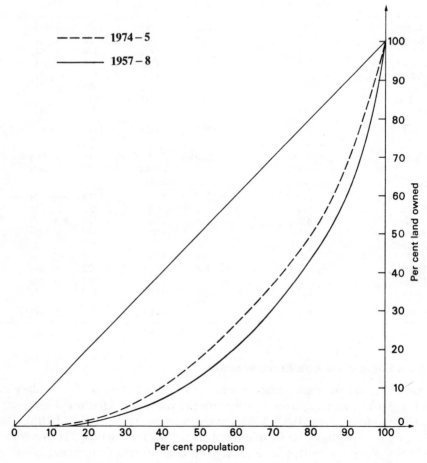

Fig. 2.3 ·

Table 2.15

Year	1957–8	1962–3	1974–5
Gini coefficient of land owned	.551	.524	.500 (.474)*

*This number is the Gini coefficient for the 112 households in our Household Survey. If the six further non-land-owning households not involved in agriculture are treated as part of the population for the purposes of calculating the Gini coefficient that coefficient would take the value .500.

This finding is interesting but should be interpreted with caution. In one sense it does indicate that, for Palanpur at least, the doctrine that the rich have been getting richer and the poor poorer does not apply where the ownership of land is concerned. However summary statistics, such as the Gini coefficient, mask a great deal of detail; that is why they are summary statistics. The number of landless households has gone from 16 to 17 between 1957–8 and 1974–5.[10] More importantly, land is the most important single component of wealth but it is not the whole of wealth. With the accumulation of other assets one would expect a shift from wealth in land to wealth in farm assets and livestock. And education should not be forgotten.

A number of comparisons with the 1957–8 survey follow.

1. According to the 1951 census the population of Palanpur was then 532. The AERC survey of 1957–8 found it to be 536, an increase of only four persons. As the AERC report remarks this was probably due to migrations, for population in the region was growing. That report included a survey of births and deaths for the period 1953–8 from which it was possible to calculate the population of the village pertaining to the households of 1958, as 469 in 1953 compared to 536 in November 1958. In this calculation the total 536 is arrived at by computing the numbers in households that could be identified as households in the village in 1958, which total is then compared to the number in those households in 1953, viz. 469. This gives only a crude indication of population growth because no account is taken of emigration from those households or immigrations into them in the interim. The rate of population growth for the period, from this calculation, was 2.4 per cent per annum. Hence it appears that population growth was rapid up to 1958 but an equilibrium of numbers was maintained by net emigration.

This state of affairs did not persist. The seventeen years since 1957–8 have seen a growth from 536 to 795[11] (48 per cent) in total village population, the equivalent of an annual rate of growth of 2.3 per cent. It seems reasonable to suppose that the main cause of the growth in village numbers is that emigration has come to play a much smaller role. Another influence would be the fall in the death rate which has occurred generally in India and to which the control of malaria and smallpox has made a great contribution. We have no data on migrations but it was not something that people talked about as a frequent occurrence while we were in the village. Nevertheless one *Murao* household did leave the village during the 1974–5 agricultural season. Our impression is of a certain amount of coming and going, particularly in the lower castes of the village. We should guess, but it is no more than a guess, that they have more or less balanced out but with a small excess of emigrations.

2. In 1957–8 the average size of a household was 5.3. This had grown by 1974 to 6.7. There were more castes listed in 1958 than we found in 1974 but the significance of this fact is unclear. The difference arises from a greater proliferation of low castes in 1957–8. This might reflect a greater inclination towards fine caste sub-divisions in the earlier year but it is more likely that some small service castes left the village for lack of work. There is, however, enough consistency between the caste groupings in the two years to enable us to say

---

[10] See Table 2.9 and the notes accompanying it.

[11] We have added the 33 persons not included in our household survey to the 762 who were—see footnote to p. 15

something about the population growth rates of individual castes. The growth rate has not been anything like the same for different castes. The number of *Thakurs*, the highest caste in the village and one in which migration has been relatively uncommon, grew 69 per cent while the *Harijans* grew 38 per cent. This difference must surely be explainêd by emigrations of *Harijans*. Certainly some of the growth rates could only be explained by emigrations or immigrations (e.g. 2 per cent for *Passis* and 366 per cent for *Dhobis*). We give in § 2.A.4. some examples of histories of families and their land constructed from a comparison of the two previous surveys and our own.

3. The wage rate in 1957–8 was reported as R1.25 a day. We found it varied over the season but, taking account of the value of a meal, R4 per day would be a central estimate for 1974–5 (see Table 4.2). Roughly speaking (and we cannot be more precise, see Table 4.12 and note) the agricultural labourers' cost of living increased fourfold from 1957–8 to 1974–5. Thus the daily real agricultural wage was not greatly altered, if anything it was somewhat lower in 1974–5 (given that the estimated wage rates in the two years are subject to errors, as is an estimate of the increase in prices, the margin of error in such a comparison must be large). What might be an explanation for the apparent fall in the real wage rate? A natural hypothesis to consider would be that population growth has been largely if not entirely balanced by land augmenting technical progress, due to increased irrigation, and so on.

4. The total credit outstanding from the Seed Store for 1957–8 was R7275. In November 1974 it was R52301. After inflation and population growth are taken into account, the Seed Store was providing roughly twenty-five per cent more real credit per head in 1974-5 than it had done seventeen years earlier.

5. In 1957–8 the Seed Store supplied *desi* as well as Punjab 391 wheat seed, and *gram* seed. In 1974–5 only wheat seed was provided and then only one variety, RR21, was available. But in 1955–6 no less than nine types of seed (including the two types of wheat mentioned) were supplied. It seems therefore that the Seed Store abandoned an early attempt to be a general supplier of seed to its members.

6. Table 2.16 gives the village cropping pattern for 1957–8, in terms of percentages of the land for the two seasons under various crops. These percentages may be compared to those in the right-hand column of Table 2.14.

Although we have not been able to calculate it precisely from the data for 1957–8, the fallow area in the *kharif* appears to have been over 40 per cent of land cultivated, and for the *rabi* between 10 and 15 per cent. Using Table 2.14 we can see therefore that there has been a big increase in double-cropping. This increase in double-cropping over the period 1958 to 1974 is associated with an augmentation of the village's irrigation facilities.

There were eleven Persian wheels in the village in 1957–8 which may be compared to twenty-five in 1974 plus seven pumping sets, counting only those in working order, in the latter year. The 1957–8 study refers in connection with the village's use of Persian wheels to irrigation as being 'a major bottleneck'. There is no question of that bottleneck existing in 1974-5. Ninety-six per cent

Table 2.16 Village-wide cropping pattern in 1957—8

Crop		Proportion of crop- ped land under various crops	Crop	Proportion of crop- ped land under various crops
Wheat		36.7	*Jowar*	.8
Wheat	*Gram*	8.1	*Bajra*	5.2
Wheat	*Barley*	.2	*Jowar—Arher*	8.3
Barley		.1	*Bajra—Arher*	38.0
Bejhar		.3	Paddy	9.6
Gram		1.2	Maize	4.4
Peas		10.2	*Sama*	.2
Masoor		.1	Sugar	24.9
Potato		.4	*Sanahi*	.2
Sugar		14.9	Spices	.3
Arher		27.8	*Jowar—Chari*	7.1

Notes: (i) For fallow, see text. We have assumed that the areas under sugar and *arher* in the *kharif* are carried forward into the following *rabi*.
  (ii) Calculations are from Table 1.3 of Ansari (1964).
  (iii) Crops included in this table but not grown in 1974—5 are not described in the Glossary.

of the land was irrigated as compared with less than ten per cent in 1957—8.

Comparing Tables 2.14 and 2.16 we can say the following: wheat is of similar importance; sugar has increased; paddy has increased; *arher* has declined sharply. We cannot put precise numbers on these changes because the mixing of crops with wheat and with *arher* was much more common in 1957—8 and, as we have just noted, we do not have an accurate measure of the fallow areas in the 1957—8 seasons.

7. In 1957—8 a sample of twenty-five households found only one man to have worked outside the village and this for only two days. This situation has changed markedly. We found work outside the village to be common and of more-than-marginal importance (see below § 4.1). Note that the increase in outside work has for some households radically changed the consequences of being landless.

8. The 1957—8 investigators report from the same sample that dung was widely used as manure, in fact all households used some, and fifteen out of twenty-five households applied a rule of thumb that half their dung should be used as manure and half as fuel. By 1974—5 manuring was an unusual practice, having been displaced by the use of chemical fertilizers.

9. The 1957—8 study reports a fascinating but not entirely credible situation with regard to tenancy. Of the land area cultivated 10.9 per cent is reported as leased-in from private owners (we are excluding here leasing from the state), but the area reported by owners as leased-out is only 3.8 per cent of the same area. Obviously leasers-out were under-reporting tenancy, knowing its legality to be in question. But this gives one cause to doubt whether either figure can be credited. If it were true that the proportionate area under tenancy in the village has more than doubled since 1958 it would be very interesting but we doubt that this has really happened.

10. In 1957–8 the village owned 94 bullocks, 28 he-buffaloes, and 90 cows or she-buffaloes. Table 2.A.3 shows that these totals had all increased by 1974–5: viz., 121 bullocks, 36 he-buffaloes, and 105 cows or she-buffaloes. However the growth was in no case as great as the growth of population between the two years, 42 per cent. An explanation would be that the number of these beasts that the village can use is more closely tied to the land area than to human numbers, but we doubt this in the case of cows.

11. The ratio of the debt for 1974–5 from the Seed Store to private debt[12] is 1.27. In 1956–7 the corresponding ratio was 0.55. Thus Seed Store debt has grown in importance relative to private debt. This shift would appear even more marked if LDB loans were included along with Seed Store loans as loans from public institutions. There can be little doubt that private money-lending has been losing its importance.

12. Table 2.17 gives the yields for some of the main village crops for the years 1974–5 and 1957–8. The large increases in yields represent the cumulative effect of all the changes that have taken place in cultivation practices since 1958. Irrigation has affected all crops to some extent while fertilizer and new seeds are particularly important in the case of wheat. In this connection it is interesting to note the very large differences in yields between the two years, a difference which is particularly marked in the case of *rabi* crops (although the paddy harvest in 1957–8 was a disaster). Ansari (1964) remarks: 'The basic problem seems to be that of irrigation' (p.95), and it is surely the great increase in irrigation since the time to which that remark applied (from about 10 per cent of the land to 96 per cent) that will mainly explain the increase in yields. Of course one should allow for differences in the weather in the two years but a large difference in yields would nevertheless remain.

Table 2.17 Comparison of yields of some major crops in 1957–8 and in 1974–5

Crop	Yield in quintals per *bigha*	
	1957–8	1974–5
Wheat	0.264	1.138
Barley	0.194	0.949
Gram	0.256	0.778
Paddy	0.026	1.024
Maize	0.214	0.619
Jowar	0.106	0.910
Bajra	0.222	0.603

13. The 1957–8 survey found no strong relationship between value of output in rupees per *bigha* and the size of holding. The averages for the size intervals given were R21.6 (below 32 *bighas*), R22.7 (32–64 *bighas*), R23.2 (64–96 *bighas*), and R23.1 (96 *bighas* and over). This is in accord with our findings in

---

[12] See Table 4.5. We have not included loans from the LDB in computing this ratio since it was not lending to Palanpur villagers in 1957–8.

Chapter 6 where we find no significant relation between farm size and yield per *bigha*.
14. The increase in the number of consumer durables in striking. We found in 1974—5 that there were seventy-four watches and thirty-eight bicycles in the village yet in a sample of twenty-five households in 1957—8 only one watch was found and not one bicycle.

This concludes the comparisons with previous years that will be presented.

§ 2.7 Concluding Remarks

We shall not attempt to summarize this chapter. We were anxious to place the more formal work of later chapters firmly against the background of the village as we knew it. In addition we hope that here and in the appendix that follows we have provided other investigators with material which might be useful in comparing Palanpur with studies of villages with very different features to which some of our findings and suggestions may not translate.

Appendix to Chapter 2

The material contained in this appendix is as follows.

§ 2.A.1 Caste
§ 2.A.2 Village politics and institutions
§ 2.A.3 Durable ownership
§ 2.A.4 Case histories of families and their land
4 2.A.5 Nearby villages.

§ 2.A.1 Caste

The castes of Palanpur were listed in rank order in § 2.1. The question of caste ranking is a delicate one and outside our range of competence (see McKim Marriot, 1965, and Cohn, 1959). The ranking that we have used is, as has been remarked, a rough guide to status, including economic status, of the various castes in the village. The precise tests that are proposed by sociologists of village India have to do with the performance of ritual functions at weddings and other ceremonies and the giving and taking of food. These tests, however, are often inapplicable to Palanpur (except in the case of the Sweepers, whose position at the bottom of caste ranking is in any case obvious) because ceremonial functions are frequently not performed by those outside the household. Similarly there is not a great deal of giving and taking of food. The Sweepers take away waste food from all households. Otherwise the traditional service castes are engaged for the most part in activities different from those which define their caste. To take an example, the majority of village households do not employ a *Dhobi* for washing clothes. However the *Dhobis* keep rugs which are used at weddings.

Exchange of food mostly takes the form of the provision of a meal for an agricultural labourer. He will nearly always be of a lower caste than his employer according to our ranking and will eat food prepared in his employer's kitchen. An interesting example where exchange of food does confirm a caste ranking, but only a fairly obvious one, is provided by Rajendra Singh, a *Thakur* who has sold most of his land and lost status by taking up with a low-caste woman, not his wife. He now lives in part from his employment as night watchman at the Seed Store and in part from agricultural labour. However when he works for an employer who is not a *Thakur* he goes home to take his lunch.

Another criterion for ranking castes which has served elsewhere is the use of names as opposed to a more honorific form of address. However this is not much help in Palanpur because, Sweepers apart, men generally call each other by their names, except that they sometimes employ a term of respect for age when addressing an old man.

We found that indicators of caste ranking such as those discussed supported the ranking that we have proposed or at least did not contradict it. But where two castes were close enough together to make the question of their relative position an acute one such criteria were often unhelpful. In our formal analysis in later chapters we shall only distinguish three groups: *Thakurs*, *Muraos*, and the rest.

The ranking of the *Passis* well illustrates the difficulties of producing an exact ranking. The *Passis* are a migrant group who came many years ago from East U.P., where there is little doubt that they were *Harijans*. However their economic status in the village is not low because they enjoy a good deal of well-paid outside employment. In talking to villagers we found disagreement as to the status of the *Passis* and people would disagree, for example, on the question of whether they ranked below or above the *Dhobis*. In general the higher the status of the respondent the more likely he was to accord a high status to the *Passis*. Those from castes at the bottom of the village often insisted that they were better than the *Passis* whom we heard described as 'lower than Sweepers'. Hyperbole in the description of other castes and individuals is quite usual, however, and throughout the world immigrants are often held in low esteem.

The *Thakurs* were traditionally warriors or soldiers but they often cultivated. At one time they used not to till the soil themselves but this has now largely changed. Under the British rule of India they provided many of the *zamindars*,[13] and today officials and village headmen are very often *Thakurs*. West U.P. villages can largely be divided into those under *Brahmin* domination and those dominated by the *Thakurs*. As has been remarked, there are no *Brahmins* in Palanpur and this is by no means unusual, for there are many villages in the locality that are likewise without *Brahmins* (see §2.A.5). When a ceremonial function has to be performed, for example when a higher caste marriage takes place, a *Brahmin* comes in from another village. However the Sweepers and *Jatabs* dispense with the services of a *Brahmin* and organize a ceremony themselves. Under the old *zamindari* system the land of Palanpur was under the control of three *zamindars*, none of whom lived in the village: the largest was a *Brahmin* while the other two were *Thakurs*.

Many *Thakurs* are keen on education for their children and they provide several examples of farmers whose agricultural practices are good within the means at their disposal. They are sometimes ambitious and dominating. At the same time they can be ruthless, quarrelsome, idle, and drunken. They are proud of their position as a superior caste and often regard lower castes as legitimate objects for exploitation. No other caste exhibits such a range of social and antisocial behaviour as the *Thakurs*. Hence it is no contradiction to say that the hard-working farmer with a high standard of practice, ambitious for his children and providing for them the best education available, and the idle drunkard dissipating a large land holding in gambling and vice, each typify certain aspects of their caste.

In Palanpur there are three sub-castes of the *Thakurs*, which in decreasing rank order are *Tomor*, *Katheria*, and *Bargujar* (only one household of the last), and this was important when there was a dispute in the *Thakur* camp, see below p. 38-9. Under the *zamindari* system the *Thakurs* generally controlled larger land holdings than the lower castes. When the *zamindari* system was abolished tenants of the *zamindar* became owners of the land that they cultivated with the consequence that the *Thakurs* are today quite well endowed with land. However, as Table 2.2 makes clear, the *Thakurs* do not monopolize the ownership of village land, indeed relative to their numbers they own less land than the *Muraos*. The *Thakurs* and *Muraos* are the predominant land-owning castes. This is shown in Table 2.A.1.

Obviously, the lower the ratio in column (iv) of Table 2.A.1 the better off, on average, is the caste concerned with regard to land-ownership for its numbers. The *Muraos* emerge as the best off but the *Thakurs* do quite well. The table should be interpreted with caution because it is based on crude areas and takes no account of the quality of the land held. Were that taken into account it would probably have the effect of making the position of the *Jatabs* in particular look less favourable.

Most of the *Muraos*, the traditional vegetable growers, belong to the sub-caste *Haldia*, or turmeric growers. The *Muraos* in turn belong to the *Sudra* grouping. However in Palanpur the *Muraos* are farmers and no more given to growing vegetables than other

---

[13]For *zamindar* see Glossary. On the *zamindari* system and its abolition see pp. 17-19.

Table 2.A.1

(i) Caste	(ii) % of village population	(iii) % of village land owned	(iv) Ratio (ii) ÷ (iii)
Thakur	22.8	30.4	0.75
Murao	24.0	40.3	0.60
Dhimar	7.7	3.4	2.3
Gadaria	8.9	7.1	1.3
Dhobi	2.9	2.3	1.3
Teli	9.3	3.6	2.6
Passi	8.0	4.2	1.9
Jatab	12.7	8.0	1.6
Other*	3.5	0.7	5.0

*Of the 4 households in this category, 3 are landless non-cultivating households.

farmers. Like the *Thakurs* they were considerable leasers of land from the *zamindars* so that they became a land-owning caste with the *zamindari* abolition. In fact some of the largest land-owners in the village are *Muraos*.[14] Moreover the *Muraos* are the most numerous caste in the village, though only slightly larger than the *Thakurs*. At the time our study was undertaken the village headman was a *Murao* but not long before the position had been filled by a *Thakur* and it was only because of a split within the *Thakur* community (see § 2.A.2) that the headmanship passed to the *Muraos*.

The *Dhimars* were water carriers. Today all but one of the *Dhimar* households cultivate land. However they do not own a great deal of land and it must be assumed that in the past they would have carried out only a little cultivation in parallel with their duties as water carriers. As they own less than 12 *bighas* per cultivating household, the smallest figure of any caste except for the *Telis* (and 'others'), it is not surprising that they take a great deal of land on lease. There must have been substantial immigration of *Dhimars* into Palanpur since 1958 since their numbers are now more than three-and-a-half times as large as they were then. Some of these families may have been ones that used to reside in the village, then emigrated, but later returned.

The *Gadarias* still look after goats but they also cultivate and like other lower castes they engage in agricultural labour for wages. They are not badly endowed with land, with nearly 20 *bighas* per cultivating household, although some of their land is of very poor quality. Since 1958 their numbers have grown more or less in line with the total village population.

To the Hindu the labour of the *Dhobis*, washing clothes, is somewhat defiling. The Palanpur *Dhobis* are Muslims and as such cannot strictly speaking be said to have caste. However throughout the book we shall use the term 'caste' loosely to include Muslims. Their numbers have grown greatly since 1958 but even now there are only three *Dhobi* households. In common with other service groups they have taken to cultivation. Two of the households are landless but the other has 58 *bighas*, some of which are leased-out. The other two households take in about 6 *bighas* each on lease.

Traditionally the *Telis* are oil-pressers, an occupation that today could not alone provide support for twelve households in Palanpur. The *Telis* are Muslims, as are the *Dhobis*, so that they are separated from the majority of their fellow villagers by a barrier of religion as well as of caste. However they form a grouping in the village, like a caste, which is separate from the other Muslim group, the *Dhobis*. Caste barriers are very strong in a village and the additional rift of a difference of faith only reinforces an

[14]See Tables 2.3 and 2.8.

already large gap. The *Telis* do not participate in such communal village activities as exist and they are not to be found among those who attend the weekly musical gatherings, although that audience is not of any particular caste.

It is the custom for about thirty people to gather beneath a tree on the edge of the village each Monday evening to make music and sing. A *Passi* performs on an old piano accordion, accompanied by drums and a whistle. *Thakurs*, *Muraos*, and *Passis* are the chief participants although no-one seems to be excluded. However the songs are Hindu songs and *Telis* and *Dhobis* are never seen there, not even their children. Yet the musical resources of the *Telis* are good: there is among their number an able story-teller and singer who used to earn money by providing entertainment. They own little land with only 9.9 *bighas* per cultivating household and seven of their households are virtually landless. They lease-in quite a lot of land. Their numbers have grown considerably since 1958, by 51 per cent. They are very dependent on selling their labour. While their children are not excluded from the primary school, their attendance there is very poor.

We have placed the *Passis* in a position in the caste ranking roughly corresponding to their position in the village in terms of general esteem. They are migrants from East U.P. where they were *Harijans*. Originally they came to Palanpur in the 1920s and 1930s as railway workers but after the railway work was finished some of them settled in the village and took to cultivating land on lease from the *zamindars*. Many still work outside agriculture with the railway or elsewhere. They improved their status by migrating because now they are fairly well-off by the standards of Palanpur. This fact is not evident from observing their ownership of land because for a number of these households farming, even when practised, is only a secondary source of income beside employment outside the village. The Palanpur *Passis* are exactly what one would expect of a mobile 'go-getting' group. They are ambitious and it is notable for example that the attendance of *Passi* children at the schools is much better than for the children of other low castes. Their mobility seems to have continued and there are now only 2 per cent more of them than there were in 1958.

The term *Harijan* is a collective term for the outcasts of Indian society. It is a romantically affectionate term, the invention of Mahatma Gandhi, meaning 'the people of God'. The British coined the term 'untouchables' to describe the same group. Although often used in the literature on Indian society and in reporting village studies, the term *Harijan* is seldom encountered in the country. The local nomenclature for the main body of these people varies from place to place and has often changed within living memory; such seems to be the case in Palanpur. The Palanpur *Harijans* were mostly *Chamars*, leather workers, the most defiled (because working with dead animals, notably cows) group in society except for the Sweepers. Today they call themselves and are usually called '*Jatabs*', a much more prestigious term implying kinship with the clan of *Krishna*[15]. They were (and still are) agricultural workers, also small-scale tenants of the *zamindar*. Despite their low status they do own some land, less per household than the castes at the top, the *Thakurs* and the *Muraos*, but more than the near landless castes, the *Dhimars*, *Passis*, and *Telis*. They also enjoy a good deal of outside employment, the reason being the government policy to favour the Scheduled Castes in public employment.

The group that we have called 'Others' is a collection of odd households not belonging to the main caste groupings in the village. Two of these are superior kinds of *Passi*, members of which have employment outside the village. These households are landless and do not cultivate but supply some agricultural labour. Another household is that of the village carpenter, a Muslim; it owns a little land but does not cultivate. A Sweeper

[15] See Wiser (1971), pp. 225–6.

household makes up the group. It owns 10 *bighas* of land, most of which is leased-out. The main activity of the Sweepers is, of course, cleaning, particularly the removal of human excreta, and the keeping of pigs, unclean animals that consume human excreta. The despised position of this group is well known. For example a Sweeper would never sit together with members of other castes, and in the presence of a member of another caste would squat, if not going about his work, in a low debased position with his eyes at a lower level than those of the man he is addressing.

There are not many occasions when the members of different castes will meet to engage in common activity. Such occasions as there are involve communal religious observances. Of course the castes are in close contact whenever a farmer of one caste employs a labourer of another caste, particularly where, as often happens, the farmer himself works alongside his labourer. Usually the labourer will be of a lower caste than his employer but even here there are exceptions. There is no awkwardness about these close meetings of different castes: an uninformed observer watching two men sowing might find it difficult to know that they were separated by a caste division. If the employer provides a meal for his labourer, which is the usual practice, this will be brought to the fields by the women or children of his household. Both men will eat their food squatting on the ground at a distance one from the other. There are exceptions to this general pattern. Should it happen that the labourer is of a higher caste than his employer, then he will not take food prepared in a low-caste kitchen and his employment arrangement will accordingly not include his being provided with a meal. In the same way, Hindus do not take food from Muslims.

When they are not occupied with schooling or assisting with household tasks, the children play like children everywhere. If, as will often be the case, they play around the household or within its immediate vicinity then they will play with children of their own caste. But sometimes they roam around and a large group of children will often be seen to be a mixture of castes. They all know each other and those who attend school sit with whichever children come. With the children as with their parents the strict separation of living and of eating, while not combined with any strict prohibition on social intercourse, leads naturally to a high degree of caste separation.

§ 2.A.2 Village Politics and Institutions

We shall shortly describe the formal political institutions having to do with Palanpur but we begin with a description of two recent feuds within the village. These are important both for understanding existing divisions in the village and as a reflection of the kind of politics which exist. The main feuds in Palanpur are not between castes but within castes and most importantly within the *Thakurs*. Currently the *Thakurs* are split along sub-caste lines into two groups, a split which dates from 1971. At the time of the 1957–8 survey the *Muraos* were seriously split as the result of a dispute concerning the question of whether a man who had formed a liaison with a woman, not his wife, and had a child by her, hence losing caste, could be readmitted to the caste. That dispute had died down by 1974. The feud between the *Thakurs* was still lively when we were in the village and it is instructive to relate how it arose. In January 1971 the Assistant Development Officer (*Panchayat*), the Block official with a particular responsibility for village government, a *Thakur* by caste, came to the village to collect a large sum of money as *panchayat* tax. In this enterprise he was supported by the then village headman who was also a *Thakur*.

There is a *Murao* in Palanpur, Man Singh, who is exceptionally well-educated for Palanpur, having graduated from a local college. When the visit of the ADO (*Panchayat*) described above took place, Man Singh chose to organize resistance to the collection of the tax and made it impossible for the tax to be levied. As a consequence of his intervention he was fined R500 and sentenced to six months in gaol but he succeeded in contesting the finding in court, won his case, and got his fine back. To avenge this insult some of the *Thakurs*, including the then headman who was a *Tomor*, hatched a plot to murder a *Jatab* and pin the crime on Man Singh. However the plot backfired: a substantial proportion of the *Thakur* community (all the *Katherias* and some of the *Tomors*) was opposed to the scheme and it was never put into effect. The split in the *Thakur* camp was a bitter and enduring one and they were unable to deliver all their votes to a *Tomor* candidate at the next headmanship election. Thus the headmanship passed to a *Murao*, Toti Ram, with the support of a good many *Thakurs*.

The remainder of this story would be a fit subject for a novel. Man Singh occupied a house immediately adjacent to the then headman's house, where the *Thakur* and *Murao* precincts share a common boundary. He had fallen in love with one of the headman's daughters and had been able to communicate with her enough to learn that his feelings were reciprocated. This was a hopeless romance. In an Indian village marriages are typically arranged and as such are not love matches, though presumably love should it happen to exist already would be no handicap. Even within a caste marriages are almost always arranged between partners belonging to different villages, hence a love match between a young couple within the same village cannot respectably occur even if they belong to the same caste. Moreover, Man Singh was soon to be involved in conflict with the then headman, as was described above, a state of affairs hardly likely to endear him to a prospective father-in-law. All these difficulties, virtually insurmountable by themselves, are insignificant beside the overwhelming barrier in a village of caste division. The houses of Montague and Capulet could be joined in marriage with ease compared to the difficulty of marrying across a caste barrier as wide as that between *Thakur* and *Murao*. Nothing came of this romance. Each lover was in due course married elsewhere, properly and correctly as custom dictates. Today Man Singh is one of the better farmers of Palanpur; the girl left the village on her marriage to join her husband's household in another village, where she died in child-bearing.

Apart from intra-village feuds, the villagers of Palanpur are affected by the political struggles which go on in the locality. These can be both ruthless and violent. An example of what can happen was provided in November 1974, when the headman of a nearby village was shot in the head at close range on the platform at Jargaon Station, dying instantly, the result of his challenge to a powerful local politician. This is an indication of the seriousness of political power struggles which can and do occur in the area. In this case the murdered man had won an election for the headmanship of his village, which was quite close to Palanpur, against the candidate of the politician, whom we shall refer to as Mahendra Pal. Mahendra Pal held amongst other things an important position in the Cane Society (see below). Great courage was required to stand up against this man who was always visibly armed and accompanied by henchmen.

Palanpur is included in a Block which takes its name from a nearby village, Baniakheda, and which has its headquarters in Chandausi. The Block is an administrative area intended to contain 1 *lakh* (100,000) persons, and is a subdivision of the *tehsil*. The Baniakheda Block is one of three that make up the *tehsil* that has its headquarters at Bilari, the next station up the line from Jargaon in the Moradabad direction. These bodies are all ultimately answerable to the Collector, the man in over-all charge of the District, in this case the Moradabad District. The Block headquarters in Chandausi house the BDO and the ADO (Agriculture). The administration at the *tehsil* headquarters is responsible for legal records of land-ownership and for the recording of land transactions, as well as for the collection of land taxes and charges. These include the development tax, which is related to land holdings, and land revenue, which is the rent paid to the state by those who became tenants of the state on the land which they acquired on *zamindari* abolition. The *patwari*, the village accountant and keeper of land records, has his office in the *tehsil* headquarters. There was a young man living in Palanpur who worked in the *patwari*'s office. We found this connection a useful one from time to time although we did not receive much help from the *patwari*.

Although the BDO and the *patwari* are important officials for the farmers of Palanpur it is unusual for either of them to visit the village. When they have business to transact the farmers will take themselves to the officer concerned. Fertilizer and some seed are obtainable at the Block headquarters as well as from the Seed Store.

The institutional arrangements for the supply of sugar to mills are important to farmers. The nearest mill is at Bilari and the organization of the flow of cane to that mill is the responsibility of the Cane Development Society. Officers of the Society are in a powerful position because they deal with the allocation of the rights to sell sugar to the mill (see § 4.5). They are elected by the members. Sugar cane is collected and weighed beside the railway line at Jargaon station. There is a weighbridge there and it was enlarged and improved during our time in the village. When cane is being collected at that weighbridge, from all around and not just from Palanpur, a clerk from the mill will come to the weighing station and keep a record of the cane collected. Farmers complain about both dishonesty at the weighing station and delays in receiving payment. After the weighing, the cane is transported further afield by rail. We shall have more to say about sugar in § 4.5.

It was at one time intended to make Palanpur a village covered by a co-operative marketing scheme and the fact that this scheme was in the offing in 1957-8 is what decided the AERC investigators to choose the village for their survey. The scheme came to nothing and at no time has there been co-operative marketing in the village.

The Seed Store serves some dozen villages including Palanpur. It was established originally by the Department of Agriculture in 1942 and is now an important and active institution. It is the headquarters of the Co-operative Credit Union, and distributes seed and fertilizer to farmers on credit. The Manager of the Seed Store is a powerful man: he controls credit and the distribution of seed and fertilizer. In principle it is part of his duties to give the members of the Co-operative Credit Union advice on agricultural practice to help improve production and quality (there is no agricultural extension worker for the village). However he is unqualified for this task even if time allowed him to do it and if he had any inclination for such unremunerative work. As is the case with most low-level officials with whom the farmer comes into contact, payment is required for any service however slight. The salaries of such official people are small and little shame attaches to such outright corruption; it is what is generally practised and people are accustomed to it. The Seed Store is a major source of seed for the village's farmers, particularly of wheat. A farmer who is a member of the union may take seed, in an amount regulated by his land holding, and in return must repay in kind the seed advanced plus 25 per cent extra at the end of the season. It would be difficult to design a scheme better guaranteed to ensure the adulteration of the seed supply. The Seed Store offered in 1974-5 only one kind of wheat seed, the so-called RR21. The features and quality of this seed are examined at length in Chapter 7.

The Village Level Worker is what his name suggests. He has responsiblity for a number of villages in the area and for these villages his duties range from acting as a go-between for farmers in their relations with higher officials, to the provision of family planning assistance. There are no family planning services in Palanpur but the Village Level Worker would have the job of dispensing contraceptives were a villager to approach him. Another of his responsibilities is giving farmers authorization to buy fertilizer from the Block. This was particularly important and lucrative when there was rationing (see Chapter 7). His visits to the village are infrequent and the farmers make it their business to seek him out when they need his services.

All the farmers of the village will come into contact with officials at some time during the course of an agricultural season. They may want to borrow money or renew outstanding loans, obtain seed or fertilizer, buy or sell land, or pay land revenue. They may be subject to compulsory purchase of grain at administered prices at the end of the season, although the great majority of Palanpur farmers are too small for the officials to waste much time extracting surplus grain from them and there was no compulsory purchase in Palanpur in 1974–5. Indeed, for the most part the village goes its own way. It has to use officials from time to time but there is no-one whom the farmers trust and to whom they can look for disinterested advice.

There is a village *panchayat* but it is inactive. Caste *panchayats* have been much more influential, since the main quarrels have been intra-caste. The maintenance of law and order is achieved to some extent by default. With serious crimes, such as murder, the police will be involved but they are far away at Kurh village, a distance of fourteen kilometres, are badly over-extended, and are thought by the villagers to be corrupt. Theft of any removable asset is a constant threat and great trouble has to be taken to protect such prize targets as diesel engines and bullocks. But guards can be overpowered, as happened in September 1974 on the edge of Palanpur when the motor that powered a tube-well was stolen[16]; and brick walls are no certain barrier, as thieves demonstrated in March 1975 at Palanpur by partially dismantling the wall of the village shop to effect an entrance and remove the contents.

The headmanship of a village can be a powerful position. The headman is a major link between the villagers and local administration, including the police and revenue officers. He might be called upon to adjudicate in disputes over land or other matters and is excellently placed to get his own way. In Palanpur however the headman, Toti Ram, was not a dynamic figure. He got elected as a consequence of the dispute which split the *Thakurs* and was probably a càndidate chosen to antagonize as few people as possible.

National politics make little direct impact on the village, although the villagers know about some of the major political figures. The local power structure was strongly Congress and most Palanpur villagers voted Congress in the past. On the breakdown of this state of affairs after 1975, see Chapter 10.

Palanpur has two schools. The Basic Primary Schools was founded in 1960 and serves two nearby villages, Bhoori and Pipli, which are without schools of their own. In addition, four children of one of the teachers attend from Chandorra village. This school is staffed by a headmaster and three teachers. The headmaster lives in Jargaon, one teacher in Chandorra, a village half-way between Palanpur and Jargaon, and the two other teachers live in Palanpur and combine their teaching with some farming. There are 150 children on the register and of these 100 – 110 attend regularly. The participation of girls is extremely poor: only 35 of those on the register are girls. Classes are held in the open,

[16] This tube-well was on Palanpur land but because of the inclination of the surrounding terrain it mostly serviced fields belonging to an adjacent village. There is no tube-well irrigation in Palanpur today and, with the small temporary exception just mentioned, there never has been. On irrigation sources in the village, see below § 4.4.

the children sitting in rows on the ground with their slates and such books as they possess. The official curriculum evokes comparisons with Dotheboys Hall: Hindi, Mathematics, Social Studies (Geography and History), Science, Agriculture, and Art. The truth is that the school is poorly run and that most children learn to count and, if they are bright, to read and write, but little else besides. This is a government school under the control of the District Board but the control is lax. The headmaster usually arrives from Jargaon on his bicycle more than an hour late, which would matter less if the other teachers felt able to start teaching seriously in advance of his arrival. There is no charge for attendance at the school but all pupils, except for those in Class I, pay 10 *paise*[17] per month to the games fund and 5 *paise* per month for Junior Red Cross.

The school has pupils from all the castes of its constituency but some castes are far better attenders than others. From Palanpur *Jatabs*, *Muraos*, and Muslims are very poor attenders. There are six *Brahmin* children and one Sweeper child. The Brahmins do not mind attending with the *Jatabs* and the Sweeper. As there is no food served during school hours the problem of eating together does not arise.

The other school is a secondary school which was founded in July 1973. It is a private concern managed by Dr Suresh Kumar who also runs a dispensary in the village. He lives outside Palanpur. Both institutions are housed in a small building on the edge of the village, near the little temple, and not far from the railway line. This building used once to serve as a rest house for rail travellers and officials on tour. There are three classes in the school, Grades 6, 7, and 8, with enrolments in the academic year 1974–5 respectively 26, 12, and 14. There was one girl in the sixth grade and two in the eighth; they were all three from the same family. As with the Primary School, children come from the surrounding areas to attend. The largest enrolment was from Pipli, a village about two kilometres to the south of Palanpur, which contributed 22 students. There were 15 from Palanpur, 10 from Chandorra, and 5 from other villages.

As this is a private school fees are payable. It cost R8 per month for the seventh and eighth Grades, but only R3 per month for the sixth Grade. Not surprisingly, when parents are paying for their children's education, attendance is good: only four or five students are absent on average. The curriculum includes English, Hindi, Sanskrit, Mathematics, History, Geography, General Science, Art, and Agriculture. This is more grand than the actual achievement. However, the school is working in difficult circumstances and its pupils undoubtedly acquire some useful, if very rudimentary, knowledge. The teaching of English appears to meet nearly insuperable barriers and not one child in the village could understand more than a phrase or two although more had been committed to memory. As might be expected, the attendance at school is heavily weighted to the higher castes and nearly all the students are *Brahmins*, *Thakurs*, or *Muraos*. But somewhat surprisingly there are five *Gadarias* at the school. This caste owns little land but one family enjoys remunerative employment outside the village. In general the relation between land-ownership and the desire for education is somewhat complex because the ownership of a large land holding can pull two ways. On the one hand, the wealth that a large land holding implies makes it easier for the family to afford the costs of education but on the other hand there is less incentive to seek employment outside agriculture and this may make education seem less attractive against other ways of investing capital.

[17] There are 100 *paise* in one Rupee.

§ 2.A.3 Durable Ownership

Table 2.A.2 shows the ownership in the village of a number of important household durables. Table 2.A.3 shows the ownership of farm animals by caste. For more on the ownership of draught animals see § 4.2.

It may be seen from Table 2.A.2 that the ownership of consumer durables is quite widespread. The numbers of bicycles, watches, radios, and sewing machines are not small. It is unsurprising that ownership is concentrated among *Thakurs* and *Muraos* but the other castes are not empty-handed. An interesting comparison is between *Thakurs* and *Muraos*, where the numbers of households and populations are similar but the *Thakurs* own considerably more consumer durables, this despite the fact that they own less land (see Table 2.8). Note that it is the *Thakurs* who own guns. This pattern of asset ownership is consistent with the view that as a group the *Muraos* are more dedicated to agriculture than are the *Thakurs*. One should not think of these assets as being on display. People in the village are quite careful not to let the world know what they own.

Table 2.A.2. Number of various durables owned by caste

Caste	Number of households	Bicycle	Watch	Transistor radio	Sewing machine	Gun	Sofa	Harmonium
Thakur	25	14	24	17	10	3	0	0
Murao	28	10	16	11	6	0	2	0
Dhimar	8	3	5	4	0	0	0	0
Gadaria	10	3	9	7	3	0	0	0
Dhobi	3	1	1	1	0	0	0	0
Teli	12	4	7	6	1	0	0	0
Passi	8	1	7	3	1	0	1	1
Jatab	14	1	3	0	0	0	0	0
Other	4	1	2	1	1	0	1	0
Totals	112	38	74	50	22	3	4	1

The commitment of the *Muraos* to agriculture is reflected in the ownership of draught animals (Table 2.A.3). They own more draught animals and a larger proportion of these are bullocks which are superior to he-buffaloes. The *Telis* and the *Jatabs* as groups, both of them badly off for land, nevertheless are quite well off for draught animals. This reflects simply the fact that they lease-in land and land cultivated is more closely related to the ownership of draught animals than is land owned (see § 4.2 and Chapter 5).

We collected data on farm assets owned by the households, such as ploughs, hand hoes, and hammers. We shall not display any statistics here; they are not very interesting as they closely reflect the agricultural involvement of the household. Of great interest however is the ownership of irrigation assets, such as Persian wheels and borings. These are examined in detail in § 4.4 where the reader will also find a description of irrigation practice in the village. Changes in irrigation resources over the last twenty years have had a great impact on the village. These changes were discussed in § 2.6.

Table 2.A.3 Ownership of farm animals by caste

Caste	Number of households	Bullocks	He-buffaloes	Cows or she-buffaloes	Young stock
Thakur	25	26	10	39	24
Murao	28	37	6	30	12
Dhimar	8	4	7	6	9
Gadaria	10	8	7	12	8
Dhobi	3	6	0	3	1
Teli	12	15	4	4	5
Passi	8	7	0	0	0
Jatab	14	18	2	9	2
Other	4	0	0	2	0
Totals	112	121	36	105	61

§ 2.A.4 Case Histories of Families and Their Land

We examined the data from the 1957–8 and 1963–4 surveys and compared it to our own household survey findings with a view to establishing the histories of families and their land holdings. It was not always easy to link up the different surveys as fathers' names are not always listed and sometimes there is a duplication of names. However in the case of 71 out of the 102 households of 1958 we were able to trace a land holding through the two subsequent survey years and infer the division of the holding and sales from it or additions to it. Table 2.A.4 summarizes the status of these holdings with regard to whether they had increased or decreased in area and according to whether there was a division of the land during the years concerned.

Table 2.A.4 Size of continuous family holdings and divisions between sons 1958–75

	Holding of family larger in 1974	Holding of family same area in 1974	Holding of family smaller in 1974
Divided	7	2	9
Undivided	21	22	10
Total	28	24	19

Note: In comparing size of holding for the purposes of this table we have added together the land owned by two or more sons to arrive at a family total. Where this has been done we have included the family under 'Divided'.

It is striking that twenty-two holdings were unaltered in the seventeen years between the first survey and our survey and were still managed by one member of the same family. On the other hand, the majority of family holdings, disregarding divisions between sons, were altered in size. Our count is incomplete and not much should be made of the difference between 19 and 28 (total smaller and total larger). Many of the changes in size were quite small, though we counted very small changes, less than 5 per cent, as no change. Clearly the land market is quite active over a run of years with the majority of families transacting in it at some time.

One might expect the larger holding category to have many divisions relative to the smaller holding category, on the argument that land purchase might be associated with dowry money coming into the family, which will happen more when there is more than one son. But we do not observe this, rather the opposite.

We give a few histories of families in Table 2.A.5. These are not chosen at random but rather are interesting examples.

Families 101/102, 108, and 109 illustrate decrease in land owned by *Thakurs*. 113/115 illustrate the effect of division when it is not accompanied by the purchase of new land. Notice that in this case the family is not much worse off than in 1963–4, despite the break-up of the holding, because the total of family members has increased little relative to the land holding. Cases 503, 703, and 804 illustrate quiet but significant accumulation of land by non-*Thakur* households.

Household 109 is Rajendra Singh, whose story is told in Chapter 4, p. 94.

The histories of individual families illustrate the characteristic attitude to land of the villagers. In general families hang on to land when they have it and sales and purchases are unusual events. But they do take place and they have had a significant effect on the distribution of land-ownership over time. An interesting question, on which we have no views to offer, is why one family will split up a land holding where another family in apparently similar circumstances will keep it as one holding. However, in this regard it is interesting that larger holdings are particularly prone to be split.

Table 2.A.5

Family nos. in 1974–5 survey	1974–5		1963–4		1957–8	
	Bighas owned	Family members	Bighas owned	Family members	Bighas owned	Family members
101	52.5	6	180	9	235	9
102	52.5	7				
108	20.75	7	49	5	49	4
109	1.66	4	20	3	10	2
113	28.67	5	79	14	123	12
114	41.75	5				
115	29.50	2				
	99.92	12				
120	28	12	46	13	33	11
125	19	9	19	9	19	7
302	6	5	6	4	6	3
503	55.25	10	40	2	40	3
602	0	6	14	7	14	9
603	0	4				
703	8.5	9	widow 6	2	7.5	8
			0	4		
804	16.84	5	9	2	7	2

§ 2.A.5 Nearby Villages

During our time in Palanpur (mainly in February 1975) we visited most of the neighbouring villages. These were in part social visits but they had a particular interest for us in that they allowed us to compare the situation of other villages with that of Palanpur. We usually spoke to the headman but there would typically be a group of farmers, sometimes as many as twenty, gathered around and joining in the discussion. Sometimes they would contradict an answer offered by the headman. These were very enjoyable sessions. There was no possibility of checking and cross-checking on answers, as we were able to do in Palanpur, but the point was not so much to gather detailed and accurate information as to gain over-all impressions and to note striking differences from Palanpur.

Our discussions were informal and we did not attempt to force them into the framework of a questionnaire. However we had a list of questions and these were asked in some form or other in most of the villages. The questions were these:

1. What is the population of the village and the numbers of the various castes ?

2. When was double-cropping first adopted on a large scale in your village ?

3. What proportion of the land is irrigated ? What are the means of irrigation and when were they acquired?

4. What wheat seeds are in use in the village and from where are they obtained ? Have you noticed a deterioration in yields in recent years from any of these seeds ?[18] What advice do you get concerning the cultivation of wheat ?

5. From where do you obtain your fertilizer ? Has the recent increase in price discouraged its use ?

6. How many households are landless? What is the daily wage at different times of the year, in cash and in kind ? How difficult is it to obtain labour at different times ?

7. Have many individuals recently migrated from your village ? Where did they go to ?

8. Is there much tenancy in your village ? How has the position changed in the last five years?

9. What is the price of an average *bigha* of land ? What was the same price five years ago ?

Sometimes these questions were appropriate and led to interesting discussions, sometimes not. We played it by ear, dropping a question and moving on when the discussion seemed not to go well. One of the interesting points in itself was which of the questions sparked off discussion and this varied to some extent from village to village.

Some brief notes on the nearby villages follow in which we note only broad characteristics and salient points that struck us.

Pipli: A village of 160 households and about 1200 people. The caste composition is very different from Palanpur. There are five *Brahmin* households and only two *Thakur* households. Half the village is Muslim and of these about half are landless. The largest Hindu group is the *Gadarias* (about twenty-eight households) and only two Hindu households are landless. Crafts are important in the village. Of the Muslim households, twenty are part-time weavers and there are five masons.

Pipli farmers began double-cropping a little later than Palanpur, mostly in the last two years. This has been accompanied, as in Palanpur, by an increase in irrigation, particularly by the purchase of pumping sets.

New seed is much less used than in Palanpur, on only 40 per cent of the area under

---

[18] Farmers in Palanpur had reported a decline in the yield from their most popular seed, RR21 (see below, Chapter 7), and we were interested to see whether this experience was typical.

wheat. Yet there is some good seed in use, for example K68, which they like for its high yield of straw. They get their fertilizer from the Seed Store and from Chandausi and complain that it is expensive. They claim that not more than four people lease-out land.

As this village is only a very short distance from Palanpur it is not surprising to find many similarities. However the land seems to be somewhat worse in quality and inequalities rather starker.

Bhoor Maresi: A village of about 150 households (1000–1200 people). There are ten *Brahmin* households as against eighty-three *Jatab* or *Dhobi* households. Nearly every household has some land, with only a few *Jatab* households being landless. Only two or three households have more than 50 *bighas* 'in their own name'.

In its agriculture this village is more advanced than Palanpur. They have been double-cropping for five to six years and have roughly fifteen pumping sets. Electricity came to the village last year and they are pressing the government to allow the use of electricity to power private tube-wells. There is one tractor in the village. There is only one field of *desi* wheat but they buy such wheat from outside for home consumption. They get a good deal of seed from the Block HQ as well as from the Seed Store. We spoke to some very educated and coherent farmers.

The wage at the time of sowing is reported as R3 plus a meal where in Palanpur and Pipli it was R4 plus a meal at that time. Yet the village imports agricultural labour. They report that there is very little tenancy now because families have enough labour to manage their land.

The impression was of a *Brahmin*-dominated village. The *Brahmins* led the discussion and others seemed to defer to them.

Ari Khera: A small village of only about 500 people. *Brahmins*, *Thakurs*, *Gadarias*, and *Jatabs* each account for about twenty households. There are six *Dhobi* households. The village is very well irrigated as it has had a shared tube-well with a neighbouring village since 1934. What is interesting is that, despite this long-established availability of water, they have been double-cropping only for the past 10–15 years. This suggests that double-cropping is a response to population pressure.

The village looks prosperous. Although they use poor seed, RR21 or home-produced seed, fertilizer use is high. Thirty-five households have more than 50 *bighas* of land, mostly the *Brahmins*, and only two are landless. Probably land-richness as much as agricultural practice accounts for the prosperity.

Villagers report much tenancy and no decline in the last five years. The wage rate is much the same as in Palanpur: R3 plus a meal at the time of asking (February) but had been R4 plus a meal earlier in the season. Labour is hard to come by only at harvest time.

Bhoori: A small village of only 87 households and 450–500 people. The *Muraos* are the dominant caste and account for fifteen households. There is one *Bania* household and all the rest are *Jatabs* (65 households) or *Dhobis* (6 households). Some village land is served by a government tube-well which started working three to four months ago, but this will not get water to the land to the west side of the village, which is high and sandy. They are double-cropping on only 20–25 per cent of their land and expect to increase this proportion to about 40 per cent because of the tube-well.

This is quite a backward village and agricultural practice is poor. Nearly all farmers use RR21 although they have noted a decline in yield from this seed over the last five years. Fertilizer use is at a very low level. They say they cannot afford fertilizer from the market or obtain it from the Seed Store.

Although only four households are landless, there are many with less than 5 *bighas*, while four or five own more than 50 *bighas*. The villagers say that there is only a little tenancy but many of them take land on lease outside the village. Wage levels were reported as much the same as in Palanpur but this village exports labour to Palanpur and Chandorra. They claim that most of their labourers work outside the village. Three *Jatab* households migrated during the last five years.

This was a strikingly poor village in comparison to Palanpur with many undernourished children. The great inequality of the distribution of land must help to account for this fact.

Chandorra: In this village lives the household of a man who was a local *zamindar* before the land reform. His fine, spacious house is a feature of the village and we were taken into it by three girls of the household whom we knew, as they are pupils at the Secondary High School at Palanpur. This is a *Thakur* village and that caste accounts for 80 of its 105 households. Two families own 1000 *bighas* between them, nearly a third of the village land. There are twenty landless households.

A few families double-cropped as long ago as 1955 but most took it up in recent years. Even now, about 1000 *bighas* of village land are not double-cropped for lack of water. There are seven private electric tube-wells in the village and one government tube-well. Use of wheat seed seems similar to Palanpur, with RR21 the most popular variety but some good seed in use as well, including UP1009.

For the last ten years big landholders have leased-out land and this has not changed much recently. There has been considerable migration of *Jatab* households to other villages in the district. More than ten have left in the past five years.

This village looked quite prosperous and had a good primary school where the teacher spoke some English.

Ahamadabad Kasaura: A village of about 100 households, 450 people, together owning about 2000 *bighas*, of which 300 *bighas* are alkaline and uncultivable. The main castes are *Jatab* (40 households), *Yadav* (40 households), and *Menna* (7 or 8 households). Very little of the village land is double-cropped, only about 200 *bighas*, although there are two private tube-wells. Use of wheat varieties is much the same as in Palanpur. Less than 50 per cent of farmers use any fertilizer though they report that 80 per cent used to before the price rise.

The distribution of land seems rather more even than we encountered in other villages. There are three landless households and a further five or six with less than 5 *bighas*. Only one household has more than 50 *bighas*. They say that there is a surplus of labour and report a lower wage at the time of sowing than was usual in Palanpur, R3 plus a meal. Five *Jatab* households left the village during the last five years and went to nearby villages. Villagers claim that there is no tenancy and that there was none five years ago which would contrast sharply with Palanpur if true.

The land of this village is poor. The price of an average *bigha* is reported as R400 where a figure close to R1000 per *bigha* is typical for the area. Nevertheless there is not the striking poverty that was observed in Bhoori, probably because the distribution of land is more even.

Umura: This is a prosperous-looking village with a good paved street and housing but in a state of war. There is a feud with a powerful local politician who, according to what we were told, had arranged for his men to damage the village's three private tube-wells. None of these was in working order at the time of our visit. The predominant caste is *Mali*

(65 households). There are five *Brahmin* households and six Sweepers. The land area is only 1200 *bighas*. About five households are landless while about four have more than 50 *bighas*.

They have been double-cropping since the tube-wells were constructed, five to six years ago, but are no longer double-cropping as the tube-wells have been damaged. The use of wheat varieties and fertilizers is similar to Palanpur. This village was unusual in our experience in that employers did not normally provide their labourers with a meal. The money wage was correspondingly higher, R5 at the time of sowing. They said that tenancy had decreased due to the subdivision of households by which they presumably meant the increase of population.

Kua Khera: This is a very small village, more of a hamlet, consisting entirely of mud huts. Our discussion was with just two men. There are three *Brahmin* households, twenty *Thakur* households, and one Sweeper household, in all about 150 persons farming 1400 *bighas*. The Sweeper is the only landless householder and no other household has less than 5 *bighas*. Two households have more than 50 *bighas*. The village imports labour. They have five private tube-wells all constructed in the last four or five years and about two-thirds of their land is double-cropped.

Agricultural practices are very similar to Palanpur. The men told us that the decline in yield of wheat in recent years was due to the fact that farmers now put on less fertilizer than formerly, a view which we never encountered elsewhere. Again here we were told that tenancy had declined because of the subdivision of households.

An examination of villages in the neighbourhood of Palanpur shows some interesting features. There are marked differences in the caste composition of different villages within a very small area, and in the distribution of land, which seems to be much more unequal in the case of some villages than others. Agricultural practices are less variable than social structures but even they vary a good deal, a fact mostly to be explained by variations in land quality, irrigation, and the educational level of the farmers.

Broadly, one can say that Palanpur does not stand out as particularly unusual compared to its neighbouring villages even though in detail it resembles none of them.

3

Theory and India

§ 3.0 Introduction

There are many theories and claims concerning the agricultural sector of less-developed countries, the structure of their village economies, and the behaviour of the participants in these economies. The purpose of this chapter is to expound, discuss, and occasionally develop certain of these theories so that in later chapters we can use them to help understand some aspects of Palanpur and comment on them in the light of the experience of Palanpur. We shall also describe some observations and propositions which have been made concerning Indian agriculture and its recent history insofar as the data from Palanpur allow us to contribute something to the discussion.

Our primary interest is in the allocation of factors of production and it will be convenient to divide our discussion into land, labour, and capital. We wish to examine the allocation of factors between activities, individuals, and groups. We must remember, of course, that markets cannot be considered in isolation. A discussion of share-cropping, for example, leads immediately to an analysis of land, labour, and capital markets and decisions, since a bargain between tenant and landlord will usually involve an understanding over the level of several inputs. The importance of a simultaneous examination of the various markets is a theme which will recur.

We shall take a fairly broad view of the definition of factors. We include migration in the discussion of labour, and irrigation and fertilizer under capital. Draught animals and power are examined together with land. We begin in § 3.1 with an examination of certain general views of the manner in which a village economy, or the economy of a less-developed country, operates. The second, and largest, substantive section of this chapter concerns land. The disposition of land must be at the centre of the study of an agricultural economy. Further the nature of the contracts governing the use of land, particularly share-tenancy, has been a popular subject with theorists both recently and amongst classical writers such as Smith, Ricardo, and Marshall. We discuss certain theories of the determination of wages and the allocation of labour in § 3.3 and examine capital inputs such as irrigation and fertilizers, and the nature of credit for their use, in § 3.4. In the course of our discussion of theories of factor markets we shall consider a variety of assumptions about the objectives of agents and we focus attention on this issue in § 3.5.

The second part of the chapter is particularly concerned with observations and propositions concerning India. In § 3.6 we examine the arguments of Hopper and others who have studied the question of efficiency by estimating agricultural production functions and comparing the value of marginal products to prices. The debate on farm-size and productivity is summarised in § 3.7. We provide, in § 3.8, a brief discussion of the geographical and historical variations in India of the form of share contract and in § 3.9 we present a review of attitudes to the so-called 'Green Revolution'. Concluding remarks are offered in § 3.10.

§ 3.1 Some General Views

Disagreement over general views of the way a poor rural economy functions often forms the basis of the most heated divisions between social scientists discussing development, and these views differ sharply in their implications for policy. The differences between the positions lie in the assumed importance of 'rational' economic behaviour on the part of individuals, the view of the competitiveness and efficiency of markets and the distribution of power and wealth, and the role of institutions, cultures, and beliefs.

Perhaps the most clearly stated of these views is that of Schultz (1964). He argues that, given its constraints of knowledge, the village economy makes efficient use of its assets. Participants in the economy make optimum decisions maximizing whichever of utility or profit is appropriate. Further, the markets which form the background to these decisions are competitive. In other words the standard model of perfect competition provides an adequate description. One can, therefore, appeal to the standard theorem of welfare economics which asserts that, under certain assumptions, a competitive equilibrium is Pareto efficient[1] (see, for example, Koopmans, 1957). By 'Pareto efficient' we mean that increases in one individual's welfare can be achieved only at the expense of another's. Improvements, apart from pure redistribution, Schultz argues, must therefore come from advances in assets or knowledge.

A second view, that of Hirschman (1958), places the emphasis on disequilibrium rather than equilibrium. He argues that entrepreneurial decision-making is in short supply and substantial and clear incentives are necessary before investment commitments will be made. This leads him to suggest, for example, the possibility of a deliberate policy of making investments before input supplies are domestically available in the hope that the increased price and/or imports will stimulate domestic production of that input. This argument makes use of the notion of 'backward linkage'. A policy of supplying an input cheaply in order to stimulate its employment places reliance on a 'forward linkage'. Hirschman was thinking primarily of industry but an example in the agricultural context would be the supply of subsidized fertilizer in order to stimulate its consumption and enable farmers to become acquainted with its use and (assumed) advantages. Prices would be raised at a later stage when the market had become established.

It is clear that there is a substantial difference between Schultz and Hirschman as to the manner and speed with which agents respond to incentives. We shall be discussing the response to incentives in Palanpur in some detail.

A third view of the behaviour of agents and the operation of markets in less-

---

[1] Those theorems are normally stated for a closed economy but the result is true, and the generalization straightforward, for a competitive equilibrium in an economy with external trading opportunities at fixed prices.

developed countries is provided by Lewis (1955).[2] He places great emphasis on the importance of incentives and the price mechanism in the allocation of resources and the generation of growth but equally regards institutions, knowledge, legal structures, and political and religious attitudes, practices, and beliefs as major determinants of the form taken by incentives and the response to them. An example of his view of the importance of knowledge is his stress on the productivity of agricultural extension work and his suggestion that from three-quarters to one per cent of agricultural income be spent on extension. On the institutional side he points to the possibility that land reform may be a prerequisite to successful extension if, without it, farmers believe that others will reap the fruits of their innovation, but ultimately he believes that, if the incentives are genuinely present, farmers will respond (see, for example, pp. 187–91).

Myrdal (1968) believes that markets and prices play a minimal role in the agriculture of South Asia. To quote (p. 912):

Thus in agriculture the relative avoidance of non-discretionary controls, especially those that depend on the manipulation of prices and the reliance instead on discretionary controls to implement policy, is justified by two complexes of facts. The first is the absence of anything like perfect markets; many transactions are not of the market type at all. The other and more basic one is that price incentives are weak. Few people calculate in terms of costs and returns, and if they do, their economic behaviour is not primarily determined by such calculations.

In contrast to an approach based on prices and markets Myrdal pleads for an institutional emphasis (p. 27).

Marxist writers have emphasized property and power. Thus Bhaduri (1973) maintains that the power which resides with the landlord in the land market goes with both a monopsony in the labour market and a tight hold on credit.[3] From his model he concludes, for example, that the landlords have an incentive to block technical change. Progress, under this view, requires expropriation.

We thus have a collection of views of less-developed economies in general and of agriculture in particular, ranging from the Schultz statement of the prime importance of prices and markets, to that of Myrdal of the central importance of institutions and culture and the minimal role of the price mechanism, to the Marxist concentration on property and power. These broad views will serve as a background to our discussion of particular markets and to the analysis of Palanpur.

We should emphasize that our division of some of our discussion into individual markets does not *necessarily* force the conclusions of our analysis of

[2] It should be emphasized that we are not attempting to summarise the work of the writers mentioned, only their general view of behaviour and markets in rural economies. Our presentation of Lewis' view concentrates on his portrayal of the traditional sector rather than the modern sector in his 'dual' economy model.

[3] But see the large-scale empirical study by Bardhan and Rudra (1977) of data from West Bengal which appears to refute the hypothesis of the model that the only buyer of labour and provider of credit is the landlord. See also the theoretical comments by Srinivasan (1979).

the Palanpur village economy towards any one of the positions just described or against, for example, the position of Myrdal. We are using the term 'market for a factor' to capture the means by which land, say, is exchanged for the use of different individuals and activities. This does not, of course, imply that there is a money transaction, a uniform price, or a fixed rent, or indeed that there is a transaction at all. Further our analysis requires a discussion of the power structure, distribution of assets, land-tenure conditions, the caste and religious structure of the village, agricultural extension services, the means by which credit is obtained, and so on. Indeed certain of these topics have already been examined in Chapter 2.

§ 3.2 Land

It is obvious that the allocation of land to individuals and uses must play a central role in agriculture, and the distribution of land has, correctly, occupied a primary position in the discussions of agricultural economies. Land was a central topic in our description of Palanpur in Chapter 2 and our presentation of theories will emphasize land too.

The market for land is in many economies, and certainly in Palanpur's, overwhelmingly in terms of its use for a limited period. The asset itself is rarely bought and sold. Transfers are usually by gift or inheritance and sales are generally associated either with some extreme personal difficulty of the seller[4] or land legislation. Most theories of the allocation of land take then the ownership of land as given and concentrate on the explanation of how that land is cultivated. We shall follow suit. This does not mean that we regard the explanation of land-ownership as uninteresting or unimportant. Indeed in Chapter 2 we have offered an historical description of how the distribution of land in Palanpur evolved. And the consequences of different land-ownership patterns in terms of land use and incomes must be an important part of any judgement of policies of land legislation and reform.

We shall include draught power in our discussion of land because access to the services of this power is in most agricultural systems a prerequisite for the cultivation of arable land. Draught animals, as we shall see, play a particularly important role in the understanding of the land market in Palanpur.

There are competing views on the consequences of great concentration in the ownership of land for the efficiency of agriculture. Griffin (1974) claims that concentration leads to inefficiency. His argument (see, for example, Chapter 2) is that certain markets, particularly those for land and credit, are biased in favour of the big farmers. In addition the marginal cost of labour to the big farmer will be higher than that for the small farmer who provides his own labour. The big farmer may be in a monopsonistic position in the labour market so that in buying an extra unit of labour he forces up the wage and thus his marginal cost is higher than the wage. There are also transaction costs in engaging in markets: the employer may take on certain social obligations together

---

[4]These do, of course, occur—see § 2.A.4.

with employment and has to find the labour (and the labourer may incur both costs in seeking and finding an employer).

The consequence of these different costs of inputs to different groups of farmers will imply, under many models of the behaviour of agents, profit maximization for example, different choice of technique. Big farmers, Griffin suggests, will select techniques which are more intensive (than those of small farmers) in the use of land and those inputs, such as fertilizer and irrigation, which are assisted by cheap credit. Similarly smaller farmers will select techniques which are more intensive in the use of labour.

Griffin goes on to argue (see, for example, p. 37) that the big farmers will adopt techniques more land intensive than is socially optimum and small farmers more labour intensive, although the claim is confused by an absence of both a criterion for optimality and a model of the rural economy in which the consequences of alternative arrangements can be described.

The Chicago view (for want of a better name) portrays the world as efficient whether or not there is concentration in the ownership of assets. Cheung (1969), for example, develops a model of a large land-owner renting out his land under share-cropping in which it is argued that the solution is efficient. We shall not only be contrasting Cheung's view of the efficient big farmer with Griffin's description but also with the view of share-tenancy that we shall call Marshallian (but see below) which portrays the institution of share-cropping as inefficient *per se*. We shall go on to discuss some recent literature on share-cropping since this is the dominant form of land contract in Palanpur (see § 5.2) and the different models have markedly different assumptions and conclusions. In order to appreciate the reasons for the differences between the results we must involve ourselves in the details of the models. Our concentration on this issue in the theory reflects its importance in our later empirical discussions. We hope that we shall provide an insight into a fairly complicated literature. Whilst our discussion will be less complex than some of the literature to which it refers, some mathematical manipulation is unavoidable.

We examine first the case where there is no uncertainty. Since the Marshallian model can be quickly described and the Cheungian questions arise naturally from the conclusions of that model, it is convenient to develop the Marshallian-inefficient picture of share-cropping first. The inefficiency arises because the tenant when choosing his variable inputs, in particular his labour, will equate some fraction of marginal product with opportunity cost. The model is set out formally as follows.

Consider a tenant who rents a given quantity of land, h, under a share contract. Suppose the landlord's share is r. The tenant chooses labour, l, to maximize his net returns. Thus l is chosen to maximize

$$(1 - r) F(l, h) - wl \tag{1}$$

where F is the production function of land (h) and labour, and w is the opportunity cost of his labour (for example, the market wage). He takes h, w, and the share r as given and thus his choice of l yields

$$(1 - r)F_1 = w \tag{2}$$

where the subscripts 1 and 2 denote the partial derivatives with respect to labour and land respectively. We have inefficiency and the so-called disincentive effect of share-cropping in the sense that the labour application is not pushed sufficiently far to yield the efficiency condition of equality between the opportunity cost and marginal product of labour. It is clear that l can stand for any variable input the cost of which is borne by the tenant.

Now let us examine the choice the share-cropper would make if he could hire as much land as he wished. Maximization of equation (1) with respect to h would yield

$$(1 - r)F_2 = 0 \tag{3}$$

In words, the share-cropper has an incentive to hire-in land wherever its marginal product is greater than zero, since the net return to him is $(1 - r)$ times the marginal product.

The implication for the model is that, where the marginal product of land is not zero, we have excess demand for land and thus some kind of rationing.[5] We should not jump to the conclusion that rationing would be inevitable in the model by assuming that the marginal product of land is never zero for an individual farmer. There may be a capacity constraint on his draught animals and no rental market for the services of others (see Chapters 4 and 5). Nevertheless, given the various options open to the tenant through his cropping pattern and sharing of assets with relations and so on, it is reasonable to suppose that for practical purposes the marginal product of land is not zero.

We are, therefore, led naturally to the complaint of Cheung (1969) – see especially his Chapter 3, § 3 – that the traditional representation of inefficiency in terms of equation (2) is unsatisfactory because it fails to examine the land market and the position of landlords. Let us examine the model which Cheung presented formally in his Chapter 2, § B. The landlord sets a labour input, l, and a share r, and decides into how many pieces, n, to split his total quantity of land M. Thus the landlord maximizes

$$nrF\left(l, \frac{M}{n}\right) \tag{4}$$

his total rent, by choice of r, n, l.

His constraint is that the tenants obtain an hourly return at least as great as they would if they sold their labour for w, the given market wage. There is perfectly elastic supply of labour, and tenants, at return w per unit of labour input. Then

$$(1 - r) F\left(l, \frac{M}{n}\right) \geqslant wl \tag{5}$$

is the constraint. Cheung used a Lagrangian approach to solve the maximiza-

---

[5] Some forms such rationing can take are discussed in Chapter 5 when we study share-tenancy in Palanpur.

tion problem presented in equations (4) and (5). The argument is more transparent if we reformulate it as follows.

Writing $R = nrF$, the landlord's total share rent, we can pose his problem as follows. Choose R, l, and n to maximize

$$R \text{ subject to } F - \frac{R}{n} \geq wl \tag{6}$$

Or, assuming the constraint binds, and substituting for R,

$$\underset{n, l}{\text{Maximize}} \; n(F(l, \frac{M}{n}) - wl) \tag{7}$$

without constraint. Differentiating with respect to l we have

$$F_1 = w \tag{8}$$

and with respect to n,

$$F - wl - \frac{M}{n}F_2 = 0 \tag{9}$$

The former first-order condition gives wage equal to marginal product and the second, using $\frac{R}{n} = F - wl$, yields

$$\frac{R}{n} = \frac{M}{n}F_2 \tag{10}$$

The landlord's rent per tenant is the land per tenant times the marginal product of land, and we have efficiency: the wage is equal to the marginal product of labour, and the rent is equal to marginal product of land. This implies that competitive shares exhaust the output, as if we were at a point on a constant-returns-to-scale production function. If we have global constant returns then n is arbitrary.

The difference between the result (8) and that in the Marshallian model (2), comes from the assumption that for the latter r is fixed and l is chosen by the tenant independent of the landlord's views, whereas in the Cheungian presentation both r and l are chosen by the landlord. In effect in the Marshallian model observation and enforcement costs are infinite and in the Cheungian model, zero.

One does not need to invoke a single landlord to make the Cheungian claim of efficiency. It can be argued that in a model with many landlords and many tenants the forces of competition amongst landlords and tenants will determine a share rent and labour allocation which is the same as the standard model where land is rented out for a given cash rent.

Thus the Cheungian conclusion is that the input levels and income distribution resulting from share-tenancy as modelled by him are indistinguishable from those that would arise if the landlord managed the land and hired in labour at the market wage. In this sense the share-croppers are effectively labourers rather than tenants making their own decisions. A third method of organization which would give the same result is for the tenants to rent-in the land at the competitive rent and undertake the farming themselves. We shall discuss the equivalence of these three methods of organization shortly but we first turn to an examination, which we think is rather interesting, of what Marshall actually said.

Marshall compares 'metayage' or share-tenancy, with the 'English system' or cash rents. Note here that the French word embodies the 50-50 share which has been traditional in a large number of countries. He would appear to be addressing the same problem as Cheung. What is surprising in view of Cheung's argument and criticism, and the association in the literature of Marshall with the inefficient solution embodied in equation (2), is that Marshall recognizes the possibility of the Cheungian conclusion, namely that the specification of input levels together with other parts of the share-contract can lead to the efficient solution of the 'English system'. Let us examine what Marshall wrote.

We reproduce here the whole of § 4 of Chapter X (Land tenure) of Book VI (The Distribution of the National Income). The marginal notes are included but not the footnotes. We shall be studying one of the footnotes in detail since it bears an important relation to the discussion just presented.

§ 4. The question whether the payments made by the cultivator for the use of his land should be reckoned in money or in produce is of growing interest with reference to both India and England. But we may pass it by for the present and consider the more fundamental distinction between the 'English' system of rental and that of holding land on 'shares', as it is called in the New World, or the 'Metayer' system as it is called in the Old.

Metayage or rental by shares

In a great part of Latin Europe the land is divided into holdings, which the tenant cultivates by the labour of himself and his family, and sometimes, though rarely, that of a few hired labourers, and for which the landlord supplies buildings, cattle and, sometimes even, farm implements. In America there are few agricultural tenancies of any kind, but two-thirds of those few are small holdings, let out to white men of the poorer class, or to freed negroes, on some plan by which labour and capital share in the produce.

has many forms in Europe and America.

This plan enables a man who has next to no capital of his own to obtain the use of it at a lower charge than he could in any other way, and to have more freedom and responsibility than he would as a hired labourer; and thus the plan has many of the advantages of the three modern systems of co-operation, profit sharing, and payment by piece-work. But though the metayer has more freedom than the hired labourer he has less than the English farmer. His landlord has to spend much time and trouble, either of his own or of a paid agent, in keeping the tenant to his work; and he must charge for these a large sum, which, though going by another name, is really ear-

It offers to the man without capital some of the advantages of cooperative production. But it involves much friction.

nings of management. For, when the cultivator has to give his landlord half of the returns to each dose of capital and labour that he applies to the land, it will not be to his interest to apply any doses the total return to which is less than twice enough to reward him. If, then, he is free to cultivate as he chooses, he will cultivate far less intensively than on the English plan; he will apply only so much capital and labour as will give him returns more than twice enough to repay himself: so that his landlord will get a smaller share even of those returns that he would have on the plan of a fixed payment.

If the control of the landlord is slight the cultivation is poor;

This is the case in many parts of Europe, in which the tenant has practical fixity of tenure; and then it is only by constant interference that the landlord can keep up the amount of labour he puts on his farm, and keep down the use he makes of the farm cattle for outside work, the fruits of which he does not share with his landlord.

but if it is effective the results may not be very different from those on the English plan.

But even in the most stationary districts the amount and quality of the stock which custom requires the landlord to provide are being constantly, though imperceptibly, modified to suit the changing relations of demand and supply. And if the tenant has no fixity of tenure, the landlord can deliberately and freely arrange the amount of capital and labour supplied by the tenant and the amount of capital supplied by himself to suit the exigencies of each special case.

It is obvious then that the advantages of the metayer system, are considerable when the holdings are very small, the tenants poor, and the landlords not averse to taking much trouble about small things: but that it is not suitable for holdings large enough to give scope to the enterprise of an able and responsible tenant. It is commonly associated with the system of peasant proprietorship; and we may consider that next.

The passage is remarkable in that it captures in a brief statement many, or most, of the important observations on share-tenancy that have been made since. It will, as it happens, prove to contain a strikingly good portrayal of the state of affairs in Palanpur.

But how does the passage compare with the view which we, and others, have described as Marshallian and contrasted with Cheung? It is clear that Marshall did not see the tenant as free to choose his own input levels. He uses the argument summarized in equation (2) above to explain why the 'landlord has to spend much time and trouble, either of his own or of a paid agent, in keeping the tenant to his work' (see above passage). And he saw too that 'if it is effective the results may not be very different from those on the English plan' (see marginal note to the above passage). Furthermore he recognizes that in order to achieve the efficient result there must be a degree of adjustment over and above the stipulation of labour input: 'And if the tenant has no fixity of tenure, the landlord can deliberately and freely arrange the amount of capital supplied by himself to suit the exigencies of each special case'. A footnote to this passage reads as follows:

This is already done in America, and in many parts of France; and some good judges think that the practice may be extended largely, and infuse new life into what a little while ago was regarded as the decaying system of Metayage. If worked out thoroughly, it will result in the cultivation being carried just about as far and affording the landlord the same income as he would have on the English plan for equally fertile and well-situated land equipped with the same capital, and in a place in which the normal ability and enterprise of candidates for farms is the same.

On the elasticity of Metayage in France see an article by Higgs and Lambelin in the *Economic Journal*, March 1894; and Leroy-Beaulieu, *Repartition des Richesses*, ch. IV.

Starting as in the last note, let the Circulating capital supplied by the landlord be represented by the distance OK marked off along OD. Then, if the landlord controls the amount OK freely and in his own interest, and can bargain with his tenant as to the amount of labour he applies, it can be proved geometrically that he will so adjust it as to force the tenant to cultivate the land just as intensively as he would under the English tenure; and his share will then be the same as under it. If he cannot modify the amount OK, but can still control the amount of the tenant's labour, then with certain shapes of the produce curve, the cultivation will be more intensive than it would be on the English plan; but the landlord's share will be somewhat less. This paradoxical result has some scientific interest, but little practical importance.

The diagrams to which the footnote refers are described in footnote 2 to p. 129 of Marshall (1959). The amount of capital expended on production is measured (in cash) by OD along the horizontal axis and the amount of produce on the vertical axis. Capital here means cost of production and the point is emphasized by his use of 'Circulating capital' in the footnote just reproduced. Thus variation in OK by the landlord involves an adjustment in the cash payment he contributes to production.

The extra degree of adjustment provided by the cash payment to the tenant will, in the circumstances described below, lead to the same outcome as when the rental share can be varied. Marshall knew and stated his result and had, he said, a geometrical proof. We offer a mathematical proof here.

Let us split the landlord's net receipts R from renting-out the land into the contribution, α, he makes to the cultivation costs of each tenant times the number of tenants n. We assume here that the only cost of production is labour and we adopt the same notation as that used for equations (1)–(10) above. We assume now that n, l, and α are to be chosen but r is fixed.

The landlord's problem is then

Maximize $\quad nrF - n\alpha$
$n, l, \alpha \quad$ subject to: $(1-r)F + \alpha \geq wl$ $\hfill (11)$

Assuming that the constraint binds we have, by substituting

$$(1-r)F + \alpha \geq wl \hfill (12)$$

into the maximand reformulated (11):

Maximize $n(F(l, \frac{M}{n}) - wl)$
n, l

We have, again, problem (7) with the Cheungian efficient conditions (8) and (10) as part of the solution.

The role of the choice of r in the problem of (4) and (5) and the choice of α in (11) is that they allow us to suppose that the constraint binds. In other words the tenant gets no more for applying his labour than the market wage w. This is the state of affairs which perfect competition amongst tenants would produce.

If we insist that the payment be made from the landlord to the tenant (so that $\alpha \leq 0$) then we require for the solution of problem (7) to be identical to the efficient configuration

$$R^* \leq \bar{r} n^* F(l^*, \frac{M}{n^*}) \tag{13}$$

where starred values denote the efficient outcome and $\bar{r}$ is the fixed rental share. In other words, where we have $50 - 50$ share-cropping the efficient solution can be achieved with the landlord stipulating the input levels and contributing part of the cost of inputs provided the competitive rent in the efficient solution is less than half the produce. Otherwise the cash payment has to go from tenant to landlord.

Marshall, as should be clear from the text and footnote quoted above, understood and stated the result which Cheung derived several decades later. Thus it seems most misleading of Cheung, after quoting part of the footnote presented in full above, to comment (p.45): 'Marshall provided no geometric proof, and it is an interesting conjecture whether he would have altered this footnote had he done so. This conjecture is interesting because the results he conceived are correct only in certain special cases, but as a matter of generality they are incorrect. They are incorrect because Marshall did not allow the rental percentage to vary'. We believe that our discussion of equations (4)—(13) above has shown that the Marshall argument is correct and that Cheung's claim to the contrary is mistaken.

One can show that any solution which can be achieved by the landlord stipulating input levels can be achieved by cost-sharing. We give an intuitive argument here but a formal proof is straightforward (see the appendix to this chapter). We saw above that the rent-maximizing landlord would wish to stipulate the quantity of the variable input labour, at a level where the marginal product is equal to the wage. A similar argument applies to the case of other variable inputs, such as fertilizer. If the landlord offers the same share in the cost of the input as he takes of the output and leaves the choice to the tenant then the tenant would indeed choose the level where the price of the input is equal to the marginal product. He will still, however, need to check that the fertilizer is actually applied to the plot in question. Where the input, such as the tenant's own labour, is not traded, then the landlord will have to stipulate the level. Note that the rental share with cost-sharing will be higher than that with stipulation of input levels since both result in the same profit level for the landlord and income for the tenant.

We can summarize our analysis of share-cropping under certainty as follows.

(i) If the tenant chooses the labour input without the intervention of the landlord and chooses how much land to cultivate then we have inefficiency and unless the marginal product of land is zero, excess demand for land.

(ii) If the landlord can enforce cultivation practice and either set the share rent or make a side payment then share-cropping is efficient.

(iii) An alternative to stipulating the cultivation procedure is cost-sharing with the tenant choosing the non-labour inputs. If there is no cost-sharing for an input (and here one thinks of labour) then the quantity must be stipulated.

(iv) In the model, efficient share-cropping/cost-sharing offers no advantages over fixed-rent tenancy or cultivation by the landlord with wage labour and vice versa.

In terms of the analysis so far there is no need to be puzzled by the question of why share-tenancy persists. We have seen that if efficient share-tenancy happens to be the traditional arrangement then there is no reason why it should be over-turned by competitive forces or technological change. The institution of share-tenancy can respond to both.

There are, however, some important aspects which have been omitted from the above analysis, particularly uncertainty as to yield. In an economy without adequate insurance markets one might expect share-cropping to play an important role in spreading risk. In share-cropping the amount the tenant will pay to the landlord depends on what the yield turns out to be. In a fixed-rent contract the tenant bears the risk and in a fixed-wage contract the cultivating land-owner bears the risk. It is natural to ask, however, whether there are circumstances in which risk-sharing equivalent to share-cropping can be achieved by combining land and labour contracts at fixed prices.

Consider an economy with just one output, labour l, and land h. Every agent has access to the same production function F which shows constant returns to scale in l, h. Output, given inputs, is a function of the uncertain parameter θ which we can think of as the weather. Thus output is $F(\theta, l, h)$. Imagine a tenant with a share-contract where he must apply labour l_o to land h_o and where the landlord's share in output is r. We want to show how the tenant can achieve the same distribution of returns as under this share-cropping contract by a mixture of fixed rent and wage contracts. The random return under the given share-cropping contract, for the tenant, is $(1-r) F(\theta, l_o, h_o)$.

We show that the same distribution of returns can be achieved by mixing contracts, by giving an example of a combination of land and labour contracts which does indeed give precisely the random returns as above.

Suppose the tenant were to hire in $(1-r) h_o$ units of land at a fixed rent P, and that $(1-r) l_o$ units of labour were applied to this land. Suppose in addition he were to hire out $r l_o$ units of labour at wage rate w. His return from this mix of contracts is

$$[F(\theta, (1-r) \, l_o, (1-r)h_o] - P(1-r)h_o \;\; + \;\; wrl_o \tag{14}$$

and this is equal to

$$(1-r) F(\theta, l_o, h_o) \; + \Big\{ wrl_o - P(1-r)h_o \Big\} \tag{15}$$

by constant returns to scale. Then if the expression in curly brackets vanishes the returns are just the same as for the share-cropping contract. The tenant takes on risk by renting land at fixed rent and spreads it by selling labour for the non-random wage. Thus share-cropping offers no *extra* risk-spreading opportunities provided a land market at fixed rental P and a labour market and wage w are available with

$$\frac{Ph_o}{wl_o} = \frac{r}{1-r} \tag{16}$$

Equation (16) says that the rent and wage opportunities in the market must give factor shares identical to those which rule under share-cropping.

Newbery (1977) (see his Proposition 2) in his extension of work by Stiglitz (1974) argues that if share-cropping is superimposed on a system with given rental P and wage w, then the only possible cultivation intensities and share-rents for which share contracts would be agreed, do indeed satisfy equation (16). A higher return to the tenant under a share-cropping contract would be unacceptable to the landlord and a higher return to the landlord would be unacceptable to the tenant, since both have the opportunity of mixing land and labour contracts as summarized in equation (15). Thus if the expression in curly brackets were positive the tenant would not accept the share contract, and if it were negative there would be a corresponding mix which would make the share-cropping contract unattractive to the landlord. Further, for a share-cropping contract to be agreed there must be a landlord and tenant with attitudes to risk such that they can concur on a production technique. In such a world share-cropping, if it were to appear at all, would be redundant. One can also argue that it is reasonable to pose the question of the role of share-cropping in the above world, where fixed-price land and labour contracts are possible and production is as described, for Newbery shows (Proposition 1 and see also Hammond, 1977) that such a competitive equilibrium exists and is constrained Pareto efficient. The constraint is the absence of contingent insurance contracts. It is known that under the standard assumptions—see Debreu (1957) —that if a full set of such markets exists a competitive equilibrium is Pareto optimum and that a given Pareto optimum can be decentralized as a competitive equilibrium.

There are, however, a whole range of circumstances in an uncertain world where the assumptions that give the redundancy of share-cropping do not apply and in which share-cropping is not redundant. The following assumptions were critical[6] to the argument which we have just given, for the superfluity of share

---

[6]The assumption of one crop is not critical to the argument. The risk characteristics of each share-contract for each crop can be replicated by the appropriate combination of land and labour con-

contracts in a model where the services of land and labour can be bought and sold at fixed prices: (i) production functions show constant returns to scale; (ii) they are identical; (iii) contracts in the labour market are riskless; (iv) contracts can be enforced without cost; (v) individuals are indifferent, for given hours of work and income, as to whether they work as share-tenants or for wage labour, or as independent farmers on their own or cash-rented land. It is clear that each of these five assumptions was used in the argument. We explain briefly how these assumptions might fail and how share-cropping can have advantages when they do fail. In each of the five cases we believe that the assumptions cannot be seen as reasonable approximations to the reality of Palanpur.

There may be indivisibilities facing the small farmer and in such circumstances the assumption of constant returns to scale is inappropriate. A particularly important example of indivisibilities can be seen in draught animals. There is no market for the services of bullocks in Palanpur (see § 4.3) and it is therefore difficult to adjust the services of bullocks to land cultivated. We suggest, and the argument is developed in Chapter 5, that, at least in the short run, the adjustment is the other way round: farmers attempt to adjust cultivated area to the capacities of their draught animals by leasing land in or out.

The risk-sharing aspects of share-tenancy then become important—a farmer may wish to cultivate quite a lot of land given the agricultural assets he owns but regard the cash rent involved as too large given the riskiness of the outcome.

It is important to recognize that the indivisibility facing a particular farmer would not necessarily appear in a production function estimated across farmers. That which is fixed for the individual can vary across cultivators. If the cultivators adjust their land cultivated to their indivisibilities there is no presumption that constant returns will be violated for the cross-section (see Chapter 6).

If farmers are not identical then there is an incentive to share in the output of a skilful farmer. Such a farmer may be willing to allow sharing because, given his skills, he may be interested in cultivating more land than he could risk on a fixed-rent basis. It is important to note here that if farming skill could be easily quantified and marketed then one might expect that a market for such a skill would emerge. Thus we are supposing that the difficulties of observation and measurement are great enough to prohibit the emergence of this market. Difficulties of observation are involved in the fourth assumption concerning the costs of enforcing contracts.

The argument on the redundancy of share-cropping used the third assumption listed above, that labour could be bought and sold on a market in which no uncertainty was involved. It is clear in Palanpur that one cannot rely on selling as much labour as one likes at a given known real wage. In such circumstances one cannot replicate the risk characteristics of a share-contract through the appropriate mix of fixed-price land and labour contracts. Share-cropping is not

tracts for that crop. Note that any given landlord can have many tenants (share-cropping or cash rent) farming many different crops and a given tenant can take on land under various terms and for various crops from many landlords.

then redundant in the sense of the foregoing discussion.

In many contracts, and particularly those concerned with labour, enforcement is not costless. It is difficult to define and monitor the obligations of contracting parties. In Palanpur it seems that landlords see the supervision as involving work on their part, although less than in farming themselves, and that the tenants dislike the interference of the landlord. The resulting compromise is well described by Marshall: 'But though the metayer [share-cropper] has more freedom than the hired labourer he has less than the English [fixed-rent] farmer' (see the text from Marshall above). We shall be discussing the degree of supervision from landlords and the residual discretion of the tenant in Chapters 5 and 7. Examples outside agriculture of the use of share-contracts to provide incentives where inputs are difficult to observe are the commission system for salesmen and, in Marshall's words, 'The relations between publisher and author on the "half-profits" system [which] resemble in many ways those between landlord and metayer' p. 535 Fn. 3). Note that uncertainty is important to this argument since in a certain world, with knowledge of the production process, output can be inferred from input.

The fifth assumption concerns preferences of individuals as to whom they work for, other things, in particular income, being equal. There appeared to be a dislike amongst many of the inhabitants of Palanpur for working as wage labourers. And, amongst the higher castes at least, issues of status were involved. There was a general and understandable wish to be left to oneself in choosing how to work. The risks of a fixed-rent system conflict with the desire to cultivate oneself and share-cropping provides an answer.

We have seen, therefore, that in an uncertain world there are strong and clear advantages to share-cropping. Further the arguments which we need to explain the possible advantages of share-cropping make it clear that there is no presumption that cultivation practices will be the same on owner-cultivated land and land under share-tenancy. And in a certain world, share-tenancy with cost-sharing or enforcement of inputs can do just as well as fixed-price land and labour contracts so that in such circumstances, if it happens to be the traditional system, there would be no reason to replace it. Our conclusion from this theoretical discussion is, then, that there is no unanswered puzzle as to the apparent absence of reasons for the common practice of share-cropping. On the contrary there is an embarrassment of riches.

There are a number of features of share-tenancy in Palanpur and aspects of discussions of share-tenancy in the literature which have not been covered in the above discussion and we shall now refer to these briefly. We have been concerned to present theory here, to retain simplicity, and to concentrate on those aspects of the simple theory which are helpful in understanding Palanpur. The details of tenancy agreements in Palanpur will be examined in Chapter 5. There is one feature of particular importance and that concerns liquidity. Whilst the sharing of some costs is almost universal in Palanpur, the tenant is usually required to provide the cash with adjustments being made at the time of harvest. Thus leasing-out can sometimes be a response to liquidity problems. A landlord lacking liquidity would look for a tenant who himself has access to liquidity. We postpone discussion of the problems of choice of tenant, choice of land to be leased-out, and the nature of the 'equilibrium' in the land market in Palanpur to Chapter 5.

We mention here certain theoretical aspects which have been omitted. We have not examined transactions costs (apart from those connected with enforcing share contracts) or the costs of establishing markets. There may well be costs associated with transacting in labour and land markets which vary with types and mix of contracts and these are relevant to a comparison between share contracts and others (see Cheung, 1969). Where there are costs of establishing markets one certainly cannot assume that all markets exist and transactions costs will have an impact on the nature of contracts in those markets which do exist. There are some interesting questions associated with the differences in the risk characteristics between crops and thus which crops might be particularly suitable for share-cropping (see Rao, 1971). And Reid (1974 and 1976) has some valuable comments on the sequential nature of uncertainty in agriculture (many issues become resolved during the growing season and at different points in time) and the ability to renegotiate contracts, particularly share contracts. Bell and Zusman (see, for example, 1976, 1977, and 1978) have provided a very interesting series of papers applying game theory to share contracts. In particular, they provide a discussion, and some calculations, of the shares which are likely to emerge in (a game-theoretic) equilibrium.

We have paid little attention in the above to the explanation of the particular share that is adopted. In this we have followed most of the theoretical literature (but see Bell and Zusman, 1976). And most recent empirical work (for example, Bardhan and Srinivasan, 1971) has been on the incidence rather than the terms of share-cropping. Thus the common occurrence of the 50-50 split has not received much in the way of theoretical explanation. Of course a vague notion of 'fairness' together with the fact that two is an easy number to divide by may be a powerful explanation of why such shares become established; and once established, shares may be hard to change (for further discussion of share contracts in India see § 3.9).

As far as the distribution of expected benefits between landlord and tenant is concerned the 50-50 split is less rigid than might appear as there is flexibility through the details of the agreement on the level of inputs and sharing of costs. However the agreement on output does indeed carry a clear consequence for it determines the way in which risk is partitioned.

We shall not, however, pursue share-cropping any further here. We shall examine tenancy in Palanpur in Chapter 5 (and on the sample wheat plots in Chapters 7 and 8) and the reader who wishes to pursue the literature further may wish to consult the references mentioned above.

§ 3.3 Labour

The theories of share-cropping described above involve simultaneous contracts for both land and labour. We shall describe briefly in this section certain theories which focus particularly on labour and which, it has been argued, have special relevance for the economies of poor countries.

There was one theory in particular which we were anxious to compare with circumstances and practices in Palanpur and this is the one we shall present first. The theory concerns the relation between productivity and consumption. The idea is that the employer may wish to pay more than the minimum wage at which labour is available because the extra consumption from the higher wages will increase the worker's productivity sufficiently to offset the cost of the extra wages. It is thought that the theory is of particular relevance to poor countries because the general level of wages may be such that incomes do not allow food consumption (measured, say, in calories) sufficient to provide for heavy or even moderate work. The theory was first stated by Leibenstein (1957) and then presented more rigorously by Mirrlees (1976) and Stiglitz (1976).

We have discussed and developed the theory elsewhere, and at some length (Bliss and Stern, 1978), so we shall concentrate on the most simple form here. Suppose a worker obtains consumption only from his employment, the working day is of fixed length, wages are all consumed, and consumption is not shared between the worker and others. We suppose that the relation between productivity and consumption is given by $E = E(c)$ where E is effective hours, or tasks performed, per day and c is consumption per day (measured, say in calories). We assume that the function $E(\ )$ takes the form illustrated in Figure 3.1. The idea is that at very low levels of consumption all or most food energy goes into body maintenance and only at higher levels do significant quantities become available for work. At very high levels of consumption the effect of extra consumption on the ability to work becomes small (and one could imagine a negative contribution).

The employer wishes to minimize the cost of buying a given number of tasks, or effective hours, by appropriately choosing the wage w and the number of employees l. We can write his problem

$$\text{Min } wl$$
$$\text{Subject to } l\, E\,(w) \geq 1 \tag{17}$$
$$w \geq \bar{w}$$

The first constraint on the minimization problem says that the employer must purchase the specified number of effective hours (and we have chosen units so that this number is one). The second says that the daily wage must be at least as large as the minimum at which labour is available, $\bar{w}$. It is supposed in this theory that the employer can get as much labour as he wants provided that he pays at least $\bar{w}$. We assume that the first constraint will bind (it is never desirable to buy more effective hours than necessary) and that the second will not.

The problem then becomes

$$\text{Min } \frac{w}{E\,(w)} \tag{18}$$

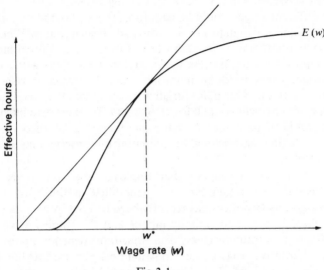

Fig 3.1

after substituting from the first constraint into the minimand. The solution is to select w^* where

$$\frac{1}{E'(w^*)} = \frac{w^*}{E(w^*)} \tag{19}$$

or where the marginal cost of an efficiency hour is equal to the average cost. The number of employees is then $1/E(w^*)$. The choice of w^* is illustrated in Figure 3.1 where $(w^*, E(w^*))$ is the point where the tangent from the origin to the E curve meets the curve. We assume that $w^* \geq \bar{w}$; were that not to be the case the assumption that the second constraint does not bind would be invalidated.

Under this theory the wage w^* would be paid by any employer hiring the type of labourer described (say, a landless labourer without dependents) and performing similar tasks—in the sense that $E(\ )$ is the same—provided sufficiently many such workers were available. Thus under the theory we should expect to see unemployment and changes in unemployment which exert no pressure on the wage. And we should expect to see the same wage in different villages. If tasks performed are similar throughout the year one would expect to see seasonal stability too.

We have argued elsewhere (Bliss and Stern, 1978) that the theory must be considered more plausible in the longer term than in the short run. The effects on strength and energy would be expected to show after weeks and months rather than a day or two. Thus one would, under the theory, expect permanent labour contracts to be rather common.[7] With day-to-day hiring of different labourers a given employer would not reap the productivity benefits of extra wages and thus would not pay them.

---

[7]Particularly where an employer can sub-contract his labourer's time. •

It is intuitively clear (and we have shown this formally in Bliss and Stern, 1978) that different wages would be paid to workers who had an independent source of consumption than to workers who had no such source. Where there is competition amongst employers such workers would be at a premium whereas with a monopsonistic employer the wages paid to the workers with a consumption background would be lower. In the latter case the employer wishes to build consumption up to the same point for all workers so that the marginal productivity of an extra payment is equal for all workers. Workers who independently have more would be paid less. We have seen then that the theory provides a number of predictions and we shall be comparing our observations on Palanpur with these results.

Another theory which suggests that employers may pay more than the minimum required to obtain labour is embodied in the 'labour-turnover models'. A rigorous treatment has recently been offered by Stiglitz (1974). In the model there is a cost to training labour and the employer will wish to minimize wage plus training costs. The 'quit-rate' depends upon the wage (relative to alternative wage-earning possibilities)—by raising the wage the employer reduces turnover. While there are set-up costs to the hiring of labour even in village agriculture we should guess that they are sufficiently small that the theory does not provide a significant reason for paying more than the minimum wage.

Much of the recent literature on labour markets in poor countries has concentrated on the migration decision, particularly rural–urban migration. The models usually describe the choice whether or not to migrate in terms of a comparison between the rural wage or utility level and the expected urban wage or expected utility level. The probabilities in the calculation of expected values depend upon urban unemployment rates. Migration was not a primary focus of this study and we refer the interested reader to the surveys by Todaro (1976) and Yap (1977).

A long-standing theme in discussions of agriculture in poor countries has been the magnitude of the marginal productivity of labour. There was an early suggestion (see, for example, Nurkse, 1953) which often recurs, that it would be possible to withdraw labourers from agriculture without reducing output. Others have argued that while the marginal product of an hour of labour may be low it is most unlikely that it will be zero since on the farm there are always additional productive tasks, such as weeding, which can be performed. And if labour has disutility it is natural to ask why anyone would work the last hour when its effect is worthless. Sen (1975), for example, has used the distinction between labour and labourers to provide a partial reconciliation of these positions.

We shall analyse Sen's model (his Ch. 4) in a little detail since we shall be discussing the marginal product of both labour and labourers in later chapters and in Chapter 6 we shall be discussing the specification of, and estimating, agricultural production functions which have as an argument the number of labourers.

The discussion can be summarized in a simple diagram which we derive below. Consider a family farm with a fixed quantity of land. Work is divided equally amongst the N members so that if total labour input is L then the labour input of an individual is $x = \dfrac{L}{N}$. Output Y is a function of L, $f(L)$. The individual obtains a share a (usually taken to be $1/N$ below) but also places a value k on output going to other members of the family. The utility function for the individual is such that individual disutility of labour can be measured in terms of consumption as a function of x only and is written $S(x)$. The individual maximizes.

$$(\alpha + (1 - \alpha)k)\,Y - S(x) \tag{20}$$

by choice of x. The special form allows a simple diagrammatic analysis.

This is the first point at which we have explicitly introduced utility functions for individuals. We shall be discussing various objectives for individuals and households in § 3.5 so that we shall not examine at this stage whether the function in equation (20) is appropriate.

We suppose first that the family member takes the labour input of other members as given. Thus although labour is equally shared at L/N each, he is trying to decide whether to do any more himself assuming the others' labour input remains constant: $Y = f(X + x)$ where X is the work of others and $L = X + x$. The equilibrium condition is

$$S'\left(\frac{L}{N}\right) = k_o f'(L) \tag{21}$$

where $k_0 = \alpha + (1 - \alpha)k$, and is illustrated in Figure 3.2 below.

We can now see the consequences for L, and hence output, of changes in the number of people on the farm N. The answer will depend on whether k_0 is independent of N. This will be the case only if $k = 1$, and then $k_0 = 1$, since α will usually depend on N. In this case $S'\left(\dfrac{L}{N}\right) = f'(L)$. Assuming α decreases with N, $S'' \geqq 0$, $f'' < 0$, and $k < 1$, a decrease in N will have the effect of shifting the S' curve up and to the left and the $k_o f'$ curve up and to the right. The effect on L is ambiguous except for the two cases: (1) $k_o = 1$, when a decrease in N implies a decrease in L and hence in output; (2) constant marginal disutility S', in which case a decrease in N implies an increase in L and output.

An alternative, and more plausible, derivation of $S'\left(\dfrac{L}{N}\right) = f'(L)$ (equivalent to case (1) above) is that the family takes both the output and labour allocation decisions together. Suppose that the individual utility function is $u(c, x) = c - S(x)$, where c is consumption of an individual, and the family wishes to maximise $\Sigma u(c, x)$, where the sum runs over the family members, subject to the production constraint $\Sigma c \leq f(\Sigma x)$. We shall have in the solution both equal labour allocation (where $f' > 0$) and $S'(x) = f'(L)$. Consumption allocation, given the above utility function, would be arbitrary but any diminishing marginal utility of consumption would imply equal consumption too. A further

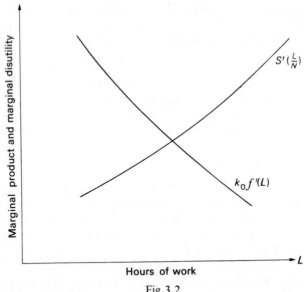

Fig 3.2

way of deriving $S'(\frac{L}{N}) = f'(L)$ (thus equivalent to $k_o = 1$ above) is that the individual maximizes as in equation (20) but that $\alpha = \frac{1}{N}$, $k = 0$ and he assumes that when he increases his labour supply all the others will too.

We call the case where the condition $S' = f'$ holds the *optimally organized farm*. We can summarize the above results in Table 3.1.

Table 3.1 Behaviour of total labour input when the number of individuals on the family farm decreases

	Constant marginal disutility labour	Increasing marginal disutility labour
Optimally organized farm $k_o = 1$	L = constant	decreases
'Inefficient' farm $k_o < 1$	increase	change in L ambiguous

The distinction between L and N is the distinction between *labour* and *labourers*. The case of equilibrium L being independent of N gives zero marginal product of labourers but not of labour. It is important not to confuse the marginal product of a labourer with the opportunity cost of labour. If output stays constant when someone leaves in the above model it is because the remaining family

[8] Stiglitz (1969) has argued that the seasonality of labour requirements in agriculture means that the production function should be written $G(N, x)$ rather than $f(Nx)$. Output is a function of peak season labour Nr_1 and slack season Nr_2. Everyone works flat out in peak season ($r_1 = \bar{r}_1$) and $x = \bar{r}_1 + r_2$. We should expect that a reduction in the number of people N, at given total labour input L, would decrease both output and the marginal product of labour.

members work harder. A extra unit of work has a cost given by the marginal disutility of labour (equal to k_0 times the marginal product of labour f').

The point we wish to emphasize from the above model and discussion is that the organizational structure of the family farm is of substantial importance not only to understanding allocation decisions and the opportunity cost of labour, but also to the form of the production function where the number of labourers is an argument.

We can by using the above analysis examine the circumstances under which the production relation would show constant returns to scale. Let us suppose that the underlying production function (where labour services, correctly measured, constitute the labour input) has constant returns. To keep things simple we assume that the only arguments are labour and land (H) – the underlying function is then written $F(L, H)$. We estimate, however, $G(N, H)$ since, we suppose, we observe only the number of workers present; $G(N, H) \equiv F(L(N, H), H)$. In the case of the optimally organized farm, G would also show constant returns—doubling N and H would not change the ratio of L to H, hence L would also be doubled. Outside this case it is clear that one cannot guarantee that G will show constant returns (take for example the case where L is independent of N). For further discussion see § 6.1.

§ 3.4 Capital and Uncertainty

Our subject matter in this section is the determination of the level of inputs other than land, labour, and draught animals. Of course, as we have emphasized previously, the decisions on the levels of each of the inputs are interrelated. We should distinguish at the outset between variables which influence output directly, such as fertilizer and irrigation, and the finance of the purchase of these inputs. We shall be discussing both topics. The capital market, meaning the market concerned with borrowing and lending, is not, of course, the market for a factor of production. It is the inputs which are purchased which affect outputs and not the loans themselves.

We examined in § 3.2 the role of the land contract in the allocation of uncertainty between landlord and tenant. We remarked also that, in a share-cropping contract, cost-sharing could be seen as equivalent to the stipulation of the levels of variable inputs by the landlord. We shall present here a simple model of the choice of input level by the owner-cultivator where output is subject to uncertainty.

We write output on a particular plot (which we think of as small for the moment) as a function of θ, $\mathbf{x}$ and $\mathbf{z}$, where θ is a random variable denoting the state of nature (we can think of it, say, as rainfall) and $\mathbf{x}$ is a vector of variable inputs. The variable inputs must be selected before the state of nature becomes known. Fixed inputs are denoted by the vector $\mathbf{z}$ – for the purpose of this discussion we can think of $\mathbf{z}$ as land. We write output y as follows

$$y = F(\theta, \mathbf{x}, \mathbf{z}).\tag{22}$$

The price of y is q and $\mathbf{p}$ is the vector of prices of the variable inputs $\mathbf{x}$. The prices **p** are given but q may be random. Given that output appears after inputs are used we are to think of these prices as present values. Complications connected with the finance of the inputs are set aside here. We are thinking of **z** as fixed and we shall, therefore, suppress it in the subsequent discussion.

We suppose that the farmer wishes to maximize the expected utility of wealth at the end of the season. We take this function as given for the time being and discuss alternative objectives in the next section. Labour is taken as fixed and we examine the choice of variable inputs.

The problem then becomes to choose **x** to maximize

$$E\,U\,(Z + q\,F - \mathbf{p}.\mathbf{x}) \tag{23}$$

where E denotes the expectation operator, U the utility function, Z wealth from other sources, and p.x is $\Sigma_i\,p_i\,x_i$ where p_i is the price and x_i is the level of the ith input. Wealth from other sources, Z, would be calculated as follows: the present value of income from jobs outside agriculture discounted to the beginning of the season, plus the present value of income from other plots cultivated this season, plus the present value from selling land and other farm assets at the end of the season (or the present value of keeping them in use whichever is the higher), less the cost of inputs which have been taken as fixed in the vector **z**, and so on.

The first order conditions for this maximization problem are

$$E\,[\,q\,F_i\,U'\,(W)\,] = p_i\,EU'\,(W) \tag{24}$$

where W is the net-wealth at the end of the season, that is $(Z + qF - \mathbf{p}.\mathbf{x})$, $U'\,(\ )$ is the derivative of $U(\ )$, and F_i is $\partial F/\partial x_i$.

$$\frac{p_i}{E(qF_i)} = \frac{E(qF_i\,U'\,(W)\,)}{E(qF_i)\,E(U'\,(W)\,)} \tag{25}$$

It is clear that we should, in general, find that $p_i/E\,(q\,F_i)$, the ratio of price to the expected value of the marginal product, would be different for different inputs. Recall that under certainty p_i/qF_i would be equal to unity for all i.

There is a special case in which we can say a little more and that is multiplicative uncertainty:

$$F\,(\theta, \mathbf{x}) = \theta f\,(\mathbf{x}) \tag{26}$$

The assumption is that the uncertainty with respect to output can be represented as a factor which merely scales output down or up. Note that here uncertainty comes in only through the product of θ and q and we can put $q = 1$. In this case the ratios of marginal products would be independent of the state of nature. In this multiplicative case we find that

$$\frac{p}{f_i E\,\theta} = \frac{E(U'(W)\theta)}{E\theta E(U'(W))}, \tag{27}$$

so that the ratio of price to the expectation of the value of marginal product would be independent of i, thus the same for all inputs. We note also that it is straightforward to establish that this ratio is less than unity using the concavity of $U(\ )$ and the fact that W increases with θ. Intuitively we can see that θ and $U'(W)$ are negatively correlated and hence $E\theta\, E(U'(W)) \geqq E(U'(W)\theta)$. From equation (25) we can see that in the non-multiplicative case the proportional excess of the expectation of value marginal product over price for an input will be higher the more strongly is the value marginal product of the input (qF_i) correlated with wealth W.

We can now ask how the choice of inputs will vary with wealth. It is clear from the results derived above and the standard theory of choice under uncertainty (see Arrow, 1970) that the answer will depend on the shape of the utility function and, particularly, on how risk aversion changes with wealth. This problem has been discussed using a model related to ours by Srinivasan[9] (1972). We first develop some results in the model we have set out above and then contrast these results with those of Srinivasan.

Let us consider an exogenous increase in the non-stochastic part of W. Writing $W(\theta, \mathbf{x}, B) = B + Y_1(\theta, \mathbf{x})$ where Y_1 increases with θ, and B is non-stochastic, we examine derivatives with respect to B. In comparing the choice of $\mathbf{x}$ for two farmers with different levels of B we are asking, for example, how two farmers would differ in their choice of farm inputs when one has a higher guaranteed income from sources off the farm.

In order to compare the choice of $\mathbf{x}$ for different B we examine first how the right hand side of equation (27) changes for constant $\mathbf{x}$. If we call this expression $\phi(B, \mathbf{x})$ we wish to examine $\dfrac{\partial \phi}{\partial B}$. From the definition of ϕ we have

$$\operatorname{sign} \frac{\partial \phi}{\partial B} = \operatorname{sign}\left\{ EU'\, E(U''\theta) - EU''E(U'\theta) \right\} \tag{28}$$

where U' and U'' are evaluated at W.

We now examine the right-hand side of (28). We assume decreasing absolute risk aversion, that is $-U''(W)/U'(W)$ decreases with W. Since W is an increasing function of θ we have, for given θ^*, where W is $W(\theta, \mathbf{x}, B)$ and W^* is $W(\theta^*, \mathbf{x}, B)$.

$$\frac{-U''(W)}{U'(W)}(\theta - \theta^*) \leqq \frac{-U''(W^*)}{U'(W^*)} \cdot (\theta - \theta^*) \tag{29}.$$

Multiply through by the positive number $U'(W)$, take expectations, and we have

$$-E\left[U''(W)(\theta - \theta^*) \right] \leqq \frac{-U''(W^*)}{U'(W^*)} \cdot E\left[U'(W)(\theta - \theta^*) \right] \tag{30}$$

We now choose θ^* so that the right hand side of (30) vanishes (in fact this involves choosing $\theta^* = \phi$ if units are such that $E\theta = 1$).

[9]See also Bardhan (1973).

$$\theta^* = \frac{E\left[U'(W)\,\theta\right]}{E[U'(W)]} \tag{31}$$

and we have, where U' and U'' are evaluated at W,

$$EU'' \frac{E(U'\,\theta)}{EU'} - E(U''\,\theta) \leqq 0 \tag{32}$$

Since EU' is positive, equation (32) says that the right-hand side of (28) is positive and thus $\frac{\partial \phi}{\partial B}$ is positive.

Hence, for given $\mathbf{x}$, the right-hand side of (27) increases as B increases.

We can now check that this result tells us that a higher B implies a higher optimum x_i for each i. The maximand (23) can be written

$$G(\mathbf{x}, B) \tag{33}$$

and the first order condition (24) as

$$\frac{\partial G}{\partial x_i} = 0 \tag{34}$$

Differentiating (34) with respect to B we have

$$\frac{\partial^2 G}{\partial x_i \partial B} + \frac{\partial^2 G}{\partial x_i^2}\frac{dx_i}{dB} = 0 \tag{35}$$

But $\dfrac{\partial^2 G}{\partial x_i^2}$ is negative from the second order conditions hence the sign of $\dfrac{dx_i}{dB}$ is the same as that of $\dfrac{\partial^2 G}{\partial x_i \partial B}$. Now

$$\frac{\partial G}{\partial x_i} = \left[\phi E\theta - \frac{p_i}{f_i}\right]EU'f_i \tag{36}$$

hence, using the fact that (34) holds at the optimum,

$$\frac{\partial^2 G}{\partial x_i \partial B} = \frac{\partial \phi}{\partial B}E\theta\,EU'.f_i \tag{37}$$

We have established that $\dfrac{\partial \phi}{\partial S}$ is positive at the optimum hence so is $\dfrac{\partial^2 G}{\partial x_i \partial B}$ and thus $\dfrac{dx_i}{dB}$. A wealthier farmer (in the sense of higher B) will apply more variable inputs.

We considered in the above an exogenous additive shift in the non-stochastic component of wealth B. If, on the other hand, we consider a multiplicative shift in the whole of W we reach a different conclusion. We analyse the consequences for choice of $\mathbf{x}$ of a small increase in λ away from unity where $W(\theta, \mathbf{x}, \lambda) = \lambda Y_2\,(\theta, \mathbf{x})$. In this case we are multiplying all components of wealth, stochastic and non-stochastic, by λ. Thus our comparison is now (for fixed B) between a farmer with $B + Y_1(\theta)$ and a farmer with $\lambda B + \lambda Y_1(\theta)$. Previously we considered an increase in B with λ fixed at unity.

As is familiar from the standard theory of choice under uncertainty (see Arrow, 1970) the effects on choices of multiplicative changes are determined by what happens to the coefficient of *relative* risk aversion, $- WU''(W)/U'(W)$ as W changes. It is usual to suppose that relative risk aversion *increases* with wealth. If we make this assumption then we can show, in an analogous fashion to equations (28) – (37), that $\frac{\partial \phi}{\partial \lambda}$ is negative and similarly that $\frac{dx_i}{d\lambda}$ is negative each *i*. Hence if we compare two farmers who have identical patterns of wealth holding, but one has more of everything than the other, the richer farmer will have lower levels of each input.

We must now ask which, if either, of these two results is relevant. Consider first a comparison between two farmers whose only source of income is the land which they own and cultivate, and one of them owns more than the other. In this case the risk associated with choice of cultivation practice (captured in the distribution of θ) applies to the whole of the farmer's wealth. Thus having more land is equivalent to a multiplicative change in wealth. The case of decreasing relative risk aversion and input per acre decreasing with size of holding would appear to be appropriate. This, indeed, was the result which Srinivasan (1972) obtained by just the kind of argument that has been presented here.

If, however, a substantial part of a farmer's wealth resides in or is allocated to assets or income streams whose value is fairly safe or whose returns are independent of θ, or the farmer regards the input choice as a short-term experiment, then the first case of decreasing absolute risk aversion and input intensities which increase with wealth would be relevant.

It is clear that neither of the two cases has an overriding claim to our attention and that many comparisons will involve a combination of the two. We should suggest, however, that the case of input intensities which increase in wealth would be of greater interest for our study. First, many of the more wealthy farmers in Palanpur have capital assets alternative to land: cash, pumping sets, stocks of grain, valuable bullocks, jewellery, guns, and so on (see § 2.A.3) which could be realized at prices which are not closely correlated with their own current agricultural conditions. Second, many groups have reliable incomes from family members working outside the village (see § 4.1). Third, alternative crops provide investments which are not perfectly correlated with the given crop. Finally the farmer need not regard his choice as permanent. He could consider renting out some land for cash rent at the end of the season, changing to a less risky cropping pattern, selling the land, and so on.

It should be noted that Srinivasan (1972) derives the result that a larger labour availability in a household will imply higher input intensities (see 1972, p. 416, remark (2)) but he does not stress the interpretation in terms of the wealth of the farmer as we have done here. Labour is interpreted as the safe asset and cultivation as the risky so higher labour is equivalent to an increase in B.

We shall be paying special attention to calculations of the ratio between price and marginal value productivity of an input based on equation (27) in Chapter 8 when we come to interpret our empirical estimates of the ratios for the sample wheat plots. Examples using specific utility functions and distributions will be provided and we shall discuss the nature of the risks faced by cultivators, in particular hunger or loss of land.

The example of land-ownership illustrates that the different forms of wealth aggregated into W in the above are not perfect substitutes. A full analysis would require a utility function with several arguments representing different components of wealth. But that would produce an analysis yet more complex than that which has already been presented and we shall not embark upon it here. We must note, however, the important link between credit and land-ownership. Loans usually require some explicit or implicit collateral and in an agricultural community this would often be land. There is a very great reluctance to risk loss of land and this, therefore, would be a strong inhibition to taking on large amounts of loans. For those without land the threat on default is starvation, although one might have the opportunity to roll a loan over to the next year or seek alternative support, particularly from the family.

Griffin (1974) and others have argued that bigger farmers will use the purchased inputs such as fertilizer and irrigation more intensively than smaller farmers for an additional reason. Credit for the finance of inputs is available more cheaply, it is claimed, because of the bias of government and financial institutions towards the larger farmers, the bias being connected with the influence larger farmers can bring to bear. This easier credit, the argument runs, would lead to more intensive use of fertilizer and irrigation than by smaller farmers.

If one finds that the use of variable (non-labour) inputs increases with wealth then one could try to discriminate between the argument presented by Griffin and that associated with diminishing absolute risk aversion by examining the way in which the markets for credit and other inputs function. Of course both arguments may be applicable but one should beware of using an observation that more wealthy farmers take on more credit for fertilizers as evidence that credit is cheaper for such farmers. If the argument concerning diminishing absolute risk aversion applies and credit is of equal price to all farmers, one may find wealthier farmers using more fertilizer per acre and using credit to finance the purchase. We shall examine credit markets in § 4.3 and the relationships between fertilizer per acre and size of holding in Chapter 6.

If on the other hand less fertilizer per acre is used by richer farmers one would incline to accept the argument associated with increasing relative risk aversion and stressed by Srinivasan (1972). Note that a lower output per acre for wealthier farmers would not necessarily provide strong evidence for the Srinivasan result since there is a range of arguments which might explain this relation (see § 3.7). Srinivasan was, however, interested in contributing a further argument which would bear on such a connection.

Most of the discussion in this section has centered on the detailed analysis of a model of choice under uncertainty. We believe that such a model has considerable explanatory power for much behaviour towards risk that is observed. We have, however, taken objectives as given and we shall provide a more general discussion of appropriate objectives for modelling the choice of farmers in the next section.

And we have not in presenting this theory concentrated on a detailed theoretical discussion of the market for credit. We believe that there is little to be gained for our empirical analysis from such a discussion. On the other hand it is very important for our analysis of input decisions to understand the structure and complications of the provision of credit as it is to be found in Palanpur. This has been discussed already in Chapter 2 and we shall have more to say in later chapters (particularly Chapters 4 and 5).

§ 3.5 Objectives of Agents

We have used explicit utility functions for choice under certainty for our discussions in § 3.3 on labour, and under uncertainty in § 3.4 on capital. For some of the discussion of share-cropping in § 3.2 we worked with profit as an objective but for much of the time in that section utility functions were implicit (for example they are required where Pareto optimality is mentioned). We shall in this section pay direct attention to the selection of objectives in modelling the peasant.

We shall point to the differences that arise between the maximization of utility or its expectation on the one hand, and profit or its expectation on the other (see in this connection Chayanov, 1966). It will be argued that profit, be it the expectation of profit or otherwise, can be rather misleading in certain circumstances. There will be no detailed development of particular models but we shall comment on those that have already been presented and give intuitive arguments for other results. There will be some brief comment on the so-called 'safety first' or 'survival algorithm' literature and on the notion that individuals do not maximize anything at all.

Uncertainty played a central role in our discussion in the previous section of the choice of (non-labour) variable inputs. In an activity such as agriculture in rural India which is characterized by much uncertainty, where many farmers are living on very low incomes, and where the consequences of crop failure can be extremely severe or catastrophic, it is very hard to believe that behaviour can be characterized by the maximization of expected profit. If the loss of R500 involves the sale of land or great hunger it is most unlikely that a farmer would accept a cultivation decision which involved a 50–50 chance of gaining R501 and losing R500, yet such acceptance would be the implication of the maximization of expected profit.

The use of utility as maximand rather than profit implies that one must take care to include income effects of prices and contracts. We give two examples both of which concern certainty. The model of share-tenancy which we called Marshallian in § 3.2 depicted the tenant as choosing his labour input whilst facing an effective tax of proportion r on the returns to his labour. It is argued that his labour input is less than it would be if that tax did not exist. Let us consider an increase in the landlord's share (r) and suppose that the share-tenancy is the only source of income for the cultivator. If we take the marginal product of labour as (locally) given this increase acts like a straight forward reduction in the price at which the cultivator sells his labour. We know from standard utility theory that the net result of such a reduction in the price of labour could be either an increase or a decrease in labour applied. The income effect will work to increase labour supply and the substitution effect to reduce it. The income effect is missed in the simple profit approach. Bharadwaj (1974, p.53) seems to have this income effect in mind when she states, 'This strategy [raising rents]will work even better if the landlord parcels out his land in such small units that the tenant has to cultivate the small piece of land intensively to raise enough crop to provide his subsistence after paying the landlord's share.' Note that the argument that labour supply may increase does not negate the inefficiency of share-cropping in the model since that arises from the difference between the marginal product and the marginal disutility of labour (expressed in terms of the output).

A second example concerns the relative level of inputs. Suppose the level x_i of input i is for some reason lowered from an initial position (one can imagine some difficulty in supply or application). If profit is the maximand, the level of the jth input would be lowered if i and j were complements in the sense of $F_{ij} > 0$, where F_{ij} denotes the second partial derivative of the production function with respect to i and j. The conclusion could be reversed where the maximand is utility, since the individual may compensate by raising x_j so as to maintain the level of his consumption.

Cost minimization for the variable purchased inputs used in the production of the selected output level does survive a change from profit maximization to utility maximization under certainty but not, in general, under uncertainty. Given other inputs we can write the problem where we have one output as: choose $\mathbf{x}$ to

$$\text{Maximize } Eu\ [F\ (\theta, \mathbf{x}) - \mathbf{p}.\mathbf{x}] \tag{38}$$

where θ is stochastic, $\mathbf{x}$ the n-vector of variable inputs, and $F(\theta, \mathbf{x})$ output (uncertainty about the price of output can be subsumed into $F(\ )$). Cost minimization, given the state of nature θ, requires

$$\frac{\partial F}{\partial x_i} \Big/ \frac{\partial F}{\partial x_j} = p_i/p_j \tag{39}$$

if strictly positive x_i and x_j are chosen. The $(n - 1)$ equations of (39) together with the specified output level give us the vector $\mathbf{x}$ to be selected. It is clear, however, that the choice would in general depend upon θ. One might try to redefine cost minimization to refer to a specified expected level of output but the solution of (38) would not in general meet this new definition. There is a special case in which equations (39) will determine input proportions uniquely and that is where uncertainty is multiplicative $(F(\theta, \mathbf{x}) = \theta f(\mathbf{x}))$.

The 'safety-first' or 'survival algorithm' approach (see Lipton, 1968, or Weeks, 1970) portrays the farmer as minimizing the probability of income falling below a given level or, alternatively expressed, maximizing the probability of avoiding disaster. We can present this formally as follows. Let $G(y, \mathbf{x})$ be the distribution function of income y given inputs $\mathbf{x}$. If the production function were as above, $G(y, \mathbf{x})$ would equal $J(\tilde{\theta}(y, \mathbf{x}))$ where J is the distribution function for the random variable θ and $\tilde{\theta}(y, \mathbf{x})$ satisfies.

$$y = F(\tilde{\theta}, \mathbf{x}) - \mathbf{p.x} \tag{40}$$

The problem is to choose $\mathbf{x}$ to

$$\text{Minimize } G(\bar{y}, \mathbf{x}) \tag{41}$$

where $\bar{y}$ is the 'disaster level' of income.

Or, rewriting, choose $\mathbf{x}$ to

$$\text{Minimize } J(\tilde{\theta}(\bar{y}, \mathbf{x}) \tag{42}$$

or equivalently

$$\text{Minimize } \tilde{\theta}(\bar{y}, \mathbf{x}) \tag{43}$$

But $\tilde{\theta}(\bar{y}, \mathbf{x})$ is defined from

$$\bar{y} = F(\tilde{\theta}, \mathbf{x}) - \mathbf{p.x} \tag{44}$$

and $F(\ )$ is an increasing function of θ. Hence the optimum $\mathbf{x}^*$ maximizes over $\mathbf{x}$, $F(\theta^*, \mathbf{x}) - \mathbf{p.x}$ for fixed θ^* where $\theta^* = \tilde{\theta}(\bar{y}, \mathbf{x}^*)$. For if a selected $\mathbf{x}$ does not maximize profits for the selected θ then changing $\mathbf{x}$ to increase profits, given θ, will allow a lower choice of θ (see equation (44)). Thus safety-first is equivalent to maximization of expected profits where we assign probability one to θ^* and, for θ^*, we have the usual marginal productivity conditions

$$\frac{\partial F}{\partial x_i}(\theta^*, \mathbf{x}) = p_i \tag{45}$$

One can interpret the 'safety-first' model as utility maximization if we write

$$\left. \begin{array}{l} U(y) = 0 \text{ if } y < \bar{y} \\ \\ 1 \text{ if } y \geq \bar{y} \end{array} \right\} \tag{46}$$

Writing the utility function in this form emphasizes the peculiarity of the case. An individual contemplating $\bar{y} - \varepsilon$ would sacrifice everything for a small probability of gaining ε (note the non-concavity at $\bar{y}$). The notion is that disaster (death) is equivalent to falling below $\bar{y}$ and all disasters are equally unattractive.

The safety-first criterion is similar to but not the same as the maxi-min criterion which is often taken as the extreme of risk aversion. Action is taken under maxi-min so that the worst possible outcome in the resulting probability distribution has the highest value amongst all those probability distributions which are feasible. The difference is that no disaster level $\bar{y}$ is specified in maxi-min. Note that one cannot in the maxi-min case produce examples of individuals accepting unfair gambles. Indeed individuals would not accept any gambles at all however large the possible winnings.

We suggest that both the safety-first and maxi-min criteria are unreasonable as models of behaviour for a substantial majority of individuals even in a poor society such as Palanpur. In the case of each model the attitude to risk involved (see the above examples) is peculiar.

Finally there is the view that individuals do not behave as if they maximize anything in particular. The problem with this view is that it is rather hard to find alternatives which give a set of hypotheses about behaviour which is anything like as productive of results as is maximization. Whether or not the hypotheses are in conflict with what one finds in Palanpur, and which of the maximization criteria look most plausible, are questions we can ask after seeing, in subsequent chapters, some of the detail of economic behaviour.

§ 3.6 The Agricultural Production Function and the Efficiency of Traditional Agriculture

In the remaining sections of this chapter we shall turn from the more general analysis of the preceding sections to arguments which have concentrated on Indian agriculture. Our starting-point is the famous work of Hopper (1965) on village Senapur in East U.P. in 1954. We have several reasons for beginning there. Other commentators, seeking to justify the general claim that traditional agriculture is efficient, have drawn on Hopper's study (see Schultz, 1964). His study included wheat, a major focus of our own work, and was concerned with a single U.P. village. It raises serious issues in the specification of production functions which will be relevant for our later work and finally, an important criticism of Hopper's work is its neglect of uncertainty in the decision-making of farmers – the topic we have just been discussing.

Hopper conducts a production function analysis designed to explain the variation for a cross-section of farms in Senapur of the expected outputs of four different crops. He fitted the following production function

$$Y_i = a_i \prod_{j=1}^{4} X_{ij}^{b_{ij}} \tag{47}$$

where X_{ij} is the quantity of the jth input to the ith crop and $i = 1, 2, 3, 4$ is for barley, wheat, pea, and *gram*, the main *rabi* crops. The four inputs $j = 1, 2, 3, 4$ are land, bullock time, labour time (other than with bullocks), and amount of irrigation water. The land measure is adjusted for quality, and the bullocks for value and feed. The parameters b_{ij} were estimated for each crop by the multiple regression of log Y_i on the log X_{ij}'s. We report his estimated coefficients for wheat, $b_{2j} : j = 1, 2, 3, 4$; 0.2354, 0.5083, 0.0201, 0.1428 (land, bullocks, labour, irrigation respectively). Each was significant at the standard 5 per cent level and the R^2 was 0.87. The sum of the coefficients is 0.9066. Constant returns to scale would imply that they sum to unity.

For each crop, he compared the value of marginal product of a given input at geometric means. He found that the value marginal products of a given input were very similar for each of his crops. He also compared the value of the marginal product of a given input with its price and again found a close similarity. This last calculation was rather more tentative since bullocks and irrigation were not marketed and guesses at costs were necessary. Further, the price of land was based on a return on capital values. 'It was readily acknowledged in the village that leased land was not as productive as owner operated land' (p. 622) and hence, Hopper argues, it was not surprising to find cash rent below estimated value of marginal product of land. He argues that his finding of efficiency in a stagnant agriculture is not surprising since substitution possibilities would have been discovered over the generations and concludes (p. 624), 'The problem of agricultural development is the problem of introducing new resources, skills and techniques in agriculture. Little progress can be expected from efforts which merely tinker with the traditional production functions, or seek to reallocate traditional resources.'

Hopper's data were collected in 1954 when, he argued, production conditions were stagnant, and ours twenty years later when farmers were using chemical fertilizers, new varieties, and more irrigation, and had not been using these inputs for very long. We should not, therefore, necessarily expect to find the same results on producer behaviour. There is, however, a basic feature of the Hopper approach which is remarkable; this is the neglect of uncertainty.

One expects uncertainty to play an important role when substantial costs are incurred on inputs prior to the value of the product of those inputs being known. For Hopper's study the main current costs seem to have been wages and the feed of bullocks. The farmer rarely cultivated himself: he owned his own bullocks and the land and he hired ploughmen and labourers to do the cultivation. The raising of irrigation water involved the employment of both men and bullocks. Thus Hopper's farmers were paying out sums which were quite substantial in relation to output. We find it hard to believe that with this level of advance commitment the farmers would show a complete absence of risk aversion and maximize expected profits.

The output Y_i was not measured output but expected output. Hopper argues, not unreasonably, that it is expected output which is the appropriate measure if the hypothesis of expected profit maximization is to be examined. In his words (1965, p. 613),

Expected yields were obtained by visiting each field with its owner and reviewing exactly what was done on the field in preparation, sowing, and irrigation, and then asking what yield he expected from the field if the winter rains came on time and disease or other hazards were not more serious than usual.

From Hopper's expression of the question it sounds as if farmers were being asked what yield would be expected in a *better* than average year, since the rains coming on time is better than average and the effect of disease on the mode output (the question asked) is likely to be less than its effect on the average.[10] Thus

[10]Imagine an individual contemplating possible outputs where the only uncertainty is connected

his finding of price equal to expected value of marginal product is yet more remarkable. Actual yields were not given.

There have been other Indian studies following the approach of Hopper. Chennareddy, for example (1967), estimates Cobb–Douglas production functions for a sample of farms in S. India in 1957–8. He takes the total value of output from the farm as the variable to be explained. The value of marginal products and prices of inputs are compared and Chennareddy claims that Hopper's conclusions are supported. Sahota (1968) uses the Farm Management Studies data for 1954–5, 1955–6, and 1956–7. He estimates Cobb–Douglas production functions for particular crops but imposes constant returns to scale by expressing inputs and output in per acre terms. This condition, he says, was a constraint imposed by the form of the data. He again claims to find efficiency thus broadly supporting Hopper.[11]

Features common to the studies include time period, techniques, and conclusion. We shall return to the issues raised in later chapters.

An important criticism of Hopper's estimation technique has been advanced by Nowshirvani (1967). He argues[12] that Hopper's statistical technique (ordinary least squares regressions using the logarithms of variables) is biased and inconsistent because the explanatory variables will be correlated with the error term. We postpone discussion of this issue to Chapter 8, where in § 8.5, certain technical statistical problems are discussed.

§ 3.7 Farm size and Productivity

The (Indian) Farm Management Surveys (FMS) for several states in the 1950s appeared to reveal an inverse relation between farm size and output per acre. The result prompted a great deal of discussion. Sen (1962) noted the result and argued that smaller farms may be using more labour per acre since he supposed, as family farms, they are not involved actively in the local labour market and may push the application of labour past the point where marginal productivity is equal to the market wage.

Khusro (1973) has argued that the magnitude of the decline in productivity per acre with farm size is reduced considerably when one takes into account the quality of land. He 'standardizes' land for quality using the land revenue ratings. Thus larger farms on average have lower land quality. Sen (1964) has suggested that an explanation may lie in a Malthusian process whereby population growth on fertile land is more rapid leading to the faster division of land holdings.

Other hypotheses have been advanced. It has been suggested that larger holdings may consist of several widely dispersed parcels which would have an

with disease and where he believes that disease will come to his fields at an average rate of once every five years. Suppose, for the sake of the argument, that disease reduces output to zero. If the 'disease-free' output is x then the mode is x, but the average is $(4/5)x$.

[11] Junankar (1976) has vigorously attacked the value of assuming profit maximization in models of Indian agriculture by econometric analysis using profit functions.

[12] See also Zellner, Kmenta, and Drèze (1966).

adverse effect on productivity. And Khusro has suggested that the proportion of land under tenancy may be larger on larger holdings and that, for the Marshallian reasons discussed earlier, one would expect lower output per acre on share-cropped land. Further, it may be that larger farms are more likely to be run by managers for absentee land-owners, and managers have less incentives than would an owner-cultivator.

We shall not attempt to select from these reasons or to analyse the arguments in further detail. There is a useful brief discussion of the literature up to the late 1960s in Bhagwati and Chakravarty (1969), and an excellent discussion of the literature up to and including the early 1970s, with a large number of references, in Sen (1975, Appendix C). For a particularly intensive study of the FMS data the reader may wish to consult Bardhan (1973). Because the two summaries mentioned exist in forms which are brief and easily available we shall not attempt a detailed exposition here. We note the finding and that there have been a number of explanations put forward. Further the empirical result has itself come under question–Rudra (1968 and 1968a), for example, has argued that it is not reflected in intra-village analyses involving individual households (the FMS data are grouped–see below).

There is one study of FMS data, however, which appeared after the two surveys we have mentioned were written, that of Bharadwaj (1974) and we shall describe it briefly here. She analysed data from the published reports 'Studies in the Economics of Farm Management' for two selected districts in each of six states for the years 1954–7. Data in the published reports are not available by individual farm but are aggregated for each district into size-groups of operational holdings. Issues such as the utilization of bullock labour, the effects of irrigation, cropping pattern, yield, the effects of tenancy, and so on are discussed, particularly in relation to the size of holding. She worked mainly with tables and simple regressions where size of holding was usually the single explanatory variable. We shall not attempt a full summary of her results but point to one or two conclusions which she chose to emphasize.

The analysis of main interest to this study concerns farm-size and productivity. Bharadwaj confirmed in general the negative relation between output per acre and size of holding but said that this was not reflected in a negative relation for individual crops. She argued that higher outputs per acre were obtained on smaller holdings by cropping more intensively and choosing higher-value crops. Her measure of area is net cropped area—that is, a piece of land is counted only once whether or not two crops are raised from it. This has been the practice in most previous studies (Rudra, 1968 and 1968a are, however, exceptions—he doubles an area if it is double-cropped in a year) and is one we shall follow here when we examine annual output (see Chapter 6).

Bharadwaj examined also the inputs of labour, draught power, and irrigation, relating each of them in particular to size of cultivated holding. Under draught power she paid particular attention to the utilization of bullocks (see Chapter 4 below where we comment briefly on her and other studies of the issue). She attempted to relate the type of tenancy to cropping pattern and intensity of cultivation but was hampered by the fact that 'The information on tenurial conditions contained in the published FMS is extremely scanty and partial so that our discussion remains highly cursory and tentative.' (p.85).

Given the fear in rural areas of the consequences of past or future land legislation for security of tenure or ownership, gatherers of official statistics are always likely to find difficulty in collecting data on tenancy(see also § 2.4 where National Sample Survey statistics on incidence are compared with our own data). These problems and the fact that most official studies aggregate in various ways, thus losing the detail of data on individuals and households, provide strong arguments for the careful collection of new data.

§ 3.8 Variations in the Form of Share Contract

We provide in this section a brief historical discussion of share contracts. Our remarks are concentrated on India although we shall refer briefly to other regions. We do not intend this section to be a survey. Our purpose is to say enough to establish two points: first, that there are records of a wide variety of share contracts where the diversity occurs in both share and understanding over inputs and costs; second, that the 50-50 share of output seems particularly common, at least in North India.

Valuable historical studies of land tenure in India which bear on the form of rental systems have been contributed by Etienne (1968), Neale (1962), and Sayana (1949).[13] The system of sharing of output has existed in India for a very long time. Etienne writes (p. 45): 'Originally the English were baffled by the Indian way of land ownership since in no way did it resemble the European system. It was based on two principles; the first man to bring land into cultivation had prior claim to part of its produce; those who had conquered the country also had a right to part of it. In fact, the harvest was divided among the grower, the sovereign and the workers who gave their services to the growers, the blacksmith, the carpenter, the sweeper, the barber'. Neale quotes from an 1878 study of Gonda by Bennett which describes in detail the rules for sharing amongst different interested parties. Various village officials and craftsmen had rights to certain shares as did the ploughman, cutters and threshers, and the washerman, barber, and so on, and finally the cultivator and *raja* split the remainder 50-50. The *raja* also had an obligation to give a little to the priest and *patwari*, as did the cultivator. Neale writes that the gross product was never evaluated and payments were always in terms of a share.

Sayana surveyed sharing systems that existed in India and Pakistan at that time and compared them with those of other countries. In Pakistan 'batai'[14] usually meant equal proportions minus 'customary deductions' which varied widely. In Sind the share of the landlord was one-third for lift-irrigated crops and one-half for flow-irrigated crops. If the landlord supplied bullocks and

---

[13]The literature on land tenure in India is voluminous and we have selected just a few from those contributions which are relevant to the issue at hand.

[14]'Batai' is derived from the verb 'batana —to be divided.

seed his share was 'much larger'. In Bihar and Bengal crop-sharing was widespread–the proportion of the cultivated area was, he suggested, around 20 per cent and increasing. In Bengal half shares were common with two-third shares to the landlord on cash crops (potatoes and sugar). Landlords supplied cattle, a plough, and seed, and took half the straw. Landlords also supplied rice for home consumption and took 50 per cent interest on this in grain at harvest. In Bihar shares varied from ½ : ½ to 9 : 7 (landlord : tenant).

More recently in his own study of Purnea district in Bihar, Bell (1975) has found the 50 – 50 share to be still very common. Ladejinsky (1977), on the other hand, has found that in the so-called 'Green Revolution' areas of Punjab and Haryana, 'The first consequence of rising land values is that rents have risen above the traditional (although illegal under the reforms) 50 – 50 share of the crop' (p. 498). He states on p. 464, 'As a consequence [of the rise in land values] not only have rents risen to as high as 70 per cent of the crop in some places but security of tenure and other rights in land the tenant might claim are in jeopardy now.' For a survey of forms of tenancy in India from FMS data for 1953–4 and 1960–1 the reader should consult Bardhan (1977), and for the changes of the 1960s Bardhan (1976).

The over-all picture for North India in recent times seems to be that the 50 – 50 share is common with a tendency for lower shares to the landlord on poor land where little inputs are provided and higher shares for better land where many inputs are supplied and the yield is likely to be of higher value. It should be emphasized again that the above is not intended as a survey but merely to give an impression of other areas and times as a background for the Palanpur study.

Share-cropping has been common in Asia, North and South America, and Europe. Again one finds that 50 – 50 is quite common (and embodied in the French word for share-cropping, 'metayage') and that there is a wide variation in shares in costs and agreement over levels for inputs. For interesting studies of other regions the reader may consult Cheung (1969) on China in the inter-war period and post-war Taiwan; Reid (1973 and 1974) for a historical study of share-cropping in the U.S.A.; Kutcher and Scandizzo (1976) on contemporary N.E. Brazil; and Higgs (1894) on nineteenth-century France.

§ 3.9 The 'Green Revolution' in India

The so-called 'Green Revolution' has produced in a short space of time a remarkable range of sentiments. Randhawa (1974) dedicates his book entitled *Green Revolution* as follows, 'To the farmers of Punjab who made the Green Revolution a reality and filled the bread-basket of India'. Ladejinsky (1977, p. 495) quotes Khusro (1972), 'One can perhaps stick one's neck out and assert that India's food problem has been solved for good'. Ladejinsky himself was one of the first to warn of difficulties. Writing his report to the World Bank in 1972 and referring to his earlier reports he says, 'Apart from environmental and other limitations, the contention propounded in these reports on previous occasions that the Green Revolution is primarily "selective" remains valid' (p.496, and see also his remarks on rental shares quoted in the previous section).

Whilst pointing to problems and difficulties, Ladejinsky was well aware of the benefits: 'To the extent that the Green Revolution makes for stability via irrigation and for higher yields via its other techniques, its role is indispensable in any attempt to modernise Indian Agriculture' (p. 534). Others have been much more sweeping:

The history of the development effort is littered with the broken promises of technology. The birth pill was going to solve the population problem. Miracle seeds were going to solve the food problem. Medical breakthroughs were going to solve the health problem. These dreams have gone sour because of a persisting belief that technology is neutral, that problems which are political, economic and social can be solved by steel, glass and plastic.

Imagine, for example, the agricultural extension worker in India who carries the good news about new strains of wheat which can yield three or four times as much per acre. He first visits the large farm of 200 acres. The farmer is at ease with a visitor from the city; he can read the literature he leaves behind; he knows how to seek further advice; he can afford the necessary pesticides, fertiliser and irrigation; and, most important, he can afford to take the risk of experimenting with the new seeds on ten of his two hundred acres.

He gets a bumper crop. So the next year he puts all his land under the new seeds. Even though the vastly increased output slightly lowers the market price in the area, he now has money to invest in more land and more mechanisation.

Next, the agricultural extension worker visits the small farmer with one acre of land. He can't read the instructions on the leaflets; he can't afford the investment in irrigation, pesticides and fertiliser; and because he and his wife and children are on the edge of subsistence with only one acre of land, he can't afford the risk.

In time, the increased yields of the larger farms depress the market price and he begins to feel the pinch and get into debt with the village moneylender who charges interest rates of 100% per annum. Meanwhile the large farmer is wanting to invest his extra profits in more land to make better use of the machinery he has just bought – so he calls on his neighbour and helps him out by buying his land and giving him seasonal employment.

The net result is that one more subsistence farmer is added to the ranks of the landless labourers and one more large farmer achieves economic 'take-off'. (*New Internationalist* May 1978, Editorial p. 3).

The literature on the 'Green Revolution' is vast and we cannot and shall not attempt to summarize it here. We hope enough has already been said to establish the first point that we wish to make: that reaction to what it is thought to be has ranged from the euphoric to the bitterly hostile.

Such extreme views have, we suppose, given rise to questions, put to us quite frequently at seminars, which embody sharp categorizations of farmers, for example, 'What proportion of the farmers in Palanpur adopted the Green Revolution ?' The language of the question is very misleading, and this is our second point. The cultivation practices in Palanpur (see later chapters and particularly § 7.3) vary across the range from 'very poor' to 'not bad' where we judge by the recommended practices of agricultural handbooks and local officials. To speak of adopters and non-adopters is not a useful way to examine what is happening.

Many farmers do now use some chemical fertilizers where previously there would have been none. New varieties of seed are used, although many are of poor quality. Nearly all the land is irrigated where twenty years ago the proportion would have been relatively small. But sowing practice is often poor, mix of fertilizer is attended to only by a few, levels of fertilizer input are very variable and for all but a very few far below recommended levels, pesticides are never used, irrigation practice is fairly haphazard, and so on. These remarks will be developed in later chapters but it is important from the outset that readers should not subscribe to the notion that, in relation to the 'Green Revolution', there is a clear division between farmers who 'practise' or 'adopt' and those who do not. We shall return to the assessment of the effects of 'Green Revolution' in Palanpur in § 7.3 and § 9.6.

§ 3.10 Concluding Remarks

Our discussion in this chapter has been wide-ranging and we shall not attempt a detailed summary here. We have concentrated in our discussion on theory and on issues of particular relevance to studies in later chapters. Thus the longest section (§ 3.2) was on tenancy and we paid special attention to choice under uncertainty (in § 3.4 and § 3.5). Similarly in our examination of various topics in Indian agriculture we have reviewed those to which, we think, later chapters have something to contribute. Thus we discussed the estimation of production functions (see Chapters 6, 7, 8) and the efficiency of Indian agriculture (see Chapters 4 and 8) in § 3.6, farm-size and productivity in § 3.7 (see Chapter 6), the variations in share contracts in § 3.8 (see Chapter 5), and the 'Green Revolution' in § 3.9 (see, in particular, Chapter 7).

In Chapter 1 we set out the organization of our study and in Chapter 2 we gave a broad description of the village of Palanpur. Chapter 3 completes the introduction in setting the background of the theoretical issues and discussion of Indian agriculture. We can now turn to our detailed studies of markets and activities in Palanpur.

Appendix to Chapter 3

We show here that in a share-tenancy contract, under certainty, any combination of input levels which can be achieved by the landlord stipulating those levels can also be achieved by cost-sharing. An intuitive argument was provided in § 3.2; a formal proof is given in this appendix.

The problem where the landlord specifies the input levels is considered first – we call it problem A. We adopt the same notation as in § 3.2, when we discussed the Cheung model, except that we generalize to include purchased inputs (we denote the inputs by the vector $\mathbf{x}$ and their prices by $\mathbf{p}$) as well as the non-purchased input labour, l. The landlord's maximization problem is as follows.

Problem A

   Maximize $\quad n\, r\, F$
   $r, l, n, \mathbf{x}$

   subject to $(1 - r)F - \mathbf{p}.\mathbf{x} \geqq w\, l$

where output from area M/n if a tenant applies labour, l, and inputs $\mathbf{x}$ is $F(l, M/n, \mathbf{x})$.

   Substituting from the constraint (it will bind at the optimum) we have, without constraint

   Maximize $\quad n\, (F - \mathbf{p}.\mathbf{x} - w\, l)$
   $l, n, \mathbf{x}$

Hence, differentiating with respect to x_i we have $\partial F/\partial x_i = p_i$; with respect to l, $\partial F/\partial l = w$; and the rent per tenant (R/n) is $F - \mathbf{p}.\mathbf{x} - w\, l$, which is equal to $M/n\ \ \partial F/\partial h$ (where $\partial F/\partial h$ is the marginal product of land) since we impose constant returns to scale. Thus, when the landlord stipulates inputs, the marginal product of each input is equal to its price.

We consider now the problem where the tenant decides on inputs but the landlord offers to contribute $C(\mathbf{x})$ when inputs are at level $\mathbf{x}$. The landlord can choose the function $C(\ )$. We call his new maximization problem, B. The tenant's income is $P(\mathbf{x}, n, r, l, C(\ )) = (1 - r)\, F - \mathbf{p}.\mathbf{x} + C(\mathbf{x})$ and he chooses $\mathbf{x}$ (but not l)

Problem B

   Maximize $n(rF - C(\mathbf{x})\,)$
   $n, r, C(\ ), l$

subject to $P \geqq w l$, and the constraint that the tenant chooses $\mathbf{x}$ to maximize P given n, r, $C(\ ), l$

   Write $R' = n(rF - C)$. The landlord's problem is

Problem B'

   Maximize R'
   $R', n, l, C(\ )$

subject to   (i) $F - \mathbf{p}.x - R\, n \geq wl$
   and (ii) the tenant chooses $\mathbf{x}$ to maximize his income.

It is now clear that the landlord can do no better in problem B than he did in problem A. For problem B' is the same as problem A with the added constraint (ii). (Note that $C(\ )$ enters B' only through (ii) and that one can write nrF as R in problem A.)

Now suppose that in problem B the landlord makes the following choices: $C(\mathbf{x}) = \beta \mathbf{p.x}$, $r = \beta$, $l = l^*$, $n = n^*$, where β is defined by the optimum total rent for problem A, $n^*r^*F^*$, being equal to $\beta n(F^* - \mathbf{p.x})$ and where the starred values are the optimum values for problem A. The tenant will now *choose* $\mathbf{x}^*$ and the landlord's rent for problem B will be the same as that for the optimum to problem A. We have, therefore, found the optimum for problem B since we saw that any result in B can be no better than the best for problem A. Note that, from the definition of β, β r^*. Thus the optimum share with cost-sharing is less than that for stipulation, although net rent and all input levels are the same.

We have seen then, that any input levels which can be achieved by stipulation can also be achieved by cost-sharing.

4

Markets in Palanpur

§ 4.0 Introduction

Having described the village in Chapter 2 and discussed some general theoretical issues concerning the economics of agriculture and development in Chapter 3, we are ready to embark upon our empirical investigations from the data that we collected in Palanpur. We shall attempt to formulate hypotheses from the theoretical models which can be confronted with our data. These exercises will be the subject matter of this chapter and of Chapters 5, 6, 7, and 8. We shall here consider in detail the operation of the major markets of Palanpur and we shall be discussing various hypotheses about these markets. A knowledge of how these operate will be important for our design of models later on and for the assessment of many of our findings.

It must be understood at the outset that we are using the term 'market' in a general, imprecise, and all-embracing sense. We intend to refer simply to the conditions under which exchange of the services of factors take place and the arrangements in force for organizing that exchange. There is no implication that the market is in any sense a formal one with a specific location; still less is there any suggestion that the market is perfect or competitive or has any other feature of markets to be found elsewhere in the world (or in the pages of economics textbooks). Indeed in one case the important thing that we shall have to describe and discuss is the near absence of a market where one might perhaps expect to find one.

In § 4.1 we examine the labour market in Palanpur. The hiring of wage labour to undertake agricultural work is widespread although there are no labour households in the village which derive all their income from agricultural labour. We shall look at the seasonal variation in the demand for labour, how easily it is obtainable, and the variation in wage rates from times of high demand to times of low demand. We shall also discuss the question of whether the wage rate can be considered as a useful measure of the opportunity cost of family labour.

In § 4.2 we shall examine the market for the services of bullocks where, as was remarked already in Chapter 2, we shall find that there is no market in the sense that the services of bullocks are not usually exchanged for cash. This fact will be of importance later on, particularly when we come to examine, in Chapter 5, the farmer's decision to lease-in land or lease it out. We shall examine some possible explanations for the absence of active trading in what might be thought to be an obvious and useful market. Since bullocks are essential for cultivation and as one cannot reliably purchase the use of bullocks for cash it might seem that a man cannot cultivate land unless he owns bullocks. However there are a few farmers in Palanpur who are cultivating (usually small) parcels of land without the benefit of owning bullocks. This they achieve by exchange of services for the use of bullocks, in most cases with relatives. So, for example, a man may work on his brother's land in exchange for the use of his brother's bullocks. We discuss some of these 'marginal cultivators' and compare them with the bullock-owning farmer.

§ 4.3 is concerned with credit in its various aspects. We shall describe where Palanpur households are able to borrow against future repayment in cash or in kind. We examine also the cost of this credit and qualitative features of the various credit sources, such as the willingness to roll over or extend loans when the borrower finds it difficult to repay, and the type of security that is demanded. Finally, we shall also discuss the extent to which lending and borrowing relations are interlinked with other market and non-market relations.

§ 4.4 is concerned with water sources, that is, the hire of the use of Persian wheels, borings, and pumping sets. This is not a market for a homogeneous product, since the demand for the use of a Persian wheel is necessarily the demand for the use of one particular Persian wheel (or one of very few) to irrigate a particular piece of land. The same is true of borings but not of pumping sets because these can be moved from place to place. The economic theory appropriate to the setting of the price for the use of a Persian wheel would apparently be bilateral monopoly. However it seems that sellers are willing to charge the 'going rate' and not 'what the market will bear'. We offer some (highly speculative) views as to why this is the case. Pumping sets are valuable assets and a considerable part of the return to their ownership takes the form of cash income from hiring them out to other farmers. We provide an estimate of the returns to owning a pumping set, gross of depreciation, and describe some characteristics of the small number of farmers who own them.

The market for the use of land will be considered in Chapter 5 which will be devoted entirely to the subject of tenancy. Apart from the use of land we shall, at the end of § 4.4, have considered all the main factor markets. The remainder of Chapter 4 will be given over to some questions to do with particular crops and cropping patterns.

§ 4.5 is devoted to an examination of some peculiarities of one particular crop, sugar. A feature which sets sugar apart from other crops is that its cultivation season is ten months so that it bridges *rabi* and *kharif* seasons. Also important are the input requirements of sugar and particularly the market for the output from its cultivation. This last feature makes sugar a significantly different crop from any other. Most cane is sold to a government mill to be processed into refined sugar. Because cane must be processed quickly after cutting and in order to keep the resources of the mills fully employed, the mill-managers run a rationing system for cane delivery. A farmer is allocated a certain area from which the mill agrees to take cane when it is mature. This means that a farmer must have a quota if he is to be able to market his cane at the best price. An alternative is to sell to the *ghur* market, but in the case of Palanpur the most popular alternative to the government mill is a private mill. Since sugar seems to be a very profitable crop we discuss the barriers to the extension of its cultivation.

§ 4.6 deals very briefly with a range of questions which could well form the basis for a separate study. A farmer typically grows several crops and the cropping pattern varies a good deal from farmer to farmer. A theory of the cropping pattern which the farmer chooses would have to take into account many features of that farmer and the members of his household, his land holding and assets, his wealth and access to credit, and his willingness to bear risk. We display a table showing the means and standard deviations of output per *bigha* for the main village crops. We show these values separately for owned and cultivated land and leased-in land and we analyse the relationship between tenancy and yield.

Without at this stage being able to demonstrate the point we incline to think that large holdings encourage diversification because on large holdings this can be achieved without the cost of diseconomies associated with cultivating very small parcels. In addition, the more wealthy farmer is more willing to undertake the risk of cultivating crops for which yield is very uncertain.

We shall not in this chapter give any consideration to the market for leased-in land. That market is of such importance that we have devoted the whole of the next chapter to its study.

During the course of our stay in the village we organized some discussions with farmers during which we put to them various questions concerning their own and village agriculture. The farmers chosen were those who cultivated plots included in our sample of wheat plots (see below Chapters 7 and 8). In § 4.7 we describe those discussion sessions which were useful and interesting to us, and detail the questions that were asked and some of the answers. At this point we leave over for § 8.5 those particular questions which were concerned with the cultivation of wheat on the sample plots.

Our concluding observations are contained in § 4.8.

§ 4.1 The Labour Market

In discussing the selling of labour time by the households of Palanpur we are going to give most of our attention to agricultural labour within the village. This is not to suggest however that the remainder is unimportant: indeed as Table 4.1(a) shows, more income is generated by the sale of labour outside the village. Of course where labour was outside the village we were observers of only one side of the transaction, since the employer might well be unknown to us. One reason for taking a particular interest in intra-village transactions is that we can examine such questions as the balance between supply and demand in the market, questions which require the buyer of labour time to be considered along with the seller.

It might seem that, out of 111,[1] forty-two households participating in non-agricultural employment would indicate a village in which agriculture, while perhaps the main activity, is not the only important source of employment. Such is indeed the case, although only thirty of the forty-two households have employment outside the village, the remaining eight being employed in service

[1] In this and all subsequent chapters we shall be dealing with a population of 111 households. As was explained in Chapter 1 (see footnote on p. 2), one household migrated from the village in November 1974.

Table 4.1(a) Households earning income from the sale of labour other than agricultural

Household	Nature or place of employment	Income from sale of labour 1974–5: non-agricultural	Income from sale of labour 1974–5: agricultural	Total income
109	Agricultural labour and night watchman at Seed Store	635	450	1267
111	Moradabad cloth mill	1501		11541
118	Teacher in Palanpur school	1485		23672
120	Service outside village	3065		11505
122	Cloth mill	2917		11493
125	Cloth mill	2387		8375
209	Cane centre	1819		3797
211	Various outside village	2293	132	4460
213	Railway employment and agricultural labour	586	525	1300
215	Teacher in Palanpur private school	4200		9920
216	Teacher in Palanpur private school	3000		11454
219	Service outside village	2543		15474
227	Doctor (*Kucca*)	6000		32174
306	Moradabad cloth mill	4653		8834
307	Service outside Palanpur	2116	525	4645
308	Railway work	2802		9527
406	Railway work	2400		10024
407	Service in Moradabad	4731		13487
408	Railway employment	3000		3400
501	Village washerman	660		2277
503	Service in mill	2352		10683
601	Railway employment	1620		2112
602	Railway and agricultural labour	1583	225	1808
603	Railway and agricultural labour	1666	150	1816
607	Service outside village	3584	360	10177
608	Cloth mill and agricultural labour outside village	3966	375	6746
609	Service in Moradabad	2483	240	2723
612	Moradabad cloth mill	2317		6672
701	A Moradabad mill	3600		6040
702	Service outside village and transport of sugar cane to the centre in his bullock cart	3543	1400	13622
703	Moradabad railway employment	6600		7942
704	Moradabad cloth mill	2680		8590
705	Moradabad cloth mill	3600		5040
706	Railway employment	1800		5151
707	A Moradabad mill	7500		10986
708	Service outside village	7915	600	8817
803	Oil mill	2485	275	6818

807	Mill employment and some dancing	1593	900	4962
813	Various within the village	227	1064	6434
901	Intermittently at Seed Store and goat trading	640	443	3243
902	Electrician and clerk in factory	1140		1140
903	Village carpenter	1117	110	2399
904	Sweeper	2535	90	4646

Notes: (i) The first digit in the household number denotes the caste of the household (see, for example, Table 2.1). The next two digits denote the number within the caste but these two digits carry no connotation of rank.
(ii) The figures are labour incomes accruing to the household. Sometimes more than one individual is involved and sometimes more than one employment.
(iii) For a definition of total income see § 6.3

occupations in the village (e.g. washing and teaching). These activities might be regarded as part of the total activity of a largely agricultural village, being service occupations to those engaged in agriculture. Even more important is the fact that we have listed a household in Table 4.1(a) whenever any of its members participates in outside employment, even if several other male family members work in the village and in farming. It is quite usual for young men to go outside the village to find work. Most of the employment from Palanpur in Moradabad is accounted for by men in their early twenties. It is likely that these men will eventually return to Palanpur to work the land when their fathers become too old to farm.

In general *Thakur* households do not hire out their services as agricultural labourers. Traditionally labour of any kind on the land would have been considered degrading and agricultural labour considered much worse than the cultivation of own (or leased-in) land. In fact no *Thakur* household in Palanpur provides agricultural labour with the exception of household 109, Rajendra Singh. We have treated this man as a *Thakur* although strictly speaking he has lost caste and should be classified separately. His story is interesting and we shall digress briefly to tell it.

Rajendra Singh was once the owner of more than 22 *bighas* of land and a respectable member of the village and of his caste. He is married and has two children. However he took up with a woman not his wife and continued an irregular liaison with her for some time. During this period he sold nearly all his land to finance his way of life and he and his family were left destitute. As a result of his behaviour he was rejected by the *Thakurs* although he remains on very friendly terms with everyone in the village. He now lives by working as a night-watchman at the Seed Store, a position that he could not enjoy but for the favour of the *Thakurs*, and by selling his labour as an agricultural labourer. He is now living with his wife again but she unfortunately has gone mad and wanders about the village behaving like a child.

Most of the households whose only labour income is from agricultural labour (see Table 4.1(b)) are *Jatabs*. None of these households gains all its income

Table 4.1(b) Households earning labour income derived solely from agricultural labour

Household	Remarks	Income earned from the sale of labour 1974–5	Total income 1974–5
301		87	1446
302	Permanent labour	1332	4357
303		127	5519
304	Permanent labour and a boy working	1581	7418
305		3571	5064
604		305	5077
606		139	3666
801		108	4386
805		461	3442
806		972	1616
809		485	4652
810		447	3787
811		532	10387
812		2880	3705
814		919	4541

from agricultural labour, and we can see that for these households agricultural labour is not even the most important part of income (and see Table 6.2).

Two types of labour contract predominate. The first is a cash wage, usually for a day's work, which may or may not include the provision of a midday meal by the employer. The second is a share contract under which the labourer receives a share of the produce of his work. The former type of contract applies in the case of most of the standard agricultural tasks, such as ploughing, sowing, or irrigating. The latter contract is used in the case in which it is most easily applied, that is, harvesting. A few other particular cases are treated by arrangements which match their requirements. So, for example, weeding is usually paid at the rate of a certain number of rupees per *bigha* weeded.

The system for paying labour for harvesting is standard and is worth describing in detail, as taking it into account will affect our measure of wheat output in Chapters 7 and 8. Harvest labourers are given a one-twentieth share of the crop. Harvesting is undertaken by teams of labourers, including women and children of the lower castes, who move about the village land cutting the crop (in the case of wheat) with small sickles and tying it into bundles. The bundles are laid beside the field and the cultivator chooses an appropriate number of bundles to give to the harvesters. This provides an incentive to the harvesters to make the bundles of equal size. The system also has the advantage that the harvesters can work at their own pace without affecting the cost to the cultivator, which is fixed at one-twentieth of his crop. Hence only general supervision is required.

Where the land has been leased to a tenant-cultivator it is his job to harvest the crop. If, therefore, the tenant hires labour to help him with the harvest then the payment to those labourers must come from the tenant's share. Suppose that the landlord's share is 50 per cent (as is always the case in Palanpur), that a proportion θ of the crop is harvested by hired labour, and a proportion $(1 - \theta)$ by the tenant or his family. Then the tenant will receive a proportion.

$$\frac{(1-\theta)+0.9\,\theta}{2}$$

of the crop after he has paid his harvest labourers. In other words, it costs the tenant one-tenth of his share to have his crop harvested for him.

Table 4.2 shows for each month of the 1974–5 *rabi* season the number of man-days of agricultural labour purchased by Palanpur farmers and the average cost of those man-days computed as the ratio of monetary outlay to number of days purchased. It should be noted that during the month of October we had not established our routine for recording the hiring of labour with the consequence that we are not able to provide a useful estimate of the number of man-days that were hired-in. The average cost figure for October is the ratio of cost for those transactions that we did record (these involved 277 man-days) to the number of man-days involved in those transactions. As such it probably represents a good estimate of the cost of hiring labour in that month. Note, however, that October is a busy month, more or less as busy as November, during which ploughing is going on every day. Hence the total of man-days bought-in must have been greatly in excess of the 277 man-days recorded. April is the main month for the harvesting of wheat so that the predominant type of wage contract is the one-twentieth share. We have not attempted to estimate the cost of labour in terms of one man-day for harvesting but it would be high, not less than R10 per day.

Table 4.2

Month	Number of man-days purchased by Palanpur farmers	Average cost in rupees per day
October	not available	4.59
November	594	4.14
December	349	3.99
January	220	4.29
February	155	3.72
March	145	3.72
April	not recorded—mainly harvesting	payment as harvest shares
May	500	3.78
June	121	3.20

Notes: (i) In calculating man-days we have given the weights 1, 1, and ½ to men, women, and children. The number of days contributed by women was tiny and the number by children was small.
(ii) Where a meal was provided it was costed at one rupee.
(iii) For movements in the price level over the year see Table 4.12.
(iv) The type of work varies over the year: for example in October it would be ploughing and in May threshing.

Another point to notice is that sometimes a meal is provided with the wage. This is the standard arrangement in October and November and in those months if no meal is provided the wage will normally be R1 higher. In December and through the turn of the year the meal will very often not be included in the hiring agreement. A meal again becomes usual in May and June. Taking the cost of a meal into account it will be seen that the real cost of one man-day's worth of labour varies with the season and that, broadly, the cost is higher when demand for labour is high.

It was generally considered that the meal served to an agricultural worker was worth R1. Whether or not the worker could take the meal depended upon his caste ranking compared to that of his employer. Rajendra Singh, for example, still regards himself as a *Thakur*, and a variation was frequently required since he could not take food prepared in a low-caste kitchen. He therefore would take his meal at home and his payment would then be R1 more. In general employers preferred the labourer to take the meal: they said it wasted too much time to have the labourer go home to take his meal rather than having the food brought out to the field, the standard practice, by the employer's wife or children. Agricultural labourers sometimes said that employers preferred to give the meal rather than the extra rupee because the meal was worth less than R1. It certainly was not worth very much less, and indeed Rajendra Singh had no difficulty in finding employment. We suspect that usually it did not make much difference to either party which arrangement was adopted.

The variability of wages with demand would appear larger if one included an implicit wage for harvesting, as a one-twentieth share of what one man can harvest in a day is, in the case of wheat, not less than R10. That wages vary with the level of demand in this way suggests that the efficiency wage model is not an appropriate one for Palanpur (see above § 3.3). Note too that the wage measured in food fluctuates more than the money wage since food prices are particularly high exactly when the money wages are low. And one cannot justify the efficiency wage model by aggregating wages over the year since an individual would usually work for several farmers. Thus no single one of them would see the returns to wages 'invested' in building up a worker.

It seemed to us that the labour market was more or less in balance at the wages that were being paid. We heard no complaints by employers of difficulty in finding labourers to carry out their work, nor did we encounter the opposite complaint, from labourers, of difficulty in finding employment. Of course such casual observations need to be approached with caution. People adjust their expectations to match their experience, so it could be for example that labourers reporting that work was not difficult to find are merely saying that work is not unusually difficult to find (no harder to find than they take for granted). Something like this very likely occurs in the slackest times of the year; there is no work going and no difficulty in finding it is experienced because no-one is looking.

It seems, however, that there is no marked over-all surplus of labour in Palanpur. The village is a (small) net importer of labour: from October to April 2450 man-days of agricultural labour were hired-in and 2399 hired-out. In some months net hirings were positive and in others negative; for example, in May and November the number of days hired-in exceeded the number hired-out and in March and June the reverse was true. Thus the importing of labour is associated with busy times. If any labour surplus exists in the area it is to be found in other villages.

The mechanism by which a wage is determined is not simple to describe – there was, for example, no obvious price leader. At any particular time everyone in the village knew what the going wage rate was. And in nearly every case that wage or something of equivalent value would be paid to every agricultural labourer. More than one farmer told us that he would incur the displeasure of his fellows if he offered more. Yet the wage altered in the course of a season, rising somewhat when the demand for labour was high, falling in slack period. Some kind of consensus operated which adjusted the wage although one could not point to any individual as the wage-setter. It is our impression that the wage was adjusted so as to more or less balance supply and demand. Employers would accept the payment of a higher wage if they were finding labour hard to get, and would want to push the wage down if labour was easy to get.

Of course there is nothing very peculiar about this example. Prices do change without there being any formal market organization or specialist traders to alter them. The labour market in Palanpur is but another example.

A notable feature of the labour contracts that were observed in the 1974–5 season is that they were nearly all of a very short-term character – mostly for one day's labour. There were two cases of 'permanent' labour in the village where a man was hired for one whole season and a few cases of contracts for one or two months. As might be expected, it would often happen that a man would regularly work for the same employer but there was no tendency for employers to try to capture labour in longer-term contracts. Nor did labourers evidence any strong wish for longer-term contracts. However, as has been remarked above (see §3.3), if there were a strong link between productivity and consumption one might expect the employer to want to gain from the benefits in terms of productivity from paying higher wages, which he could only do if the employment contract were for a longer term than one day.

Finally we turn to the question of whether the wage rate ruling at any time measures the opportunity cost of family labour. From what has already been said it will be clear that it cannot generally be so considered. *Thakur* households do not usually hire-out their labour for agricultural work. Hence a *Thakur* household with an excess of family labour cannot solve that problem by having some of its members seek employment as agricultural labourers. This helps to explain why young *Thakur* men in particular have found employment in the inconvenient location of Moradabad.

For households whose caste rules do not constrain them not to sell out family labour as agricultural labour the position is different. We have argued that employment is not too difficult to come by. Moreover it can be obtained on a very short-term basis. Hence a man who works on his own farm is in a real sense losing the opportunity to gain wages elsewhere. On the other hand, since most households in Palanpur do cultivate, the man who works as an agricultural labourer does forgo the opportunity to work on his own land. However, even though those who are unconstrained by caste rules from working for others have the real possibility of finding work they do not in general regard the possibility with enthusiasm. There is the disutility of work itself and the special disutility of working for others – to the villagers of Palanpur both seemed important. In addition the possibility of finding work on a particular day was not a certainty.

We shall return to a consideration of the decision to sell family labour outside, or to buy-in labour, in Chapter 6.

§ 4.2 The Market for the Services of Bullocks

It will be useful to establish some terminology at the outset. Where human muscle-power is inadequate the most usual source of motive power in Indian agriculture is the draught animal, most commonly the bullock. Tractors have been introduced into some parts of India and their use is quite widespread in some areas, but there is no tractor in Palanpur and this form of motive power need not concern us. We shall refer below to the possibility of hiring tractor services from the village Amar Pur Kashi some six kilometres from Palanpur, but since our farmers do not do this our discussion of the possibility will be brief. In Palanpur ploughing and other activities requiring animal power are carried out with the aid of bullocks or with the aid of he-buffaloes. Later in this section we shall refer to some differences in the performances of these two types of animal, but in general the term 'bullock' will be used to cover bullocks or he-buffaloes without distinction. This usage avoids the tedious repetition of some such formula as 'bullocks or he-buffaloes as the case may be'.

The term 'the market for bullocks' might cause confusion since it could be taken to refer either to the market in which the ownership of bullocks is transferred or to the market, were any such to exist, in which the use of bullocks would be transacted. In the latter case, which is the one chiefly at issue in the present section, we shall refer to the 'bullock-hire market'. Bullocks, like cows, goats, and other farm animals, are regularly bought and sold and the fact that farmers can put a price to a farm animal and that they agree broadly on what that price would be indicates that these markets function fairly efficiently. Such transactions would not normally take place within the village since, as one would expect, Chandausi or a village which organizes a regular cattle market would be more promising locations and we have no detailed knowledge of their functioning. However it can be safely assumed that a bullock or a bullock pair have a price at which they could be sold and that a similar bullock could be bought for that money. Obviously one would not expect in either case to be able necessarily to find a buyer or a seller at the right price in a hurry and, again naturally, the price could very well fluctuate with the season.

The idea that there is a natural or economic area that a bullock pair can cope with has been an influential one. But the calculation of what that area would be is beset with difficulties. The most commonly used calculation of the optimal size of farm for a pair of bullocks is that quoted by Bhattacharjee (1947) of 6.8 acres (43.5 *bighas*). This is based on the area that draught animals kept in average conditions can plough. The matter is discussed in detail by Khusro

(1973, Chapter 5) who concludes that, in the case of U.P., a pair of bullocks would be seriously under-utilized on a holding of less than 10 acres (64 *bighas*). He however decides upon a conservative estimate of 7.5 acres (48 *bighas*) as the minimum holding for a standard bullock pair. Farm Management Surveys, as reported by Bharadwaj (1974), show that area cultivated per pair of bullocks varies very widely and is correlated positively with farm size. This is the case of the U.P. observations as for those for other states. The range is enormous: expressed as *bighas* per bullock pair[2] it is 17.9 for the smallest farms (less than 2.5 acres) to 75.5 for the largest (25 acres or above). In Palanpur the ratio of cultivated *bighas* to pairs of draught animals is 32.5. Note that the Farm Management data reported by Bharadwaj refer to 1954–7.

The basic problem is that the bullock pair is by no means a standard unit of motive power. True, given a particular pair of bullocks, a particular cropping pattern, and a particular package of practices (number of ploughings, irrigations, and so on), one might hope to define a maximum area that could be cultivated at least within narrow limits. However, this is to hold constant a number of variables. The work output that a pair of bullocks can produce varies greatly with the age and health of the bullocks. In addition, a well-matched pair do better than an ill-matched pair because a weak bullock will tend to hold back a strong one to the pace which it itself can manage. Recall furthermore that some of our bullocks are he-buffaloes. These are inferior to true bullocks with regard to their strength and particularly with regard to their stamina. He-buffaloes have inefficient sweat glands and they refuse to work in the afternoon. For this and various other reasons, the use of low-value bullocks demands more labour per acre than is the case with high-value bullocks. This becomes obvious when one considers that a weak pair of bullocks which take longer to plough a given area will require a man to walk behind them just as will a strong pair, so that more of that man's time will be involved in getting the area ploughed.

Table 4.3 gives the frequency distributions of numbers and values of draught animals owned. As might be expected, owning an odd number of bullocks is unusual, and only nine out of the 111 households do so. We shall have more to say about these cases below. The table makes it clear that there is a great spread among households which do own bullocks in the value of the bullocks owned.

Table 4.3 Number of draught animals owned/Value of draught animals owned

Number	Frequency	Value (R)	Frequency
0	34	0	34
1	7	0–400	9
2	64	401–800	33
3	2	801–1200	20
4	4	1201–1600	7
	⎯	>1600	8
	111		

Mean ≈ 662.95   median of positive values = 800   mean of positive values = 955.68.

[2]See Bharadwaj (1974) p. 35.

Because bullocks are so variable in quality we have taken the view that the number of bullocks owned by a household is not a sensible variable to explain, for example, the productivity of the family farm. This is interesting in that we thereby depart from the approach of Khusro who lays emphasis on the area that a bullock pair can manage, but the difference may be more apparent than real. In principle one could base everything on the abilities of a standard pair of bullocks and regard a farmer owning a stronger (or weaker) pair than the standard as owning, say, 1.2 (or 0.7) standard pairs. This leaves outstanding two problems which arise in field studies. First, what is one to do with the farmer who owns only one bullock? Second, how is one to estimate the relative productivity of different bullocks ?

In Palanpur there are seven farmers owning only one bullock. They must perforce participate in some kind of exchange agreement and this is commonly done in such cases. An example would be the following: two brothers each own one bullock, so they in turn borrow the other bullock to do their own ploughing. Given the co-operation that one might hope for between brothers, it is as good as having the use of a bullock pair on every second day.

A way of measuring the productivity of different bullock pairs would be to time them in ploughing a given field. The relative times would then give a good estimate of relative productivities. This is quite a demanding exercise. We did it implicitly in the case of farmers owning one of our sample wheat plots and that involved a lot of work. We did not command enough resources in time and observers to do it for the whole village and we therefore had to employ another measure of bullock power.

The measure that we used is certainly imperfect but may not be too bad in practice. This is the value of bullocks owned by the household. This measure is not ideal for our purposes because market value is a forward-looking evaluation of the future stream of services which bullocks may be expected to provide—it is not an assessment of current strength and stamina, although those factors come into the total assessment. Thus a good young pair of bullocks would be valued highly even though their strength might be no more than that of an old and not very good pair, unlikely to be able to work at all next year, currently able to pull as well.

What we are doing here is a familiar practice in production function studies where the treatment of capital is concerned. We are assuming that the flow of current services is proportional to the value of the stock. Since that assumption is unlikely to be strictly accurate our measure is less than ideal. We give in Table 4.4 the distribution of b (bullock value per area cultivated). Note that not all the variability in b is to be explained by variations in the flow of services from a unit of bullock value: variations in the extent to which bullock services are utilized on the farm would give rise to variations in b as well.

Table 4.4 Distribution of *b* (bullock value relative to area cultivated)

Range (Rupees/*bigha*)	Number of households
0 (cultivating without bullocks)	15
0–10	2
10–20	9
20–30	23
30–40	22
40–50	8
50–60	5
60–70	4
70–80	2
80–90	2
not cultivating	19
Total	111

Table 4.4 is reassuring in the following regard: although bullock value per *bigha* cultivated shows considerable spread, there is a clear bunching of cases in the range R20–40 per *bigha* cultivated. Forty-five out of ninety-two cases fall in this range. Moreover, we shall argue below that the fifteen cases recorded as zero in the table (cultivating without bullocks) must in every case have had some kind of access to the services of bullocks, so that for these households at least the recorded level of *b* is misleading. Setting them aside, we should find forty-five out of seventy-seven cases falling in the range R20-40.

The value of draught animals in a household's ownership per *bigha* cultivated is non-monotonic when related to size of the area cultivated; it first increases then decreases (the data are not displayed here). We would explain this in terms of very small cultivators making use of borrowed bullocks, or exchange relations and then, when the curve turns down, in terms of economies of scale in matching bullocks to the needs of a large holding rather than a small one. The 1957–8 study reports the result of undertaking a different calculation in which the number of draught animals is expressed in ratio to the number of *bighas*. The relation between this value and the area cultivated is unclear; it goes up and down according to no clear principle. This may indicate some real effect but may mean no more than that value of draught animals is a better measure than crude numbers. What is common to the two years 1957–8 and 1974–5 is that very small areas only were cultivated by households owning no bullocks.

The foregoing discussion makes sense only in terms of the presumption that the flow of bullock services available to a household is governed solely by the bullock power in its ownership. Such would not be the case were there to exist a bullock-hire market. But generally there is no such market in Palanpur. We first describe the exact position with regard to obtaining the use of bullocks without owning them and we then go on to discuss the question of why there should not be a bullock-hire market.

With rare exceptions, bullocks are not hired out for cash. Many people told us that it never happened but this is not quite accurate. There are a few cases known to us where land was ploughed in return for a cash payment. The cost was R2½-3 per *bigha*. However the areas involved were, taken alone or together, small and it is doubtful whether bullocks could be obtained on hire to plough larger areas. A good indication of the unimportance of this practice is that even people who knew that it happened did not know the price that was charged (and in most cases people seem to know the price of everything). Also significant is the case of Birbal, a *Passi*, whose land (only one acre) was ploughed for him in return for cash by a *Dhimar*. Yet this same man told us that he could not obtain land on tenancy because the landlords would not give land to someone without his own bullocks.

This observation should be considered in conjunction with the point that other researchers have noted the absence of a market for the services of bullocks in Indian villages. These include Hopper for Senapur village, Jaunpur District (see Hopper, 1965, p. 621) and Bell for Purnea District in Bihar (see Bell, 1975 and 1977).

While hiring of bullocks for cash is very unusual, exchange of the use of bullocks for other services is more frequently encountered. More often than not such cases involve arrangements between relatives. A typical example would be this: a man without bullocks does work on his brother's land; in return his brother lends him his bullocks so that he can plough and thresh and cultivate his own land holding. That such arrangements work, where cash renting apparently does not, seems to us significant as we shall shortly explain.

There are eight households in the village cultivating without owning bullocks. A further seven households are cultivating jointly without bullocks but where the other joint cultivator (or one of the others where there is more than one) does own bullocks. Obviously the latter case explains itself. The average size of the area cultivated by these fifteen households is almost exactly one acre (6.4 *bighas*) but not all of this was under crops in the *rabi* season of 1974–5. The average cropped area was 5.44 *bighas*, the maximum was 16 *bighas*, and the median area was 4 *bighas*. That one household managed to cultivate 16 *bighas* (that is 2.5 acres) without owning bullocks is impressive but cannot be regarded as typical.[3] It requires very good relations with the lender to manage such a large area with borrowed bullocks. This example apart, the areas that households managed to cultivate without bullocks are less than one acre. Only two of these households depended solely upon agriculture for their livelihoods. It seems that cultivation without bullocks is a marginal activity.

The absence from Palanpur of a bullock-hire market is a fact that we shall have to take into account in later chapters when we come to construct models of various aspects of the agriculture of the village. However it is worth spending some time in asking whether this is something that we can explain. Bullock hiring seemingly has a function to perform. If it were the practice, then farmers who owned bullocks would be enabled more easily to ensure their full utilization, while farmers who did not own bullocks would be able to cultivate land that they otherwise might be unable to cultivate, or which they could cultivate

---

[3]Most of this land was under sugar which, as it has a ten-month growing season, requires less ploughing than other crops.

only with difficulty. Why then is bullock hire so unusual ?

The answer to this question must be assessed in the light of the argument that will come in Chapter 5 when we consider tenancy. There we shall argue that the leasing-in and the leasing-out of land serve the function of adjusting cultivated land areas to the stock of inputs owned by the household. If this view is correct then the absence of bullock-hiring leads to a partial adjustment of bullocks to area cultivated by other means.

Where bullocks have been hired-out a member of their owners' household worked with them, rather than the hirer providing the labour to go with the bullocks. This is not fortuitous since bullocks are valuable animals and an owner is anxious to avoid their being misused. When the owner works the bullocks himself the danger that the bullocks might be maltreated is overcome. However, if the hirer wants to cultivate land in order to provide an outlet for family labour then having to hire-in labour with the bullocks is unattractive from his point of view. Moreover, there is the problem that the hired worker may not have sufficient incentive to do the work well unless he is supervised (which is costly in labour time) or unless a family member is working alongside him. Given that supervision of the employment of bullocks has to be under-taken by a member of the hirer's family, the upper castes of the village (par-ticularly the *Thakurs* but the *Muraos* to some extent as well) are in effect dis-qualified from hiring-out bullocks, since were they to hire-out bullocks they would have to do something too much like hiring-out their labour.

Finally one should note the general point, which applies here, that having to rely on the market for the supply of an input is often less certain than owning the input. The farmer need not doubt that he will be able to get the input even-tually through the market; it is enough that he should be worried about timing. Where bullocks are very much in demand as would be the case in the peak weeks for ploughing prior to the *rabi* season, owners will give preference to their own land unless the price payable for bullock hire rises by just the right amount at that time, but it is asking a lot of a small market to expect it to operate that well.

It remains to mention one related point. There is a progressive village not far from Palanpur, called Amar Pur Kashi. The head of this village runs a tractor-hire service and he told us that he would bring a tractor to Palanpur to plough or do whatever work there was for a tractor if the farmers of Palanpur re-quested this. But it would be difficult to get a tractor from Amar Pur Kashi to Palanpur because there is no good direct road, and if a tractor came the users would have to pay for the costs of the journey.

It would seem that tractor-hire is even more problem-ridden than bullock-hire. A group of farmers would have to co-ordinate their demands to provide a full-day's employment for the tractor when it came and then divide the overhead cost of the journey amongst them. The tractor driver would come from outside and once again there would be no outlet for family labour. And the farmers would have to command the cash to pay for the services of the trac-tor. Taking all these considerations together we do not feel that tractor-hiring has any great merits from the point of view of Palanpur households.

§ 4.3 The market for credit

Credit is not an input like labour and bullock power but it enables the farmer to buy inputs and it therefore plays a central role in agriculture. The market for credit in Palanpur consists of several sources which provide credit under different conditions. We shall first describe these sources and then offer an assessment of how easy it is to obtain credit.

The important sources of credit in the village are the Seed Store, the Land Development Bank at Bilari, and some of the richer farmers in the village. We shall refer to these sources respectively as the Seed Store, the LDB, and the private market. Table 4.5 gives the amount outstanding from each source by caste. More detailed examination of what this table shows will follow a discussion of the individual sources.

Table 4.5 Amount outstanding from various loan sources by caste, *rabi* 1974–5

Caste	Number of households	Debt to seed store	Private debt	Debt to LDB	Total debt	Debt per household	Income per household
Thakur	25	19823	2200	5000	27023	1081	8799
Murao	27	6395	7800	9000	23195	859	8596
Dhimar	8	3070	1750	4500	9320	1165	5851
Gadaria	10	12118	1100	—	13218	1322	6101
Dhobi	3	220	800	—	1020	340	4928
Teli	12	1400	1350	—	2750	229	4530
Passi	8	5640	3800	—	9440	1180	8274
Jatab	14	3635	5200	—	8835	631	4954
Other	4	—	—	—	—	—	5422
All castes	111	52301	24000	18500	94801	854	7083

Notes: 1. The sums outstanding from the Seed Store refer to November 1974. The figures for the LDB and private loans were collected in March and April 1975.
2. There were four LDB loans, each for the purchase of a pumping set.
3. The sum for private loans is an underestimate, if only because two households declined to provide the information. However we believe that the magnitude is not wildly wrong.
4. The average income per capita is R1039 (see Table 6.14).
5. Most of the private loans are within the village and thus involve credits as well as debts—only the debts have been included here.

The Seed Store (more accurately the Co-operative Credit Union run from the Seed Store) is the most important source of loans. It provides seed on credit and this is its most common form of lending. Taking seed from the Seed Store in this way has severe drawbacks. The seed is inferior (for the reasons, see § 2.A.2) and will provide only a poor yield. The borrower could eat it, but the amount available is limited by the quantity of seed judged appropriate to the land holding so that borrowed seed would not provide a substantial source of consumption.

The Co-operative Credit Union has 1000 members, 107 of them from Palanpur (a household may have more than one member). Membership enables a farmer to get seed on credit from the store, as has been described, and also urea when it is available. In each of these cases the advance is on credit. Seed must be repaid with seed plus twenty-five per cent, urea is paid for in cash at the end of the growing season and not later than 30 June for the *rabi* season. The official rate of interest for fertilizer loans is 13 per cent per annum (we shall discuss the rate of inflation at the end of this section). A member of the Credit Union may borrow money for agricultural purposes subject to a limit which is governed by the number of shares the member has purchased, up to a maximum of fifty shares, and the size of his land holding. No member may owe more than five times his share capital. Each share costs R20, so the limit for a member with the maximum of fifty shares would be R5000. In addition the cash loan outstanding cannot exceed R100 per acre and the kind loan must not exceed R200 per acre. Thus there is no point in buying the full allowance of shares unless one has 50 acres, more than any Palanpur household owns.

Nearly all the credit advanced is short term, usually one season. It is inexpensive when compared with the private market and 800 farmers out of the 1000 members are borrowing the maximum permitted to them. There are a few medium-term loans advanced, for three years. In 1974 the medium-term loans were advanced only to those wishing to use the money to buy shares, but two years previously an advance of R1500 was used to purchase a thresher. However such cases seem to be unusual. There is of course no guarantee that money advanced will be used for the overt purpose mentioned by the borrower and even an advance in kind need not be applied as the authorities might stipulate. The Manager complained that some households used seed advances for consumption and that others sold fertilizer for cash instead of applying it to the crops.[4] There are, of course, conceptual problems in allocating loans to uses.

Thirty members of the Co-operative are without land. They can borrow a maximum of R150, cash or kind, and are subject to the same time limits for repayment as other members.

The Seed Store is an important source of urea to the village, although it can be purchased on the open market in Chandausi. The great advantage of the Seed Store from the point of view of a household hard-pressed for cash is that the fertilizer is advanced on credit, while the merchants in Chandausi demand cash with the purchase. There are however some serious drawbacks to the Seed Store as a source of urea. The fertilizer comes in bags which nominally weigh 50 kg and the price in November 1974 was R105.25 per bag. There were frequent allegations, which we believe were justified, that the bags weighed less than 50kg.

The total amounts outstanding on loan from the Co-operative Credit Union are seldom large. The most important items are money loans. Fifty-nine Palanpur households owed seed in 1974–5 and this was in every case either 50kg, 100kg, 150kg, or 200kg. The most usual amount was 100kg, which would have been worth about R160 as consumption grain at the time (October 1974). Only thirty-four bags of urea were issued: one farmer got three bags, four got two

[4] A man entitled to borrow R300 who asked in our hearing for a loan of R1000 for his daughter's wedding was refused.

bags, the rest one each. Most cash loans outstanding were for less than R500. The size distribution of these amounts is given in Table 4.6. From the table it will be seen that the loans taken from the Seed Store by members are on average approximately one-tenth of average income per household in the village.

There is an advantage to borrowing from the Seed Store which makes it particularly attractive to a farmer whose resource position is weak. The Seed Store manager is fairly easy-going about rolling-over loans and extending the period of repayment. Moreover, there is no mortgage of the borrower's land involved. The worst that can happen is that the borrower would lose his membership of the Credit Union, a serious matter but not as bad as forfeiting land.

Table 4.6 Size distribution of amounts outstanding to Co-operative Credit Union from Palanpur households who were members of the Union at 31 October 1974 (Rupees)

Amount outstanding	Number of households
0	14
> 0	29
> 500	12
> 1000	7
> 1500	1
> 2000	1
> 2500	1
> 3000	3
> 3500	2
4000 +	1
	71
Total Amount Outstanding	R52 301
Average Amount Outstanding	R 737

Notes: (i) The upper bound to a range given in a row is the figure indicated in the subsequent row
(ii) Average income per household in the village is R 7083

The Land Development Bank (LDB) at Bilari is the source of long term credit for agricultural improvements. In the case of Palanpur it has been used to finance the purchase of pumping sets (see below § 4.4). There are only four loans outstanding; the amounts are R5000, 5000, 4500 and 4000. The rates of interest are 11 per cent or below, lower than for both the private market and the Seed Store. The period of loans is ten years, repayable in instalments. For the enterprising farmer this has been an attractive proposition and the availability of these loans is the reason why Palanpur has been provided with pumping sets in recent years, indeed the village now has about as many as it can use given the competition from Persian wheels. Because pumping sets can be hired-out for cash they provide a source of income to their owners on top of the convenience in using them for their own irrigation. On the returns to owning pumping sets, see below § 4.4.

The private market is the remaining source of credit. Tables 4.7 to 4.11 summarize our information on loans outstanding in early 1975 not including those taken from the Seed Store or the LDB. As Table 4.11 shows, in thirty-three out of thirty-five loans where the source was known to us, it was in the category we have designated 'village money-lender'. In the 'unknown' case the respondent told us that he owed over R2000 but declined to provide any other details. Interesting is the fact that only one loan is reported as coming from a relative. This may be misleading because some respondents may have felt that loans from relatives fell into a different category and not reported them. Only three households refused to disclose their debt position.

The village money-lender is not one person and in no case is he a specialized money-lender not involved in agriculture in any other way. Some of these loans are from outside the village. From within the village they come mostly from four or five farmers who combine money-lending with other activities.

It is interesting to note that there are only two cases where a tenant has a loan from his landlord (there are thirty-five households with private debts, forty households which take in land under tenancy, and thirty-seven which lease-out land). A *Murao* household borrowed R150 rupees from a *Thakur* landlord who was leasing him land and similarly a *Dhimar* household borrowed R300 from a *Thakur* landlord. In both cases the loans were for home consumption and at usual rates of interest for private loans (see below). Thus the model described by Bhaduri (1973) where a tenant's landlord is his lender is clearly inapplicable to Palanpur.

There are, however, two types of example in which the tenant advances credit to his landlord. First, it is common for tenants to pay all the costs of shared inputs such as fertilizer, and the landlord then pays for his share of the cost of the input at harvest time. We have not recorded these implicit loans but they are obviously intimately connected with share-cropping. Usually there seems to have been no interest charged for these loans. Second, a type of situation can arise such as the following. A borrower defaults on a loan and it is agreed between him and his lender that the borrower will cultivate his land for one or more seasons in lieu of the loan repayment. Default on a loan gives rise to tenancy. This happened in the village in one case known to us.

Most loans are for one year but this could be misleading. Very often a loan is renewed and sometimes the reason for borrowing was given as the repayment of debt. We have not listed that as an independent reason but have tried to go back to the original purpose of the borrowing. The very small number of doubtful cases have been listed as 'consumption'.

Rates of interest are high but not astronomic. The most usual interest rate for a private loan was 24 per cent, the next 36 per cent. The latter was more likely to be the cost where the loan was for consumption, where a marriage was being financed, or where the borrower was a *Jatab*. The highest recorded rates were all for loans to *Jatabs*, three cases of 50 per cent. One reason for this might be that lending to *Jatabs* is frowned upon by the law, and repayment could thus not be enforced in a court; hence the rate is correspondingly higher.

We devoted considerable energy to trying to discover how easy it is to obtain credit for the purchase of agricultural inputs from the private market.[5] As

---

[5]See below Chapter 10 for details of the discussion sessions in which this question figured.

Table 4.7 Size distribution of private debt outstanding*

Debt	Thakurs	Muraos	Others	All castes
not disclosed	I	2	—	3
zero	23	15	35	73
1–200	1	3	3	7
201–400	—	—	11	11
401–600	1	1	4	6
601–800	—	—	3	3
801–1000	—	—	—	—
1001–1500	1	1	1	3
1501–2000	—	2	1	3
2001–3000	—	1	1	2
Totals	27	25	59	111

*The figures in the table denote numbers of households with total debts in the range indicated.

Table 4.8 Rates of interest on private loans*

Interest rate (per cent)	Thakurs	Muraos	Others	All castes
zero	1	1	1	3
21–30	2	4	13	19
31–40	—	2	8	10
41 +	—	1	2	3
Totals	3	8	24	35

*In the few cases where a household had more than one loan we have used in this and the following tables the attributes of the major loan.

Table 4.9* Period of private loans

Period	Thakurs	Muraos	Others	All castes
6 months	1	1	—	2
1 year	1	6	19	26
2 or 3 years	1	1	5	7
Totals	3	8	24	35

*See note to Table 4.8

Table 4.10* Reasons given for private loans

Reason	Thakurs	Muraos	Others	All castes
Consumption	2	2	15	19
Marriage	—	3	5	8
Seeds	—	1	2	3
Home construction	—	1	1	2
Buffalo	1	—	1	2
Agricultural input	—	1		1
Totals	3	8	24	35

*See note to Table 4.8

Table 4.11* Sources of private loans

Source	Thakurs	Muraos	Others	All castes
Unknown	1	—	—	1
Relative	—	—	1	1
Village money-lender	2	8	23	33
Totals	3	8	24	35

*See note to Table 4.8

Table 4.10 shows, this was an unusual reason for borrowing money. However there was a clear consensus that one could borrow to purchase agricultural inputs, including fertilizer. Cases in the past were called to mind and there does not seem to be any clear-cut prohibition on the part of lenders against using credit to improve agricultural productivity. Nevertheless, the habit of borrowing from the private market for the purchase of agricultural inputs is not well-established and farmers think of the Seed Store as the natural place to obtain credit for those purposes.

A possible explanation for the farmers' borrowing habits would be the following. Certain expenditures, notably weddings, take priority and where the household cannot find the money from its own resources it will perforce borrow, even if it has to run the risk of a forced sale of its land. Borrowing for the purchase of agricultural inputs is seen as a luxury, on the other hand, and most farmers are unwilling to take the risk that there may be a loss of the crop requiring a sale of land if the loan is to be repaid. Loans from the Seed Store fall into a different category because the Seed Store manager is expected to take a tolerant attitude in the case of difficulty and if the worst came to the worst one could always default and lose membership.

We are now in a position to consider the over-all incidence of debt amongst the castes in Palanpur. Returning therefore to Table 4.5 we note that the over-all debt to income ratio (12.1 per cent) is not large. It should be borne in mind that credits have not been included—where private debt is concerned a loan usually involves a credit within the village as well as a debit. We conclude from Table 4.5 that neither Palanpur in general nor any particular caste is over-burdened with debt.

The amount of debt per household varies considerably between castes. In general the richer castes owe more debt. Thus, far from it being the case that the lower castes are overburdened with debt their problem would appear to be gaining access to credit. In the case of the *Jatabs* the reason has been mentioned above. The lowest debt to income ratios are for the *Dhobis* and *Telis*—the two Muslim castes. Here the Muslim attitude to borrowing at interest may be of importance.

There are six households with debts in excess of R4000. Four of these owe the money to the LDB—the loan was for the purchase of a pumping set (see Table 4.13 below). Of the four households one is *Thakur*, two are *Murao*, and one *Dhimar*. The two remaining households which owe more than R4000 are one

Thakur (R4935 from the Seed Store) and one *Murao* (R3800 from the Seed Store plus R2000, long-term, from a powerful local figure from outside the village). This last *Murao* household has, therefore, the largest total debt in the village. The head of household is a young man (aged 28) with a good job in the Cane Society. He owns little land and it seems that he got into debt five years ago for the marriage of his sister.

Amongst the low castes large debts are unusual and where they occur the source is usually a private money-lender and the reason marriage.

From Table 4.12 it will be seen that the year 1974–5 was one in which the rate of inflation was low, indeed prices fell somewhat, but in the previous year it had been very high. In the circumstances it is very difficult to know what value to use for the expected real rate of interest and we have arranged our discussion around nominal rates. Given the actual rate of inflation we doubt that this is seriously misleading.

Table 4.12 Index numbers of consumer prices for U.P. agricultural labourers

	1965	1966	1967	1968	1969	1970	1971	1972	1973	1974	1975	1976
Food	177	187	284	214	198	210	190	231	286	393	374	272
General	165	173	250	196	184	194	180	214	260	353	342	262

Month of Index: June

1974–5

	July	Aug.	Sept.	Oct.	Nov.	Dec.	Jan.	Feb.	March	April	May	June
Food	399	411	435	452	437	439	450	448	436	399	377	374
General	354	368	389	403	390	392	401	400	391	362	344	342

Base 1960 = 100
Source: Monthly Abstract of Statistics, Central Statistical Organization, Department of Statistics, Ministry of Planning, Government of India. Vol. 22, No. 12, Table 50; Vol. 27, No. 12, Table 50; Vol. 30, No. 12, Tables 53 and 54; Vol. 29, No. 12, Table 54.

Note: We have not been able to find these index numbers for 1957–8, the year of the first AERC survey. We suppose that a fourfold increase in prices between that year and 1974–5 would not be wildly inaccurate.

This completes our description of the institutions concerned with credit in Palanpur. However the availability and price of credit will figure importantly in our discussions in the remaining chapters.

§ 4.4 The Market for Water Sources

As was described in Chapter 2, most of the land of Palanpur is irrigated and there is abundant ground water. The main difference between methods of irrigation is the means used to raise the water from beneath the ground to the surface. This is either by means of a Persian wheel or a diesel-powered pumping set.

The method of irrigation is as follows. The field is divided up by low ridges into small rectangular portions each a few feet by a few feet. Channels are constructed from the source to the field. Main channels are often made with brick or cement but more usually mud, and smaller channels of mud. The area inside a rectangular portion is flooded to a depth of two or three inches and then the area is closed off from the water source and the ridges into another portion are opened to allow that to be flooded. Several rectangular portions will be irrigated simultaneously and progress around the field will be governed by topography and the positions of the main channels. The land is very flat by the standards of most parts of the British Isles but the surface flow is governed by gravity so the topography is very important. The pumps and Persian wheels serve only to lift the water from the underground water table. The Palanpur land is sufficiently undulating by the standard of the Indo-Gangetic plain to make it very unlikely that Government tube-well water will be provided to cover the whole of the village land.

The Persian wheel is a large horizontal wheel which is drawn around by bullocks. It is linked by gears to a chain of buckets in a vertical plane which descend into a well about ten feet in diameter. The water is lifted in the buckets. Someone has to drive the bullocks round and round, a role often played by children, while someone else in the field itself attends to the rectangular portions and changes the flow from one to another by breaking and mending the dividing ridges appropriately. It takes approximately thirty hours to irrigate an acre by Persian wheel. The hire of a Persian wheel is up to two rupees per *bigha* (0.16 of an acre) to be irrigated. The price is a little more variable across the village than that for a pumping set, since if a pumping set is not feasible the cultivator and owner of the Persian wheel strike a bargain unrestricted by competition (usually only one Persian wheel would be a possible source for a given piece of land).

The alternative form, where a boring is available, is a pumping set. This is a small diesel engine which is transported on a cart. The borings are vertical tubes approximately four inches in diameter set in the ground. The price of the hire of a pumping set in 1974–5 was 5.5 rupees per hour (including the fuel—worth roughly 1.5 rupees per hour—and supervision by the owner of the set). It takes approximately five hours to irrigate an acre by pumping set.

There are two different markets for water sources to which rather different considerations apply. Consider first the hire of Persian wheels. A particular plot of land will typically be serviced by one, or at most two or three, Persian wheels. Hence the owner of the Persian wheel is in theory a monopolist or oligopolist and one might expect that he would charge different prices to different users, charging what the market would bear in the case of each particular user. This does not however, happen; the charges to different users are uniform and there is no evidence of discriminating monopoly. No doubt the owner gives preference to his own needs when it comes to the timing of irrigation but this is not a very important problem: there is always a fair degree of flexibility in the timing of an irrigation within a range of, say, plus or minus two or three days, and the pressure on the water sources in the village is not such that it will prove difficult for the hirer to obtain use of a Persian wheel within that time span. He may need to be a bit better organized than would an owner but it is not a critical matter. Far more important is ownership of bullocks where the pressure on the stock is very high at certain times and a household shopping for an idle bullock pair would sometimes have to wait a long time.

Pumping sets are mobile and therefore the element of a seller's monopoly does not arise. A boring close to the field will have to be used and here there will be a single owner or only one or two. But again the monopoly element is too weak or not exploited. Of course the presence of pumping sets weakens the monopolistic element for Persian wheels and conversely.

Because there is an advantage to owning a water source rather than having to rely on the market, we have used two variables below to represent this advantage. Pumping sets are much faster than Persian wheels and this led us to think at an early stage that the ownership of a pumping set would be particularly significant. Hence we make use of the variable NPSO, number of pumping sets owned, in later chapters to represent this advantage. NPSO is a zero-one variable[6] because no household owns more than one pumping set.

Whether pumping sets are really so important as compared to Persian wheels remains to be seen (see § 7.3). The cash cost of using a pumping set is higher but the employment of a Persian wheel requires the use of other inputs, such as bullock time, which are not charged in cash. The construction of Persian wheels has continued in recent years which would suggest that they have not been entirely superseded by pumping sets. It makes sense anyway to look at all water sources together, and this we do by means of the variable VALWATS which is the sum of the values of all water sources owned by the household (Persian wheels plus pumping sets plus borings).

Table 4.13 gives some details on the households who own pumping sets. The

Table 4.13 Households owning pumping sets

Household no.	Value of pumping set (R)	Remarks	Land owned (*bighas*)
107 Mirahi Singh	3000		50.00
116 Sahab Singh	4500		63.00
117 Narain Singh	4000 (if working)	Not in working order	23.00
*118 Tilok Singh	3500		70.50
122 Vinish Singh	2200		24.50
208 Toti Ram	4000 (if working)	Not in working order	52.50
*217 Kishan Lal	5000		25.63
219 Bhajan Singh	4000		60.70
*227 Man Singh	4000		73.50
*305 Mithu	4500 (if working)	Not in working order	16.00

Note: NPSO was taken a zero in the case of households 117, 208, and 305 whose pumping sets were not functioning for long periods during the season. Households marked with an asterisk have a loan outstanding from the LDB for the purchase of the pumping set.

[6]The definitions of variables will be found in Tables 5.5, Table 6.3, and Table 8.1.

purchase of a pumping set might be regarded as showing a certain degree of initiative or access to credit in excess of the average for the village. If that were the case, then NPSO might turn out to represent initiative and enterprise as well as the ownership of the pumping set *per se*.

Table 4.14 shows the cash income that our pumping-set-owning households earned from renting out their sets month by month for the 1974–5 *rabi* season. Note that there is quite a bit of variability. These are not net returns since there are fuel and maintenance costs and depreciation to take into account. Household 118 has a ten-year loan of R5000, repayable in ten annual instalments of R800. The gross return during the *rabi* season as a percentage of the capital tied up is 23.7 per cent. Probably most of the cash returns accrue during the *rabi* season and after these have been reduced by deductions for maintenance and so on they might seem poor compared to the going return on capital in the village. However, recall that the household has the use of the pumping set for itself on top of any cash income that is derived from the ownership.

Table 4.14 Returns to owning a pumping set

Month/Household	107	116	118	122	217	219	227
October	—	—	—	—	400	400	400
November	100	120	200	175	500	500	600
December	40	100	225	150	300	400	400
January	120	150	160	150	100	300	300
February	150	150	250	175	150	300	300
March	150	120	300	200	100	350	100
April	80	—	50	100	—	100	100
Total	640	640	1185	950	1550	2350	2200

§ 4.5 The Market for Sugar

The arrangements for selling sugar to the government mill were described in § 2.A.2 and again in § 4.0 above. The outstanding question to which this section is devoted is why the area covered by sugar is not more extensive than is presently the case. Is it that the rationing by quota of mill acceptance is the effective constraint in the long run, or is it that there are other barriers in the way of the farmers of Palanpur expanding their acreages under sugar ?

Both the private mill and the government mill operate a system whereby a grower is allocated an acreage according to the average of his previous three years' area under sugar. We heard complaints that the government mill officials were corrupt and in league with the influential farmers in the village. The mill was accused of paying very late for cane delivered. Thus, although the government mill paid R1 per quintal more than the private mill (at the time farmers received around R 12 per quintal) it was widely felt that on balance there was little to choose between them and many farmers sold both to the government mill and to the private mill.

While we took seriously the claims that the Cane Society was dishonest, we were not convinced that it was impossible for a farmer who wished to take up the cultivation of cane to do so and to obtain in due course an allocation of land for mill processing. Many farmers from all castes had done so and it was hard to see the barriers as insuperable. It is true that the Cane Society is dominated by the *Thakurs* and other influential groups and it is natural that this should be resented by outsiders. However, we think that the really important barriers to the expansion of the cultivation of sugar are to be found elsewhere and this is in line with what many respondents told us.

Sugar cane is a high-value crop but it is usually held to require a high level of inputs. First, the soil should be of reasonable quality and able to retain moisture. Some of the soil of Palanpur is too sandy to make it worthwhile to try to grow cane. Second, the crop needs plenty of water and responds well to fertilizer. It should not be newly sown on the same land more than once every three of four years (ICAR, 1969, pp. 199–200). Sugar cane repays care and attention to soil preparation and to maintenance when growing. It is thus by its nature a labour intensive crop.

The most obvious explanation why the cultivation of sugar has not gone further in Palanpur should now be apparent. Many farmers simply do not command the resources in terms of capital and labour to make a success of cane growing. Even those who do would not necessarily be able to grow more cane than they have planted presently without it making impossible demands on the family's labour and other resources.

§ 4.6 Some Observations on Cropping Patterns

The choice of cropping pattern is an important decision. This decision will reflect *inter alia* the resources under the control of the household, the quality of its land, the amount of family labour allocated to agriculture, and the willingness of the household to undertake risk. We have not attempted to construct a formal model of the choice of cropping pattern although we see no reason in principle why that should not be done. One factor which we believe would be important is the trade-off between average yield and the riskiness of the yield. Our data do not suffice to determine these quantities. However we can report mean gross yields per *bigha* for each of the main crops and sometimes one can say a *priori* whether the crop is a risky one or relatively safe. (Potatoes, for example, being a disease-prone crop, are risky in this sense.)

Table 4.15 gives the mean gross value yields and the coefficients of variation of the yields for our households and for each of the main village crops. We include in the table a comparison of leased-in land with other land but this will be discussed in Chapter 5 on tenancy.

A number of points emerge from the columns concerned with 'All land' in Table 4.15. First, a comparison of the mean yields from the various crops for the right-hand block shows how some crops have far higher gross yields per *bigha* than do others. Of course one has to take into account also the costs associated with the various crops which vary a good deal and usually with the yields in terms of rupees per *bigha*. Thus, for example, sugar which has a high value per *bigha* is also an expensive crop to cultivate. It demands the use of the land for ten months. Furthermore, it needs plenty of irrigation and fertilizer if

Table 4.15 Yields of various crops comparing owned and leased-in land (R per *bigha*)

	Owned and cultivated land			Leased-in land			All land			Coefficient of variation (all land)
	mean	standard deviation	no. of cases	mean	standard deviation	no. of cases	mean	standard deviation	no. of cases	
1. Wheat	136.8	36.4	75	147.0	40.3	32	140.3	33.3	84	.24
2. Barley	106.1	78.9	27	66.1	17.4	7	97.8	72.6	34	.74
3. Pea	129.3	30.3	31	122.9	32.8	6	127.1	30.9	35	.24
4. Mustard	172.5	72.9	12	71.9	12.8	3	158.5	68.4	14	.43
5. *Gram*	134.6	35.0	22	135.8	12.7	9	134.5	30.6	30	.23
6. Sugar	260.2	80.9	55	295.5	70.0	16	265.0	73.8	61	.28
7. *Lahi*	134.0	48.7	9	—	—	0	134.0	48.7	9	.36
8. Paddy	120.7	32.9	29	118.0	28.4	7	120.9	32.2	35	.27
9. Maize	77.8	16.4	42	77.2	6.4	5	77.8	15.6	47	.20
10. *Jowar*	106.7	59.8	29	137.0	52.9	6	109.2	61.3	32	.56
11. *Bajra*	79.8	20.9	64	80.0	19.8	19	78.9	20.4	73	.26
12. Ground-nut	158.9	33.6	23	177.0	57.3	6	162.6	40.4	29	.25

Note : A household contributes a case under the heading attached to a given column if it grows the relevant crop on the type of land specified. If it does so contribute, the yield for that household for leased-in land, for example, is total output for the crop concerned from leased-in land divided by acreage of leased-in land under that crop.

the soil is not to be depleted. Second, there are wide variations between crops in the variability across farms of yields per *bigha*. This is measured by the coefficient of variation (standard deviation divided by the mean). This number is only 20 per cent in the case of maize but is 74 per cent in the case of barley. It is tempting to use this number as a measure of the riskiness of different crops and it may well reflect that factor to some extent. However strictly it measures the differences in performance between different farmers in growing one crop. These differences do indeed reflect certain aspects of their common risk experience but, on the one hand, they fail to include some of the risk that is only manifested in a run of seasons and with regard to which 1974–5 might have been a fortunate or an unfortunate year throughout the village for the crop concerned.[7] On the other hand, they include along with risk, differences between the cultivation techniques of the various farmers. As we shall see when we come to look closely at the case of wheat in Chapters 7 and 8, these last differences are considerable.

Table 4.15 is derived from a large body of data on cropping patterns for individual households which it is our intention to make the subject of a special study in the future.

§ 4.7 The Discussion Questionnaire

During February 1975 we had lengthy discussions with thirty different farmers. These farmers were the cultivators of our random sample of wheat-growing plots (see below, Chapter 7). In this section we present the questionaire around which our discussions were organized and note some of the interesting conclusions which emerged from these discussions. Although our respondents were all cultivators of sample wheat plots, not all our questions were concerned with those plots, or even with wheat. In part we took advantage of the fact that we were having these discussions to ask whatever questions were on our minds at that time and on which we thought these farmers could throw some light. Those of our questions which were concerned explicitly with the cultivation of wheat will be listed in this section but we will defer the discussion of these questions until Chapter 8 when they can be considered in context.

Our sessions usually lasted for about one hour. They were informal and we did not try to fill in any formal questionnaire. We were anxious to let the cultivators expound their views and we encouraged them to speculate a little on possible consequences of different cultivation practices. In general, they were happy to indulge in such counter-factual discussions and found no difficulty with hypothetical questions. Not all the questions were hypothetical and we tried to build up to the more speculative or controversial questions so that these were put after a warm atmosphere had been established.

The sessions were conducted in the evenings at our rooms in the Seed Store and we usually provided the cultivators with one or two cigarettes or 'biddies' during the discussion. On the whole we found these sessions very enjoyable and had the impression that the cultivators did too.

---

[7] It was not a bad year for wheat—see Ch. 7 and 8.

While the sessions were informal we did try to ask similar questions to each cultivator and for our own purposes drew up the list of questions which is presented in Table 4.16. We did not always ask all the questions and often wandered outside the issues in that Table.

Table 4.16 Questions on which discussions with cultivators were based

---

0. When did you shift to double-cropping? Why not before?
1. Has there been a big shift to late planting in the village?
2. Why did you choose your seed type?
    (Ask about, reversion to *desi*, adulteration, risk, labour requirements, timing, and quantity.)
3. What are the returns to leaving a wheat plot fallow in the *kharif*? Why did you choose your rotation?
    (Land, labour availability, consumption requirements)
4. How do you decide your source of water?
    (Cost, speed, getting it when wanted, includes labour availability)
    Why not one more irrigation?
    (Compare other farmers if appropriate. Effect of an extra irrigation on yield and risk of pests)
5. How do you decide which fertilizers to apply and their rates of application?
    How do you choose your source? How certain are you of covering the cost?
    What effect would 25 per cent less fertilizer (translate into kg or bags) have on yield and the riskiness of yield?
    For how much could you sell your fertilizer on the open market?
    How much fertilizer would you use in the absence of any credit limits?
    How certain would you be of covering the cost?
    How serious is the problem of adulteration of fertilizers?
    Effect of Seed Store having fertilizer this year?
6. How and at what times could you increase productivity by applying more labour?
    (How much more labour and how much more production? Why don't you do it?)
    (Hiring in if necessary)
7. How do you choose which labourers to hire? (Wages, reliability, health and strength, caste)
    Do you pay different wages to different labourers? Do you pay different wages at different times?
8. Is a member of your household always working alongside a hired labourer? Why?
9. Do you give your labourer the choice of lunch or a higher wage? (Cost of lunch; which choice do you like him to take; would you employ him if he took the other option? Why offer a choice at all?)
10. Could you arrange to cultivate more (or less) land?
    (Informal tenancy, or joint cultivation)
    Why don't you? (Terms, labour requirements, supervision)
11. Why don't you grow a greater (smaller) variety of crops in the *rabi* season? (Concentration on the most profitable, spread of risk if this is vital)
12. Has the acreage leased out under informal tenancy increased over the last five years? What is the reason for this?

There was only one of the forty-seven sample wheat plots for which no discussion session occurred. This was plot number 88 (see Chapter 7) which was under tenancy. There was rather a complicated arrangement where two farmers from different castes (a *Dhimar* and a *Thakur*) were renting the plot from another *Thakur* and cultivating jointly. Our informant on cultivation details was the *Dhimar* (Ram Kumar) and he was rather reluctant to come. For all the other plots we spoke to the cultivator who in most cases co-operated with some enthusiasm. The person we spoke to was not always the nominal cultivator of the plot. For example Naresh Pal Singh (a *Thakur*) was the cultivator of two plots (numbers 377 and 379) but most of the cultivation decisions appeared to be taken by his son Poppu Singh who also did most of the work on the plot. Naresh Pal Singh was asthmatic and Poppu Singh, who had left high school in Chandausi two years before our survey, had spent three months training in plant production at a local Block headquarters. And Man Singh, while he is the nominal cultivator of just two plots (157 and 360) plays an active role in the cultivation decisions of his relatives Baboo Ram (plot 500) and Kishan Lal (plot 475) who are part of the same household. This is the very large *Murao* household of twenty-seven members which was mentioned in § 2.2. Thus we spoke to Man Singh about all four plots. With some cultivators or landlords discussing more than one plot and the omission of plot 88 we conducted sessions with thirty different people. Of the nine cases of tenancy, one (plot 88) was omitted, and three sessions were conducted with the landlord rather than the tenant. In each of these three cases the landlord had been giving the activity details on the plot and it would have been regarded as impolite if we had then gone to the tenant to ask about the decisions. These are also cases where it is reasonable to suppose that the landlord was playing an influential role in the decision-taking.

Before discussing the responses to the different questions we shall record our general impressions. There is wide variability in the practices of Palanpur farmers and this dispersion is apparent in their attitudes as well. We have variation from Man Singh, a young *Murao*, who is well-informed, analytical, and alert to opportunities; to Ompal Singh, an older *Thakur*, who while thoughtful was neither analytical nor well-informed. If we are to speak of an average we should say that farmers were fairly well aware of the productivity of inputs, although many were badly informed about sowing technique. They were, however, lacking in confidence in their estimates. This is, we presume, a result of their experience in the vagaries of agriculture and their comparative inexperience with the more intensive use of inputs such as fertilizers and irrigation.

This lack of confidence may be connected with the apparent reluctance of many of the cultivators to invest the effort and the capital required to obtain certain inputs such as newer seeds or fertilizer at the time of sowing. We had the strong impression that the perceived effort was indeed viewed as a substantial cost by certain of the farmers. One should not be surprised to find that amongst thirty people a significant minority show a fairly apathetic attitude to their occupation. We shall have more to say about these issues in connection with wheat in Chapters 7 and 8.

The answers to the question on how long they had been double-cropping (Question 0) varied from one year to ten or fifteen years. The answers were, however, concentrated around three or four years. The beginning of double-cropping was generally associated with the arrival of easier irrigation in the form of pumping sets and borings.

The answer to the question why planting of wheat had been late that year told a lot about the farmer. Some farmers associated late planting with the frost in the previous *rabi* season which had severely damaged plants which had not been planted late. The idea was that, if there was a repeat frost at the same time, later planted wheat would still be in a stage where it was safe. These farmers were, on the whole, less well-informed and analytical. The implied prediction that this year's weather would be the same as last year's even though last year was (correctly) regarded as peculiar, is clearly unconvincing. The sharper farmers gave the answer that this year's *kharif* harvest was late because of late rains in the *kharif* season. While it was possible to harvest and prepare for timely sowing the problem was more difficult than for an average year.

Questions 2 to 6 were mainly concerned with the cultivation of wheat and we shall take up the answers that those questions elicited where they belong in context in Chapter 8.

In asking Question 7 we had in mind the efficiency theory of wages (see § 3.3) and in particular the possibility that our cultivators would refer to differences between the productivities of different workers and the influence of a meal on the worker's productivity.

Most farmers said that they were prepared to hire whichever labourer was available and that they found no problem in obtaining labour at the going wage whenever they needed the work. The usual practice was to make an arrangement the day before. Others mentioned that there were two or three known as particularly good workers. They agreed that the money wage fluctuated a little during the season, dropping from R4 plus meal in October/November to R3 plus meal in February but they did not discriminate amongst workers as to the wage paid. In nearly all cases the employee worked alongside a family member so that there was proper supervision.

The hirer of labour generally offered the worker the choice of the meal or an extra rupee. There were special circumstances when the offer was not made: for example the wife of the cultivator was ill or the hirer of labour was a Muslim and the Hindu worker would not take food from him (or vice versa). Hirers differed in their opinions on whether they preferred the worker to choose the meal or the rupee. Some said that it was easy to find an extra meal at little cost, others thought that the food was worth more than a rupee, and others did not mind which the worker chose.

An advantage of the worker electing to take the meal, which was indicated by some, was that everyone eating at the same time was a more efficient arrangement. The day was disrupted if the worker went home to eat at midday. If a meal was provided this was taken together in the field. Only one farmer (Ompal Singh) suggested that food at lunchtime improved the worker's productivity in the afternoon.

With regard to Question 10, most farmers had a clear idea of how much land they could or wanted to cultivate. This quantity varied across households according to individual circumstance, in particular with the presence and health of other male members and of draught animals. Thus the general response to why they do not lease-out less or lease-in more was that they could not manage any more land. One farmer, however, claimed that it was more profitable to hire permanent labour than to lease-out. There was only one permanent labourer, see above § 4.1.

Most farmers thought that it would be possible to adjust the amount of land cultivated, by leasing-out or leasing-in more or less. There was one *Teli* cultivator who claimed that he would like to lease-in a little more but could not get it. We had the impression he was a poor farmer and he turned out to have below average yield on his sample wheat plot.

One farmer, who said he could cultivate more, did not want to hire-in because, he claimed, landlords want to lease-out land that is exhausted after the *kharif* season and they would bother him with how much labour should be done. This potential interference was also mentioned by other farmers who were leasing-in land as an argument for not leasing-in more.

Another farmer whose son had been ill for two years had considered leasing-out land. Prospective tenants, he claimed, thought that he was in a weak bargaining position and tried to get him to agree to provide seed (an unusual practice in tenancy arrangements in the village) and he had not been able to conclude a deal. He did not want a permanent labourer as he could not trust him to work alone.

One *Murao* farmer claimed that it was degrading to hire-in land from others and would much prefer to take it from his father. Another *Murao* farmer said that he wanted to lease-in more land (he was already leasing-in a little) but this year his bullocks were weak. A *Thakur* cultivator pointed out that if he were to cultivate more it would be a lot more because he would have to buy another pair of bullocks. He was considering this possibility.

Farmers mentioned both profitability and riskiness in our discussions of the mix of crops. For example pea was considered profitable (inputs were not as high as wheat) but rather risky, and large areas were eschewed. Potato was also considered a profitable possibility but the large inputs of labour and water were viewed as a deterrent. The production of straw to feed the animals was an important consideration.

Many farmers claimed that they were producing primarily for their own consumption and sold only if they happened to find themselves with a surplus. Sugar, however, was viewed with some enthusiasm as a cash crop.

The final question on our list was concerned with changes in the incidence of tenancy over the last five years and with reasons for those changes. There were four farmers who thought that tenancy had increased. The remainder were roughly equally split between saying that there had been a decline and no change. Those who estimated the magnitude of the decline mentioned figures of around 25 per cent over the last five years.

The most common reason advanced for the decline in tenancy was the increase in population. It was suggested that landowners now had more labour available inside the family and were less willing to lease-out land. Another reason mentioned was the increase in irrigation—it had been the custom to lease-out only unirrigated land—which made the land more profitable for one's own cultivation. Two cultivators mentioned land reform as making tenancy more difficult.

Two of the four who claimed that tenancy had increased said that the increased intensity of cultivation that had accompanied irrigation meant that land-owners could cope with less land.

This concludes our analysis of the responses to our questions during the discussion sessions. In going through the questions in order we may have made these sessions sound more structured than they were. In fact they were informal and cheerful and provided a pleasurable way to pass the February evenings. While there was a general willingness to join in the discussion it was not universal. By February we had allayed most of the suspicion of the villagers, in particular because both our wives had visited the village by then. Again, while there was a willingness to respond to counter-factual or speculative questions, there were some who remained blank or answered, 'I do not know, I have never tried'.

While many were anxious to discuss ways of improving their practice, most were resigned to the uncertainty of agriculture and God was often mentioned as an important determinant of the course of events.

§ 4.8 Concluding Remarks

As we have surveyed a number of different markets in the chapter and found in them disparate features it would be pointless to attempt a summary of our findings, for this would have to amount to a brief statement of the argument section by section. However there are some general statements which we offer as a conclusion.

Economists have often attempted to classify markets into types—competitive, oligopolistic, and so on. Others have asked whether markets are competitive in the rural areas of developing countries. This makes little sense for Palanpur: the perfectly competitive market of the textbook is an unlikely object to look for in a small village, yet there are prices which farmers treat as 'givens' for some inputs at least; the bilateral monopoly model seems not to find much application even where one might expect it to be applicable. People find it convenient or right to use a standard price for a day's labour or the hire of a Persian wheel rather than fighting out the price for each bargain.

Few generalizations could be made concerning the markets in the village. Each has its peculiar features and in one case, the market for the hire of bullocks, it is not to be found at all. Nevertheless our somewhat vague concept of a market has proved to be useful in our research and this in itself is significant. It would not make sense to think about the labour market on its own or the market for the hire of pumping sets on its own (and in the following chapter we shall add the land market) if a transaction with an individual in one market were to imply a transaction with that same individual in another market. The theorists of 'semi-feudalism' have proposed a model in which people transact simultaneously over a range of markets so that, for example, a landlord will buy his tenant's labour and lend him money because the two enter into a wide-ranging relationship when land is leased from one to the other. One cannot in such a case usefully discuss the labour market in isolation.

Of course two individuals will frequently transact with each other in more than one market and there is reason why they should do so. In many cases the 'good' that is being sold is not absolutely standard and the more the transactors know of each other the better placed they will be to assess what is being bought and sold. But Palanpur is clearly a market economy in which the model proposed by the theorists of 'semi-feudalism' does not work. That it is not a perfectly competitive economy adds to its interest and in the following chapters we will frequently make use of the particular features of the various markets we have described to explain what we find in our later studies.

5

Tenancy

§ 5.0 Introduction

Share tenancy is important in Palanpur, accounting for about 20 per cent of the cultivated area at any time. And share-cropping has attracted a lot of attention recently from economic theorists. Tenancy will be the subject matter of the whole of this chapter.

The theory of share-cropping tenancy was examined in detail in § 3.2 above. In that section we also looked at the question of why share-cropping tenancy arises and saw how it might be related to risk-sharing or to the incentive to labour.

In § 5.1, starting from the theory presented in Chapter 3, we note some further explanations for tenancy (not only share-cropping) which have to do with the abandonment of some critical assumptions in the formal analysis of that chapter, notably the assumption that the production function is the same for all cultivators and that there are constant returns to scale in cultivation. In giving up these assumptions we refer to management as a kind of input and stress its importance.

In § 5.2 we turn to a detailed description of the form which share-cropping tenancy takes in Palanpur, the division of costs and output, the extent to which tenants are supervised and their decisions subject to negotiation, and the balance of supply and demand in the market for leased-in land. Bringing theory and institutions together we are enabled to see how far theory throws light on why tenancy arises at all in the village, what role it plays, and why it takes the form of share-cropping rather than some other arrangement such as cash tenancy. Another central question to which we shall address ourselves is this: given that leasing takes the form of share-cropping, what determines the shares of landlord and tenant?

We examine statistically in § 5.3 the notion, a central feature in the discussion of § 3.2, that output per *bigha* will differ between owner-cultivated and tenanted holdings. The hypothesis that there is a difference can be tested in various ways according to what is being compared. We shall investigate output per *bigha* for all crops taken together at the level of the farm in Chapter 6 and for individual wheat plots in Chapters 7 and 8. In § 5.3 we examine individual crops (particularly wheat) and sum across plots within the farm. The issues which these different approaches raise are not the same and will be compared in Chapter 9.

§ 5.4 is concerned with the detailed location of tenanted plots, where they lie in relation to landlord's and tenant's owned and self-cultivated holdings. This allows us to see to what extent leasing performs the role of land-consolidation—allowing cultivators to arrange their land in convenient parcels of adjacent plots. We present maps showing the broad location of land parcels leased and look at the patterns that emerge. We look at the hypothesis that leasing is playing the role of land consolidation and also at some other hypotheses on the location of tenanted plots.

In § 5.5 we present a simple stylized model of land-leasing (leasing-in or leasing-out) by the household. This model works with a notion which we call 'desired cultivated area' (*DCA*) for that household. Leasing is then accounted for by the difference between *DCA* and the land area owned. *DCA* is determined in the model by certain fixed or less-than-perfectly-marketable factors in the ownership of the household. A household owning less (more) than its *DCA* will want to lease-in (lease-out) land and the larger the gap the more it will want to lease-in (lease-out). The approach is analogous to the capital stock adjustment principle in the theory of investment. We make use of our knowledge of the factor markets in the village, which were the subject of Chapter 4, to decide which will be the factors exerting a determining influence on *DCA* and hence on the leasing decision.

The functional form of the relation between factors owned and *DCA* will be left very general in the discussion of § 5.5. However in § 5.6 we go into more detail concerning this issue and discuss the relationship between the substitutability of different inputs and the *DCA*.

In § 5.7 we discuss the sample and the full list of variables in the regression analysis and in § 5.8 we estimate the model. § 5.9 will be given over to the discussion and evaluation of these results. The final section of the chapter § 5.10 draws the argument together and notes what conclusions we have been able to reach and which questions remain unresolved. Thus in this chapter we shall be concerned with the features of tenancy in Palanpur and with developing our own model to explain quantities of land leased-in and -out.

§ 5.1 The Theory of Share Tenancy

We can begin by asking why land need be leased at all. If agricultural production were to be subject to constant returns to scale; and if every other factor, land apart, were to be perfectly marketable at the same fixed prices for each household, whether buyer or seller; and if finally the output market were perfect; then the household could adjust its use of factors to the size of its land holding and would have no need to adjust the size of its cultivated land area one way or the other.[1] Of course we are here supposing that each household would be subject to the same production function so that, given the co-operating factors, it would not make any difference which household cultivated a particular plot of land. An important force of this assumption is to exclude the influence of differences in non-marketed managerial ability between households. This is hardly plausible. Certainly some households are, for whatever reason, 'better farmers' than others. On the other hand, once one allows management to be an important factor then it is no longer reasonable to assume constant returns to scale in agricultural production, unless management or some proxy for it is included as an argument of the production function. Otherwise one would expect

---

[1] More generally with constant returns to scale, identical production functions and n factors, only $(n-1)$ factor markets are necessary. Hence, if there are set-up costs to markets it may be efficient to have less than n factor markets.

a range of increasing returns to scale followed by a range of diminishing returns to scale giving rise to the characteristic U-shaped cost curve.

If management is the non-marketed factor to which size of cultivated area is adjusted then leasing-out land would serve the role of buying-in management services. True the 'seller' of the management service pays a rent for the land but he will receive payment for his management services in the sense that his net return from farming the land will be higher than it would be to someone who supplied less or poorer management services. We show formally in the footnote[2] that under profit maximization and constant returns to scale the household obtains the same net return as it would if it could sell out its management services and earn their marginal product. This conclusion depends upon the doubtful assumption of the absence of uncertainty and that all other factor markets are perfect. By an exactly similar argument one can show that a household leasing-in land is in effect selling management services.

If one were to take the view that the function of tenancy is to combine land and management, then the arguments in Chapter 3 would be importantly affected. The Cheung model (see § 3.2) in which the landowner closely supervises the activity of the tenant seems to suppose that such supervision imposes no cost and that is unlikely to be the case. On the other hand, it may be that a somewhat general and irregular supervision meets the landlord's needs, which supervision is less costly and time-consuming than the attention which cultivation demands of the manager of the land.

In a sense, management is serving in this discussion the role of any non-marketed input and one can duplicate the conclusion that tenancy would have a role to play whenever any productive input is less than perfectly marketable. To cite another example, suppose that labour is not bought and sold in a market such that its opportunity cost is constant and the same for each household.

---

[2] Let H be the area cultivated, L the level of other variable inputs, and $\bar{M}$ the quantity of management service available to the household. Let agricultural production be a constant returns to scale function F of H, L, and $\bar{M}$. $\bar{M}$ is a constant and cannot be varied by the household. We assume that land can be leased-in or-out in any quantity at a rent μ per *bigha*, and that the variable factor (which can be interpreted as rupees spent optimally on all the variable inputs) costs 1.0 per unit Where a household is maximizing profit, H and L are chosen to maximize:

$$F[H, L, \bar{M}] - \mu H - L \tag{1}$$

Assuming that the solution will give H and L positive, this requires:

$$F_H = \mu \text{ and } F_L = 1.0 \tag{2}$$

where F_I $(I = H, L, M)$ is partial derivative of F with respect to I. Since F is homogeneous of degree one in H, L and $\bar{M}$ we have by Euler's Theorem:

$$F[H, L, \bar{M}] = F_H + F_L L + X_M \bar{M} \tag{3}$$

The net profit to the household from leasing-in (or using rather than leasing-out) the land that it cultivates is:

$$F[H, L, \bar{M}] - \mu H - L, \tag{4}$$

which from (2) and (3) can be seen to equal $F_M \bar{M}$.

Then, once again, tenancy could serve the function of 'bringing land to the labour'.

It should be clear that one can dispense with any one market without essentially affecting the outcome, at least where there are constant returns to scale, perfect markets, and profit maximization. On the other hand, it should also be clear that tenancy can fulfil only imperfectly the dual function of bringing both management to land and labour to land.

None of this implies share-cropping, since any form of lease would serve to transfer the use of land to the households with the non-marketable factors to cultivate it. However, as we saw in § 3.2 above, share-cropping has merits as a means of spreading risk.

§ 5.2 Tenancy in Palanpur

The first point to note concerning tenancy in Palanpur is that it is a phenomenon of substantial importance. This is so despite the legal restrictions' described in § 2.4. Obviously tenancy achieves something for landlord, tenant, or both which is not easily achieved by alternative arrangements. We shall offer some views on what it is that tenancy achieves for the households of Palanpur but we first describe the arrangements under which land is leased-out in more detail.

With only a handful of exceptions, leasing in Palanpur takes the form of share-cropping. Moreover it is significant that the exceptions nearly all take the form of cash tenancy between a village tenant and a landlord whose time is heavily committed outside the village. The interpretation which suggests itself is in accord with the theory of share tenancy. An efficient share-cropping contract requires enforcement by the landlord, but where the landlord cannot afford the time to supervise, say because he has a job outside the village, cash tenancy may be the only[3] feasible alternative even if the unwillingness of the tenant to undertake the risk involved means that the cash rent obtainable is only a low one.

In the vast majority of cases the arrangements for the share-cropping agreement are as follows. For the use of land the tenant pays 50 per cent of the yield. The tenant must pay from his 50 per cent any harvest shares paid to hired labourers. The traditional costs, that is the labour for cultivation, the use of bullocks to plough and draw water, and seed are paid entirely by the tenant. If no extra costs are incurred beyond these then the landlord bears no costs at all. If the landlord's Persian wheel is used to irrigate the leased-in land there is no charge for this, but the tenant must use his own bullocks. However contemporary agricultural practice has added to the list of costs that may be incurred, through the use of fertilizers and irrigation by the use of diesel pumping sets (these are the only such costs that apply to Palanpur). Moreover the use of Persian wheels is sometimes paid for in cash where a tenant hires a Persian wheel from a third party (not the landlord). These last costs are divided equally between landlord and tenant, that is, in the same proportion as the product is divided between landlord and tenant. Some arrangement of cost-sharing or en-

[3] No farmer in Palanpur is large enough to make it worthwhile to employ an agent.

forcement is necessary if the undertaking of variable costs is not to be discouraged; for a discussion of various possibilities, see Chapter 3. It is useful to have a collective term for those inputs whose cost is shared by landlord and tenant. In Palanpur these costs are, as we have seen, for fertilizer and where a cash payment is involved in raising water. We shall refer to these costs as 'discretionary'.

An important point is that all discretionary costs are normally borne initially by the tenant. Thus if R100 worth of fertilizer is applied to leased land, the tenant will have to find the R100 at the time of fertilizer application. At the time of the harvest, the landlord will reimburse the tenant for half the cost, here R50, either in cash or by adjusting his share of the produce. This detail of the tenancy arrangement has important implications. A land-owner who is short of credit has an incentive to lease-out land if he can find a tenant with cash or access to credit.

At the time that landlord and tenant agree that the land will be leased from the former to the latter they come to an agreement concerning the crop or crops that will be grown and the use of inputs. The agreement is supervised by the landlord who will regularly observe the progress of the cultivation. Indeed we often heard the complaint that landlord interference was onerous (see § 4.7). This accords with Cheung's view that a leasing arrangement will usually involve specification and enforcement of input levels, and Marshall's description of the 'time and trouble' of the landlord (see § 3.2). However the discretionary inputs are not the critical ones here since the discouragement to the provision of inputs by the tenant does not operate directly where the costs are divided in the same proportion as the product. That discouragement applies to the tenant's own labour where he is able to vary it and the labour input here should be taken to cover both the quantity and the quality of the labour provided, notably the care and attention that the tenant gives to cultivation. Important though this is, it is hard to measure hence hard to lay down what it should be in an agreement covering only one season.

It would however be misleading to think of the tenancy contract for one season as an isolated negotiation concerning that particular season only. In interviews with farmers we were frequently told that a landlord would prefer a 'good cultivator' to a poor one as his tenant. Thus a tenant might serve his own short-term interest by skimping on his labour in one season but would find it progressively harder to obtain land on lease in future seasons. The conditions subject to which would-be tenants can obtain land on lease will be discussed below.

One cannot hope to discover whether the market for land on lease is exactly in equilibrium but any gross imbalance, say a large excess demand, might be expected to make itself evident. The majority of our informants (see § 4.7) concurred in the view that a would-be landlord would experience no difficulty in finding a tenant in Palanpur, while a would-be tenant wishing to lease-in land would usually be able to find a landlord. These views were governed by the presumption that a would-be tenant had to be 'qualified' if his desire to lease-in land was to count seriously. To be qualified a tenant must have the means to cultivate, notably he has to own bullocks. (Recall that we are using the term bullock to cover all draught animals.) This is not surprising in view of our observation (see above § 4.2) that it is very nearly impossible to obtain the use of bullock-services through the market or even, with the exception of rather marginal cultivation, through exchange arrangements. Along with the expectation that a tenant will have his own bullock power goes a parallel presumption that he will have other resources including his family's labour power sufficient to allow him to manage and cultivate the land he takes on lease at the intensity required of tenants (allowing for some hired-in labour). Further, if his landlord expects him to apply fertilizer, he will have to have access to the credit to pay for it. Whether the intensity that will be required of tenants would be the same as that of owner cultivators is a question which will be examined statistically in § 5.3, Chapter 6, and Chapters 7 and 8 in the sense that we shall compare the output per *bigha* on tenanted and non-tenanted land.

Where share-cropping is concerned the landlord's share is the charge for the use of land. Given that the landlord's share in Palanpur is always 50 per cent and has been the same for a very long time, right back to the time of the *zamindars*, one might reasonably expect an imbalance of supply and demand—the economist's normal expectation where a price fails to adjust. As we have said, that imbalance if it exists is not very marked. Yet that observation, while true as it stands, could be misleading. Suppose, as seems likely given that there are quite a few landless or near-landless families in the village and that population has been growing rapidly, that the general tendency has been towards an excess demand for land to lease. If, for whatever reason, the share of the landlord does not increase then the market will nevertheless find a kind of equilibrium through the process of land rationing, followed by an accommodation by the households which fail to get the land they would like to lease to the state in which they find themselves. It works in the following manner. Given an excess demand for land to lease and the minimum amount he is prepared to lease to one person, or the minimum that would be accepted, the landlord will choose as tenants those he regards as the best cultivators and the remainder will be disappointed. In the medium term the disappointed would-be tenants may divest themselves of bullocks and other means of cultivation and may thereby take themselves out of the market. Eventually this process will cause an excess demand to disappear given that such people no longer meet the minimal conditions to be tenants, namely the ownership of the resources with which to cultivate land.

Tied up with the issue of supply and demand is the question of why the shares have remained unaltered in Palanpur for a long time. It would be extraordinary if it just happened that the market clearing share was always 50 per cent or very close to it. Since there are legal restrictions on tenancy in U.P. (see Chapter 2) it might seem that there could be no local restriction on what the share could be. In other parts of India, in the Punjab and in West Bengal, shares have sometimes been altered in favour of landlords in the last decade. Why not in Palanpur?

Probably the share has not altered because there has not been sufficient pressure to overcome the substantial inertia. Since 50 per cent is a convenient percentage in dividing output and one hallowed by time it is not going to be changed unless the pressure of demand for land is so great that a large excess demand emerges. Further there are other methods of adjustment to changes in market conditions. Other prices can change and the details of the tenancy contract can be adjusted. The prices of a bullock pair and of fertilizer, for example, vary freely and cost-sharing for discretionary inputs has been introduced. Whilst there is a certain presumption that the tenant provides the credit for discretionary costs the arrangement can be altered following negotiation. And the market for leased land can accommodate some excess demand by the simple system of setting a higher standard for the would-be tenant. The unsuccessful tenant will in due course disappear from the demand side of the market, and one will have the situation we have described in which tenants can find as much land as they are qualified by their ownership of resources to cultivate and landlords can find qualified tenants for as much land as they would like to lease out. We are not claiming that the land market has been in full equilibrium at 50 per cent shares but merely that any disequilibrium has been too small, given the other adjustment possibilities, to push the share away from its established value.

Important questions for a household which is considering leasing-out some land are whom to choose as tenants, which land to lease-out, and how to match type of land with different tenants. Similarly a prospective tenant will be concerned with quality as well as quantity of land. It was our impression that tenants who farm better could obtain or lease better land than could worse farmers. There was no variation in shares according to quality of land or quality of tenant, although variations in the detail of the contract may have been governed by these factors.[4] We formed no strong impression as to whether landlords leased-out their worst land. Neither did it seem the case that leased-out land was on average worse than owner-cultivated land (which could occur, for example, if landlords, on average, owned poor land). Hopper (1965), on the other hand, claimed that leased land was not as productive as owner-operated land (see § 3.6).

The question of what economic theory would lead one to expect concerning these matters is complex. We illustrate this complexity with some examples. Suppose that λ *bighas* of good land ($\lambda < 1$) are a perfect substitute for one *bigha* of poor land. A prospective landlord would be indifferent between leasing-out 1 *bigha* of poor land and λ *bighas* of good land, assuming the share to be the same in each case and the variable inputs on the good land to be $1/\lambda$ those on the poor land. These last two assumptions would be satisfied in competitive equilibrium. Thus on these assumptions there is no presumption that landlords lease-out their worst land. It is implausible, however, that there exists an area of good land which gives exactly the same results for associated inputs as does the Sahara desert. An answer to the question as to whether landlords choose to lease-out worse land will depend upon the way in which differences in land quality affect production and on the equilibrium.

---

[4]For example a good tenant might be able to persuade his landlord to provide credit for fertilizer, or the owner of good land might demand an usually high level of labour from his tenant.

The notion of a good tenant involves different issues from those raised by good land since it would be absurd to suppose that a good tenant is equivalent to a poor tenant with a larger family. A good tenant provides higher quality management than does a poor tenant. Thus a good tenant, or a better farmer, obtains higher output from inputs given in quality and quantity. One would expect therefore that he could command a higher share. If shares are invariant one might expect him to have a greater chance of obtaining land on lease thus obtaining a return for a contribution which is not directly marketable. The example we gave above concerning differences in land quality shows that there is no logical necessity that a better tenant would prefer, better quality land.

Given our discussion of the operation of factor markets in Chapter 4, the function of tenancy in Palanpur seems fairly obvious. There are at least two inputs that are less-than-perfectly marketable, the services of bullocks and of labour.[5] The market for the use of water sources works much better but, as we remarked above, cannot be completely perfect because the product is by its nature not a homogeneous one. Our view is that the major function of tenancy is to bring land to its co-operating inputs in a situation in which the opposite method, bringing inputs to the land, works nothing like as well. This view of tenancy in Palanpur forms part of the model which is set out in § 5.5 and § 5.6, and estimated in § 5.7 and § 5.8.

Given that tenancy exists in Palanpur there remains the question of why it should take the form of share-cropping. Since the picture that we have presented of the leasing contracts in Palanpur includes agreements explicit and implicit concerning the level of inputs and since there is a fairly close supervision by the landlord, with the implicit threat that poor cultivation will mean that the tenant will not get the land under lease next season, one might expect share-cropping to be efficient as suggested by Cheung's account. However, this is not a positive advantage for share-cropping as against, for example, a fixed-rent contract.

In the case of Palanpur there is a possibility that the legal restrictions on tenancy in U.P. have had the effect of encouraging share-cropping. This is because the obvious thing for a landlord who wants to cover up tenancy to do is to claim that he is the cultivator and that the tenant is his wage labourer. He can do this anyway, but it is easier and more convincing if the contract is a share-cropping agreement. With cash tenancy there is a payment from tenant to landlord and the product all belongs to the tenant, clear evidence that it is tenancy. With share-cropping it is not too difficult for the landlord to claim that the product belongs to him and that he is making from that product a payment to the tenant in return for his labour. Indeed the difference between share-cropping tenancy and wage labour paid a share of the product rather than a fixed wage lies in who manages the land and makes the decisions concerning its cultivation. We have noted that the landlord is involved in decision-making with share tenancy so in fact this arrangement is not very far from wage labour paid a share of the harvest. Indeed it is not as clear as many farmers of Palanpur

---

[5]Formally speaking credit is not an input but it has some of the effects of a less-than-perfectly marketable input. However it would not generally be easy to find a would-be tenant with access to extra credit.

imagine that their form of share tenancy, with the landlords present in the village and performing a supervisory function, is in fact illegal in U.P.[6] In any case the existence of the legislation reinforces the traditional system.

Apart from the effect of legal restrictions on tenancy, the main positive reason for share-cropping as opposed to another tenancy arrangement is that it shares risk betwen landlord and tenant. We judge this to be an important influence in sustaining the institution of share-cropping. With regard to the particular situation of Palanpur there is little to add to the theoretical discussion of § 3.2 above concerning superior alternatives to share-cropping. In § 3.2 we gave five conditions *all* of which have to be satisfied to establish that share tenancy, as a risk-sharing institution, is redundant. It should be clear from what has been said in Chapter 4 and above in this chapter that none of these five conditions applies in Palanpur.

Apart from its potential advantages associated with risk, it is far from clear that share-cropping as practised in Palanpur does push the use of inputs on leased land below efficient levels. The discretionary inputs have their costs divided so that there is no direct discouragement to their use. Other inputs, particularly care and attention to cultivation and the general intensity of cultivation, are somewhat controlled by negotiation between landlord and tenant and policed by some direct supervision and by the tenant's interest in getting land on lease in the future. Hence there seems to be no strong presumption that share-cropping tenancy in Palanpur is a very inefficient institution.

Since we have put stress on supervision costs it will be clear that an important merit of share-cropping to the landlord, compared with farming himself, is that it economizes on these costs. True the landlord does supervise in a general way in that he takes an interest in what is happening on the plot and he is involved in some of the decisions. However this is less demanding than the close and continuous supervision that is required when wage labour is employed. Another way of looking at the point is this: a wage labourer lacks the incentive for hard and careful work which a share-cropping tenant has. Indeed, even if the landlord took all the decisions in detail so that the tenant was in effect his wage labourer it might be in the landlord's interest to pay a wage related to the size of the crop as an incentive to good work.

A further deficiency of wage labour from the labourer's point of view is that the demand for his labour is uncertain. By taking land on lease he guarantees himself employment. This point was underlined by Newbery (1977) (see § 3.2).

The market for credit is also potentially important but its effect is hard to assess. There is a sense in which this market could not be perfect. A landless household without assets can offer no collateral for a loan and in an uncertain world will find it impossible to borrow very much. However, while the ownership of wealth is important in that it allows the household to borrow against future income or to use the wealth to buy now things that would otherwise be unobtainable, it is not clear what effect it will have on the decision to lease. Given the typical arrangements in Palanpur wealth might provide an argument

---

[6]We discussed this question with a lawyer in Delhi who specializes in land litigation.

against leasing as the landlord's need to obtain credit in this manner is diminished. On the other hand one could argue just as plausibly that a wealthy household would be more likely to want to free itself of the burden of cultivating land with its own labour or of supervising the labour of others by leasing-out. We have not been able to think of an effect of wealth which is clearly a dominant one and the direction of which is unambiguous. We shall have occasion to mention this factor again in assessing our regression results in § 5.8.

§ 5.3 Comparisons of Productivity on Tenanted and Non-Tenanted Land

There are various ways of comparing productivity on tenanted and non-tenanted land. In this book we shall employ three levels of aggregation for land: the farm (Chapter 6), land under one crop (this section) and, finally, the plot (Chapters 7 and 8). The questions involved are different and we should not necessarily expect to get similar answers. We therefore defer until Chapter 9 the over-all evaluation of the influence of tenancy on productivity.

Our present concern is this: for a particular crop we examine the yield obtained by households on tenanted and non-tenanted land. For a given crop, which for the moment we shall take to be wheat, we define two variables Y_1 and Y_2, yield per *bigha* on respectively non-tenanted and tenanted land. A household contributes an observation for Y_1 if it grows any wheat on non-tenanted land and likewise a household contributes to observations for Y_2 if it grows any wheat on tenanted land. Thus a particular household may contribute observations to both Y_1 and Y_2, to just one of them, or to neither. The number of cases for Y_1 and Y_2 will typically differ and is small for some crops. The number of cases is much larger for wheat than for any other *rabi* crop and for this reason we shall concentrate on wheat.

Of the households in the village, seventy-five grow wheat on non-tenanted land, and thirty-two on leased-in land. Each of these includes twenty-three cases of households growing wheat on non-tenanted and also on leased-in land (see Table 5.1).

We shall make use of the standard t-test to examine the hypothesis that observations on Y_1 and Y_2 are drawn from the same underlying normal distribution. Columns I and II only of Table 5.1 will be employed for this purpose. The reason is that the t-test requires observations to be independent and where an observation on Y_1 and on Y_2 are contributed by the same household it is not sensible to suppose them to be independent. We shall examine households contributing to both Y_1 and Y_2 in the discussion of Table 5.2.

Where the $t-$test is used in comparing two samples one must make the hypothesis that the variance of the normal distributions from which the samples are drawn is the same in each case. We test this hypothesis first, still considering wheat. On the hypothesis that the population variances are the same,

$$\frac{\sum_i (Y_{1i} - \bar{Y}_1)^2}{(M_1 - 1)} \Big/ \frac{\sum_i (Y_{2i} - \bar{Y}_2)^2}{(M_2 - 1)}$$

Table 5.1. Output in rupees per *bigha* on tenanted and non-tenanted land

Crop	Households growing the crop only on non-tenanted land I			Households growing the crop only on tenanted land II			Households growing the crop on non-tenanted land III			Households growing the crop on tenanted land IV		
	Mean	Standard Deviation	No. of Cases	Mean	Standard Deviation	No. of Cases	Mean	Standard Deviation	No. of Cases	Mean	Standard Deviation	No. of Cases
Wheat	141.1	36.9	52	146.4	23.7	9	136.8	36.4	75	147.0	40.3	32
Barley	115.5	89.2	20	68.9	17.4	4	106.1	78.9	27	66.0	17.4	7
Pea	126.6	31.6	24	138.6	1.4	2	129.3	30.3	31	122.9	32.8	6
Gram	142.8	32.9	14	128.3	15.8	2	134.6	35.0	22	135.8	12.7	9
Mustard	146.8	59.2	5	62.9	0	1	172.5	72.9	12	71.9	12.8	3
Sugar	274.0	62.2	36	240.0	0	1	260.2	80.9	55	295.5	70.0	16
Lahi	124.5	36.8	7	—	—	0	134.0	48.7	9	—	—	0
Paddy	119.9	28.4	15	134.0	27.9	3	120.7	32.9	29	118.0	28.4	7
Maize	78.8	13.7	29	82.6	0	1	77.8	16.3	42	77.2	6.4	5
Jowar	106.5	60.4	18	103.3	63.3	2	106.7	59.8	29	137.0	52.9	6
Bajra	78.1	22.5	42	85.3	25.2	4	79.8	20.9	64	80.0	19.8	19
Groundnut	162.0	30.0	18	210.0	42.4	3	158.9	33.6	23	177.0	57.3	6

Note: Columns I and III refer to Y_1, II and IV to Y_2—see text.

is distributed as F_{M_1-1, M_2-1}, where sub-sample one is defined so that the ratio is greater than unity, there are M_1 observations on Y_1, M_2 observation on Y_2, Y_{ji} ($j = 1,2$; $i = 1,\ldots,M_j$) is the ith observation on Y_j and $\bar{Y}_j$ is the sample mean of Y_j. It can be calculated from Table 5.1 that, for the case of wheat, the variable Y_1' in the test we have just given is in fact the variable Y_1 defined as output per *bigha* on non-tenanted land.

For wheat it can be calculated from the first rows of columns I and II that the above ratio takes the value 2.20. This is to be compared with the 2½ percentile[1] of $F_{51,8}$. The null hypothesis that the population variances are the same is comfortably accepted.

On the hypothesis that the population means (and variances) are the same,

$$\frac{\bar{Y}_1 - \bar{Y}_2}{W} \quad \text{where } W^2 = \left(\frac{1}{M_1} + \frac{1}{M_2}\right)\left[\frac{\sum_i (Y_{1i} - \bar{Y}_1)^2 + \sum_i (Y_{2i} - \bar{Y}_2)^2}{M_1 + M_2 - 2}\right]$$

is distributed as t with $M_1 + M_2 - 2$ degrees of freedom. For the case of wheat the degrees of freedom are 59 and $(\bar{Y}_1 - \bar{Y}_2)/W$ takes the value -0.40. One can comfortably accept the null hypothesis that the population means are the same at the 5 per cent significance level.

We have not carried out these tests for the other crops of Table 5.1 because the number of cases in column II for crops other than wheat is rather small.

For wheat, therefore, we may conclude that the difference between yields on tenanted and non-tenanted plots is insignificant. Inspection of Table 5.1 in-dicates that the same appears to be true for most of the other crops.

We shall now examine in some detail the wheat yields for households growing the crop on both tenanted and non-tenanted land. There were twenty-three such households (the number of cases in column III of Table 5.1 minus the number of cases in column I). It will be seen that for most of the other crops, the number of households doing both is small. Details of the twenty-three households are presented in Table 5.2.

We wish to examine the hypothesis that a household growing wheat on both tenanted and non-tenanted land will obtain the same expected yield on each. Accordingly we ask whether the mean of $Y_1 - Y_2$ is significantly different from zero. Writing X for $Y_1 - Y_2$, $\bar{X}$ for the sample mean, and s^2 for $(X_i - \bar{X})^2/(n-1)$ where n is the number of observations, we have under the null hypothesis that

$$\frac{\bar{X}}{s/\sqrt{n}}$$

is distributed as t with $(n - 1)$ degrees of freedom. Here we can see from the note to Table 5.2 that X is -21.4 and s is $43.7\sqrt{(23/22)}$ or 44.7. The ratio given

---

[7] The test is one-tailed since we have selected the sub-sample to make the F-value greater than unity.

above is then -2.3 which must be compared with the quantiles of the t distribution with 22 degrees of freedom: the 5 per cent level is 2.07. Thus for this particular comparison yields on tenanted land are significantly different from those on non-tenanted land with the former being the larger.

A parallel exercise for $(B_1 - B_2)$—see Table 5.2—yields a t-value of -0.80 and for $(T_1 - T_2)$ a t-value of -0.51. Thus the fertilizer inputs on tenanted and non-tenanted land are not significantly different.

The results from our analysis of the figures presented in Table 5.1 are in accord with Cheung's view that cultivation on tenanted land would, with appropriate share-cropping contracts, be just as it is on non-tenanted land. The difference in yields we find in Table 5.2. is, however, striking. The expectations suggested by the theories were that there would be either no difference (Cheung) or lower productivity on tenanted land (so-called Marshall).

The second exercise (based on Table 5.2) comes closer to being a test of the hypothesis at issue than the first. For in comparing outputs on tenanted and non-tenanted land for a given farmer one is automatically holding constant, across tenanted and non-tenanted land, the attributes of the cultivator. It is interesting to speculate on why this surprising significant difference has emerged. Where a tenant is growing the same crop on his own land as he is on the landlord's, the landlord may feel that he must be especially on his guard to avoid the tenant transferring the use of inputs from his leased-in land to his owned land. He must endeavour to, as Marshall puts it with reference to draught power, 'keep down the use he [the tenant] makes of the farm cattle for outside work, the fruits of which he does not share with his landlord' (Marshall, 1959, p. 536). We have in mind that such watchfulness on the part of the landlord might enforce on these tenants a higher intensity of cultivation than is usual for tenants in general. If there is anything in this idea it is not reflected in significant differences in fertilizer use.

A further explanation of the result would be the following. We have described in § 4.3 the system in Palanpur where the tenant provides credit for the purchase of irrigation and fertilizer. We also described the difficulty encountered by some lower castes in obtaining credit and also the apparent reluctance to use the private credit market for agricultural loans. Where it is easier for landlords to find tenants than vice versa (see above § 5.2) one would expect landlords to try to use the power which this position entails to shift the use of the tenant's limited credit in the landlord's direction. Again this idea is not reflected in significant differences in fertilizer use although an informal inspection of our records on irrigation suggests that the effect may operate in the case of water usage. In this case too the landlord might assist the tenant in obtaining the use of a pumping set at a good time.

The final speculative view we shall offer is that the quality of owned land in Table 5.2 may be lower than of the tenanted land. The households involved are mainly from the lower castes (particularly the *Jatabs*) whose land may be inferior.

We have done our best to explain the result based on Table 5.2 but we find none of the reasons we have offered very convincing and incline to the view that

Table 5.2 Yields and fertilizer applied to wheat for households with tenanted and non-tenanted land

	Owned				Tenanted			
Household no.	Owned area (bighas)	Basal (kg/bigha) B_1	Fertilizer/area TD (kg/bigha) T_1	Yield in rupees per bigha Y_1	Leased area (bighas)	Basal (kg/bigha) B_2	Fertilizer/area TD (kg/bigha) T_2	Yield in rupees per bigha Y_2
103	8.0	6.25	6.25	136.5	5.0	6.00	6.00	156.0
107	20.0	4.00	7.50	155.4	2.0	—	5.00	130.0
111	6.4	4.69	6.25	215.3	9.5	4.74	4.74	131.4
113	15.74	2.86	3.18	152.4	7.5	5.33	5.33	208.0
225	10.0	4.00	5.00	143.0	3.0	4.00	5.00	130.0
306	3.2	—	—	130.0	6.0	—	5.00	125.7
402	2.0	—	5.00	130.0	5.0	—	4.00	117.0
404	2.25	—	11.11	150.2	5.0	—	5.00	145.6
406	9.0	—	5.00	122.8	4.0	12.50	12.50	260.0
503	13.0	—	1.92	102.0	4.0	—	6.25	117.0
606	7.5	—	4.67	149.1	6.0	—	4.00	177.7
610	0.75	—	—	69.3	13.0	—	5.38	130.0
611	0.75	—	—	69.3	16.0	—	5.125	142.2
612	6.0	—	5.00	156.0	4.0	—	—	260.2
704	6.0	—	5.00	134.3	18.5	—	5.03	116.0
801	5.0	—	—	93.6	12.0	—	—	114.4
802	3.9	—	3.85	120.0	8.0	—	4.375	130.0
803	4.48	—	—	104.5	3.0	—	—	108.3
804	4.48	—	4.46	127.7	5.0	—	6.00	156.0
805	1.79	—	11.17	163.4	6.0	—	5.00	156.0
808	8.58	—	3.50	125.8	5.0	—	4.00	156.0
809	5.57	—	—	104.0	5.0	—	—	130.0
811	6.0	—	3.33	156.0	10.0	—	3.00	156.0

		$Y_1 - Y_2$	$B_1 - B_2$	$T_1 - T_2$
	Mean	−21.4	−0.47	−0.37
	Standard deviation	43.7	2.75	3.43

Notes:
(i) Mean / Standard deviation
(ii) TD means top-dressing and is nearly always urea;
(iii) Basal fertilizer is usually some NPK mixture.

the statistical difference may have emerged by chance. This feeling is supported by our failure to find significant differences in our analysis in later chapters (6, 7, and 8).

§ 5.4 The Location of Tenanted Plots

The quantitative analysis of tenancy which will be presented from § 5.5 onwards is entirely concerned with the question of how much land a farmer will lease-in (or lease-out). While this is an important and central issue it by-passes a different and essentially less tidy question: which particular plots will a farmer choose to lease-out and, given a choice, which plots will tenants try to lease-in ?

More than one detailed aspect of leasing is subsumed under these questions. A tenant may prefer one plot to another because of its location relative to water sources or relative to owned land holdings. A landlord may prefer to lease-out a plot close to one which he will cultivate himself to facilitate the supervision of his tenant's activity. Furthermore, tenancy might serve as a partial substitute for land consolidation. This would be the case were a farmer to arrange by leasing-out to cultivate a smaller number of plots, or plots closer together than those of his total land holding.

Table 5.3 Households whose leasing pattern seems to conform to the proximity hypothesis

Household number	R e m a r k s
Leasing-in	
103	added to own plots by leasing-in adjoining land
111	added to own plots by leasing-in adjoining land
121	leased-in one piece by owned land but others remote from other plots and generally his cultivated holding is very dispersed
119	leased-in all land in one area
304	leased-in several plots near to each other but has other dispersed pieces
306	leased-in one piece by an owned piece but owns another piece far away
704	leased-in extra land adjacent to two owned plots
Leased-out	
108	leases-out all of a remote plot, but also part of a cultivated plot. His own-cultivated plots are close to each other
114	leases-out owned land in Kasaura village
125	leases-out two plots remote from his cultivated plot but close to each other
209	leases-out two adjoining plots remote from one that he cultivates
210	cultivates three plots close to each other, leases-out another three remote plots
218	leases-out one remote plot but also another plot by his cultivated land
220	leases-out land in Bhoori village
503	leases-out his most remote plot; part-cultivates other plots and leases-in another remote plot

On the basis of this kind of reasoning we may advance some hypotheses concerning particular features that one might expect to observe in the leasing behaviour of households. The following hypotheses could all be seriously defended on *a priori* grounds, and their effects would not all be in the same direction.

1. Leasers-in will tend to take on lease plots adjacent to other cultivated land. This will serve to establish larger contiguous holdings and give the cultivator any economies of scale with regard to plot size.

2. Leasers-out will tend to lease plots remote from their main holdings.

We shall refer to the hypotheses 1 and 2 together as the 'proximity model'. The following are further hypotheses:

3. There will be a number of cases of leasing of more than one plot to one person or from one person. This has conveniences to both parties and allows easier supervision and consultation.

4. Land will be leased-out close to own-cultivated holdings to facilitate the supervision of the tenant's cultivation. Note that this is exactly the opposite tendency to the one detailed in 2.

5. Recently acquired land will tend to be leased-out more frequently than long-owned land. Possibly such land will have been acquired due to availability rather than its natural desirability in terms of the new owners' existing holdings and will not yet have been absorbed into the owner's cultivation pattern.

6. Land will frequently be leased to brothers or close relatives.

Generally, points 1 and 2 were those that occurred to us in advance of our close inspection of the data on leases and the maps showing the locations of tenanted and owned plots, while points 3 to 6 emerged from the examination of the maps and the household data. Enough examples apparently falling under one or other of these last headings came to light for us to note the particular feature concerned. On the other hand, the data were unsympathetic to our own favoured hypotheses (points 1 and 2) and on the whole they were poorly supported. Of course, given almost any hypothesis, one can find the odd example conforming to it but looking for many cases of a particular type led us to conclude that the proximity model does not do well in explaining leasing patterns.

The test of the various hypotheses is the examination of the leasing patterns of individual households. We consider examples under the numbered headings above.

Taken as a whole we find this evidence unimpressive. Some of the above examples do conform nicely to the proximity hypothesis but as we have displayed all the most likely looking examples it seems less than convincing that there are only fifteen of them (seventy-seven households were involved in leasing). Even among these few, some are far from being unambiguous. Household 121, for example, is cultivating all over the place and the fact that one of his leases fits into the proposed pattern is quite likely due to chance. Similarly 304 and 306 cultivated dispersed holdings despite having consolidated a little through leasing.

On the leasing-out side, two of the examples are of households leasing-out owned land in another village. This is unsurprising from one point of view as it is inconvenient to cultivate in another village, but it is equally inconvenient to supervise cultivation outside the village so that the point is not so straightforward as might at first seem. In saying this we are doing no more than to note that points 2 and 4 are always in tension since they propose opposite tendencies. Examples 209 and 218 are somewhat ambiguous: really only 108 and 210 are ideal examples of this feature. Household 210 is Mohi Lal, *Murao*, who tried to keep his leasing-out secret from us.

Given that these are the only examples that we can produce, it seems reasonable to conclude that the proximity motive taken alone is not of great importance is deciding the pattern of leasing in Palanpur. Table 5.4 is concerned with examples conforming to hypotheses 3 & 4.

Table 5.4 Various examples of leasings conforming to hypotheses 3 and 4

Hypothesis	Household	Remarks
3. leasing to or from one person	608	leases in one large block from Mohi Lal 210
	125	125 leases two plots close together but not adjacent to 805
	119	leases-in the whole of two large plots leased-out by 101, 102, and by 104 respectively
	209	leases two close plots to 811 while keeping one remote plot
4. leasing-out part of larger plots	102	
	116	also leases to one person
	226	
	401	
	503	
	813	
	210	
	202	
	203	lease-out plots beside cultivated land
	205	
	218	

There were in each case several examples conforming to hypotheses 5 and 6, but as these cases are not to be seen by inspection of the maps which we shall now introduce there is no point in giving the household numbers.

In the course of our investigation of leasing patterns we had maps prepared, two for each caste, showing the location of own-cultivated and leased plots. Figures 5.1 to 5.3 show examples of these maps for the largest castes, the *Thakurs* and the *Muraos*. Most of the examples given above, where they involve *Thakur* or *Murao* households, can be traced on the maps. The numbers appended to plots refer to the households of the caste concerned.

On Figure 5.1 note in particular household 1-11 (centre of the map near the railway line) leasing-in a plot next to his owned plot. Note also the wide dispersal of 1-21's holding, including his leased-in fragment. Household 1-19 has

Thakurs: Location of plots leased-in

Other land leased in:
08 cultivates 2 *bighas* near the river
19 leases 3 *bighas* near the river from a *Murao*

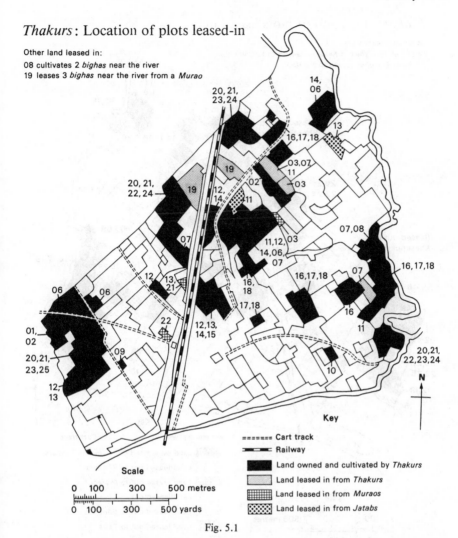

Key

===== Cart track
▬▬▬ Railway

▉ Land owned and cultivated by *Thakurs*
▨ Land leased in from *Thakurs*
▦ Land leased in from *Muraos*
▧ Land leased in from *Jatabs*

Scale

0   100   300   500 metres

0   100   300   500 yards

Fig. 5.1

leased-in a tidy holding (though the railway line cuts across it) by taking two large plots.

On Figure 5.2 note the leasing-out behaviour of household 1-08. He leases out completely a remote plot (centre to the left of the railway line) and part of his main holding (right-hand side by the river). Household 1-25 is seen to have confined his cultivation to the west (left-hand) side of the village while leasing-out two neighbouring plots on the east side. Household 1-02 has leased-out part of his large plot at centre top by the railway line while cultivating on the other side of the path, yet he cultivated his plot at the far west of the village land. Finally 1-16 is interesting. His holding is dispersed east of the railway line) and he has leased-out land from part of his holding near to the river and from part of his holding at the north of the village, while leaving himself with an isolated central plot.

Thakurs: Location of plots leased-out

Other land leased out:
14,15 own 16 *bighas* in Kasaura leased to Kasaura man
24 owns 5 *bighas* leased to a *Jatab*

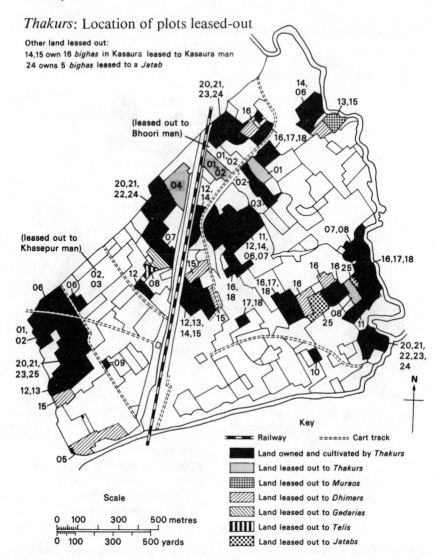

Key

═══ Railway   ══════ Cart track

■ Land owned and cultivated by *Thakurs*

▨ Land leased out to *Thakurs*

▦ Land leased out to *Muraos*

▨ Land leased out to *Dhimars*

▨ Land leased out to *Gadarias*

▥ Land leased out to *Telis*

▨ Land leased out to *Jatabs*

Scale

0 100   300   500 metres

0 100   300   500 yards

Fig. 5.2

On Figure 5.3 notice how 2-09 has leased-out two adjacent plots near the river (both to household 8-11) while cultivating a small holding of 2.7 *bighas* near the village (not marked on the plan). Household 2-10 will be seen to have kept land close to the village and leased-out plots to the north by the river and to the west of the railway line. Household 2-18 cultivates by the Jargaon road on a plot part of which he has leased-out, while leasing-out his other plot (bottom centre to the east of the railway line). Household 2-02 is seen to lease-out part of a larger plot to the south of the village land by the river. Household 2-03 does the same near the railway station and 2-05 in the centre of the village land to the east of the railway line.

Muraos : Location of plots leased-out

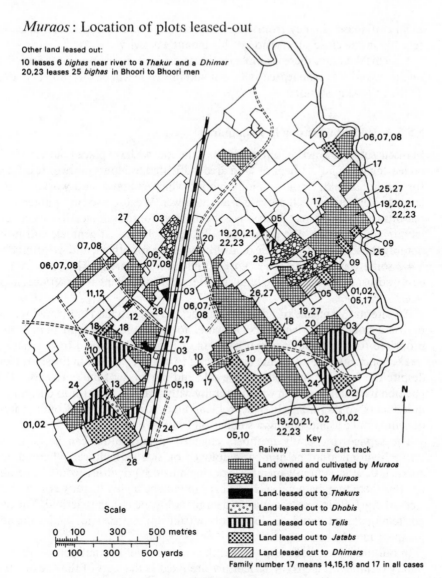

Other land leased out:

10 leases 6 *bighas* near river to a *Thakur* and a *Dhimar*
20,23 leases 25 *bighas* in Bhoori to Bhoori men

Fig. 5.3

Our conclusion concerning the location of tenanted plots would be that location as such does not seem to be a very important issue. The proximity hypothesis is certainly not well supported. Some other patterns, points 3–6 above, do appear frequently enough to attract notice but they do not predominate. We doubt that tenants are in a position to lease-in land wherever they would like to but even leasers-out have not found it easy, or have not taken trouble to arrange tidy holdings for themselves. A desire to have a tenant cultivating close by seems as common a feature and this is interesting because it fits in well with the theory of share tenancy from which one would expect the landlord to be interested in the close supervision of his tenant's activity.

It seems then that there is ample justification for concentrating our attention on the quantity of land leased-in or-out and this issue will be the subject matter of the following sections.

§ 5.5 A Model of Leasing in Palanpur

In discussing the function of tenancy in Palanpur we have placed our emphasis on leasing as an adjustment of land area cultivated to inputs more or less fixed for the household, notably family labour which manages and works on the land, and bullocks which provide draught power. We discussed in Chapter 4 the reasons for the imperfect function of the markets for the services of respectively labour and bullocks. We argued in § 4.1 that villagers in general, and most notably those of the *Thakur* caste, dislike working for others, and we offered in § 4.2 some views on the absence of a bullock-hire market. Thus one cannot easily adjust factor services to land cultivated through hiring these services in or out.

An alternative means of adjusting bullock services to land cultivated would be for a household wishing to cultivate, for example, less land than is appropriate for the bullock pair it owns to sell the bullocks and to purchase a weaker pair. Such adjustments are difficult to achieve, at least in the short run, despite the fact that markets for the sale and purchase of bullocks exist. The position is similar to that in which a family with a car too large for its current requirements would find itself. The problems associated with renting out a seat or of selling the car and buying a smaller one will be clear.

The services of family members engaged in agriculture can be adjusted through variation in the number employed outside agriculture. Where an increase is desired, a family member working outside agriculture would be recalled. But there may be none such, or his job may be highly lucrative or the services of one full-time person may be a larger adjustment than is desired. The opposite adjustment entails finding a job outside agriculture and, again, the adjustment may be too large.

In our model we shall suppose that the value of bullocks and the number of family members engaged in agriculture are fixed at the start of the season. We wish to examine the determination of the quantity of land that the household will cultivate that season. We shall proceed as follows. We introduce the concept of 'desired cultivated area' (*DCA*) for the household, being that area which (roughly speaking) accords best with the factor supplies available to the household. We have used the term *desired* cultivated area because there is no implication that the household will cultivate its *DCA*. However, and we shall make this our definition, if the household owns an area equal to its *DCA* then it will neither lease-in nor lease-out.[8] The concept of *DCA* is parallel to the con-

---

[8]Note that on this definition the *DCA* need not be unique, for there might be more than one area such that, owning it, the household would wish neither to lease in nor to lease out, but we shall assume that this problem does not arise.

cept of desired capital stock in the theory of investment and subject to some of the same difficulties. In our discussion sessions with farmers (see § 4.7) most of them had an idea of how much land they could manage to cultivate, which quantity varied across households according to individual circumstances. Thus the concept of a *DCA* finds some justification in the stated views of these farmers.

On what will the household's *DCA* depend ? In presenting this theory we simplify and consider those factors on which we wish to place our greatest emphasis, bullocks and family labour. In our statistical analysis we also examine the influence of other variables but here, for the sake of presentation, we include only the two main variables. We shall measure bullock power by the value of the draught animals owned by the household. (On the justification for this, see above § 4.2.) Family labour will be measured by the number of family males[9] between sixteen and sixty whose only occupation is agriculture.

As presented so far we have viewed the household as a production unit in parallel with capital stock adjustment processes for the firm. We shall incorporate the notion that households maximize utility rather than profit in the other variables just mentioned (in particular, *LOFA*, see below).

The term 'desired cultivated area' refers to the demand side. But when we come to consider leasing we must bear in mind that a tenant can only lease-in land if his potential landlords regard him as qualified, by virtue of his ownership of resources, to do so. We shall assume in our model that rationing by landlords if it exists does not do other than confine the household to its *DCA*: what it would like to cultivate anyway.

Leasing-in or -out is now seen as an adjustment of land owned towards *DCA*. If that adjustment were complete, land area leased-in minus land area leased-out[10] (that is, net leased-in, denoted *NLI*) would be simply the difference between *DCA* and land owned. However more generally *NLI* will be a function of *DCA* and land owned. The land area owned by the household will be denoted *LANDO*.

$$NLI = h(DCA, LANDO) \tag{7}$$

A more special form would make *NLI* depend only upon the difference between *DCA* and *LANDO*. This is a natural restriction upon *h*, but may be invalid, see below. So we have:

$$NLI = h(DCA - LANDO) \tag{8}$$

The adjustment of land cultivated to *DCA* will not, in general, be complete. There are various costs and difficulties associated with involvement in the market for leased land and these are represented by the difference between the function *h* ( ) and the identity function ($h(x) = x$). The prospective tenant will be better informed about his own land than that of others; he will possibly encounter difficulty in finding landlords wishing to lease to him the land he would

---

[9]Women seldom work in the fields.

[10]Apart from one case involving debt repayment, in no case did a farmer lease-in some land in the *rabi* of 1974–5 whilst leasing-out other land.

desire to cultivate; he may dislike leasing-in as such because the landlord will interfere with his cultivating the land as he would choose were it his own. The prospective landlord will have to negotiate with tenants, or he may encounter difficulty in finding a suitable tenant. From what has been said in § 5.2 we suggest that the difficulties facing the tenant in adjusting are in general more severe than those facing the landlord.

In comparing our model to the capital stock adjustment principle note that in describing the $h(\ )$ function we have referred only to difficulties in making the adjustments. It is common in capital stock adjustment theories to attribute partial adjustment to uncertainty about future developments. These aspects make the use of the term 'desired' in that theory somewhat inappropriate as given the uncertainty the specified stock is not desired. This point does not apply to our model.

The restrictions on h are obvious and necessary. First, $h(0)$ should equal 0; a household which owns its *DCA* will cultivate its *DCA*, that is, neither lease-in nor lease-out, by definition. Second, h should be a non-decreasing function of *DCA* − *LANDO*; the more *DCA* exceeds the amount the household owns the more it will wish to lease-in and certainly it will not wish to lease-in less.[11]

Figures 5.4 (a), (b), and (c) illustrate three possible forms of h which satisfy both restrictions.

In Figure 5.4(a), h is a linear function with slope less than 1. *NLI* is simply proportional to the difference between *DCA* and *LANDO*, so that a certain proportion of the difference is made up by leasing and this proportion is independent of the size of the difference. Figure 5.4 (b) illustrates one possible non-linear version. When the absolute value of the gap between *DCA* and LANDO becomes large, the slope of h becomes larger. In other words the response of leasing to the difference between *DCA* and *LANDO* is weak when land owned is close to *DCA* but becomes stronger when the gap is a wide one. Figure 5.4 (c) illustrates a further possibility which is only an extension of Figure 5.4 (b).[12] Here *NLI* is zero unless the absolute value of *DCA* − *LANDO* is quite large. In other words, the household does not bother with leasing unless the land area it owns is far different from its *DCA*.

In all the figures the slope of h to the right of zero is the same as the slope to the left. This implies that the household responds as strongly to an excess of land by leasing it out as it does to a deficit of land by leasing it in (though in the case of Figure 5.4(c) it does not respond to a small difference in either direction). This is not very plausible and when we come to discuss our regression results in § 5.7 we shall return to this matter again.

Our next task in formulating the model is to express *DCA* as a function of the variables upon which it depends. We are considering only *V1*, the value of draught animals and *F3*, male workers of age 16–60[13] engaged only in

[11]We are supposing that a household which leases will either lease-in or lease-out, not both.

[12]In defining *DCA* as *the area* which a household would have to own not to lease-in or-out we were implicitly ruling out this case.

[13]The numeral *3* following *F* (family) is to distinguish this measure of family labour from other definitions denoted *F1* and *F2*. Similarly *V1* denotes draught animals where *V2* denotes all animals.

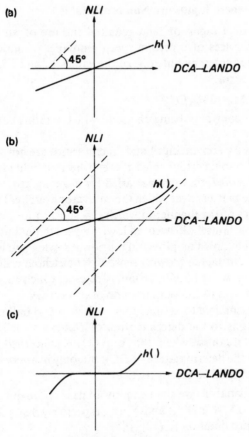

Fig. 5.4 (a), (b) and (c).

agriculture. The only obvious restriction is that *DCA* should not decrease with either of these variables. We write:

$$DCA = \phi \ (V1, F3) \tag{9}$$

At this point the only variable we have explicitly excluded as a determinant of *DCA* is *LANDO*. This might not be correct. *LANDO* could, for example, influence access to credit, and thus *DCA*, through the opportunity to purchase non-fixed inputs. We should be unable to distinguish such an influence from partial adjustment, see § 5.8.1. and § 5.8.3. Other variables will be introduced below.

Combining (8) and (9) we obtain:

$$NLI = h \ [\phi(V1, F3) - LANDO] \tag{10}$$

This is our model of leasing for Palanpur and the one that we shall eventually test. However we first need to say more about the functional form of ϕ and this is the subject of the next section.

§ 5.6 Substitution where Inputs are Non-Marketable

If the cultivation of a *bigha* of land required the use of an exact value of bullocks and the services of a certain specific number of agricultural males, *DCA* would be determined by only one of the values *V1* and *F3*. Then ϕ would take the following form:

$$\phi\,(V1, F3) \;=\; \mathrm{Min}\,(\alpha V1, \beta F3) \tag{11}$$

where α and β are constants being the land—factor ratios for, respectively, bullocks and men.

This idea is not very convincing. Land—factor ratios are not so rigidly fixed, they can be varied to some extent at least, even where an individual crop is concerned. Hence, *a fortiori*, they can be varied for a whole farm whose cropping pattern is one of the matters over which the cultivator exercises his choice. Consider some examples of the manner in which this substitution can be achieved. In growing wheat a household well endowed with labour but badly off for bullock power can cut down on ploughings prior to sowing and instead weed by hand once or more during the growing season. A household well off for labour and credit can grow sugar, a labour-intensive crop which makes no greater demands on the services of bullocks than do other crops.

It is therefore reasonable to assume that both men and bullocks make their separate contributions to the determination of *DCA*. This is the assumption that we shall test. Of course where the form (11) is concerned both men and bullocks matter for the determination of *DCA* but only in a very special manner and one that we judge to be too restrictive.

In our regression analysis we shall employ a linear approximation to (9) and (10). Let $\gamma = dh/dDCA$ and ϕ_V and ϕ_F be respectively $\partial\phi/\partial V1$ and $\partial\phi/\partial F3$. Then the linear approximation to (10) is:[14]

$$NLI \;=\; \gamma\cdot\phi_V V + \gamma\cdot\phi_F F - \gamma\cdot LANDO + K \tag{12}$$

where K is a constant. Then the coefficient on *V1* should be interpreted as the product of terms each of which has an economic interpretation. The term γ measures the responsiveness of leasing to a deviation of *DCA* from *LANDO*, while ϕ_V measures the marginal responsiveness of *DCA* to the value of bullocks owned by the household. The coefficient on *F3* can similarly be regarded as the product of two terms.

While the linear approximation is valid in the sense that any differentiable function can be approximated locally by its linear form, it is special because only a local approximation. Indeed we know that the true form of ϕ is most unlikely to be linear and it is worthwhile considering whether we might make use of a more general form. There are however difficulties in the way of doing this, mainly because it is very far from clear which would be a more appropriate form and also because some forms which might suggest themselves would not be amenable to simple regression analysis. What we have done is a compromise

---

[14]To ease notation we write *V1* as *V* and *F3* as *F* in equations (12) and (13).

between the ideal from the theoretical point of view and what is feasible.

An important deficiency of equation (12) is that it allows no scope for interaction between bullocks and men in the determination of DCA. Thus the marginal increase in DCA from a given increase in $F3$ is independent of $V1$ and this runs counter to intuition. To test how serious this mis-specification may be we tried also a quadratic approximation to (9), the approximation which includes one further term in the Taylor series expansion. The quadratic approximation takes the form:

$$NLI = \gamma \cdot \phi_{VV} V^2 + \gamma \cdot \phi_{FF} F^2 + 2\gamma \cdot \phi_{FV} VF + \gamma \cdot \phi_V V + \gamma \cdot \phi_F F$$
$$- \gamma \cdot LANDO + C \tag{13}$$

where ϕ_{ij} $(i, j = F \text{ or } V) = \partial^2 \phi / \partial i \partial j$.

A way of evaluating the linear approximation for $h(\ )$ is to look at the residuals from the fitted regression line. This approach has the advantage that it allows one to see how misleading is the assumption, implicit in the linear approximation, that h is a linear function (with slope γ). By looking at the households for which the absolute value of the residual is large and seeing whether they exhibit extreme values of $DCA - LANDO$ one may hope to form a judgement concerning the accuracy of the linear approximation. We examine these residuals in § 5.7 and discuss them in § 5.8.

The reader will notice that we have specified the problem of constructing a model of leasing as the problem of explaining NLI. However, given $LANDO$ and the decision which gives us NLI, the land area cultivated by the household, denoted $CULT$, follows from the identity:

$$CULT \equiv LANDO + NLI. \tag{14}$$

Why not then try to explain $CULT$ directly from the relation

$$CULT = DCA(V1, F3) \tag{15}$$

and its derivatives, through linear approximation, and so on ?

As it happens, (15) gives us a special case of equation (8), because subtracting LANDO from both sides of (15), and taking into account (14), we have:

$$NLI = DCA - LANDO, \tag{16}$$

which is equation (8) with h constrained to be the identify function. In the linear formulation this is equivalent [15] to requiring γ to equal 1. The restriction in (15) is clearly very strong, in that it says that the household cultivates its DCA rather than merely gravitating towards it but we nevertheless submit it to a test in § 5.7.

In § 5.7 we first discuss the criteria on which our sample of households for the regression analysis were selected, and the characteristics of those households, and then we present our results. The evaluation of these results is the subject matter of § 5.8.

---

[15] Note that there is a contribution to K in equation (12) both from linearizing $h(\ )$ and $\phi(\ )$.

§ 5.7 Regression Analysis of the Model of Leasing: The Sample and the Variables

For the purposes of this section we shall use a slightly narrower definition of involvement in agriculture than that of § 2.1. Specifically we exclude households for which all of the following variables, just introduced— *V1, F3, LANDO*, and *CULT*—take the value zero. Not surprisingly, there are few such households, four in all. The justification for excluding the four households is that their involvement in agriculture is somewhat marginal, being limited to agricultural labour, and that not full-time.[16] To interpret their decision not to lease-in land as a decision involving their desired cultivated area seems artificial. The same cannot be said of non-cultivating households whose members are involved in agriculture as full-time labourers,[17] if no land is owned.

As well as *V1, F3*, and *LANDO*, our main variables which might be influential on the decision to lease-in land, we shall examine the possible influence of certain others, offering in each case a brief rationalization.

We have declared already above and in § 4.4 our view that the markets for water sources in Palanpur function fairly effectively and so our *a priori* judgement was that a proxy for ownership of water sources did not belong in the list of variables importantly influencing *DCA*. However we decided to test this view and we experimented with two measures of ownership of water sources. One variable was designated *VALWATS*. It is defined as the estimated value of all water sources (being Persian wheels, borings, and pumping sets) owned by the household. We thought this the most appropriate variable to capture the notion of ready access to water.

Another variable was the number of pumping sets owned by the household, denoted *NPSO*. Since pumping sets are faster than Persian wheels in delivering water one might expect that the ownership of this superior type of source would bestow a particular advantage on a household and make it more ready to lease-in. We were sceptical about this idea for two reasons. In the first place we felt that the use of pumping sets was something that could be purchased through the market and, secondly, we doubted whether the superiority of pumping sets was quite so great. In the latter view we were influenced by the observations that Persian wheels are not being wholly displaced by pumping sets, that the construction of them has continued into recent times, and that they seemed adequate if less convenient to provide irrigation.

We wanted to examine the effect of a variable which would represent 'pressure on the land' for a household. The idea is, for example, that a family with large consumption needs relative to its land holding would want to lease-in more than a family with a lower need relative to its land holdings. We experimented with a variable called *LOFA* (land owned over family) defined as

$$LOFA = \frac{LANDO}{1.0 \text{ MEN} + 0.8 \text{ WOMEN} + 0.5 \text{ CHILDREN}}$$

[16]Some kind of involvement in agriculture was required for inclusion in the sample of 111 households (see above p. 15).

[17]We designate involvement in agriculture as full-time if a worker has no other occupation.

We shall experiment again with *LOFA* in Chapters 6, 7, and 8. *MEN* is the number of adult males in the household, *WOMEN* the number of adult females, and *CHILDREN* are under 16. Naturally the denominator was never zero for any household. This denominator, which we refer to later as the number of 'standard family members', is intended to represent food needs of sthe household. The numbers 1.0, 0.8, and 0.5 are based on standard calculations of energy requirements for men, women, and children. For discussion of such calculations, see Bliss and Stern (1978).

We thought that caste might make a difference to leasing behaviour. The *Thakurs* are the high caste with a traditional distaste for agricultural work while the *Muraos* are traditionally cultivators. We therefore examined the effect of two zero-one variables, *CASTE1* and *CASTE2*. *CASTE1* = 1 if the household is *Thakur*, = 0 otherwise. *CASTE2* = 1 if the household is *Murao*, = 0 otherwise. Employing these variables is equivalent to an analysis of covariance comparing two populations, on the one hand *Thakurs* (or *Muraos*) and on the other the remainder (see Scheffé, 1959).

Table 5.5 gives the variables that we employed in our linear regression analysis together with their definitions, means, and standard deviations.

§ 5.8 Regression Analysis

§ 5.8.0 *Introduction*

In the present section we shall be concerned with the results of regression analysis designed to test the model of leasing that was introduced in § 5.5. In § 5.8.1 we describe the regression package SPSS from which we obtained our regression results and interpret the *F* statistics which that package uses as significance tests. In § 5.8.2. we present and discuss the correlation matrix between the variables of the basic model and various other variables included in order to see whether such variables would be significant in a single-variable regression with *NLI*. We then go on to discuss the results for a linear regression analysis of the basic model and of two variants of that model. In § 5.8.3 we shall be concerned with interpreting the coefficients on *V1* and *F3* in the basic model as products of marginal effects of these variables on *DCA* and a coefficient which measures the extent to which land area cultivated is adjusted through leasing to *DCA*. § 5.8.4 will be concerned with the discussion of the residuals of the basic model, § 5.8.5 with some statistical problems to which our approach gives rise, and § 5.8.6 with conclusions.

§ 5.8.1 *The SPSS Package*

Calculations for our regression analysis and of the correlation coefficients were on the Oxford University ICL 1906A using the package of programmes 'Statistical Package for the Social Sciences' (SPSS). SPSS presents the *F* statistic for the test of significance of coefficients, rather than the *t* which is more usual in econometric work (the *t* statistic is simply the square root of *F*). The *F* statistic can be used to test the hypothesis that a coefficient is zero. It is

Table 5.5 Definitions of means and standard deviations of variables used in the regressons

Variable	Definition	Mean	Standard Deviation
LANDO	Land area owned by the household (in *bighas*)	23.4	20.3
CULT	Land area cultivated in *rabi* 1974-5	22.8	17.4
NLIR	Net area leased-in* in *rabi* 1974-5	– 0.6	16.5
F3	Number of agricultural males aged 16-60	1.2	0.9
VI	Value in rupees of draught animals owned by the household	693.9	660.8
NPSO	Number of pumping sets owned (always 0 or 1)	0.07	0.25
VALWATS	Estimated market value or cost of all owned water sources (rupees)	1077.6	1967.1
LOFA	Land owned per standard family member	5.2	4.7
CASTE 1	= 1 if *Thakur*, = 0 otherwise	0.23	0.43
CASTE2	= 1 if *Murao*, = 0 otherwise	0.25	0.44

Number of cases   107

*A negative figure for the mean implies that more land is being leased-out than -in —the excess is 2.6% of the village land (Palanpur) and 11.3% of the Palanpur land leased-in.

conventional to accept a coefficient as significantly different from zero at the 5 per cent level if F takes the value 4 or greater (this corresponds to the conventional level of 2 for t). The value 4 is an approximation but the number of degrees of freedom involved here will make the approximation a good one. The regression programme allows one to see what the coefficients and significance levels of a given variable which is excluded from the equation would be if it were included as a single variable additional to those already included. These coefficients with their F statistics are included in the tables in which we present regression output. Our criterion for significance is in general the 5 per cent level, or $F = 4$.

An irritating feature of the version of SPSS which was available to us was that one could not obtain standard errors and F statistics for the constant term of an equation. The other attractions of SPSS led us nevertheless to use it and we have calculated standard errors for the constant term in certain cases. These cases are where there is a single explanatory variable apart from the constant term itself. In these circumstances the standard error of the constant term can be calculated rather easily and they also correspond to circumstances where the size of the constant term is of particular theoretical interest (see Chapter 6).

The significance of correlation coefficients may be judged by the result that the statistic

$$t = \left\{ (n-2)\frac{r^2}{1-r^2} \right\}^{\frac{1}{2}}$$

where r is the correlation coefficient in a sample of size n from a bivariate normal distribution is distributed as Student's t-distribution with $(n - 2)$ degrees of freedom (see Kendall and Stuart, 1973, p. 308) on the hypothesis that the population correlation coefficient is zero. The 5 per cent significance level for t with 105 degrees of freedom is 1.98 (see Kendall and Stuart, 1973, p. 653) and thus for our sample we have a 5 per cent significance level for r of 0.190 (these levels are to three significant figures). From now on we shall be using significance levels of 5 per cent unless otherwise stated.

The significance of a simple correlation coefficient is equivalent to significance of the coefficient on the independent variable in a simple linear regression.

§ 5.8.2 *Correlation and Regression Results*

Table 5.6 presents the correlation matrix of the variables listed above. The sample size is 107.

Table 5.6 Correlation matrix of variables

CULT	NLIR	LANDO	F3	VI	LOFA	CASTE1	CASTE2	VALWATS	NPSO	
1.00	0.28	0.63	0.61	0.81	0.27	0.11	0.20	0.50	0.48	CULT
	1.00	-0.57	0.27	0.16	-0.70	-0.13	-0.29	-0.29	0.05	NLIR
		1.00	0.30	0.57	0.80	0.19	0.40	0.67	0.37	LANDO
			1.00	0.58	-0.07	0.11	-0.06	0.27	0.37	F3
				1.00	0.24	0.10	0.16	0.57	0.43	VI
					1.00	0.20	0.45	0.48	0.15	LOFA
						1.00	-0.32	0.26	0.21	CASTE1
							1.00	0.30	0.11	CASTE2
								1.00	0.52	VALWATS
									1.00	NPSO

From an inspection of the correlation matrix we can see which if any of the variables that we have considered on *a priori* grounds would prove significant in a two variable regression with *NLIR* as the dependent variable. Five variables pass this test. They are, in order of significance, *LOFA*, *LANDO*, *VALWATS*, *CASTE2*, and *F3*. *VI* is nearly significant but if we adhere to the 5 per cent level then the hypothesis that the coefficient on *VI* in a two variable regression with *NLIR* is zero is not rejected.

Some remarks are in order. Bear in mind that significance in simple pairwise regression is not equivalent to significance in multivariate regression and we shall shortly see that the variables do rather differently when we consider them in groups. Note that *LOFA* is highly correlated with *LANDO*, another variable that is highly correlated with NLIR, but there is some residual variance in *NLIR* not explained by *LANDO* which LOFA can explain. This finding can be understood as follows. A household with a low value of *LOFA* is one under strong pressure to survive and this it can only do, if there is no opportunity to work outside agriculture, by either selling agricultural labour or by leasing-in land. Such pressures are emphasized by Chayanov (1966) and may be interpreted as the income effects mentioned in § 3.5.

Of the three variables which we expected to play the central role in explaining *NLIR*, two have significant correlation coefficients. These are *LANDO*, which has the expected negative correlation with *NLIR*, and *F3*. By itself *V1* is not significant. However, note that there are a large number of high values for cross correlation coefficients so that pairwise regression could be misleading.

In moving to multiple-variate regression analysis we have to take a decision concerning which variables to include in our regression. Having included a set of variables, the SPSS print-out will give us the *F*-statistics for the excluded variables. These statistics will depend upon the included variables and will indicate only whether the coefficient on an excluded variable would be significantly different from zero at the 5 per cent level were that variable only to be added to those already in the equation. However, we have clear prior views as to which variables will prove significant and make use of these prior views to decide the order in which the variables should be introduced. We work from something which we shall refer to as the basic model. This model will include only those variables which appear explicitly in equation (12). The effect of the other variables may then be judged by their *F*-statistics relative to the basic model. Our regression equation, from the basic model, is

$$NLIR = aV1 + bF3 + cLANDO + K + \varepsilon \qquad (19)$$

where ε is an error term with mean zero, and where errors for different households are independent and identically normally distributed.

Table 5.7 gives the regression results for the basic model. In the case of each variable, whether included or excluded, we give *B* (the coefficient on the variable when included) and the associated *F*-statistic. The size of the coefficients on the main variables is the subject of § 5.8.3.

All the explanatory variables of the basic model, that is *LANDO*, *F3*, and *V1* are highly significant. Moreover their coefficients have the expected signs (negative for land, positive for the other two). Of the five variables not included in the basic model only one has an *F*-value greater than or equal to the critical value for a 5 per cent confidence interval, $F = 4.0$; this variable is *LOFA*.

Neither of our water source variables does well in terms of *F*-values. *NPSO* does slightly better than *VALWATS*. The meaning of this superiority is unclear if only because the ownership of a pumping set may represent something in addition to control of water. We have in mind here wealth, access to credit, or an unusual degree of enterprise. We think that these possibilities are plausible but would not like to make too much of it as the *F*-value on *NPSO* is less than 4. The *F*-value of *VALWATS* is even lower; moreover it would have a negative coefficient if it were introduced into the equation. It seems that this variable is not useful for explaining leasing decisions.

Table 5.7 Regression results: basic model dependent variable *NLIR*

Multiple *R*	0.84	Number of cases	107
R Squared	0.70	Number of variables	3
Standard error	9.18	*F*-value for equation	79.43

Variables in the equation

Variable	*B*	Standard error of *B*	*F*
LANDO	−0.78	0.05	213.4
F3	4.42	1.29	11.8
V1	0.014	0.0019	53.9
Constant	2.35		

Variables not in the equation

Variable	*B* IN	*F*
LOFA	−0.773	4.21
NPSO	6.33	2.43
VALWATS	−.0007	1.05
CASTE2	1.04	0.21
CASTE1	1.97	0.20

Notes:
  (i) *B* is the coefficient on the associated variable in a regression with *NLIR* as dependent variable and 'variables in the equation' as explanatory variables
  (ii) $F = (B/\text{standard error of } B)^2$
  (iii) For discussion of the 'Constant' and 'Variables not in the equation' see § 5.8.1.

In the correlation matrix our *CASTE2* dummy had a significant negative correlation coefficient with *NLIR*. However this is accounted for by its correlation with other variables. Once we come to the basic model both caste variables are completely insignificant. A number of implications follow for ideas that one might have in advance of analysis. For example, *Thakurs* might be expected to lease-in more frequently, other things being equal, because they are normally prohibited from selling out their labour. On the other hand they may enjoy agricultural work less than other castes.

We referred above in § 5.6 to the possibility of working with a model of the choice of cultivated area rather than the choice of area to lease-in or-out. This has the effect of constraining the adjustment coefficient γ in the linear version to be 1. In Table 5.8 we present the regression results for the basic version of this model, that is, the model where *F3* and *V1* are included as independent variables. *LANDO* does not belong in the basic model in this case (see § 5.6).

An inspection of Table 5.8 shows that both the basic variables have high *F*-values, well above the value for significance at the 5 per cent level. What has changed is the *F*-values on the excluded variables now that *LANDO* is no longer in the main equation. *LANDO* itself has an *F*-value exceeding 4.0 so that the hypothesis that the choice of cultivated area is not influenced by the land area owned (perfect adjustment through leasing) is decisively rejected.

Table 5.8 Regression results: basic model dependent variable *CULT*

Multiple R	0.83	Number of cases	107
R Squared	0.68	Number of variables	2
Standard error	9.87	F-value for equation	112.3

Variables in the equation

Variable	B	Standard error of B	F
F3	4.18	1.38	9.15
V1	0.018	0.0018	103.5
Constant	5.01		

Variables not in the equation

Variable	B IN	F
LANDO	0.22	17.2
LOFA	0.50	5.39
NPSO	9.09	4.56
CASTE2	4.21	3.54
VALWATS	0.0007	1.29
CASTE1	0.51	0.05

Notes:
(i) B is the coefficient on the associated variable in a regression with *NLIR* as dependent variable and 'variables in the equation' as explanatory variables.
(ii) $F \equiv (B/\text{standard error of } B)^2$
(iii) For discussion of the 'Constant' and 'Variables not in the equation' see § 5.8.1.

We turn next to the fitting of the quadratic formulation (13). Once again we include the basic variables *LANDO*, *V1*, and *F3* (and in the case of the last two variables their squares and products). Table 5.9 gives the definitions of the new variables that are introduced for the purposes of the quadratic case.

Table 5.9

Variable	V1SQ	F3SQ	V1F3
Definition	V1 squared	F3 squared	Product of V1 and F3

The results of the regression for the quadratic case are presented in Table 5.10. Introducing the quadratic variables makes some notable differences. However *LANDO* remains highly significant and the coefficient is hardly altered (-0.77 as opposed to -0.78). *V1* is the next most significant variable but its coefficient is now rather different (0.023 as opposed to 0.014). *F3* is now insignificant, although this is perhaps not surprising in view of the fact that *F3* now enters into two other variables. None of the quadratic variables of Table 5.9 is significant in Table 5.10. Among the non-included variables, only *LOFA* does well and the coefficient on it is once again significantly different from zero at the 5 per cent level.

Table 5.10 Regression results: dependent variable *NLIR* quadratic formulation

Multiple *R*	0.85	*Number of cases*	107
R Squared	0.75	Number of variables	6
Standard error	8.93	*F*-value for equation	43.5

Variables in the equation

Variable	*B*	Standard error of *B*	*F*
LANDO	−0.77	0.05	206.5
F3	1.56	2.87	0.29
V1	0.023	0.004	39.8
F3SQ	1.71	1.32	1.67
V1SQ	0.00	0.00	0.67
V1F3	−0.003	0.003	1.18
Constant	0.68		

Variables not in the equation

Variable	*B* IN	*F*
LOFA	−0.96	6.50
NPSO	5.06	1.53
CASTE2	1.75	0.59
CASTE1	−1.19	0.31
VALWATS	−0.0003	0.22

Notes:
  (i) *B* is the coefficient on the associated variable in a regression with *NLIR* as dependent variable and 'variables in the equation' as explanatory variables
  (ii) $F \equiv (B/\text{standard error of } B)^2$
  (iii) For discussion of the 'Constant' and 'Variables not in the equation' see § 5.8.1.

The quadratic case does not produce results that are more convincing than those obtained in the linear case. Only two variables are significant, *LANDO* and *V1*, whose predominance is confirmed, but the additional contribution of *F3* is obscured. It seems therefore that the non-linearities in the determination of *DCA* (equation (9)) which one feels must be there are not well captured by a quadratic approximation.

§ 5.8.3 *The Interpretation of the Coefficients in the Basic Model*
We argued above in § 5.6 that there is a possibility of substituting between the two less than perfectly marketable inputs, bullocks and men. Hence it makes sense to discuss separately the marginal effects on leasing of bullocks and family labour taken separately. A somewhat lower (greater) stock of either will tend to cause the household to lease-in less (more). In this section we want to attempt to quantify these responses. We shall use the coefficients in the regression of the basic model (see Table 5.7) to estimate the quantitative response of leasing to the basic variables.

The coefficients on *F3* and *V1* in the regression are our estimates of the marginal response of area leased-in to these variables. However to interpret these numbers it is necessary to bear in mind that the effect of, say, bullocks on land area leased-in is in our theoretical formulation an indirect one. A household with more bullocks will have a larger *DCA*; a household with a larger *DCA* will wish to lease-in more or lease-out less. Our regression analysis indicates that a unit increase in land cultivated implies a less than unit increase in *DCA*—one lies outside the 95 per cent confidence interval for the coefficient on *LANDO* in Table 5.7 and the hypothesis that the adjustment coefficient was 1 was rejected in Table 5.8. Therefore the coefficient on *VI* (or on *F3*) has to be modified if we are to obtain an estimate of the marginal response of *DCA* to an increase in bullocks (or in men).

The regression results from Table 5.7 indicate that the response of land cultivated to an increase in land area owned is 78 per cent of the increase. To estimate (see equation 12)) the response of *DCA* to a marginal increase in *F3* or *VI* we should divide the coefficients on those variables by 0.78. By doing this we obtain estimates of the marginal effects of *F3* and *VI* on *DCA* as follows:

Coefficient on *F3* (= 4.42/0.78) = 5.67
Coefficient on *VI* (= 0.014/0.78) = 0.18.

We shall discuss the plausibility of these magnitudes.

The estimated coefficient of *DCA* on *F3* indicates that a household with one extra agricultural man would wish to cultivate (would have the capacity to cultivate) 5.67 *bighas*, that is, just less than one acre. The average *CULT/F3* ratio for Palanpur is 19.2 *bighas* per man in comparison with which the value of 5.67 looks small but we would expect the marginal value to be below the average value given that factors other than *F3* are being held constant.

The estimated coefficient on *VI* indicates that a household with R1000 more of *VI* (we choose a reasonably large value to correspond to the market price of an average pair of bullocks) would wish to cultivate 17.9 *bighas* extra, that is about three acres. The ratio for the village of land area cultivated to units of bullocks value of R1000 is 32.9 *bighas* or 5.1 acres. Again the estimated marginal value comes out at below the average and the gap is quite a large one.

§ 5.8.4 *The Residuals of the Basic Model*

The standard error of the equation relating *NLIR* to *LANDO*, *F3* and *VI* is 9.18 *bighas* (see Table 5.7) which indicates that the equation typically makes quite large errors in predicting exactly how much a particular farmer will lease-in or -out. The residual with the largest absolute value had the value −22.08. It is interesting to see what can be said about cases in which the residual from the fitted equation was large relative to the standard error. We chose to pay special attention to those residuals of absolute value larger than 14.5, which is a little more than 1.5 times the standard error. There were eleven such cases and they are displayed in Table 5.11.

We include also in Table 5.11 some cases in which the absolute value of the residual was not quite as large but where the equation predicted leasing-out where in fact the farmer leased-in (or leasing-in where he leased-out) and the

Table 5.11 Residuals from basic equation for NLIR

Household number	Y1	F3	LANDO	Residual	Estimated value of NLIR	NLIR		Comment
106	1300	1	55.02	17.76	−17.76	0	Predicted to lease-out but does not, Hires-in a lot of labour.	Son is a schoolteacher. Employs Yograj a permanent labourer.
118	2000	2	70.50	15.53	−15.53	0	ditto.	Cultivates jointly with 217, who does own bullocks. Is a schoolteacher
215/16*	0	0	25.63	17.61	−17.61	0	Part-time cultivation without bullocks.	
219	3500	4	60.70	−22.08	22.08	0	Predicted to lease-in but does not.	
224	0	0	80.12	−20.06	−60.06	−80.12	Leased-out all his land where the equation predicts only 60 bighas.	
605	1700	2	22.75	−17.43	17.43	0	Predicted to lease-in but does not	Has a 16 year old son. Counting the son as one unit of F3, effective family labour maybe over-estimated. Son is an agricultural labourer.
607	1000	2	19.75	−14.90	9.90	−5.0	Leased-out when he was predicted to lease-in.	
610	600	1	.75	19.36	14.64	34.00	Leased-in much more than the equation predicted.	
611	800	1	.75	21.54	17.46	39.00	Leased-in more than the equation predicted.	Has poor soil and also sons aged 15 and 11 (may work on farm but not included in F3)
704	1200	1	19.00	15.61	8.89	24.50	ditto.	
811	400	2	23.00	19.59	−1.09	18.50	Leased-in when he was predicted to lease-out.	Does work in mill, has son of 15
223	1000	1	22.76	−8.14	3.14	−5.00	Leases-out where the equation predicts leasing-in	
225	5000	1	21.50	3.93	−2.93	11.00	Leases-in when he was predicted to lease-out	Newly married to a widow
227	2200	5	73.50	11.80	−1.80	10.00	Predicted to lease-out but leases-in	Man Singh.
812	0	2	8.00	−12.95	4.95	−8.00	Predicted to lease-in but leases-out.	
814	0	2	8.57	−8.86	4.51	−4.35	ditto.	Is an agricultural labourer.

*Separate households whose heads are brothers cultivating together (and with 217). They are treated as separate observations in the regression analysis but data on only one of them are presented and discussed here. The data on the other will be the same (but 217 is different).

residual was greater than 8 *bighas* in absolute value.

Five of the eleven cases with the largest residuals have *NLIR* zero, that is no leasing at all, where the model predicts a transaction of at least 14.5 *bighas*, in or out as the case may be. The model as such attributes no significance to not transacting at all whereas in reality one avoids a certain amount of bother by not involving oneself in leasing. It is striking, however, that there are so many non-transactors amongst the cases with large residuals since one might expect to find the inconveniences of transacting to exert their influence where the calculated required adjustment is small. Of the total population of 107 households, 30 are non-transactors (*NLIR* = 0), 37 lease-out (*NLIR* < 0), and 40 lease-in (*NLIR* > 0).

A phenomenon similar to the one just described, in that the model attributes no particular significance to it, is the convenience associated with leasing-out all one's land. Thirteen farmers did just this (*NLIR* = *−LANDO*) but only one (224) appears in the list of large residuals.

In some cases additional unsystematic information helps to throw light on the leasing decision concerned but in other cases one simply has to note an unexplained departure from the theory. A rather general feature concerns *F3*. This is in some cases a very imperfect measure of the labour available to a household. Consider for example household 704 which leased-in more land than the equation predicted. There were two sons in this household aged fifteen and eleven. Boys of these ages are not included in *F3* and it would not always be appropriate to include them if, for example, they were studying. But in reality they do very often work in the fields, especially at busy times. If *F3* were on the low side for this household we would expect a large positive residual. Another example in which *F3* is certainly misleading is provided by household 118 which employs Yograj, *Dhimar*, as a permanent labourer. As this is not family labour it is not reflected in *F3*. One would expect a positive residual in this case and indeed it is positive. However the equation predicts that one extra unit of *F3* would involve the cultivation of 4.37 extra *bighas* so that the residual in this case is even so very large. This family has a schoolteacher and part-time cultivator among its members and perhaps the ability to manage land is larger here than would typically be the case. Finally on this case, it would be expected that Yograj would have a negative residual as his *F3* value overestimates the availability of family labour to his farm. Such is indeed the case, the residual for his household (302) is −1.87.

One might reasonably ask why hired labour is not being included generally but it would not be correct from the theoretical point of view to do so. First, the model is built on the assumption that family labour has a lower opportunity cost than hired labour, so that we expect it to be precisely family labour that is crucial in determining *NLIR*. Second, it is obviously and necessarily the case that the labour to cultivate land comes from somewhere. Hence when we observe a household cultivating more land than we should expect given the value of *F3* we will usually find that a lot of labour is being hired-in. This however is a consequence of the low value of *F3* and the choice of *NLIR*, not an explanation of why *NLIR* is large. Household 106 illustrates this point—it is predicted to lease out 17.67 *bighas* but cultivates all the land it owns with only one family man engaged full-time in agriculture. This is only possible because it hires-in a lot of labour.

In some other cases the *V1* value may be misleading. This is necessarily the case where *V1* is recorded as zero, since we know that cultivation without the use of bullocks is impossible. A good example is provided by households 215/16 whose heads are brothers cultivating jointly. According to the data there are no bullocks and no family men engaged in agriculture. For such a household the equation predicts that the number of *bighas* leased-in will be 2.35 (the constant term) less 0.78*LANDO*, which in this case is −17.6 *bighas*; in fact they do not lease-out at all. But these brothers cultivate jointly with household 217 which does own bullocks. The value of *V1* for household 217 is 1600 and the ratio of *V1* to *CULT* for the village is 30.6. Applying the average, which could be misleading, one can say that these bullocks might serve for the cultivation of 52.3 *bighas*. Household 217 cultivates 26 *bighas* so that he surely has excess bullock power at his disposal. We would therefore expect his residual to be negative and it is in fact −13.8.

On the other hand there are some cases where the explanation for the misfit is completely unclear. Households 409, 610, and 611 are all in this category. So perhaps are households 812 and 814 but in these cases it is interesting to note that they are both households cultivating without owning bullocks and they both have negative residuals. The average residual for a non-bullock-owning household is -2.92 whereas the population mean for the residuals is, of course, zero. There are thirty-five farmers without bullocks and the standard error of the equation is 9.18. The standard error of the mean of thirty-five observations from that distribution is 1.55 (that is $9.18/\sqrt{35}$). We should not quite reject the hypothesis that the model is correct and that there is no difference between the errors for non-bullock-owners and bullock owners. But it does seem that the model is not right for households cultivating without bullocks. An example will illustrate the point. Take a household which has *V1* = 0 and *F3* = 2; the estimate for *NLIR* will be 2.35 + 8.84 − 0.78*LANDO*. If *LANDO* were zero, the household would lease-in 11.2 *bighas*. This is not credible, for we know that a household which genuinely was without bullocks could not obtain 11 *bighas* of land on lease.

Our examination of the residuals from the basic equation suggests that some of the departures from the leasing behaviour predicted by the model can be explained by looking at the particular circumstances of the household concerned. However such is not always the case and there is evidence of certain misspecifications. The model may perform badly for farmers who lease no land in or out, or who lease-out all the land that they own. It may be incorrectly specified for farmers who own no bullocks at all. The *F3* variable is a rather crude measure of the labour power at the disposal of a cultivating unit and inspection of some particular cases indicates that a more detailed measure would lead to more accurate prediction.

§ 5.8.5 *Problems With the Basic Model*

With any regression analysis there are numerous problems and possible pitfalls and ours is no exception, but rather than noting these while presenting the model we have saved the consideration of some of them until the end, by which time the reader will have a clear idea of what we are attempting. We concentrate on the basic model with *NLIR* as dependent variable and no quadratic terms, since this is the most successful of our models. There are two particular problems with our approach which deserve cautionary notes.

The first has to do with the relation between our 'independent' variables, *V1* and *F3*, and our 'dependent' variable *NLIR*. Our theory of leasing assumes that the household has a certain owned land area *LANDO*, a certain number of family men working in agriculture, and a certain level of bullock power *V1*, all given at the beginning of the season. The household then decides how much land to lease-out or to lease-in as the case may be. In the longer run the direction of causation is not all as one-way as that account would suggest, and what we observe of a moment in time is partly constituted of long-run adjustments. Putting aside *LANDO*, which is not the cause of greatest concern, we note that *V1* and *F3* are each to some extent decision variables. The household has some control over the value of bullocks that it holds, at least it can sell some of what it has and hold less. The number of males 16–60 is more or less given to the household but whether they work in agriculture or not will reflect a decision in many cases.

We have, in our model, taken *V1* and *F3* to be fixed in the short run, that is, for the season under discussion. But even if this assumption is accepted problems may still arise. Suppose, for example, that *V1* is determined by land cultivated in the previous season (denoted *CULT (−)*). *CULT (−)* will be determined in the previous season, if our model applies, by an equation such as (12) with an error term, that is (19). If the errors in this equation for the current season and the last season are positively correlated then *V1* for this season will be positively correlated with the error term for this season. In this case the ordinary least squares estimator is biased and inconsistent. A positive correlation between errors in the two season will arise whenever there is an unmeasured and continuing feature of a household which is relevant to leasing and which distinguishes it from other households. The possibility does not seem fanciful.

One way round this problem would be an explicit model of the movement of a household's assets and cultivation over time. The data problems would obviously be enormous. An alternative would be to attempt to construct instrument variables for *V1* and *F3* which would not suffer from the similar defect of correlation with the error term. Many possible variables associated with the household will be disqualified because they too will be corelated with how much land was cultivated last year. We were unable to think of useful instruments.

There is another problem with the econometric testing of the basic model which has to do with the validity of the linear approximation which was employed in going from equation (10) to equation (12). Obviously any linear approximation is likely not to be strictly accurate but there is a particular reason for feeling uncomfortable about it in the present case. To approximate the function $h(\ )$ by a straight line is to assume the adjustment of land cultivated to land owned to operate in the same way and with the same force regardless of the sign of $DCA - LANDO$. In other words, the model as tested does not allow adjustment to operate more freely and easily for leasers-in than it does for leasers-out, or conversely. This specification is doubtful and we should obviously try to examine the consequences of relaxing the restriction.

We have undertaken a number of exercises which have a bearing on the question, but none of them is the ideal test. We tried including as an explanatory variable, additional to the basic model, the square of land area owned ($LANDOSQ$) and found that it was not even remotely significant at the 5 per cent level (F was 0.01). It may be seen, however, from inspection of (10) that the inclusion of $LANDOSQ$ is not a satisfactory way of incorporating non-linearities of the $h(\ )$ function.

Another thing which we have done is to look at the residuals from the basic model. One might hope that a marked non-linearity in h would show in those residuals but again this test is not satisfactory. As the residuals are obtained from a line fitted by a least squares, they must be correlated with the dependent variable and uncorrelated with the independent variables. Hence looking at correlations between errors and independent variables will tell us nothing about the linearity of h. There are, however, numerous exercises that one might perform on the residuals to check for evidence of non-linearity. For example, it might be thought that if the model is being forced to fit a relationship with different slopes on the two sides of the origin, then those at the origin, i.e. neither leasing-in nor leasing-out, tend to have residuals of one sign. This test would not appear to be conclusive: of the thirty non-leasers, two have negligible residuals, thirteen have negative residuals, and fifteen have positive residuals. A further exercise would be to plot the graph of the residuals against dependent variables and look for particular patterns. This is not something we attempted.

It is tempting to split the sample into leasers-in and leasers-out, fit equation (17) to the two sub-groups using least squares, and compare the results. This is not legitimate. Suppose that the basic model as specified is correct—there is no difference between the response of land cultivated to a discrepancy between DCA and $LANDO$ for those owning more than DCA and those owning less. There is however an error term. On the hypothesis that the model is correct, some of those who fall into the sub-group 'leasers-in' will have done so only because the error term in their case is large and positive. Equally, some of those who fall into the sub-group 'leasers-out' will have done so only because the error term in their case is large in absolute value and negative. The result of splitting the sample will be violations of the standard assumptions on the error terms. For illustration, consider the case in which $NLIR$ is a function only of $F3$. Households with high $F3$ will be included in the sub-group $NLIR > 0$ provided that the error term exceeds a certain level. Households with lower $F3$ will be included in this sub-group only if the error term exceeds a higher level. It is

clear then that for the sub-group $NLIR > 0$ the error term is not independent of
F3. The problems presented by truncating samples are familiar in other contexts; see, for example, Hausman and Wise (1976).

It is possible to develop an approach to handle the above problem but we
have not attempted to do so. In the absence of such an approach one should
refrain from reporting the results of fitting regression lines by least squares to
the two samples treated separately. Nevertheless, the results of that exercise are
suggestive, and as we have warned the reader to treat these results with caution,
perhaps it may be in order for us to report them. Table 5.12 gives the two regression equations in summary. The *F*-values for all the non-included variables are
tiny (less than 1.0 in every case, except for *LOFA* in the equation for leasers-out
which has $F = 1.7$) and we have thought it not worth reporting them. Note that
households which neither leased-in nor leased-out ($NLIR = 0$) have been excluded from both sub-groups. The numbers in brackets beneath the regression
coefficients are the *F*-statistics.

Table 5.12

(1)	Leasers-in ($NLIR > 0$):

$$NLIR = \underset{(15.7)}{-0.61LANDO} + \underset{(3.7)}{3.85F3} + \underset{(4.5)}{0.009VI} + 9.38$$

Number of cases = 40. $R^2 = 0.31$.

(2)	Leasers-out ($NLIR < 0$):

$$NLIR = \underset{(203.1)}{-0.80LANDO} + \underset{(3.1)}{2.46F3} + \underset{(60.5)}{0.019VI} - 2.60$$

Number of cases = 37. $R^2 = 0.87$.

We may compare the results shown in Table 5.12 with those of Table 5.7. The
signs on the variables are in every case the same. The coefficient on *LANDO* in
Table 5.12 is little changed from that in Table 5.7 for the leasers-out but is much
smaller for the leasers-in. The interpretation that suggests itself is that adjustment is stronger for leasers-out than for leasers-in. There could be many explanations for this finding, if one accepted the interpretation, but an obvious
one would be that the market for leased land is somewhat a seller's market in
that it is easier for a land-owner to find a tenant than for a tenant to find a land-
owner. But there are other explanations which are equally plausible. It might
be, for example, that a disutility attaches to taking land on lease to which there
is no corresponding disutility to leasing-out.

The coefficients on *F3* are both lower than in the case of Table 5.7 but this, of
course, is not the relevant comparison. One ought to compare the ratio of the
coefficient on *F3* to the coefficient on *LANDO* (see above, § 5.8.3) in the two
cases. For equation (1) of Table 5.12 we should then compare 6.31 (3.85/0.61)
with the 5.67 computed from Table 5.7 (4.42/0.78). In the case of (2) of Table
5.12 we would be comparing 3.08 (2.46/0.80) with 5.67, a much larger difference. However, note that the coefficient on *F3* is now in neither case dif-

ferent from zero at the 5 per cent level of significance. Such was not the case with the pooled sample.

Where the coefficients on $V1$ are concerned, again there is a large difference. We should compare, from equation (1) of Table 5.12, 0.015 (0.009/0.61) with 0.018, calculated from Table 5.7. From equation (2), we should compare 0.024 again with 0.018. In the latter case the numbers are closer but one must take into account that the F-statistic on $V1$ for (2) is very large, while $V1$ in (1) is only just significant. What this suggests is that it is the leasers-out who are playing a dominant role in determining the fit, the sizes of the coefficients, and the F-statistics for the equation fitted to the pooled data. This idea would gain support from the observation that with $LANDO$, as with $V1$, the F-statistic is much larger with (2) than with (1) and the coefficient is very little different from the coefficient on $LANDO$ in the equation fitted to the pooled data.

We have explained that the splitting of the sample according to the sign of an endogenous variable and ordinary least squares regression with data from the two parts of the split sample is statistically illegitimate. However, we suspect that the results of this exercise are, in the present instance, not wholly nonsensical. In so far as the findings seem to suggest that the specification that says $h(\ )$ is the same for leasers-in and leasers-out is incorrect, then this finding is not implausible; indeed the picture we get seems quite reasonable. We infer that adjustment of land area cultivated to DCA is stronger on the side of the leasers-out; also, that bullocks play a stronger role in explaining leasing-out than in explaining leasing-in.

§ 5.9 Conclusions

Our discussion of tenancy in Palanpur has taken us in two directions. One is towards the examination of the institutional aspects of tenancy in the village: what the arrangements are and the division of labour where supervision is concerned. Since the predominant form of tenancy is share-cropping we naturally drew on the substantial literature on the theory of share-cropping tenancy. We think that that literature does help to throw light on what happens in Palanpur. Share-cropping is associated with considerable supervision by the landlord as Marshall and Cheung suggested would typically be the case. Given the presumption that our farmers have a high degree of risk aversion (for evidence on this see below), share-cropping would commend itself because it spreads risk between landlord and tenant.

We are not convinced that share-cropping in Palanpur leads to a considerable inefficiency due to a lack of incentive either on the part of the tenant or on the part of the landlord. Large and critical 'discretionary' costs, as we called them, are shared in the same ratio as the output is divided. Other non-monetary costs, such as care and attention to doing a good job, are to a great extent controlled by supervision by the landlord. These were our impressions. We provided some formal tests in § 5.3 of the hypothesis that yields on tenanted and non-tenanted land are the same. Broadly speaking the hypothesis is accepted with a suggestion that outputs on tenanted land are higher rather than lower than those on non-tenanted land. Yields on the two types of land will be compared in different ways in Chapters 7 and 8 and we shall postpone any over-all assessment of the influence of tenancy on productivity until Chapter 9. Hence our interest in tenancy does not come to an end with the close of the present chapter, but is carried on through the following chapters.

The other aspect of tenancy which attracted our attention is the quantitative one: how much land does a household lease-in, or -out. We have tried to relate this decision to fixed or less than perfectly marketable factors in the ownership of the household, specifically, bullocks and family labour. The exercise of estimating this model in its most simple linear form is successful according to the following criteria:

(i) nearly 70 per cent of the variance of land leased-in (*NLIR*) is explained by land owned (*LANDO*), value of bullocks owned (*V1*), and full-time agricultural males (*F3*);

(ii) the signs of the coefficients on the three independent variables are as expected and the magnitudes plausible in so far as one can judge what value to expect;

(iii) the simple version of the model does better than the version constrained to have full adjustment and better than the quadratic form.

We do not wish to claim too much but in an area where it is all too easy to come up with poor or nonsensical results we find the above reassuring. There are nevertheless good reasons to approach our findings with caution. The equation for *NLIR* may be mis-specified in that it treats leasing-in as determined by exactly the same equation and the same coefficients as leasing-out. Also, because *V1* and *F3* are to some extent determined simultaneously with *NLIR* by a single decision there is reason to fear bias and inconsistency in the coefficients.

6

Output and Income

§ 6.0 Introduction

In the previous two chapters we have studied the allocation of factors to different uses. We shall now examine the output a household generates by the employment of these factors and, using simple regressions, we investigate how the value of output for a season or a year is explained by land cultivated, family labour, and bullock power. Water sources and the use of fertilizers will also be considered.

We must immediately draw a sharp distinction between the production relations discussed in this chapter and those to be examined in Chapters 7 and 8. The output studied here is the sum of the value of the outputs from different activities. The inputs are, in general, stocks available to the individual household. Thus the production functions as formulated and estimated are not simply technological relations but contain important behavioural elements in that they embody decisions about cropping patterns and the use of stocks of the factors. In contrast, in our study of the sample wheat plots, reported in the next two chapters, we have concentrated on a single crop and have measured inputs actually used. Although behavioural components cannot be entirely eliminated, the relationship which is estimated in that study is, in the main, a description of the technical aspects of the activity in question—wheat production.

Each of the two varieties of production function has its own interest. It is important, however, to recognize the behavioural component of the functions analysed in this chapter. We showed, for example, in Chapter 3 that output could be either an increasing or decreasing function of the number of family members present on the farm, given different assumptions on utility functions and sharing arrangements. Thus the range of possible outcomes of the investigations in this chapter is rather wider than those of the study to follow since in the latter case we have extensive information on the technical relations from previous agricultural studies.

The aggregation in this study is accompanied by a wider data base. For the analysis of our sample wheat plots the details required implied a restriction on the number of plots we could cover. We had forty-seven observations drawn from thirty-seven households. Here we have output and income data for all the 111 households involved in agriculture in some way although some, of course, do not cultivate. Our primary concern in this chapter is with agricultural output. We concentrated our attention in the collection of data on the outputs of various crops and devoted rather less resources to attempting to measure costs and other sources of income. The space devoted to the analysis of income is accordingly smaller.

In the next section we shall discuss some theoretical preliminaries and in § 6.2 the collection of the data. The construction of our output and income measures is presented in § 6.3 We restrict the use of the term output to gross value of crops produced from land cultivated. In income we shall include other sources and deduct certain costs. The specification of regression equations to explain output and income is discussed in § 6.4 and the results from estimating output equations are presented in § 6.5. The economic implications of these results are discussed in § 6.6. In § 6.7 we present some simple regressions designed to examine the views that the intensity of cultivation will vary with land cultivated or with wealth. We use two measures of intensity: the proportion of cultivated land left fallow and the amount of fertilizer per cultivated area. In § 6.8 we examine the determination of income and its distribution across households. Concluding remarks are contained in § 6.9. The results for output and income discussed in § 6.4 and 6.8 refer to the whole agricultural year. We present in the appendix to this chapter results for the separate components of output for the different seasons and for sugar.

§ 6.1 Some Theoretical Preliminaries

Suppose output Y is a function of land cultivated H and a vector of other inputs x as shown in equation (1)

$$Y = f(H, x) \tag{1}$$

Let us assume that f shows constant returns to scale and that there are no problems with the measurement of inputs used and output produced. We assume, in addition, that the function f is the same for all farmers. Suppose further that there are perfect markets for all inputs in the village. Cost minimization under certainty would imply that the ratio x_i/H, of the level of input i to land, would be the same for all cultivators in the village. Output would be proportional to land cultivated, and a regression of the logarithm of Y on the logarithm of H would yield a coefficient of one. The same result would be obtained by regressing the logarithm of output on that of any one single factor and it would be pointless to include two factors in a regression equation since we shall have perfect multicollinearity.

The above is what one would expect to see in a simple neoclassical world. From what has already been said in Chapter 4 and elsewhere we know that Palanpur should not be seen as a close approximation to such a world but the above model will be useful for making comparisons.

Given that (1) is an appropriate model of the production process we can immediately see several important ways in which Palanpur differs from the circumstances described above. For example the markets for inputs are not perfect—see the discussion of the markets for labour and the services of bullocks in Chapter 4 and our discussion of the land market in Chapter 5. Farmers facing different prices or constraints in the market will choose different factor proportions. Further, it is obvious that peasant agriculture is an occupation for which uncertainty is important. Different attitudes to risk would lead to different input choices. And management skills are clearly neither irrelevant nor marketed.

Thus, even given (1), we need have no fear of strong multicollinearity amongst the factors.

It is not only the structure of markets and the behaviour of agents which distinguish our estimations form those which one might perform for a village characterized by the assumptions of the simple neoclassical model. Our data do not provide precise measures of factor services actually used. The resource requirements for the collection of data on the use of factor services on each farm for the whole agricultural year would have been far beyond our means. The detailed examinations were reserved for the sample wheat plots (see the next chapter). The absence of these data has important implications for our view of the production relation estimated. The clearest and most important example concerns labour.

We shall be arguing in the next chapter that labour in terms of hours worked or number of people present should not enter production functions of the more 'technical' kind described there. The appropriate input measure is the numbers of various tasks carried out by labour—for example, the number of ploughings. If a full description of activities is not available one would hope to have labour hours and as a third best the number of workers. Let us examine how a production relation with the number of workers as argument might differ from that expressed in (1).

We can first ask whether we should expect to see constant returns to scale when output is expressed as a function of land cultivated, H, and number of family workers present, N. Consider a family farm where there is a given amount of land under cultivation and no uncertainty. We assume that output is a constant returns to scale function of H and hours worked. We examine three cases: the family hires-in no labour; the family hires-in (or hires-out) labour up to the point where the marginal product is equal to the market wage; the family is involved in the local labour market, hiring-in or -out, but the wage is not equal to the marginal product (there may, for example, be perceived costs of engaging in the market over and above wage payments). An example of a perceived cost of hiring-out labour would be any shame attached to working for someone else, and of hiring-in would be the necessity to seek out, and make the arrangements and bargain with, the hired labourer. We assume that H is fixed outside the model.

In the first case we can appeal to the analysis of § 3.3 and our development of the Sen (1975) model. Where the farm is 'optimally organized', where the household maximizes the sum of utilities of its members and there are constant returns to scale in production we saw (§ 3.3) that the changes in the size of farm accompanied by equal proportional changes in the number of workers would leave the marginal product of labour unchanged. Hours worked per worker would be unchanged and constant returns to scale in the underlying production function would be reflected in constant returns to output as a function of H and N. We saw also that in the inefficient farm of that section, the effort per worker might decline with the number of people present, since each worker supplies hours up to the point where the marginal disutility of work to him is equal to his perceived fraction of the marginal product. That perceived fraction would decline with the number of workers present, N. In this circumstance one should expect to see diminishing returns to scale for production as a function of H and N.

The second case, that of the standard competitive model, is straightforward. The marginal product of labour is independent of the size of farm and is given by the wage rate. The number of workers present is irrelevant. With a given amount of land the family hires-in or hires-out labour until the wage is equal to the marginal product. Output is proportional to land and the number of workers would be insignificant in a regression equation.

The answer in the third case is a little more complicated. Suppose first that there is a fixed relationship between the market wage and the perceived cost of hiring labour-in or -out. Thus the family with a relatively large quantity of land per family worker hires-in labour but equates the marginal product to $w + \alpha_1$ where w is the wage and α_1 is the perceived cost per labourer hired. The family with a relatively small amount of land applies family labour to its own land up to the point where the marginal product is equal to $w - \alpha_2$, where α_2 is the perceived cost of hiring labour out, and hires-out its labour for w. Where α_1 and α_2 are fixed the situation is analogous to the competitive model of the preceding paragraph.

If α_1 and α_2 depend upon H and N, then we should not expect in general to find output proportional to H, because the marginal product of labour will vary with H and N. One might suppose that α_1 decreases with H for fixed N since there may be economies of scale to hiring-in labour. We may suppose also that α_2 increases with H for fixed N since the fewer are the family members who hire-out their labour the greater the stigma may be.

A dependence of the costs of hiring on H for fixed N of the kind just described would lead to a relation between output and H for fixed N as sketched in Fig. 6.1. At low levels of H the family hires-out much labour, the perceived cost α_2 is low, and the marginal product of labour is approximately equal to the wage. As H increases α_2 increases and the land – labour ratio falls. For a range of H the family neither hires labour in nor out. As H increases still further the family starts to hire-in labour. The cost α_1 starts to fall and for very large H the land – labour ratio is similar to its level for very low H. The argument is close to that of Sen (1962 and 1975) in his comment on the empirical results from Farm Management Surveys that output per acre decreases with size of farm over a certain range (see § 3.6), but adds the further point that output per acre for very large farms should, in the model, start to increase with farm size.

We have seen that in the first case it is possible that one would discover output to be a constant returns to scale function of H and N. But the functional form would not be the same as the underlying production function since total hours worked per family worker would depend on the H to N ratio. We have also seen that in the second case output would not be a function of N at all but merely proportional to H. The third case can approximate either the first or the second. The possibilities are legion.

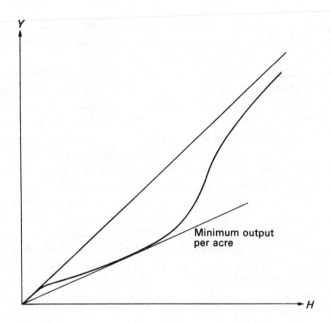

We have, in the above, assumed that output is homogeneous. This would be acceptable if all crops could be sold in any desired quantities at prices which were fixed and the same for everyone[1]. If, however, access to certain markets depends upon influence and influence is correlated with the household's size of holding, or size of holding per family member, then any underlying constant returns to scale in production might be disturbed by the composition and valuation of output. It is possible that the market for sugar, sales to which are in part controlled by a government mill, could provide an example of the kind described. This is a particularly valuable crop and, if large farms have an advantage in the sale of sugar, a higher proportion of sugar in large farms could give rise to apparent increasing returns to scale or could offset decreasing returns.

Finally on N, as an argument of the production function, it is possible that the number of family members engaged in agriculture can be varied in addition to the hours worked per family member. This could be through migration from the village or different occupations within the village. In an extreme form this could imply a perfect correlation between N and H and we should have an analogy with the simple neoclassical model.

A third explanatory variable in the production function we shall be estimating is the value of draught animals. Whilst these may be bullocks or he-buffaloes we shall, once more for simplicity, refer to bullocks. We again have the problem that we have observations on a stock variable and not the flow—the

[1]In that case the maximized value of output provides an aggregate.

activities performed by bullocks. The problem would not be serious if we could assume that bullock services were proportional to bullock values. Let us ask whether such an assumption could be plausible.

If there were a market for the services of bullocks one could not assume that the work performed by bullocks was entirely on the land cultivated by the owner of the animals. But we have already remarked that such a market hardly exists in Palanpur. There are, however, exchange arrangements between households. Unless animals involved in exchanges are worked more intensively than others the existence of exchange arrangements would not violate the assumption of services proportional to value since exchanges would, if they really are exchanges, average out over the agricultural year.

Given that the market for the services of bullocks is severely limited, there are three ways in which one can adjust the services per rupee of bullock value owned. One can choose a cropping pattern which uses bullocks intensively, hire land in or out, and adjust the value of the bullocks by better or worse treatment or the purchase of better or worse animals. There is no doubt that adjustments in Palanpur occur in all these ways.

Nevertheless it is not the case that the services per value of bullocks owned are equal across households (see Table 4.4). Firstly, there are a few households that cultivate without owning bullocks. The exchange arrangements in such cases are usually in terms of human labour for bullock labour. Such arrangements do not involve large pieces of land and never occur on tenanted land. Thus someone who owns a very small amount of land may cultivate it by exchanging labour for ploughing. Secondly, bullocks can be, to some extent, prestige goods. Thus one might buy good bullocks in part for the pleasure and admiration that came from owning them and not only because they plough well. Note here that bullocks play an important part at weddings. And the whole literature on the optimum size of farm for a pair of bullocks (see § 3.7) is predicated on the assumption or observation that bullocks are imperfectly divisible. Finally, at a given point in time different bullocks will have different expected lifetimes. On this ground alone one would not expect value proportional to services.

A further example where we were, on account of limitations of data, forced to use a stock but where we should have preferred a flow measure, concerns water. For each household we have data on water sources owned but not on water used. There is an active market for the use of water sources, particularly pumping sets, and one would not therefore expect water used by a household to be very closely correlated with sources owned. Nevertheless there are certain advantages concerning timing (§ 4.4) attached to owning one's own source. And the fact that a household has been prepared to make a substantial agricultural investment indicates a certain seriousness about the occupation. The variables we shall use to capture the role of water sources are discussed in § 6.4.

The conceptual problems with the use of fertilizers as an input are not as severe as with the other factors we have been discussing. There are, however, some measurement problems and these are discussed in the next section.

The remaining variables we shall be using in our regressions are intended to capture attitudes, skill, effort, or other advantages connected with the production activity and cannot so readily be considered as direct inputs themselves. An example is the zero-one variable for whether the farmer is a member of the traditional cultivating caste—the *Muraos*. These variables will be discussed when we introduce the regression equations themselves in § 6.4.

§ 6.2 The Collection of the Data

The data we shall be using in this chapter concern land owned, land cultivated using different crops, outputs of each crop, prices of crops, family composition, ownership of animals, other assets, and so on. They were collected on questionnaires by asking for information directly from the head of the household. Many of the replies, such as those concerning land under different crops, could be and were checked by direct observation.

Many of the replies were, however, not susceptible to precise checking. These concern in particular the outputs. This is in contrast with our sample wheat plots (see Chapter 7) where our research investigators were, in general, present at the weighing of threshed outputs. Even in the case of outputs, however, partial checks were available, for the *rabi* season, from observation of the fields in question.

The basic unit of observation was the household. Households, in general, own or cultivate a number of parcels of land and are concerned with several crops. The data on output and cropping patterns formed a very substantial file. The size of our sample implied that we could not collect detail on inputs used on each plot and for each crop. That detail was reserved for the sample wheat plots discussed in the next chapter.

The valuations of animals, water sources, and other assets came from the head of household. We were, of course, able to check whether the valuations were reasonable. The prices for the outputs were those at which the farmer could sell at harvest time and such data were collected ourselves from local market sources.

Our data permit the calculation of gross output for each household. They provide also the raw material to construct income measures although these are incomplete in respect of certain costs and revenues. For example, the quantity of fertilizer purchases in the 1974 *kharif* season was not recorded and labour incomes and hirings were recorded only from October 1974 (when we arrived in the village) until June 1975. We have made certain adjustments to allow for these defects (see § 6.3). We shall have more to say about the data in the next two sections when we discuss the measurement of output and income and the specification of our regression equations. We shall present simple summary statistics for our data in § 6.5 after we have introduced the variables to be used in our analysis.

§ 6.3 The Measurement of Output and Income

We shall be using four different measures of gross output and just one measure of income. The output measures are for the *rabi* season, the *kharif* season, for sugar (a ten month crop), and for the sum of these three. This last measure is the gross annual output (*GAO*). Unless otherwise stated, *rabi* output will always exclude sugar (which is normally harvested in that season) and sugar is similarly excluded from *kharif* output. It seems reasonable to suppose that farmers take the full agricultural year as the basic unit for their cultivating decisions and in this case *GAO* is the appropriate output measure to study. The over-all decisions for the agricultural year fall, however, into three parts—the annual crop, sugar, and the two separate cropping seasons, *rabi* and *kharif*. Each of these three provides important contributions to *GAO*—*rabi* contributes roughly half with *kharif* and sugar contributing approximately equally to the other half (the precise percentages for *rabi*, *kharif*, and sugar in total *GAO* for the village are 48.7, 26.3, 25.0). And the nature of cultivation decisions for these three categories of crop are rather different. Further, the number of households involved and the quality of data are not the same for these categories. It is therefore of interest to analyse the three components separately and we provide in the appendix to this chapter results using these three separate components of *GAO* as dependent variables.

In this section we shall describe how our measures of output and income were constructed. We begin with the output figures. As stated above figures on weight were obtained directly from farmers. The prices used for both *rabi* and *kharif* output figures were taken from those ruling in the market when the main sales were made. The prices were intended to represent those a farmer would actually receive from the purchaser, for example a wholesaler from the local market. There are sharp movements in the market prices from week to week (see Chapters 7 and 8 for a description of the movements of wheat prices). Thus the data selected for the valuation of output can make a substantial difference to the result calculated. We selected 30 June 1975 for the valuation of *rabi* output. Many farmers had sold output by that date and for all but a few the harvest was in and available for sale. One can argue that those farmers who could have, but did not, sell by that date placed an implicit value on their output higher than the one we have selected. We have made an implicit adjustment for transport to the market at Chandausi, thus the price must be interpreted as a farm gate price, that is, net of allowance for marketing costs. In the case of Palanpur such costs are small in relation to the value of output since the market is only seven miles away—transport of large quantities would be by bullock cart and smaller quantities with the farmer on the passenger train. Prices for the main crops are shown in Table 6.1.

The valuation of *kharif* output was based on principles similar to that for *rabi* with the data of valuation of output 31 October 1974. Our figure for the valuation of sugar output was the total revenue agreed on delivery of the sugar to the weighing station—thus we do not multiply price by quantity to arrive at a value figure. As the weighing centre is in Palanpur itself the marketing costs are

Table 6.1 Prices of main crops for the estimation of output and income

Crop		Price (Rupees/quintal)	Crop		Price (Rupees/quintal)
Rabi	Wheat	130	*Kharif*	Paddy	120
	Barley	100		Maize	130
	Pea	150		*Jowar*	120
	Gram	180		*Bajra*	130
	Mustard	200		Groundnut	180
	Potato	25		*Urd*	200
	Arhar	170			
	Masoor	160			
	Lahi	200			

minimal. The actual payment is received by the farmer some time after delivery.[2]

Our output figures represent gross concepts—we have not deducted any costs. The figures are to be used in an analysis of the determinants of the value of production from the land area cultivated by the family. Thus we shall attempt, in § 6.5, to explain output by the levels of inputs used rather than deducting costs of inputs in order to calculate a profit or net income figure. We shall examine income, and its distribution, in § 6.6 and 6.7 and we discuss its definition below.

Items of potential importance which have been excluded from the gross output figures are: the by-products from crops, for example sugar-cane tops and straw from grain crops, which are mainly used for fodder; the value of milk production; and labour incomes. The last two are excluded because we wish to analyse the output of the land cultivated by the household. The by-products have been left out because they are in the nature of intermediate products which are used on the farm for feeding animals. These by-products would be roughly proportional in value to the main product; thus it is fairly easy to make an adjustment for their inclusion if so wished. The value is relatively small compared with the main product, although it is not so easily estimated since the by-product is usually neither weighed nor marketed.

We did not include, because we did not have the data, the value of the output of mangoes. The area under mangoes owned by Palanpur households is only 88 *bighas* (out of a total of 2400), and the trees are young, producing little output at present.

For our calculation of income we attempt to measure the net returns to the assets owned by the household—land, family labour, and draught animals being the most important. We must adjust the annual output figure (*GAO*) described above in several ways. We add sources of income other than from crops produced on land cultivated and we subtract the costs of certain inputs.

Our first adjustment of the *GAO* figure is to take account of tenancy. For a given tenanted plot we added half of the value of the output of that plot to the *GAO* figure for the landlord and subtracted it from that of the tenant. The adjustment clearly requires precise information on the owner and cultivator of

[2]We have followed the standard practice in the computation of annual figures of ignoring the fact that revenues accrue and costs occur at different times within the year. As real interest rates are high (see § 4.3) this practice is less attractive than would otherwise be the case.

each plot. Rental payments are a very important constituent of the incomes of some households. For example *Thakur* households 104 and 105 lease-out all their land (28 and 12 *bighas* respectively) producing a rental income of 3822 and 1075 rupees (respectively) for the year 1974–5. Household 608 (*Teli*) owns no land at all, cultivates 25 *bighas*, and pays 2609 rupees (half its *GAO* of 5218) in rent.

We used the adjustment of half to the landlord and half to the tenant since the predominant form of the tenancy (uniform except for one or two cases) is 50–50 sharecropping. There are occasional variations in sharing arrangements for inputs but output is invariably split in two (§ 5.2).

The second adjustment is to deduct the cost of purchased feed for animals and to add the value of milk produced. Most of the milk is for home consumption although a local market does exist. We have data on the number of kilogrammes produced each month and we used an average price over the year of 1.6 rupees per kg for buffalo milk and 1.5 rupees per kg. for cows' milk. We count only purchased feed as a cost since the by-products from crop production which are eaten by the farm animals are intermediate goods.

We next deduct the cost of fertilizers. We have data only for *rabi* fertilizers. We multiplied this by 1.5 to obtain a crude estimate of fertilizer purchased for the full year. The *rabi* output is roughly equal in value to *kharif* and sugar output taken together: total *rabi* output for the village is 254 924 rupees, *kharif* 140 189 rupees, and sugar 130 370 rupees. As a crude rule of thumb we decided to assume that fertilizer use in *rabi* is twice that for *kharif* and sugar, since rationing and supply difficulties occurred during *kharif* 1974 (also the period when fertilizer would have been applied to sugar), but were relaxed in November 1974. We cannot pretend that this estimate is other than a guess but it seems obvious that a multiplier of 1 would be too low and of 2 would be too high.[3]

Our final adjustment is for labour hired-in and hired-out. Many households (see Table 4.1) have a member in some full or part-time employment outside the village. This work is not usually on the land but in a mill or government establishment. In addition there is an active labour market in Palanpur (§ 4.1) and households buy and sell agricultural labour. Our data on labour incomes and purchases covered only the nine months October 1974 to June 1975 and it was again necessary to make some crude adjustment to estimate a twelve month figure. We multiplied our nine month figure by 4/3. For someone earning a regular monthly salary this adjustment will be accurate. Where income or labour payment sources are less regular small errors will be introduced.[4]

The calculation of the final figures for income can be expressed formally as follows:

[3]For our treatment of fertilizer as an input see § 6.4.
[4]Responsibility for the omissions connected with income rests unambiguously with ourselves and not with our research investigators S.S. Tyagi Jr. and V.K. Singh. We had not intended originally to attempt income figures for the full year but became more ambitious as we saw the success with the collection of the other data.

$$INCOME \equiv GAO + NET\ RENT\ RECEIVED + MILK - FEED -$$
$$1.5\ FERTILIZER + 4/3\ NET\ LABOUR\ INCOME\ RECEIVED \qquad (2)$$

The income figure thus calculated is intended to estimate the returns to assets owned by the household—it is analogous to *GNP* for a nation. There are, of course, a number of ways in which our calculations are unsatisfactory. We have already mentioned the 'grossing-up' necessary because our data on fertilizers and labour incomes did not cover the full year. We have made no deduction for the purchase of seed and water. And the figure contains no allowance for the deterioration of assets. We have excluded interest payments too. Our reason here was that we wished to analyse the income figure in terms of the assets generating it. Interest payments are returns to capital lent and we did not collect data on assets owned by households, other than farm equipment. Our data on interest cover only those payments made by households and not the income received. The difficulties that we should have encountered in the collection of such data would have been very large.

We decided, again for data reasons, to exclude payments for the renting out of farm assets. Whilst our data on the ownership of these assets are quite good, our data on rental payments for the use of these assets is rather patchy. In particular we do not have records of payments by farmers for the hiring of Persian wheels or pumping sets. The returns to renting out water sources were discussed in Chapter 4. The sums involved in rentals are not huge and we hope that the omission is not serious. A further omission concerns income from services performed. For most households this would be zero but for a few, such as sweepers and carpenters, the omission would be serious. The components of income for each caste are set out in Table 6.2.

Our second use of the income figure is the calculation of statistics on the distribution of income. These are presented in § 6.8. We now turn to the specification of the regression equations which are intended to model the determination of output and income.

§ 6.4 The Regression Equations

We shall examine, using single equation linear regressions, the determinants of output and income. We have four different measures of output (although only *GAO* results are presented in the body of the chapter) and thus five variables to be explained. Our main explanatory variables are, as described above, land, labour, and draught power. In this section we shall consider the specification of our regression equations. Relevant theory, the data, and the measurement of output and income have been discussed in the previous three sections. These discussions provide the background to our choice of equation to be estimated. We begin with the output regressions.

The first variable to be considered in the explanation of agricultural output is, naturally, land. For the case of *rabi* output we used the land cultivated in the *rabi* season excluding land left fallow in that season and land under sugar (recall that *rabi* output here excludes sugar). For *kharif* output we used land cultivated

Table 6.2 The components of income

1	2	3	4	5	6	7	8	9	10
Caste	NRNSO	NRSUO	NKNSO	NKSUO	MILK	4/3 (VLO–VLI)	1.5 FERT	FEED	INCOME
Thakur 1	80 200	31 539	45 610	4300	68 451	6 399	10 055	6480	219 964
Murao 2	84 198	63 446	45 011	0	38 343	12 251	8 119	3050	232 080
Dhimar 3	9 699	6 485	6 274	0	9 387	16 795	909	920	46 811
Gadaria 4	20 811	5 170	11 825	300	16 674	9 461	1 623	1605	61 013
Dhobi 5	4 710	2 020	1 724	0	3 888	3 012	176	395	14 783
Teli 6	17 418	5 090	8 720	120	6 720	18 775	1 596	890	54 357
Passi 7	13 025	1 750	6 711	0	6 891	39 237	762	660	66 192
Jatab 8	21 798	8 850	13 602	300	13 845	13 275	790	1520	69 360
Other 9	1 024	0	114	0	4 464	16 335	0	250	21 687
Total	252 883	124 350	139 591	5020	168 663	135 540	24 030	15770	786 247

Notes : (i) Column (10) = Columns (1) + (2) + (3) + (4) + (5) + (6) + (7) − (8) − (9)
(ii) Notation is defined in Table 6.3.
(iii) Units are rupees.
(iv) The number of households in castes 1–9 respectively are 25, 27, 8, 10, 3, 12, 8, 14, 4.
(v) Omissions and errors concerning income are discussed in the text at the end of § 6.3.

Table 6.3 Definitions of variables

Variables	Definitions
INCM	Total income earned by household
GAO	GRNSO + GKNSO + SUGAR
GRNSO	Gross value of *rabi* non-sugar output
NRNSO	Net value of *rabi* non-sugar output
SUGAR	Gross value of sugar output
NRSUO	Net value of *rabi* sugar output
NKSUO	Net value of *kharif* sugar output
GKNSO	Gross value of *kharif* non-sugar output
NKNSO	Net value of *kharif* non-sugar output
F3	Number of males aged 16–60 whose sole occupation is agriculture
F1	Number of males aged 16–60
V1	Value of draught animals owned
V2	Value of animals owned
FERT	Value of fertilizer used in *rabi* season
LANDO	Quantity of land owned in *rabi* season
CULT	Quantity of land cultivated in *rabi* season
SUCLT	Quantity of land cultivated under sugar in *rabi* season
NSCULTR	CULT – SUCLT—land left fallow in *rabi* season
NSCULTK	CULT – SUCLT—land left fallow in *kharif* season
NPSO	Number of pumping sets owned (0 or 1)
CASTE1	1 if household is member of *Thakur* caste, 0 if otherwise
CASTE2	1 if household is member of *Murao* caste, 0 if otherwise
OWCU1	See Text (§ 6.4)
OWCU2	See Text (§ 6.4)
LOFA	See Text (§ 5.7)
MILK	Value of milk production
FEED	Value of purchased animal feed
VLI	Value of labour services bought
VLO	Value of labour services sold
FLRONCLT	Land fallow in *rabi* divided by CULT
FLKONCLT	Land fallow in *kharif* divided by CULT
FLONCLT	FLRONCLT + FLKONCLT
FRTONCLT	FERT/CULT

Notes : (i) *LN* preceding a variable name denotes logarithm to the base *e*.
(ii) Net (denoted by *N* in place of *G*) means after adjustment for share rent paid and received.

in the *rabi* season less land left fallow in the *kharif*. The land cultivated in the *rabi* and *kharif* seasons (including fallow land in each case) were nearly always identical and we chose the *rabi* figure since, as we were present in that season, we felt our confidence in the accuracy of the *rabi* figures to outweigh small differences between *kharif* and *rabi*. The differences between our figures for *rabi* and *kharif* were so small that there would have been a negligible change in results had we made the alternative choice. The land variable for sugar was the land under sugar in the *rabi* season, since sugar output results almost entirely from cane harvested in the *rabi* season. Our land variable for *GAO* was land cultivated in the *rabi* season including fallow land and land under sugar. Our reasons for this last choice are as follows. Sugar is included in *GAO* and it is therefore obviously appropriate to include land under sugar. No land was left fallow in both seasons and land cultivated (including fallow land) was almost always the same. Thus the total land cultivated in any one season measures the land employed by the household during the agricultural year. We chose the *rabi* season measure.

One possible alternative to our land measure for *GAO* would be count twice land which is double-cropped. There are a number of reasons for rejecting this. We are interested here in the output a family gets from the land at its disposal and this is the land it has available to it for the year. The output it achieves will depend upon its cropping pattern and this has been aggregated in *GAO*. There is no strong argument for singling out land fallow in a season as the sole aspect of the yearly cropping pattern to be used in explanation of output.[5] Indeed the choice of cropping pattern is itself an important constituent element of the production relation under examination and should not in this context be used as an explanation of the production level. And if one were to decide to try to take account of it there is not a strong argument in favour of multiplying by two. The seasons are of different length and have different potential. Further, one would have to take account of sugar which is a ten month crop.

We did not correct our area measurement by land quality. There are various possible methods but for our circumstances all were unsatisfactory. We did not split irrigated and unirrigated land since virtually all of Palanpur land has access to some water source. We shall be including a variable on the nature of these sources—see below. The assessments for land taxation (used for example by Khusro (1973) to correct for quality—see § 3.6) are, for Palanpur, very unrealistic as indicators of land value. Finally our own attempts to classify soil quality turned out to be rather unsuccessful as explanations of output in our detailed wheat plot study (see Chapters 7 and 8), and we did not feel justified in introducing them into this analysis. Thus we decided that no reasonable improvement on the crude figure, total land cultivated, was available.

Neither did we make any adjustment to land cultivated for the number of plots. One might expect that a given area which is cultivated as a large number of fragments rather than a single piece might be less productive. It is not at all easy, however, to define the number of fragments from this point of view—for example, two pieces close together might present negligible additional problems over and above those for a single piece of equivalent area. Further, in Palanpur the number of fragments per land holding had been reduced by land consolidation schemes, so that one might suppose that the problems of so-called fragmentation were not severe. And we did not find (§ 5.4) that the pattern of geographical location of plots owned provided a useful explanation of leasing.

A second explanatory variable is the value of draught animals owned by the household. In using value we are supposing that the price of an animal represents its productive potential. We have already stated (§ 6.1) that we should have liked to use a variable representing the flow of services of draught

---

[5]We are influenced here by the knowledge that in Palanpur nearly all the land is irrigated, so that double-cropping is possible. Where double-cropping is frequently impossible the case for counting double-cropped land twice to take account of this quality difference would be stronger.

animals rather than the stock measure, explained the data constraints which dictated our choice, and discussed associated problems of interpretation.

Thirdly we have the number of family workers engaged in agriculture. This is also a stock variable where we should have liked to use a measure of flow and again we discussed associated problems in § 6.1. We concluded that the use of this variable as an explanation of output introduced a behavioural element into the production relation being examined. Thus, for example, we pointed to the possibility that in certain models output might not be an increasing function of the number of family workers. With this note of caution we must decide how the variable may best be measured. There are a number of possibilities.

Our data on household composition give age, sex, and occupation of each member. Many of the occupations are joint—agriculture and other. We decided to restrict ourselves to the number of males aged 16–60 inclusive, engaged only in agriculture (*F3*). It is true that some children under sixteen are engaged full-time in agriculture, that some lower-caste women work in the fields, that some men under sixty whilst having no occupation other than agriculture are not particularly active, and that some of those giving their occupation as joint are predominantly engaged in agriculture. However the difficulty of collecting data on the precise breakdown of each individual's time forces us to use a fairly simple criterion. The age band reflects our impression of the predominant working pattern, and the narrow definition of occupation the fact that the joint occupation category covered such a wide variety of involvement in agriculture as to be potentially misleading.

The final factor which we wish to include as a direct input is water. Again we have to use a stock variable. We tried the two variables described in § 5.7: the value of water sources owned (*VALWATS*) and the number of pumping sets owned (*NPSO*). The former variable proved insignificant in nearly all the regressions which we tried and we decided to omit it from the results presented here. The variable *NPSO* is zero-one since no household owns more than one set. In fact there are only seven households in the village owning a set in working order (§ 4.4). The few households which made the effort to purchase pumping sets may have special features which influence productivity other than through the pumping set; we must bear this point in mind when we come to interpret our results.

Our next group of variables refers to features of the household which are not direct inputs but which may affect productivity through their effects on cultivating practice. There are the zero-one variables for membership of each of the two highest castes—the *Thakurs* and the *Muraos* (see § 5.7). We tried two variables representing possible effects of tenancy on productivity. The variable *OWCU1* takes the value of the ratio of land owned to land cultivated if this ratio is greater than one, and one otherwise, and *OWCU2* takes the value of the ratio if it is less than one, and one otherwise. Land cultivated refers here to total land cultivated (including sugar) in the *rabi* season and households which did not cultivate in that season are excluded.

The variable *OWCU2* should be positively related to output if the argument that tenancy discourages effort is correct—a low value of *OWCU2* indicates that much of the cultivated land is leased-in. If *OWCU1* is high then much of the land which a household owns is leased-out. If this indicates an absence of interest in agriculture or some difficulty with cultivation (for example, sick bullocks) then we might expect to find a negative relation with output.

We tried at one stage the explanatory variable called *LOFA* defined as land owned per standard family member, see § 5.7. The idea is that those families with a large number of mouths to feed from a small acreage of land owned would try particularly hard. The variable was used, with qualified success, in Chapter 5 and in the next chapter.

The variables *LOFA*, *OWCU1* and *OWCU2* were thoroughly insignificant wherever they were incorporated. We decided therefore to exclude them from the results presented here. Notation is summarized in Table 6.3.

We have six explanatory variables in our output regressions: four are measures of direct inputs and two measure a feature of the household, caste, which is not directly connected with production. We have one more input for the *rabi* output regressions—the value of fertilizer used in the *rabi* season. We have not included this variable in the other regressions since it may not be a reliable indicator of fertilizer use for crops other than *rabi*. This decision is in contrast to our deduction of 1.5 times fertilizer as a cost in the calculation of income. There are three reasons for this different treatment. Firstly, the introduction of an error into a dependent variable (such as income) does not bias estimators of coefficients unless the error is correlated with an explanatory variable, whereas errors in an explanatory variable do introduce bias. Secondly, we are interested in the over-all level of income, and not just its variance across households, and we know that fertilizer is a cost and one which is greater than that for the *rabi* season taken alone. Finally, the errors in the measurement of income associated with the deduction of fertilizer as a cost are proportionally much smaller than in the measurement of fertilizer itself.

One might expect to find that our explanatory variables referring to direct inputs are highly correlated with each other. In the preceding chapter, for example, we have offered a partial explanation of land cultivated using the number of family members and the value of draught animals. The correlation matrix will be discussed in § 6.5 and we shall indeed find pairwise correlation coefficients which are quite high. However the correlations are far from perfect and we may hope that multicollinearity is not a serious problem. Further discussion is postponed until we have presented the results.

We turn now to the question of functional form. We emphasized in our discussion of underlying theory (§ 6.1) that one should be wary of interpreting the production regressions as estimates of purely technical production functions. To the extent, however, that such functions are important components of the relationships under examination one would expect to find diminishing returns to each of the four variables (taken separately) representing direct inputs. The most convenient way of representing such diminishing returns in a linear regression is to regress the logarithm of output on the logarithm of input.

This was one of the procedures we adopted. The variables logged were output and the direct inputs land cultivated, the number of family members aged 16–60 solely occupied in agriculture, and the value of bullocks. We did not take the logarithm of variables which are not direct inputs or the logarithm of the number of pumping sets owned (a zero-one variable).

The second procedure was to use the linear (unlogged) form for each variable. This latter procedure, if we exclude the assumption that the world is linear, amounts to taking a first order approximation to the production relation.

The logarithmic form has one particularly irritating feature for our analysis and that concerns the treatment of observations which take the (unlogged) value zero; the logarithm of zero is, of course, minus infinity. In our logarithmic regressions we excluded observations which took zero values for included variables which were logged. This can involve substantial reductions in the number of observations, particularly if the value of draught animals is included (see § 6.5). And the same is true for the case of fertilizer in the *rabi* season. This problem provides an additional reason for not using the value of fertilizer used in the *rabi* season as an explanatory variable for *GAO, kharif*, and sugar output measures.

We tried at an early stage to avoid the problem of zeros in logarithmic runs by replacing the logarithm of value of fertilizer used by the logarithm of (value plus a constant times acreage). The reasoning behind this experiment was that the land contains its own nutrients and the fertilizer used provides additional nutrient over and above that which is already there. Some detailed calculations along these lines are presented in the next chapter. It is not surprising that this experimental variable proved too highly correlated with the logarithm of land to yield helpful results.

We did not for this study experiment with functional forms other than those already mentioned. We pursue other possible specifications in a little more detail in our wheat study reported in the next chapter, in particular we tried some quadratic approximations. These experiments did not prove successful and we decided not to repeat them for our study here. Delicate experiments with the functional form would be out of keeping with the other parts of the raw material, since it must be recognized that our input measures are rather crude.

Having defined the full list of explanatory variables and the functional form, the remaining problem concerns the list of variables to the included in a particular equation. We noted above that for logarithmic forms this choice will have consequences for the numbers of observations in a regression.

For the linear functional form we present the simple regression of output on land cultivated. In this way we can examine the relation between output per acre and size of area cultivated. This relation has been a central feature of both theoretical and empirical discussion on Indian agriculture—see § 6.1, § 3.3 and § 3.7. In the linear case our estimated relation will have output per acre decreasing (increasing) with area cultivated if the estimated constant term is positive (negative).

Our second regression for the linear functional form includes as explanatory variables the four direct inputs, land cultivated for the relevant output, the number of males aged 16–60 working solely in agriculture (*F3*), the value of draught animals (*V1*), and the number of pumping sets owned (*NPSO*). For *rabi* output we include also the value of fertilizer used in that season (*FERT*). This is the closest we can come, given our data, to a technical production function, although we have already remarked that this is not particularly close.

For the logarithmic form we also follow the above procedure, presenting results for the case of just one explanatory variable, land cultivated, and then the collection of direct inputs. Where land cultivated is the only explanatory variable we have output per acre decreasing (increasing) with area cultivated if the estimated coefficient on land is less (greater) than one. We give two separate cases for the logarithmic form. First we include the logarithm of *V1* in the list of variables and then we exclude it. We provide both sets of results since the inclusion of *V1* causes a sharp drop in the number of observations. For the *rabi* output logarithmic equations we provide a third set of results where the logarithm of fertilizer is included, causing the number of observations to drop still further.

In each regression we give the coefficients together with their standard errors for the variables in the full list which are not included in the regression; the coefficient on an excluded variable is that which would result from the inclusion of that single variable in addition to those already included.

We now turn to the income regressions. Our concept and measurement of income were presented in § 6.3. We use the measure as an attempt to capture the net returns to the assets owned by the family. The list of measures of direct inputs included in a regression to explain income is, consequently, different from those for the output regressions. First, we have land owned in place of land cultivated. Second, we have replaced the narrow definition (*F3*) of family workers by the number of males aged 16–60 in the household (*F1*). The definition accords with our counting in income the payments from all sources, agricultural and otherwise. Our measure of animal assets is extended to include the value of all animals (*V2*). This corresponds with our inclusion in income of the value of milk. The variable *NPSO* is included as before. Our notation for variables is summarized in Table 6.3.

The 'indirect' variables included are again just two:*CASTE1* and *CASTE2*. We did not experiment with the variables *OWCU1* and *OWCU2*. These were tried previously to examine differential outputs on tenanted and owner-cultivated land. We are now looking at the full allocation of the household resources over possible activities rather than focusing on a particular one. The proportion leased-in or-out is really a consequence rather than a determinant of this full set of decisions. One can take a similar view of the decision to work inside or outside the village. We did, however, consider the use of a zero-one variable for whether or not at least one family member had a job outside the village. It might be supposed that the acquisition of a job outside the village was in the nature of an exogenous piece of luck for the household. However we doubt this supposition (see § 4.1) and even if it were acceptable there are also practical difficulties in defining an outside job – if it is to be viewed as an exogenous boost to output one would wish to exclude the more minor activities. We wished to avoid a classification by income since the variable would be used in the explanation of income, yet our data were not sufficiently precise to enable us to draw a useful distinction on any other lines. Thus we have no additional variable for whether or not there is some employment outside the village.

Our selection of functional form is similar to that for output. We present results for both linear and logarithmic forms of the relationship. In the latter case we take the logarithm of income, land owned, the number of male family members aged between 16 and 60, and the value of animals. The wider definition of animals in $V2$ implies that there are fewer zeros and thus we drop fewer observations when we take logarithms. We have therefore not provided separate regressions with and without the logarithm of $V2$. We provide results for the simple equation where land owned is the only explanatory variable and where all the variables representing productive assets, land owned, family members, value of animals, and the number of pumping sets owned, are included.

§ 6.5. The Results

We have, in the preceding sections, discussed theory, our data, the measurement of variables, and the specification of equations. In this section we shall present the results from estimating those equations.

We shall begin with a brief discussion of the simple summary statistics on our variables: means, standard deviations, and simple correlation matrices. Before we can do this we must explain the number of observations used in different circumstances. We confined our attention in the analysis of the determinants of output to those households which were actually cultivating in the sense of having a strictly positive *GAO*. This yields 93 cases. Note that this is less than was used for Chapter 5 (where there were 107 cases) since in our analysis of tenancy in that chapter the appropriate criterion for inclusion of a case was potential involvement (defined in Chapter 5) in agriculture. For the income regressions we include all 111 households.[6] We explained in § 6.4 that our use of the logarithmic form for some our regressions makes the number of observations in such a regression depend upon the pattern of zeros for the included variables. Accordingly in Table 6.4 we present this pattern in a simple diagrammatic form. The means and standard deviations of variables in linear form are given in Table 6.5(a) and (b) and we present these statistics for the logarithmic form in Table 6.5(c) and (d). We have two linear tables corresponding to 93 and 111 observations (see above). The reason for presenting two logarithmic tables also concerns the number of observations. Where we have only a few logarithmic variables in a regression the number of observations will be larger than when the list is extended. We give the means and standard deviations when just a few important variables are logged in Table 6.5(c), and similar statistics in Table

[6]As was explained in § 2.1 we exclude from our analysis of output and income the household (number 212) which emigrated.

Table 6.4 Zeros in the Data

Villages 1–2

Household	GRNSO	GKNSO	SUGAR	F3	V1	FERT
101	×	×	×			×
102	×	×	×			
103	×	×			×	×
104	×	×	×		×	×
105			×			
106					×	
107						
108	×	×	×		×	×
109					×	×
110						
111						
112						
113						
114						
115	×				×	×
116					×	
117	×					×
118						
119						
120						
121						
122						
123						
124						
125	×					

Village 2

Household	GRNSO	GKNSO	SUGAR	F3	V1	FERT
201						
202						
203						
204		×				
205			×			
206						
207						
208		×		×		
209			×	×	×	×
210		×	×	×	×	×
211		×	×	×	×	×
212		×	×	×	×	×
213		×	×	×	×	×
214						
215			×	×		
216			×	×		
217						
218	×	×	×	×	×	×
219						
220						
221		×	×	×		×
222						×
223						
224	×		×	×	×	×
225						
226						
227						
228						

Villages 3–5

Household	GRNSO	GKNSO	SUGAR	F3	V1	FERT
301	×	×	×			×
302	×	×	×	×	×	×
303		×				
304						
305			×		×	
306						
307						
308						
401						
402		×	×			
403		×	×			
404						
405					×	
406						
407						
408	×	×	×	×	×	×
409					×	×
501			×	×	×	×
502		×	×	×		×
503						

Villages 6–7

Household	GRNSO	GKNSO	SUGAR	F3	V1	FERT
601	×	×	×	×	×	×
602	×	×	×	×	×	×
603			×		×	×
604			×			×
605			×			
606			×			
607			×			
608	×				×	
609	×	×	×	×		
610						×
611						
612						
701	×	×	×	×	×	×
702	×		×		×	×
703	×	×	×	×		
704						
705	×	×	×	×	×	×
706	×	×	×	×	×	×
707						
708	×	×	×	×	×	×

Villages 8–9

Household	GRNSO	GKNSO	SUGAR	F3	V1	FERT
801						×
802						×
803						
804						
805						
806			×			
807			×	×	×	
808			×			
809			×		×	×
810					×	×
811						
812	×				×	×
813		×	×	×	×	×
814		×	×	×	×	×
901	×	×	×	×	×	×
902	×	×	×	×	×	×
903	×	×	×	×	×	×
904	×	×	×	×	×	×
Total 'x' for village	19	23	51	21	34	42

Notes : (i) '×' in a column denotes a zero in the data for that variable.

(ii) Notation defined in Table 6.3.

(iii) 'SUGAR' is value of sugar harvested in *rabi* season (there are very few cases of sugar harvested in *kharif*.)

(iv) Household 212 migrated in November 1974

Table 6.5 Means and Standard Deviations
(a) All Households, Linear Variables

Variable	Mean	Standard Deviation
INCM	7,083.294	4,831.960
GAO	4,734.081	4,465.435
GRNSO	2,296.611	2,139.295
SUGAR	1,174.505	1,653.896
GKNSO	1,262.966	1,187.446
F1	1.820	1.029
F3	1.189	0.869
V1	668.919	661.508
V2	836.532	722.144
FERT	144.324	232.468
LANDO	22.507	20.413
CULT	21.942	17.583
SUCLT	4.173	5.498
NPSO	0.063	0.244
CASTE1	0.225	0.420
CASTE2	0.243	0.431
NSCULTR	16.201	13.336
NSCULTK	14.415	11.781

Number of cases 111

Variables appearing in 6.A.8

SUGAR	2137.213	1709.690
SUCLT	7.560	5.427
F3	1.492	0.868
V1	977.869	670.418
NPSO	0.115	0.321
CASTE1	0.262	0.444
CASTE2	0.328	0.473

Number of cases 61

(b) Cultivating Households (*GAO > 0*), Linear Variables

Variable	Mean	Standard Deviation
INCM	7,595.416	4,980.018
GAO	5,650.355	4,313.687
GRNSO	2,741.116	2,059.203
SUGAR	1,401.828	1,717.096
GKNSO	1,507.411	1,146.044
F1	1.850	1.021
F3	1.376	0.793
V1	798.387	647.086
V2	937.688	731.783
FERT	172.258	244.439
LANDO	24.553	20.148
CULT	26.081	16.181
SUCLT	4.980	5.664
NPSO	0.075	0.265
CASTE1	0.247	0.434
CASTE2	0.258	0.440
NSCULTR	19.337	12.302
NSCULTK	17.097	10.957

Number of cases 93

Variables appearing in 6.11(a) (b) (c) (d)		
FRTONCLT	5.4421	5.2676
LANDO	24.6418	20.3172
LOFA	5.1393	4.1130
CULT	26.6544	15.8805

Number of cases 91

(c) Logarithmic Variables (excluding *LNVI* and *LNFERT*)

Variable	Mean	Standard Deviation.
LNGAO	8.480	0.770
LNGRNSO	7.764	0.772
LNGKNSO	7.195	0.675
LNINCM	8.809	0.608
LNF1	0.501	0.493
LNF3	0.298	0.403
NPSO	0.090	0.288
LNCULT	3.159	0.689
LNCULTR	3.074	0.701
LNCULTK	2.997	0.681
LNNSCLTR	2.868	0.660
LNNSCLTK	2.766	0.649
LNLANDO	2.903	0.975
CASTE1	0.256	0.440
CASTE2	0.256	0.440

Number of cases 78

Variables appearing in 6.13(a) and (b)		
LNINCM	8.8606	0.5294
LNLANDO	2.9776	0.8500
LNF1	0.4871	0.4975
LNV2	6.8222	0.6406
CASTE1	0.2716	0.4476
CASTE2	0.2469	0.4339

Number of cases 81

(d) Logarithmic Variables (including *LNVI* and *LNFERT*)

Variable	Mean	Standard Deviation.
LNGAO	8.766	0.477
LNGRNSO	8.031	0.466
LNGKNSO	7.429	0.488
LNINCM	8.969	0.509
LNF1	0.530	0.514
LNF3	0.334	0.426
NPSO	0.123	0.331
LNCULT	3.367	0.445
LNCULTR	3.301	0.448
LNCULTK	3.226	0.452
LNNSCLTR	3.064	0.419
LNNSCLTK	2.969	0.421
LNLANDO	3.049	0.963
CASTE1	0.281	0.453
CASTE2	0.281	0.453
LNV1	6.806	0.523
LNFERT	5.206	0.793

Number of cases 57

Variables apearing in 6.A.3 and 6.A.7		
LNGKNSO	7.3339	0.5381
LNGRNSO	7.9327	0.5584
LNF3	0.3264	0.4129
NPSO	0.1014	0.3041
LNNSCLTR	3.0147	0.4904
LNNSCLTK	2.9064	0.5083
CASTE1	0.2464	0.4341
CASTE2	0.2609	0.4423
LNV1	6.7728	0.5393
Number of cases 69		

Notes to Table 6.5
(i) For definitions of variables see Table 6.3
(ii) For logarithmic variables the numbers of cases depends upon the number of logged variables (see text § 6.4 and §6.5).

6.5(d) where we take the logarithms of all the relevant variables. Note that none of the eighteen (111−93) households with zero *GAO* would be included in a logarithmic output regression.[7]

The correlation matrices are presented in Tables 6.6(a), (b), (c), and (d). We have four tables for the same reason as that just described concerning mean and standard deviations.

Our regression results are presented as follows. In this section we examine the determination of gross annual output (*GAO*). The results for the linear regression are presented in Table 6.7 and for the two logarithmic regressions in Tables 6.8 and 6.9. The income regressions are in § 6.8 and those for the components of *GAO* (*rabi*, *kharif*, and sugar) in the appendix to this chapter.

For each of the output regressions we give the results first where the only included explanatory variable is land cultivated and second where all the relevant direct inputs are included. Thus each table of these estimates is divided into two parts.

In each of the regression tables we have a list of coefficients for variables not included in the regression. Corresponding to each such variable there are two numbers: *B* and its associated *F*-value. *B* is the coefficient which would be estimated for that variable if it were included as the only additional variable in the equation.

We give a preliminary discussion of the results in this section and relate these results to some wider issues in the next section. We discuss the Tables 6.4 to 6.9 in the order presented.

We can see from Table 6.4 that certain of the households are not involved in cultivation and have zeros for all, or nearly all, of the important variables. Such households would have one or a mixture of the following occupation: self-employed outside agriculture and performing a service role in the village; agricultural labour; a job outside the village. They would not be included in our

---

[7] They can however be included in logarithmic income regression provided that none of *LANDO*, *F1*, and *V2* are zero. We decided not to include yet further tables on means, standard deviations, and correlation coefficients to cover this case.

Table 6.6 Correlation Matrices
Table 6.6 (a) All Households, Linear Variables

	INCM	GAO	GRNSO	SUGAR	GKNSO	F1	F3	V1	V2	FERT	LANDO	CULT	SUCLT	NPSO	CASTEI	CASTE2	NSCULTR	NSCULTK
INCM	1.00																	
GAO	0.83	1.00																
GRNSO	0.80	0.95	1.00															
SUGAR	0.73	0.85	0.68	1.00														
GKNSO	0.66	0.87	0.83	0.56	1.00													
F1	0.52	0.33	0.42	0.17	0.25	1.00												
F3	0.49	0.63	0.66	0.43	0.55	0.62	1.00											
V1	0.66	0.79	0.81	0.59	0.68	0.33	0.60	1.00										
V2	0.63	0.53	0.53	0.43	0.43	0.14	0.32	0.53	1.00									
FERT	0.67	0.77	0.80	0.56	0.69	0.39	0.55	0.76	0.52	1.00								
LANDO	0.67	0.62	0.58	0.59	0.48	0.14	0.34	0.58	0.47	0.49	1.00							
CULT	0.74	0.94	0.92	0.77	0.82	0.32	0.63	0.82	0.49	0.71	0.65	1.00						
SUCLT	0.64	0.79	0.61	0.94	0.55	0.16	0.44	0.56	0.38	0.53	0.55	0.76	1.00					
NPSO	0.59	0.58	0.51	0.61	0.43	0.26	0.37	0.43	0.41	0.46	0.37	0.47	0.57	1.00				
CASTEI	0.19	0.18	0.20	0.07	0.23	-0.01	0.13	0.12	0.31	0.29	0.21	0.13	0.08	0.22	1.00			
CASTE2	0.18	0.22	0.14	0.35	0.07	0.15	0.03	0.18	0.22	0.14	0.41	0.22	0.30	0.11	-0.31	1.00		
NSCULTR	0.73	0.91	0.94	0.63	0.83	0.35	0.63	0.83	0.51	0.73	0.61	0.96	0.59	0.41	0.14	0.18	1.00	
NSCULTK	0.68	0.88	0.90	0.58	0.88	0.33	0.61	0.79	0.46	0.72	0.57	0.92	0.55	0.41	0.24	0.11	0.95	1.00

Number of cases 111

Table 6.6(b) Cultivating Households (*GAO*>*0*) Linear Variables

	INCM	GAO	GRNSO	SUGAR	GKNSO	F1	F3	V1	V2	FERT	LANDO	CULT	SUCLT	NPSO	CASTE1	CASTE2	NSCULTR	NSCULTK
INCM	1.00	0.86	0.83	0.73	0.66	0.52	0.47	0.65	0.63	0.67	0.71	0.77	0.63	0.60	0.19	0.20	0.75	0.70
GAO		1.00	0.94	0.83	0.83	0.38	0.54	0.73	0.46	0.76	0.65	0.93	0.75	0.60	0.15	0.22	0.88	0.84
GRNSO			1.00	0.64	0.77	0.49	0.59	0.76	0.46	0.79	0.59	0.90	0.54	0.52	0.17	0.12	0.93	0.87
SUGAR				1.00	0.50	0.18	0.35	0.53	0.38	0.52	0.61	0.75	0.93	0.61	0.04	0.37	0.57	0.52
GKNSO					1.00	0.27	0.44	0.60	0.34	0.66	0.47	0.76	0.47	0.43	0.21	0.04	0.78	0.85
F1						1.00	0.73	0.37	0.18	0.43	0.19	0.37	0.16	0.28	0.01	-0.15	0.41	0.39
F3							1.00	0.51	0.20	0.52	0.32	0.53	0.35	0.38	0.11	-0.06	0.52	0.51
V1								1.00	0.47	0.74	0.60	0.77	0.49	0.43	0.08	0.17	0.79	0.73
V2									1.00	0.49	0.48	0.41	0.31	0.41	0.29	0.25	0.43	0.38
FERT										1.00	0.50	0.70	0.48	0.45	0.28	0.13	0.72	0.71
LANDO											1.00	0.69	0.55	0.38	0.19	0.38	0.64	0.58
CULT												1.00	0.73	0.49	0.08	0.21	0.94	0.89
SUCLT													1.00	0.57	0.04	0.31	0.51	0.47
NPSO														1.00	0.21	0.11	0.42	0.41
CASTE1															1.00	-0.34	0.10	0.22
CASTE2																1.00	0.17	0.07
NSCULTR																	1.00	0.93
NSCULTK																		1.00

Number of cases 93

Table 6.6 (c) Logarithmic Variables (excluding LNVI and LNFERT)

	LNGAO	LNGRNSO	LNGKNSO	LNINCM	LNFI	LNF3	NPSO	LNCULT	LNCULTR	LNCULTK	LNNSCLTR	LNNSCLTK	LNLANDO	CASTE1	CASTE2
LNGAO	1.00	0.94	0.87	0.74	0.26	0.35	0.40	0.94	0.96	0.95	0.90	0.86	0.57	0.02	0.23
LNGRNSO		1.00	0.82	0.71	0.37	0.38	0.35	0.92	0.93	0.89	0.95	0.89	0.54	0.003	0.16
LNGKNSO			1.00	0.64	0.27	0.38	0.33	0.81	0.82	0.87	0.81	0.87	0.49	0.10	0.09
LNINCM				1.00	0.51	0.36	0.47	0.61	0.67	0.66	0.64	0.62	0.62	0.22	0.16
LNFI					1.00	0.72	0.26	0.27	0.28	0.29	0.34	0.36	0.23	0.01	0.16
LNF3						1.00	0.38	0.36	0.35	0.37	0.35	0.36	0.31	0.05	-0.01
NPSO							1.00	0.34	0.37	0.37	0.31	0.28	0.31	0.23	0.12
LNCULT								1.00	0.98	0.96	0.94	0.90	0.54	-0.05	0.20
LNCULTR									1.00	0.96	0.96	0.88	0.54	-0.02	0.24
LNCULTK										1.00	0.91	0.94	0.52	0.05	0.17
LNNSCLTR											1.00	0.93	0.52	-0.02	0.19
LNNSCLTK												1.00	0.49	0.08	0.08
LNLANDO													1.00	0.18	0.35
CASTE1														1.00	-0.34
CASTE2															1.00

Number of cases 78

Table 6.6 (d) Logarithmic Variables (including *LNVI* and *LNFERT*)

	LNGAO	*LNGRNSO*	*LNGKNSO*	*LNINCM*	*LNFI*	*LNF3*	*NPSO*	*LNCULT*	*LNCULTR*	*LNCULTK*	*LNNSCLTR*	*LNNSCLTK*	*LNLANDO*	*CASTEI*	*CASTE2*	*LNVI*	*LNFERT*
LNGAO	1.00																
LNGRNSO	0.85	1.00															
LNGKNSO	0.74	0.59	1.00														
LNINCM	0.69	0.67	0.52	1.00													
LNFI	0.27	0.44	0.25	0.60	1.00												
LNF3	0.44	0.47	0.42	0.45	0.76	1.00											
NPSO	0.55	0.48	0.36	0.55	0.28	0.40	1.00										
LNCULT	0.91	0.81	0.65	0.54	0.23	0.38	0.46	1.00									
LNCULTR	0.93	0.84	0.66	0.57	0.25	0.41	0.50	0.97	1.00								
LNCULTK	0.89	0.72	0.73	0.59	0.27	0.39	0.48	0.91	0.91	1.00							
LNNSCLTR	0.80	0.90	0.65	0.55	0.33	0.38	0.40	0.87	0.90	0.77	1.00						
LNNSCLTK	0.75	0.75	0.76	0.55	0.34	0.36	0.34	0.79	0.78	0.89	0.83	1.00					
LNLANDO	0.43	0.37	0.35	0.55	0.16	0.29	0.32	0.37	0.37	0.33	0.36	0.31	1.00				
CASTEI	0.19	0.16	0.25	0.29	0.08	0.12	0.24	0.12	0.13	0.23	0.12	0.26	0.29	1.00			
CASTE2	0.15	0.05	0.001	0.05	-0.23	-0.03	0.12	0.12	0.15	0.07	0.09	0.03	0.32	-0.39	1.00		
LNVI	0.63	0.66	0.38	0.54	0.32	0.43	0.46	0.61	0.64	0.56	0.62	0.50	0.42	0.12	0.14	1.00	
LNFERT	0.68	0.79	0.47	0.55	0.35	0.43	0.43	0.66	0.68	0.67	0.69	0.68	0.32	0.34	0.04	0.63	1.00

Number of cases 57

Table 6.7(a) *GAO* on Land Cultivated—Linear.

Multiple R	0.93	Number of cases	93
R Squared	0.86	Number of variables	1
Standard error	1627.06	F-Value for equation	555.66
		Dependent variable	*GAO*

Variables in the equation

Variable	B	Standard error of B	F
CULT	247.12	10.48	555.66
Constant	−794.89	62.95	159.46

Variables not in the equation

Variable	B IN	F
F3	359.51	2.07
VI	0.35	0.75
NPSO	3186.27	23.42
CASTE1	757.68	3.85
CASTE2	236.66	0.36

Table 6.7(b) The Determinants of *GAO*—Linear

Multiple R	0.94	Number of cases	93
R Squared	0.89	Number of variables	4
Standard error	1467.14	F-Value for equation	176.83
		Dependent variable	*GAO*

Variables in the equation

Variable	B	Standard error or B	F
CULT	213.34	15.67	185.30
F3	166.64	234.22	0.51
VI	0.15	0.38	0.16
NPSO	3079.36	672.34	20.98
Constant	−496.72		

Variables not in the equation

Variable	B IN	F
CASTE1	421.53	1.37
CASTE2	286.96	0.62

Notes : (i) See notes to Table 5.7
(ii) For definitions of variables see Table 6.3

cultivator questionnaires (see § 1.2) unless they owned land (and thus lease it out) or are involved in agricultural work. However it seemed unreasonable to attempt to explain, through 'inputs' involved, the output of those who do not produce at all. Our criterion for the inclusion of households in the linear regressions is that gross annual output (*GAO*) be strictly positive. This we take as a

Table 6.8(a) *GAO* on Land Cultivated—Logarithmic (excluding *LNVI*)

Multiple *R*	0.94	Number of cases	86
R Squared	0.89	Number of variables	8
Standard error	0.27	*F*-Value for equation	682.99
		Dependent variable	*LNGAO*

Variables in the equation

Variable	*B*	Standard error of *B*	*F*
LNCULT	1.08	0.04	682.00
Constant	5.06	0.06	6,292.26

Variables not in the equation

Variable	*B* IN	*F*
LNF3	0.01	0.03
NPSO	0.23	4.44
CASTE1	0.12	3.37
CASTE2	0.07	1.01

Table 6.8(b) The Determinants of *GAO* —Logarithmic (excluding *LNVI*)

Multiple *R*	0.95	Number of cases	86
R Squared	0.90	Number of variables	3
Standard error	0.26	*F*-Value for equation	236.07
		Dependent variable	*LNGAO*

Variables in the equation

Variable	*B*	Standard error of *B*	*F*
LNCULT	1.05	0.05	542.78
LNF3	− 0.03	0.08	0.15
NPSO	0.24	0.11	4.51
Constant	5.13		

Variables not in the equation

Variable	*B* IN	*F*
CASTE1	0.09	1.98
CASTE2	0.06	0.71

Notes : (i) See notes to Table 5.7
(ii) For Definition of variables see Table 6.3

definition of a 'farmer' or cultivating household for the purposes of the regressions. Note that the use of the logarithmic form automatically excludes non-cultivating households in the output regressions.

There are 34 zeros for the value of draught animals (*VI*), 42 for the value of *rabi* fertilizer (*FERT*), and 51 for the value of sugar output. The inclusion of *VI* or *FERT* reduces the number of observations substantially for the logarithmic regressions. We can see that the absence of a family member solely involved in

Table 6.9(a) *GAO* on Land Cultivated—Logarithmic

Multiple *R*	0.90	Number of cases	75
R Squared	0.81	Number of variables	1
Standard error	0.26	*F*-Value for equation	313.89
		Dependent variable	*LNGAO*

Variables in the equation

Variable	*B*	Standard error of *B*	*F*
LNCULT	1.03	0.06	313.89
Constant	5.25	0.14	1402.42

Variables not in the equation

Variable	*B* IN	*F*
LNF3	0.05	0.46
NPSO	0.28	6.59
LNVI	0.16	6.01
CASTE1	0.13	3.73
CASTE2	0.06	0.74

Table 6.9(b) The Determinants of *GAO* —Logarithmic

Multiple *R*	0.91	Number of cases	75
R Squared	0.84	Number of variables	4
Standard error	0.25	*F*-Value for equation	89.11
		Dependent variable	*LNGAO*

Variables in the equation

Variable	*B*	Standard error of *B*	*F*
LNCULT	0.89	0.07	148.39
LNF3	− 0.002	0.08	0.00
NPSO	0.23	0.11	4.08
LNVI	0.13	0.07	3.71
Constant	4.81		

Variables not in the equation

Variable	*B* IN	*F*
CASTE1	0.10	2.25
CASTE2	0.03	0.22

Notes : (i) See notes to Table 5.7
(ii) For definition of variables see Table 6.3

agriculture is associated with the absence of draught animals (with two exceptions, 205 and 501).

We concentrate our discussion of the means, standard deviations, and correlation coefficients on the linear variables, in particular on Tables 6.5(a) and

6.6(a). We can calculate from an examination of the means[8] in Table 6.5(a) that *rabi* output contributes 32.4 per cent of income for the 111 households, *kharif* output 17.8 per cent, and sugar output 16.6 per cent (for further detail on income breakdowns see Table 6.2).

We see from Table 6.5(a) that the mean of $F1$ is approximately 0.6 above that of $F3$, corresponding to the wider definition of $F1$ which includes all males aged 16–60 and not just those solely engaged in agriculture. Of the adult males in the 111 households, 65.3 per cent $(F3/F1)$ are engaged full-time in agriculture. Comparing the means of the value of draught animals $(V1)$ and the value of all animals $(V2)$ we can see that draught animals constitute the major proportion (80.0 per cent). Land owned $(LANDO)$ is slightly more than land cultivated $(CULT)$. The extra comes from net land leased from Palanpur households to outside the village. Of the total land cultivated 19.5 per cent is devoted to sugar.

The pairwise correlations amongst the set of output, income, and direct input variables are in general high—a high proportion of the entries in Table 6.6(a) in the matrix formed by excluding the rows and columns $CASTE1$ and $CASTE2$ are above 0.5. This is unsurprising. Households with high outputs from one constitutent will have high outputs from others and high inputs. Our problem is to isolate the contribution to output and income variations from the variations in different inputs—that is the purpose of the multiple regression analysis. The correlations connected with the variables $CASTE1$ and $CASTE2$ of Table 6.6(a) are in general not particularly high. The picture from Table 6.6(b), (c), and (d), containing the logarithmic correlations is broadly similar to that for the linear variables and they are not discussed further here.

We turn now to the regression equations for gross annual output (GAO). We find in Table 6.7 (a) a coefficient for the linear form with land cultivated the only explanatory variable, of 247.1. This indicates that an extra *bigha* of land contributed an extra 247.1 rupees. The constant term is negative indicating that output per *bigha* increases with area cultivated (its value, R 795, may be compared with the mean GAO for the sample, R 5650). A relationship which is very slightly increasing can be seen in the logarithmic runs where we have a coefficient in Table 6.8(a) and 6.9(a) of 1.08 (0.04) and 1.03 (0.06) respectively (standard errors in brackets). Thus we have a relationship from the logarithmic regression which is very close to proportional.

We do not provide a formal test of the hypothesis that the coefficient is exactly equal to one. It is straightforward, however, to see whether 1.00 lies inside a 95 per cent confidence interval for the true value of the coefficient. Such an interval is $(B-2\sigma, B+2\sigma)$ where B is the estimated coefficient and σ the estimated standard error (the factor 2 is approximate here).

The introduction of other direct inputs (see Table 6.7(b), 6.8(b), and 6.9(b)) yields only $NPSO$ as significant. In the logarithmic form however $LNV1$ is close

[8].The mean of *GRNSO*, *GKNSO*, and *SUGAR* has been divided by the mean of *INCM*. For an individual farmer his output for a season may be less than his agricultural income if he receives agricultural rent. For the village as a whole these differences cancel out except where rent is received from outside the village. Such rent is a very small proportion of village income.

to significance (see Table 6.9(b)) with a coefficient of 0.13 and a standard error of 0.07. In this case the sum of coefficients on *LNCULT* and *LNV1* is slightly above one.

We can sum up our results on the direct inputs for our output variables as follows. The results from estimations using the components of gross annual output (*rabi*, *kharif*, and sugar) are anticipated here (the detail is contained in the appendix). We have for all the crops a relationship between output and area cultivated which is not far from proportional. Only in the case of *kharif* logarithmic models does output per *bigha* show any tendency to decline with area cultivated and this effect does not come through in the linear *kharif* model or in aggregate annual output. Land cultivated is always highly significant. The variable *NPSO*, indicating whether or not a pumping set is owned, is generally significant with a large positive coefficient. The variable denoting use of fertilizer in the *rabi* season yields a positive significant coefficient for *rabi* ouput. The value of draught animals is occasionally significant with a positive coefficient, and the number of family members solely engaged in agriculture is never significant. The economic implications of these results are discussed in the next section. The caste variables were always insignificant.

§ 6.6 The Economic Implications of Our Results

There are two particularly striking features of our results from the output regressions. The first is that output is roughly proportional to area cultivated. The second is that the number of adult males engaged solely in agriculture (*F3*) is insignificant throughout.

Our result that output per *bigha* is independent of area cultivated is in strong contrast with some earlier discussions of Indian agriculture (see § 3.7) and it is interesting to speculate on the reasons. We suspect that an important factor is the absence of any very large farms in our sample —no household cultivates more than 100 *bighas* (15.6 acres). They can all be described as family farms. The hiring of permanent labour is very rare in the village, although there is a great deal of hiring on a day to day basis (see § 4.1). Some of the explanations for declining output per *bigha* would not therefore be as strongly relevant for our sample as for samples which include large farms. We are thinking here of the arguments which refer to lower complementary inputs, in particular labour, per unit area on large farms, either because of the prevalence of tenancy on such farms or because labour inputs which are hired would not be used to the same extent as family labour. Such farms are sometimes called 'capitalist' to distinguish them from family farms.

The apparent absence of the two effects just mentioned on the larger farms in Palanpur may be associated with the high degree of supervision of both hired labour and tenanted land which is possible where farm sizes are relatively small, even for the larger farms of the village. It is notable here that the variables *OWCU1* and *OWCU2* representing the proportion of area under tenancy were completely insignificant as explanations of output. Also relevant is the insignificance of *F3*—if hired labour can work efficiently alongside family labour the effect of lower family labour per *bigha* on productivity may be less marked.

A further factor associated with the constancy of output per *bigha* in Palanpur may be the absence of large farms comprising a high percentage of poor land. We recall that Khusro has argued (see § 3.7) that the finding of a declining output per acre can be explained by correcting the acreage for land quality, which he suggests reduces, relatively, the effective area cultivated on the larger farms.

The insignificance of the number of family members engaged solely in agriculture (*F3*) accords not only with the proportionality finding just discussed but also with our discussion of the Sen model of the application of family labour in § 3.3 and § 6.1. Thus the insignificance of this variable may be associated with its being a stock (the number of family members) rather than a flow (actual labour input). Where the number of family members is fewer, output from a given area may be kept up either by those members working harder or by hiring more labour.

We note here that this argument is not inconsistent with our conclusion in Chapter 5 that families with higher *F3* will attempt to cultivate more land—by leasing-in more or leasing-out less. The family which seeks more land to lease must also take a decision, given the land it manages to obtain, on cultivation intensity. We have seen that this decision may not involve intensity increasing with *F3*, and there will in addition be pressures from the landlord not to let that intensity differ too much from that of other cultivators.

Since our variables are stock variables we cannot in general make simple comparisons between the marginal product of an input and its price. There is one exception to this, however, and that is fertilizer in the *rabi* season. We recall that our input is the value of fertilizer applied to *rabi* (non-sugar) output. Output is measured in value terms and thus in a perfectly competitive world with no uncertainty the coefficient in the linear form should be 1.0. If the value of the marginal product is equal to the price for the (geometric) mean of the sample in the logarithmic form, then the coefficient on fertilizer should be equal to the mean of the value of fertilizer divided by the (geometric) mean of the value of output.

We find in Table 6.A.1 (b) that the coefficient on the value of fertilizer in the linear form for *rabi* output is 1.78. It is highly significant. The coefficient in the logarithmic form (Table 6.A.4 (b) is 0.15 and the ratio of (geometric) mean fertilizer to (geometric) mean output is 0.06 (calculated from Table 6.5 (d)). Thus we find that the value marginal product of a kilogramme of fertilizer is substantially above twice its price using the logarithmic method and not far short of twice its price using the linear method. The results are consistent with those we shall be reporting in Chapter 8 and we postpone further discussion until that chapter.

The remaining two direct inputs are the value of draught animals and the number of pumping sets owned. We have seen the number of pumping sets owned is generally quite strongly significant. The coefficient for gross annual output in linear form (see Table 6.7 (b)) is 3079.4. Thus the gross returns, from crops alone, to owning a pumping set would appear to be above 75 per cent of the value of the set (assuming a price of 4000 rupees). There are a number of reasons for supposing that this overstates the productivity. First, we have not deducted the cost of using the set. Second, the marginal return to increasing the number of pumping sets in the village is likely to be rather smaller than the average. It is already fairly easy to rent the services of a set. Finally, our knowledge of those farmers who do own pumping sets leads us to suppose that they are amongst the most astute farmers in the village. Thus one is picking up in the regressions, in addition to returns to the pumping sets themselves, returns to characteristics of such farmers.

The value of draught animals seems to do rather better in terms of significance levels in the logarithmic regressions. One excludes from such regressions those households with no draught animals. This suggests the possibility that farming activities with and without draught animals may be qualitatively different. In Table 6.9 (b) for example we can examine the returns to gross annual output around the (geometric) mean from owning an additional rupee of value of draught animals: $0.13 \times$ mean $GAO \div$ mean $VI = 0.85$. Thus an extra R100 of bullock earns a gross revenue of R85 in a year. Given that one must deduct certain costs and that the health of a bullock is subject to some uncertainty the figure does not seem unreasonable.

It is quite commonly remarked that higher castes have special advantages in agriculture in India. Thus our finding that the caste variables are insignificant is of some interest. It may be, of course, that if such advantages exist they operate through access to assets and not in their use. An examination of Table 6.6 (b) indicates that the *CASTE1* variable is significantly[9] positively correlated with *FERT* and *NPSO* but not with *VI* and *CULT* and the *CASTE2* with *CULT* but not with *VI*, *FERT*, or *NPSO*. There is therefore some evidence of greater access to assets but it is not impressive.

§ 6.7. Cultivation Intensity

It has been suggested by some theorists (see § 3.7) that smaller farmers will achieve higher outputs per acre by cultivating more intensively. Thus one might suppose that the proportion of fallow land on smaller farms would be lower. And other economists (see § 3.9) have argued that larger farmers will have privileged access to inputs associated with the new methods of the 'Green Revolution'. Thus one might expect to find higher ratios of fertilizer input to area cultivated for the larger farmers. In this section we test both these hypotheses.

In Table 6.10 we present a correlation matrix for the proportion of land cultivated which is fallow in each season, the sum of the land cultivated by households in each season which is fallow divided by area cultivated, the wealth

---

[9] For a sample of size 93 a correlation coefficient of over 0.204 is significant at the 5 per cent level—see § 5.8.1.

variable *LOFA,* and the area cultivated (precise definitions for and names of those variables are given in the notes to Table 6.10). All households with strictly positive land cultivated are included.[10] It can be seen that the proportion left fallow is completely unrelated to either *LOFA* or land cultivated.

The second hypothesis described above is examined with the aid of Table 6.11. A correlation matrix of (*rabi*) fertilizer per *bigha* with land owned, *LOFA,* and land cultivated is presented in Table 6.11 (a). Again all households with positive land cultivated in the *rabi* (*CULT*>0) are included. For ninety-one observations a correlation coefficient of above 0.204 is significant at the 5 per cent level. It can be seen that the correlation of fertilizer per *bigha* with both land owned and land cultivated is significant although that with *LOFA* is not. The correlation with land cultivated is strong compared with the correlation with *LANDO.*

In Table 6.11 (b), (c), and (d) we present the simple regression of fertilizer per *bigha* on land owned, *LOFA,* and land cultivated. As one should expect from the correlation matrix the coefficients on the explanatory variable are significant in Tables (b) and (d) but not in (c). The relation with land cultivated is much stronger than with land owned (as measured by R^2) and the coefficient on land cultivated is twice that of land owned. Thus it would seem not to be wealth that goes with high fertilizer per *bigha* but concern and ability to be involved in agriculture.

§ 6.8 Income

§ 6.8.1 The Determination of Income

The income regressions are presented in linear form in Table 6.12 and logarithmic form in 6.13. We find in the linear form that the regression of income on land owned (Table 6.12(a)) yields a coefficient of 159.1 rupees per *bigha* with a constant of 3502.3. The average is 314.7 rupees per *bigha.* The positive constant indicates that income per land area owned declines with land owned. This is unsurprising, as income includes returns to assets other than those directly involved in crop production, for example income earned outside the village by family members, and the value of milk. The direction of the relationship is confirmed in Table 6.13(a) where we find a coefficient on land owned which is much less than one, 0.35 with a standard error of 0.06.

On introducing the directly productive assets we find that for both linear and logarithmic forms all three of male family members aged 16-60 (*FI*), value of animals owned, *NPSSO* are significant. The sum of the coefficients of the logged explanatory variables in Table 6.13(b) is quite close to one, 0.92. It is notable in this table that the coefficient on *LNFI* has a high *F* value (as does that on *FI* in Table 6.12(b) and is more than twice as large as the coefficient on

---

[10] This gave 91 cases. This is two less than the 93 cases defined under the criterion *GAO* > 0 since two households with small positive *kharif* output did not cultivate in the *rabi* season. Our *CULT* variable is land cultivated in the *rabi* season.

Table 6.10 Correlation Matrix on Cultivation Intensity Variables

	FLRONCLT	FLKONCLT	FLONCLT	LOFA	CULT
FLRONCLT	1.00	0.29	0.67	−0.02	0.01
FLKONCLT		1.00	0.91	−0.03	−0.003
FLONCLT			1.00	−0.03	0.002
LOFA				1.00	0.43
CULT					1.00

Number of cases 91

Notes : (i) $FLRONCLT$ = Land fallow in *rabi* divided by $CULT$
   $FLKONCLT$ = Land fallow in *kharif* divided by $CULT$
   $FLONCLT = FLRONCLT + FLKONCLT$
   $LOFA$—see § 5.7
   $CULT$ = Land cultivated in the *rabi* season (including fallow land).
   (ii) For definitions of variables see Table 6.3

Table 6.11(a) Correlation Matrix concerning Fertilizer per Cultivated *Bigha*

	FRTONCLT	LANDO	LOFA	CULT
FRTONCLT	1.00	0.22	0.09	0.37
LANDO		1.00	0.82	0.70
LOFA			1.00	0.43
CULT				1.00
Number of cases 91				

Note : (i) $FRTONCLT = FERT/CULT$.
   (ii) For other variables see Table 6.3.

Table 6.11(b) Fertilizer per Cultivated *Bigha* on Land Owned

Multiple R	0.22	Number of cases	91
R Squared	0.05	Number of variables	1
Standard Error	5.17	F-Value for equation	4.51
		Dependent variable	FRTONCLT

Variables in the equation

Variable	B	Standard error or B	F
LANDO	0.06	0.03	4.51
Constant	4.04	0.14	828.37

Table 6.11(c) Fertilizer per Cultivated *Bigha* on *LOFA*.

Multiple R	0.09	Number of cases	91
R Squared	0.01	Number of variables	1
Standard error	5.27	F-Value for equation	0.75
		Dependent variable	FRTONCLT

Variables in the equation

Variable	B	Standard error of B	F
LOFA	0.12	0.14	0.75
Constant	4.84	0.15	1,063.05

Table 6.11(d) Fertilizer per Cultivated *Bigha* on Land Cultivated

Multiple R	0.37	Number of cases	91
R Squared	0.14	Number of variables	1
Standard error	4.91	F-Value for equation	14.52
		Dependent Variable	*FRTONCLT*

Variables in the equation

Variable	B	Standard error of B	F
CULT	0.12	0.03	14.52
Constant	2.13	0.21	106.96

Notes : (i) See notes to Table 5.7.
(ii) For definitions of variables see Table 6.3.

Table 6.12(a) Income on Land Owned—Linear

Multiple R	0.67	Number of cases	111
R Squared	0.45	Number of variables	1
Standard error	3593.98	F-Value for equation	89.83
		Dependent variable	*INCM*

Variables in the equation

Variable	B	Standard error of B	F
LANDO	159.11	16.79	89.83
Constant	3502.31	71.74	2383.36

Variables not in the equation

Variable	B IN	F
F1	2,030.46	54.18
V2	2.66	31.22
NPSO	7,822.03	35.22
CASTE1	620.79	0.55
CASTE2	− 1,330.86	2.36

land. The inclusion of labour incomes and the corresponding widening of the definition of family members transforms the insignificant *F3* into the highly significant *F1*. The caste variables were again insignificant.

Whilst the R^2s are in general lower than for the output regressions the significance levels of the direct input variables other than land are much higher. We find also that income per *bigha* decreases quite sharply with area cultivated, the reason, we presume, being that we are measuring the returns to assets other than land in activities not directly associated with crop production. The result indicates that any relationship of farm size to productivity will be sensitive to the way in which output or income is measured. We should emphasize that previous discussion has concentrated on a measure close to our gross annual output. And if one is discussing the crop production per unit area, that seems the obvious measure to use.

Table 6.12(b) The Determinants of Income—Linear.

Multiple R	0.88	Number of cases	111
R Squared	0.77	Number of variables	4
Standard error	2347.05	F-Value for equation	90.06
		Dependent variable	*INCM*

Variables in the equation

Variable	B	Standard error of B	F
LANDO	94.44	12.74	54.95
F1	1696.23	225.83	56.42
V2	1.96	0.37	28.48
NPSO	4483.81	1054.42	18.08
Constant	− 50.90		

Variables not in the equation

Variable	B IN	F
CASTE1	− 350.09	0.38
CASTE2	− 318.28	0.29

Notes :   (i) See notes to Table 5.7
 (ii) For Definition of variables see Table 6.3

Table 6.13 (a) Income on Land Owned—Logarithmic.

Multiple R	0.56	Number of cases	81
R Squared	0.31	Number of variables	1
Standard error	0.44	F-Value for equation	35.36
		Dependent variable	*LNINCM*

Variables in the equation

Variable	B	Standard error of B	F
LNLANDO	0.35	0.06	35.36
Constant	7.83	0.07	11,646.11

Variables not in the equation

Variable	B IN	F
LNF1	0.46	27.47
LNV2	0.35	23.12
NPSO	0.66	15.23
CASTE1	0.05	0.19
CASTE2	0.004	0.001

§ 6.8.2 The Distribution of Income

The distribution of income by caste is displayed in Table 6.14. The two richest castes are the *Thakurs* and the *Muraos*. Between them they share 57.5 per cent of the income although they contribute 46.8 per cent of the households and 46.5 per cent of the population. They are themselves roughly equal in income—the *Thakurs* have a slightly higher income per household and the *Muraos* a very slightly higher income per capita. The next caste in terms of income is the *Passis*. We saw in Chapters 2 and 4 that the *Thakurs* and *Muraos*

Table 6.13(b) The Determinants of Income—Logarithmic

Multiple R	0.82	Number of cases	81
R Squared	0.67	Number of variables	4
Standard error	0.31	F-Value for equation	39.02
		Dependent variable	LNINCM

Variables in the equation

Variable	B	Standard error of B	F
LNLANDO	0.18	0.05	16.24
LNF1	0.42	0.07	33.76
LNV2	0.32	0.06	28.46
NPSO	0.31	0.14	5.08
Constant	5.88		

Variables not in the equation

Variable	B IN	F
CASTE 1	−0.01	0.02
CASTE 2	0.02	0.04

Notes : (i) See notes to Table 5.7.
(ii) For definitions of variables see Table 6.3.

at the end of § 6.3.

Table 6.14 The caste distribution of income

Caste	Number of households	Number of individuals	Total income (rupees)	Share in total %	Income per household	Income per capita
Thakur 1	25	174	219964	28.0	8799	1264
Murao 2	27	178	232080	29.5	8596	1304
Dhimar 3	8	59	46810	6.0	5851	793
Gadaria 4	10	68	61013	7.8	6101	897
Dhobi 5	3	22	14783	1.9	4928	672
Teli 6	12	71	54356	6.9	4530	766
Passi 7	8	61	66192	8.4	8274	1085
Jatab 8	14	97	69360	8.8	4954	715
Other 9	4	27	21687	2.8	5422	803
Total	111	757	786245	100.1	7083	1039

Notes: (i) Income figures are taken from column (10) of Table 6.2. There is a slight discrepancy with figures in Table 6.15 because of rounding. (ii) Omissions and error concerning income are discussed in the presentation of Table 6.2 at the end of § 6.3.

are particularly well endowed with land and the *Passis* have a relatively high number of outside jobs (particularly with the railways). Table 6.2 on the components of income confirms the importance of labour income for the *Passis* and the high income from land of the *Thakurs* and *Muraos*. All the other castes have below average income per household or per capita with the poorest being the *Dhobis* and the *Jatabs*.

Observe that the caste ranking by income per household is not exactly the same as income per capita. For example the ranking between the *Thakurs* and *Muraos* is reversed, and *Telis* who have the lowest income per household exceed both the *Dhobis* and *Jatabs* in income per capita. The spread of caste income per household, measured by the ratio of maximum to minimum (1.94), is equal to the spread of caste income per capita.

The average income per household is 7083 rupees and per capita is 1039 rupees. This last figure is quite close to an estimate of the average per capita income for India[11] in 1974–5 of 1022 rupees.

The distribution of income by household is presented in Table 6.15. One should not infer from the ranking of average income by caste just discussed that there is an overwhelming relationship between caste and income for the individual household. For example the bottom five households contain one *Thakur*, two *Muraos*, one *Dhimar*, and one *Gadaria* household. On the other hand the top fifteen households are all *Thakur* or *Murao* with the exception of the ninth and tenth households in the ranking (*Passi* and *Gadaria* respectively).

Table 6.15 The household distribution of income

Decile	Rank order of households in decile (bottom=1, top=111)	Income of decile (rupees)	Share in total %	Cumulative income (rupees)	Share in total %
1 (Bottom)	1-11	17 844	2.3	17 844	2.3
2	12-22	34 435	4.4	52 279	6.6
3	23-33	46 202	5.9	98 481	12.5
4	34-44	52 610	6.7	151 091	19.2
5	45-55	58 246	7.4	209 337	26.6
6	56-66	70 003	8.9	279 340	35.5
7	67-77	79 368	10.1	358 708	45.6
8	78-88	97 183	12.4	455 891	58.0
9	89-99	119 565	15.2	575 456	73.2
10 (Top)	100-111	210 743	26.8	786 199	100%

Maximum income R 32 174; Minimum income R 1149.

Note : Omissions and errors concerning income are discussed in the presentation of Table 6.2 at the end of § 6.3.

The lowest households in social status, the Sweepers and the *Jatabs*, are on the whole in the lower half of the order but not right at the bottom. For example there are only two *Jatab* households in the bottom twenty and the Sweeper household, with an income of 4646 rupees per annum (six members of the family), is 36th from bottom[12].

The five richest households have incomes in rupees per annum 32 174 (27), 23 682 (11), 20 524 (5), 19 357 (8), 16 074 (8) respectively, where we have shown

[11] See 'Report on Currency and Finance 1975-6 Vol.I', Reserve Bank of India, Bombay.

[12] Recall that one of the deficiencies of our measure of income is that we have not been able to include income from service employment. Thus we underestimate the Sweeper's true income quite considerably.

the number of household members in brackets. The five poorest households have incomes 1149 (1), 1235 (6), 1267 (4), 1299 (1), 1446 (3). Note how the richest households generally have more household members than the poor. Thus measuring inequality with households as the basic unit would appear to give a greater dispersion of incomes than would a measurement with individuals as the basic unit. Note that one cannot infer that big households necessarily have a higher proportion of children since the very large households will usually involve more than one family. A common way of dealing with income comparisons between households of different sizes and compositions is to use household equivalence scales (one calculates income per 'equivalent' family member). We did not attempt to perform these calculations.

The household with highest income is *Murao* and that with lowest income is *Gadaria*. However the household with highest income per capita is *Thakur* (third in the household income ranking) with 4105 rupees per member per annum, and that with the lowest is *Murao* (second from bottom in the household income ranking) with 206 rupees per member per annum.

We have used two types of summary measure of the inequality of the income distribution. The first is the Gini coefficient and the second the Atkinson index. The former is defined as

$$1 + \frac{1}{n} - \frac{2}{n^2 \bar{y}} \left\{ ny_1 + (n-1)y_2 + \ldots + 2y_{n-1} + y_n \right\} \tag{3}$$

where n is the number of individuals y_i is the income of individual rank i ($y_1 \le y_2 \le y_3 \le \ldots \le y_{n-1} \le y_n$), and $\bar{y}$ is the mean income. It represents the area between the Lorenz curve and the 45° line as a proportion of the area below the 45° line in the standard diagram—see Fig. 6.2 (the Lorenz curve is the graph of

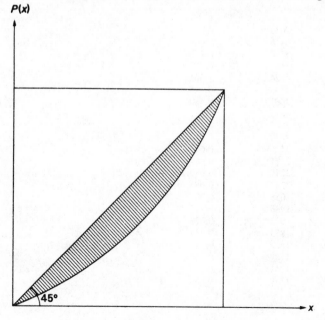

Fig. 6.2

A Lorenz curve of income distribution

$P(x)$ the proportion of income received by the poorest x, expressed as a fraction, of the population). The Atkinson index is constructed as follows. We calculate first the equally distributed equivalent income, $\hat{y}$, which is defined as

$$nu(\hat{y}) = \sum_{i=1}^{n} u(y_i) \tag{4}$$

where $u(\ )$ is a social valuation or utility function. Thus, if each individual had exactly the income $\hat{y}$, the level of social welfare would be regarded as equivalent to the distribution $(y_1, y_2, \ldots y_n)$. The Atkinson index of inequality is then defined as $1 - (\hat{y}/\bar{y})$. Properties of both the Gini coefficient and the Atkinson index are discussed in Atkinson (1970).

The Gini coefficient for the distribution of household income in Palanpur is 0.326. This may be compared with indices for the distribution of incomes in poor countries of around 0.4 and 0.5 which are calculated in Anand (1978) and Atkinson (1970), although it should be remembered that such statistics are for the whole country rather than for individual villages.

The Atkinson index for various utility functions is presented in Table 6.16. We use the isoelastic form $u(y) = y^{1-\eta}/1 - \eta$, $\eta > 0$. When $\eta = 1$, $u(y) = \log_e y$. When $\eta = 0$, we have $\hat{y} = \bar{y}$ and as $\eta \to \infty$, $\hat{y}$ tends to the minimum income.

The numbers in Table 6.16 may be compared with the following numbers reported by Atkinson in his paper (1970): for n = 1, $1\frac{1}{2}$, and 2 he finds for India in 1950 an index of inequality of 0.297, 0.359, and 0.399. These are to be compared with 0.175, 0.261, and 0.341 from Table 6.16.

Table 6.16 Atkinson index for distribution of household incomes

η	$\hat{y}$	$1 - \hat{y}/\bar{y}$
0	7083	0
½	6418	0.086
1	5790	0.175
1½	5190	0.261
2 .	4624	0.341
2½	4105	0.415
3	3651	0.480
3½	3272	0.534
4	2965	0.578
4½	2720	0.612
5	2526	0.640
5½	2371	0.662
6	2246	0.680
6½	2143	0.695
7	2058	0.707
7½	1986	0.717
8	1925	0.726
8½	1873	0.733
9	1827	0.740
9½	1787	0.745
10	1751	0.750
∞	1149	0.836

Thus the income distribution in Palanpur appears rather more equal than that for poor countries in general, whether we measure inequality by the Gini coefficient or the Atkinson index. We must bear in mind, however, that we are here comparing inequality in one village with that for a country. One can clearly find greater extremes of poverty and wealth in a country than in one village.

We should emphasize here that specifying the household as the unit for measuring income distribution may imply more inequality (as measured by the above indices) than would arise from taking the individual as a unit since, on the whole, larger households have higher incomes. This arises because the larger households usually involve more than one family living together and taking cultivating decisions together. But one must take care here, because it does not necessarily follow that a positive correlation between income and household size implies that an inequality index is lower for the distribution of income across individuals (where one supposes, for example, equal sharing of income inside the household) than for households (for a thorough analysis of these problems see Anand, 1978). Further, our omission of service incomes under-states the incomes of some of the poorer households, although this may be partially offset in the measurement of inequality by the omission of income from interest and rental of farm assets. Such income would accrue to richer households.

§ 6.9 Concluding Remarks

We shall be brief here since our main economic conclusions have been set out in § 6.6. We have studied in this chapter, using simple regression analysis, the determinants of output and income in Palanpur. Certain striking conclusions have emerged.

We found that output was roughly proportional to land cultivated, in clear contrast to several other studies of Indian agriculture. We argued in § 6.6 that this should not be seen as puzzling since many of the arguments advanced, in the discussion surrounding previous studies, to explain the apparent diminishing relation between output per acre and cultivated area do not apply, or do not apply strongly, to Palanpur. In particular we should stress the absence of large farms from the village.

The number of adult males engaged in agriculture was not a significant variable in the explanation of any of the outputs. We argued that this finding was consistent with the theory discussed in § 6.1 and § 3.3. Both the theory and our finding cast serious doubt on the use of the simple variable, number of workers, in production functions for peasant agriculture.

We found that the value marginal product of fertilizer in the *rabi* season was around twice the marginal cost, where competitive conditions and certainty should imply equality. We discuss possible explanations for our finding in detail in § 8.6 and we shall there lay particular stress on the role of uncertainty.

The value of draught animals was only occasionally significant as an explanation of output. Where it was significant the gross annual returns, in cultivation, to ownership of draught animals appeared to be around 85 per cent of the value of the animals.

All of the variables, land owned, number of adult males, value of animals owned, and number of pumping sets owned, were significant explanations of income.

We found that the propensity to leave land fallow bore no significant relation to wealth or size of cultivated holding. On the other hand, the intensity of cultivation, as measured by fertilizer per cultivated area, was positively correlated with wealth but yet more strongly correlated with size of cultivated holding.

The level of income per capita in Palanpur was found to be around the average for India. It seems that the distribution of income in Palanpur is rather more equal than one generally finds for the whole of a poor country such as India.

Appendix to Chapter 6

In this appendix we present our regression analysis of the determinants of output for the three components *rabi* (non-sugar), *kharif* (non-sugar), and sugar. The *rabi* results for the linear model are given in Table 6.A.1 and for the three logarithmic cases in 6.A.2, 6.A.3, and 6.A.4. We have separate logarithmic results since, as explained in § 6.5, the number of observations decreases with the number of included explanatory variables: in Table 6.A.2 we have as logged explanatory variables, land cultivated in *rabi* and *F3*; for Table 6.A.3 we add *V1*, and for Table 6.A.4 *rabi* fertilizer. Table 6.A.5 gives *kharif* linear results and 6.A.6 and 6.A.7 the logarithmic cases. There are just two such cases since we do not include fertilizer (we have data only for *rabi* fertilizer). Table 6.A.8 contains the linear sugar results and 6.A.9 and 6.A.10 the logarithmic.

Our criterion for the inclusion of an observation in both *rabi* linear and *kharif* linear regressions was that the household concerned be involved in cultivation in the sense of strictly positive *GAO*. For the case of the single crop sugar we included in the linear regression only those households with strictly positive sugar output. In the logarithmic regressions those households with zero outputs are automatically excluded.

The main features of the results have been summarized at the end of § 6.5 and certain other aspects such as the role of fertilizer in the *rabi* season, in the main body of the chapter. We do not therefore present any further discussion here.

Table 6.A.1 (a) *Rabi* Output on *Rabi* Land Cultivated—Linear

Multiple *R*	0.93	Number of cases	93
R Squared	0.86	Number of variables	1
Standard error	764.89	*F*-Value for equation	575.79
		Dependent variable	*GRNSO*

Variables in the equation			
Variable	*B*	Standard error of *B*	*F*
NSCULTR	155.54	6.48	575.79
Constant	− 266.57	28.55	87.21

Variables not in the equation		
Variable	*B* IN	*F*
F3	375.20	11.36
V1	0.23	1.36
FERT	2.07	24.46
NPSO	1224.33	15.83
CASTE1	372.41	4.21
CASTE2	− 189.03	1.06

Table 6.A. 1(b) The Determinants of *Rabi* Output—Linear (Excluding *LNVI* and *LNFERT*)

Multiple *R*	0.95	Number of cases	93
R Squared	0.91	Number of variables	5
Standard error	634.53	*F*-Value for equation	176.38
		Dependent variable	*GRNSO*

Variables in the equation

Variable	*B*	Standard error of *B*	*F*
NSCULTR	124.20	9.38	175.22
F3	225.35	102.62	4.82
V1	−0.23	0.18	1.60
FERT	1.78	0.44	16.52
NPSO	−868.03	286.87	9.16
Constant	−158.75		

Variables not in the equation

Variable	*B* IN	*F*
CASTE1	53.09	0.10
CASTE2	−147.00	0.88

Notes : (i) See notes to Table 5.7.
(ii) For definitions of variables see Table 6.3.

Table 6.A. 2(a) *Rabi* Output on *Rabi* Land Cultivated—Logarithmic
(Excluding *LNVI* and *LNFERT*)

Multiple *R*	0.95	Number of cases	78
R Squared	0.90	Number of variables	1
Standard error	0.24	*F*-Value for equation	703.24
		Dependent variable	*LNGRNSO*

Variables in the equation

Variable	*B*	Standard error of *B*	*F*
LNNSCLTR	1.11	0.04	703.24
Constant	4.57	0.06	5463.81

Variables not in the equation

Variable	*B* IN	*F*
LNF3	0.08	1.34
NPSO	0.17	3.06
CASTE1	0.04	0.38
CASTE2	−0.04	0.31

Table 6.A. 2(b). The Determinants of *Rabi* Output—Logarithmic (Excluding *LNVI* and *LNFERT*)

Multiple *R*	0.95	Number of cases	78
R Squared	0.91	Number of variables	3
Standard error	0.24	*F*-Value for equation	240.13
		Dependent variable	*LNGRNSO*

Variables in the equation

Variable	*B*	Standard error of *B*	*F*
LNNSCLTR	1.08	0.05	568.39
LNF3	0.05	0.08	0.45
NPSO	0.15	0.11	2.12
Constant	4.64		

Variables not in the equation

Variable	*B* IN	*F*
CASTE1	0.01	0.05
CASTE2	− 0.04	0.38

Notes : (i) See notes to Table 5.7
     (ii) For definitions of variables see Table 6.3.

Table 6 A. 3(a) *Rabi* Output on *Rabi* Land Cultivated—Logarithmic (Excluding *LNFERT*)

Multiple *R*	0.91	Number of cases	69
R Squared	0.84	Number of variables	1
Standard error	0.23	*F*-Value for equation	344.43
		Dependent Variable	*LNGRNSO*

Variables in the equation

Variable	*B*	Standard error of *B*	*F*
LNNSCLTR	1.04	0.06	344.43
Constant	4.79	0.13	1,409.90

Variables not in the equation

Variable	*B* IN	*F*
LNF3	0.11	2.65
NPSO	0.22	5.46
CASTE1	0.09	2.24
CASTE2	− 0.03	0.26
LNVI	0.12	4.12

Notes: (i) See notes to Table 5.7.
     (ii) For definitions of variables see Table 6.3.

Table 6.A. 3(b) The Determinants of *Rabi* Output—Logarithmic (Excluding *LNFERT*)

Multiple *R*	0.93	Number of cases	69
R Squared	0.86	Number of variables	4
Standard error	0.22	*F*-Value for equation	95.20
		Dependent variable	*LNGRNSO*

Variables in the equation

Variable	*B*	Standard error or *B*	*F*
LNNSCLTR	0.94	0.07	202.64
LNV1	0.08	0.06	1.82
LNF3	0.07	0.07	0.87
NPSO	0.15	0.10	2.31
Constant	4.50		

Variables not in the equation

Variable	*B* IN	*F*
CASTE1	0.07	1.08
CASTE2	−0.05	0.70

Notes : (i) See notes to Table 5.7
(ii) For definitions of variables See Table 6.3.

Table 6.A. 4(a) *Rabi* Output on *Rabi* Land Cultivated—Logarithmic.

Multiple *R*	0.90	Number of cases	57
R Squared	0.82	Number of variables	1
Standard error	0.20	*F*-Value for equation	244.77
		Dependent variable	*LNGRNSO*

Variables in the equation

Variable	*B*	Standard error of *B*	*F*
LNNSCLTR	1.00	0.06	244.77
Constant	4.95	0.19	663.47

Variables not in the equation

Variable	*B* IN	*F*
LNF3	0.16	5.95
NPSO	0.19	5.10
CASTE1	0.06	1.02
CASTE2	−0.03	0.25
LNV1	0.14	4.90
LNFERT	0.18	20.54

Table 6.A. 4(b) The Determinants of *Rabi* Output—Logarithmic

Multiple *R*	0.94	Number of cases	57
R Squared	0.88	Number of variables	5
Standard error	0.17	*F*-Value for equation	73.07
		Dependent variable	*LNGRNSO*

Variables in the equation

Variable	*B*	Standard error of *B*	*F*
LNNSCLTR	0.73	0.08	82.04
LNFERT	0.15	0.04	12.23
LNF3	0.08	0.06	1.56
NPSO	0.09	0.08	1.17
LNV1	0.03	0.06	0.17
Constant	4.80		

Variables not in the equation

Variable	*B* IN	*F*
CASTE1	− 0.04	0.41
CASTE2	− 0.03	0.32

Notes: (i) See notes to Table 5.7.
(ii) For definitions of variables see Table 6.3

Table 6.A.5(a) *Kharif* Output on *Kharif* Land Cultivated—Linear

Multiple *R*	0.85	Number of cases	93
R Squared	0.72	Number of variables	1
Standard error	613.75	*F*-Value for equation	229.78
		Dependent variable	*GKNSO*

Variables in the equation

Variable	*B*	Standard error of *B*	*F*
NSCULTK	88.53	5.84	229.78
Constant	−6.11	22.67	0.07

Variables not in the equation

Variable	*B* IN	*F*
F3	15.07	0.03
V1	− 0.07	0.21
NPSO	411.02	2.44
CASTE1	64.54	0.18
CASTE2	− 34.07	0.05

Table 6.A.5 (b) The Determinants of *Kharif* Output—Linear

Multiple *R*	0.85	Number of cases	93
R Squared	0.73	Number of variables	4
Standard error	613.68	*F*-Value for equation	58.21
		Dependent variable	*GKNSO*

Variables in the equation

Variable	*B*	Standard error of *B*	*F*
NSCULTK	89.02	8.84	101.36
F3	−1.75	98.11	0.00
V1	−0.12	0.15	0.59
NPSO	453.52	274.69	2.73
Constant	45.81		

Variables not in the equation

Variable	*B* IN	*F*
CASTE1	14.89	0.01
CASTE2	−39.28	0.07

Notes : (i) See notes to Table 5.7.
      (ii) For definitions of variables see Table 6.3.

Table 6.A.6 (a) *Kharif* Output on *Kharif* Land Cultivated—Logarithmic (Excluding *LNV1*)

Multiple *R*	0.87	Number of cases	78
R Squared	0.76	Number of variables	1
Standard error	0.34	*F*-Value for equation	234.58
		Dependent variable	*LNGKNSO*

Variables in the equation

Variable	*B*	Standard error of *B*	*F*
LNNSCLTK	0.90	0.06	234.58
Constant	4.69	0.08	119.78

Variables not in the equation

Variable	*B* IN	*F*
LNF3	0.12	1.36
NPSO	0.21	2.29
CASTE1	0.04	0.22
CASTE2	0.04	0.17

Table 6.A.6 (b) The Determinants of *Kharif* Output—Logarithmic (Excluding *LNVI*)

Multiple *R*	0.87	Number of cases	78
R Squared	0.76	Number of variables	3
Standard error	0.33	*F*-Value for equation	79.97
		Dependent variable	*LNGKNSO*

Variables in the equation

Variable	*B*	Standard error of *B*	*F*
LNNSCLTK	0.86	0.06	183.03
LNF3	0.08	0.11	0.54
NPSO	0.17	0.15	1.45
Constant	4.76		

Variables not in the equation

Variable	*B* IN	*F*
CASTE1	0.02	0.04
CASTE2	0.03	0.10

Notes : (i) See notes to Table 5.7.
(ii) For definitions of variables see Table 6.3.

Table 6. A 7(a) *Kharif* Output on *Kharif* Land Cultivated—Logarithmic

Multiple *R*	0.79	Number of cases	69
R Squared	0.62	Number of variables	1
Standard error	0.34	*F*-Value for equation	107.62
		Dependent variable	*LNGKNSO*

Variables in the equation

Variable	*B*	Standard error or *B*	*F*
LNNSCLTK	0.83	0.08	107.62
Constant	4.92	0.16	899.61

Variables not in the equation

Variable	*B* IN	*F*
LNF3	0.12	1.39
NPSO	0.24	2.92
CASTE1	0.11	1.36
CASTE2	0.0001	0.00
LNV1	0.04	0.27

Table 6 A.7(b) The Determinants of *Kharif* Output—Logarithmic

Multiple *R*	0.80	Number of cases	69
R Squared	0.64	Number of variables	4
Standard error	0.33	*F*-Value for equation	27.89
		Dependent variable	*LNGKNSO*

Variables in the equation

Variable	*B*	Standard error of *B*	*F*
LNNSCLTK	0.78	0.09	74.44
LNV1	−0.01	0.09	0.02
LNF3	0.08	0.11	0.51
NPSO	0.21	0.15	1.89
Constant	5.12		

Variables not in the equation

Variable	*B* IN	*F*
CASTE1	0.09	0.82
CASTE2	−0.01	0.02

Notes :   (i) See notes to Table 5.7
(ii) For Definition of variables see Table 6.3

Table 6.A.8 (a) Sugar Output on Sugar Land Cultivated—Linear

Multiple *R*	0.89	Number of cases	61
R Squared	0.79	Number of variables	1
Standard error	783.44	*F*-Value for equation	226.74
		Dependent variable	*SUGAR*

Variables in the equation

Variable	*B*	Standard error of *B*	*F*
SCULT	280.62	18.64	226.74
Constant	15.71	37.77	0.17

Variables not in the equation

Variable	*B* IN	*F*
F3	95.25	0.60
V1	0.33	4.31
NPSO	803.93	4.61
CASTE1	−29.34	0.02
CASTE2	439.13	4.14

Table 6.A. 8(b) The Determinants of Sugar Output—Linear

Multiple R	0.90	Number of cases	61
R Squared	0.82	Number of variables	4
Standard error	755.83	F-Value for equation	62.75
		Dependent variable	*SUGAR*

Variables in the equation

Variable	B	Standard error of B	F
SUCLT	247.22	22.40	121.83
F3	−68.76	136.41	0.25
V1	0.30	0.18	2.67
NPSO	673.64	391.48	2.96
Constant	4.14		

Variables not in the equation

Variable	B IN	F
CASTE1	−219.22	0.89
CASTE2	461.29	4.70

Notes : (i) See notes to Table 5.7.
(ii) For definitions of variables see Table 6.3.

Table 6.A. 9(a) Sugar Output on Sugar Land Cultivated—Logarithmic

Multiple R	0.94	Number of cases	54
R Squared	0.88	Number of variables	1
Standard error	0.27	F-Value for equation	384.29
		Dependent Variable	*LNSUGAR*

Variables in the equation

Variable	B	Standard error of B	F
LNSCULT	1.01	0.05	384.29
Constant	5.59	0.03	26,239.29

Variables not in the equation

Variable	B IN	F
LNF3	−0.05	0.36
NPSO	0.05	0.18
LNVI	0.18	5.67
CASTE1	−0.07	0.66
CASTE2	0.12	2.14

Table 6.A. 9(b) The Determinants of Sugar Output—Logarithmic

Multiple R	0.95	Number of cases	54
R Squared	0.90	Number of variables	4
Standard error	0.25	F-Value for equation	108.15
		Dependent variable	*LNSUGAR*

Variables in the equation

Variable	B	Standard error of B	F
LNSCULT	1.00	0.06	270.6
LNF3	−0.14	0.09	2.57
NPSO	0.01	0.13	0.002
LNVI	0.23	0.08	7.55
Constant	4.15		

Variables not in the equation

Variable	B IN	F
CASTE1	−0.08	1.10
CASTE2	0.08	1.06

Notes : (i) See notes to Table 5.7.
         (ii) For definitions of variables see Table 6.3.

Table 6.A.10 (a) Sugar Output on Sugar Land Cultivated—Logarithmic (excluding *LNVI)*

Multiple R	0.93	Number of cases	57
R Squared	0.87	Number of variables	1
Standard error	0.29	F-Value for equation	361.63
		Dependent variable	*LNSUGAR*

Variables in the equation

Variable	B	Standard error of B	F
LNSCULT	1.00	0.05	361.63
Constant	5.59	0.03	26,398.15

Variables not in the equation

Variable	B IN	F
LNF3	−0.08	0.66
NPSO	0.09	0.46
CASTE1	−0.04	0.18
CASTE2	0.16	3.34

Table 6.A. 10(b) The Determinants of Sugar Output—Logarithmic

Multiple R	0.93	Number of cases	57
R Squared	0.87	Number of variables	3
Standard error	0.29	F-Value for equation	120.15
		Dependent variable	*LNSUGAR*

Variables in the equation

Variable	B	Standard error of B	F
LNSUCLT	0.98	0.06	272.14
LNF3	−0.10	0.10	1.12
NPSO	0.13	0.14	0.92
Constant	5.63		

Variables not in the equation

Variable	B IN	F
CASTE1	−0.04	0.20
CASTE2	0.15	2.97

Notes : (i) See notes to Table 5.7.
(ii) For definitions of variables see Table 6.3.

7

WHEAT : The New Varieties and Practices in Palanpur

§ 7.0 Introduction

Wheat is of special interest for several reasons. It is the most important *rabi* crop in Palanpur, covering 42 per cent of cultivated land in *rabi* 1974–5. The cultivation of wheat plays a central role in the Indian economy in general. It occupies 76 per cent of the area under winter cereals. About 87 per cent of that area lies in North and Central India (ICAR, 1969, p. 151). Wheat is central to the North Indian diet, mostly eaten in the form of *chapatis*, and the straw is an important source of feed for cattle. Finally the cultivation of wheat in India in general and Palanpur in particular has undergone interesting and rapid changes over the past decade with the introduction of new varieties and the extension of irrigation. The new varieties and associated practices are discussed in § 7.1.

One of the centre–pieces of our study was the collection and analysis of data on our sample of forty–seven wheat plots in the village. The collection occupied a great deal of the time of our research investigators and ourselves while we were in the village. The discussion and analysis of this body of data are the main topics of this and the next chapter. The selection of sample plots and the method of our observations are described in § 7.2. In § 7.3 we shall discuss the cultivation practices of the farmers in Palanpur. We shall introduce the notion of 'good practice'. The choice of agricultural technique has been a major theme in discussions of development, particularly in relation to the new varieties and the so–called 'Green Revolution' (see § 3.9). A second major issue in the literature has been the relation between tenancy and agricultural practice. An analysis of the differences in cultivation between tenanted and owner-cultivated plots is the subject matter of § 7.4. The final section is devoted to concluding remarks.

We are concerned, therefore, in this and the next chapter with a detailed analysis of farmers' input decisions for just one crop, wheat. We shall be paying particular attention in the next chapter to a comparison between our estimates of the relation between inputs and outputs and the farmers' beliefs about the productivity of their inputs. In this chapter, however, we concentrate on the background of the new varieties in India, practices in Palanpur, and tenancy. The outcome of our regression analysis and the interpretation of estimated coefficients is postponed until Chapter 8. The reader who knows about, or is not interested in, the detail of the technicalities of the cultivation of the high–yielding varieties may wish to pass straight to § 7.2.

§ 7.1. The New Varieties, the Recommended Level of Inputs, Agricultural Practices and Problems.

§ 7.1.1. The New Varieties

The 'high-yielding varieties' of wheat, or *HYVs* as they became known, were introduced into India in the mid–1960s. The original advances in the development of these new types of wheat were made in Mexico by Dr Norman Borlaug in the 1950s. He first gave samples for trial plantings in North India in 1963. The first year of large–scale adoption by farmers was 1966. Thereafter the acreage under these new varieties built up very quickly. For example, in the Punjab it grew from 130 000 acres in 1966–7 to 5 000 000 acres in 1971–2 (Randhawa, 1974, p.69). The most popular of the new varieties in the initial expansion in the Punjab were called Kalyansona and *PV18*, and in U.P., Sonalika.

These new wheats are bred to accept, in a sense to be discussed below, high doses of nitrogenous fertilizers and controlled irrigation. There is a continuous stream of new varieties which have been developed in different countries and regions with an emphasis on different properties. We shall concentrate here on Indian varieties for discussion of the properties relevant for our study.

One should distinguish at the outset between various terms such as dwarf, improved, Mexican, and high-yielding which are often applied interchangeably to wheat varieties. Dwarf, semi-dwarf, and tall clearly refer to the height of the wheat. Roughly speaking, at maturity the dwarf wheats are 75 cm, semi-dwarfs 110 cm, and tall wheats are 140 cm, although there is substantial variation within categories. Most of the new varieties which have been extensively adopted in North India in the late 1960s and early 1970s are semi-dwarf. For example, RR21 (the most popular variety in Palanpur) averages 110 cm (Gill, 1974, p.6.).

The height is determined by the number of dwarfing genes: the number is 0, 1, 2, or 3. The traditional wheats have no dwarfing genes. We call a triple-gene variety a dwarf, and varieties with one or two dwarfing genes semi-dwarfs. RR21 has one dwarfing gene and Kalyansona, with two dwarfing genes, averages 95 cm at maturity. (For further detail see ICAR, 1968, pp.43-52.)

'Improved' is obviously a nebulous term. Formal study of wheat varieties has been going on in India since the turn of the century with work by Milne in U.P. in the 1890s (Gill, 1974) and by the Howards, who began research in 1905, at the Imperial Institute of Agricultural Research at Pusa in Bihar. The varieties the Howards developed won prizes at International Grain Exhibitions in 1916–20 and were used as parents in wheat development programmes in many countries (see Kohli, 1968, p. 17). The most popular of the domestic improved wheats in Palanpur was K 68, a tall variety developed in Kanpur. The domestic strains are known as *desi* wheats and, where they have been subject to selection, improved *desi*. Thus K68 is improved *desi*. Currently the variety C306 released by the Punjab Agricultural University at Ludhiana in 1965 is considered the best of the improved *desi* varieties (see Gill, 1974).

Attractions of the improved *desi* varieties, as against the newer varieties discussed below, are that their *chapatis* are considered tasty, they are generally hardy and fairly resistant to pests (see below § 7.1.3), and the longer straw provides (for a given grain output) more fodder. The grain-to-straw ratio, by weight, for C306 is 1:2.1 but for *PV18* 1:1.5. Of course, a shorter strawed variety can provide equal fodder if the number of straws is sufficiently large. Some of the early Mexican varieties (such as Lerma Rojo) were considered unattractive because the grain was red as compared with the amber of *desi* varieties.

The significance of the material brought to India by Borlaug from Mexico in 1963 was that it possessed the desired maturity period for North Indian conditions (where temperatures rise very rapidly in March) as well as significantly superior lodging and rust resistance (see § 7.1.3). (Lodging is the name given to the buckling of the straw so that the plant falls over.) Lodging had been the major obstacle to the achievement of high yield with high doses of fertilizers with traditional varieties because the heavy ear resulting from the fertilizer caused the straw to collapse. The imported Mexican varieties were either dwarf or semi-dwarf and this shorter stature went with a resistance to lodging which was crucial to the provision of high yield from high applications of fertilizer.

The variety RR21 is a strain of Sonalika (the descriptions are often used interchangeably—see Pantnagar, 1974) which in turn was a selection from one of the original 1963 Mexican samples S308. Sonalika was the most popular new variety in U.P. in the early 1970s. Similarly Kalyansona, the most popular variety in the remarkable expansion of the new varieties through the Punjab from 1966–7 to 1971–2, was a selection from one of the original Mexican samples S227. It is to Kalyansona and Sonalika that most new varieties are compared (see Gill, 1974).

The term Mexican clearly refers to the geographical origin of a seed type and Mexican wheats can be semi-dwarf (such as Kalyansona or Sonalika) or dwarf, but the varieties of the first 1963 batch were semi-dwarf.

Wheat-breading stations throughout India are now developing new varieties from combining through crosses, mutations, and selections, the superior plant type of the Mexican varieties with the excellent grain qualities (in particular taste and colour) of the Indian varieties (Kohli, 1968, p.65). An example of the newer crosses which was used in Palanpur is Hira. This is a triple-gene variety which has been studied at the U.P. Agricultural University at Pantnagar (Pantnagar, 1974). This was adopted by one of the more analytic and enthusiastic of the farmers (Man Singh see § 2.A.2 and § 7.3) in 1971 at the same time as its properties were being examined at Pantnagar. A second example of the newer crosses is 2009, also used by Man Singh, which had been released only in *rabi* 1974-75.

In Palanpur, therefore, we have examples of *desi*, improved *desi* (K68), Mexican semi-dwarfs (Sonalika—*RR21*), and the newer crosses (Hira—which is a dwarf). The term 'high-yielding varieties' or '*HYVs*' is generally used to cover all the dwarf and semi-dwarf varieties, but usually excludes the improved *desi* varieties.

The responsiveness of the different varieties to varying input levels is discussed in the next sub-section (§ 7.1.2) and resistance to various pests in § 7.1.3.

§ 7.1.2. The Recommended Level of Inputs and Agricultural Practice

We shall describe briefly the work at research institutes on the effect of varying input levels. It is on such research that recommended agricultural practices are based. First, however, we summarize these packages and the High Yielding Varieties Programme (*HYVP*) which was launched by the Government of India to promote the new varieties in the later 1960s. The HYVP was an important part of the New Agricultural Strategy of the Indian Fourth Plan (1969–1974) under which about 30 per cent of the area under wheat, rice, maize, *jowar*, and *bajra* was designated to be under HYVs. The Programme followed the experience of the Intensive Agricultural District Programme (seven districts in 1961) and the more widely spread Intensive Agricultural Area Programme (114 districts in 1965).

The HYVP was adopted by the U.P. government in 1966 – 7. In 1970 – 1 32 per cent of the area under wheat in U.P. was 'targeted' for HYVs (see Chaudhari and Sirohi, 1973) and 49 per cent of the targeted wheat acreage was in the Western Region of U.P. (there being five regions in all). The State organizes, through the Districts and Blocks, the allocation of fertilizers and attempts to provide the new varieties of seed. Advice on agricultural practice is, in theory, available from the Village Level Worker who is responsible to the Block Development Officer. As we pointed out in Chapter 2, the Village Level Worker in Palanpur in 1974–5 was responsible for nine other villages and had insufficient time to give such advice. And it was not clear that he was qualified to provide it even had he had the time. Some credit in Palanpur was made available through the Block and in particular the Co-operative Seed Store, subject to certain rules (see § 4.3), for the purchase of fertilizers and seeds. The construction of irrigation facilities was not usually financed by the agencies of the Block, but where credit was available, by official bodies through various agricultural organizations.

The aim of the HYVP was to promote the adoption of 'appropriate' high-yielding variety 'package' of practices and inputs. This meant sowing at a certain time, depth, seed rate, and spacing; irrigating at particular times; applying recommended types and quantities of pesticides. The administration of the advice and the organization of the supply of inputs was, to put it mildly, patchy. The adoption of the full package by farmers in our area was very rare and in Palanpur itself, absent. The particular practices in Palanpur are discussed in the next section.

We now summarize the main recommendations. These differ between varieties and areas but are broadly similar for the high-yielding varieties. We give the suggested practices for RR21, the most popular wheat in Palanpur, and they apply to that locality and medium quality soils. Most of the information on recommended practices was given to us (on 8 February 1975) by Shri Kumar of IFFCO in Moradabad. He is the agronomist in charge of fertilizer advice in the District. The advice is delivered through IFFCO and the State agricultural administration and generally emanates from agricultural research stations and university departments, such as Pantnagar in U.P.and Ludhiana in the Punjab. Shri Kumar visited the Seed Store from time to time and while we were there conducted a 'seminar' on fertilizer use for a group of local farmers.

The recommended sowing date for RR21 is 10 November. The growing season is 120–5 days. The recommended seed rate is 40kg/acre[1] and the depth of sowing should be two inches. The depth of sowing is significantly different from the more traditional varieties which were normally sown at around four inches deep. The recommended number of irrigations (excluding pre-irrigation) is six for 'timely' sowing. In the *rabi* season 1974–5 there were quite good winter rains and Shri Kumar suggested that for later sowing three to four irrigations were sufficient. The six stages for irrigation (with 'timely' sowing) are at the following days after sowing.

21	40	60	80	100	115
Crown root initiation	Late tillering	Late jointing	Flowering	Milky stage	Dough

The most important irrigation, in the sense of its omission causing the greatest loss, is the first, since the effect on the number of tillers can be substantial.

The recommended dose of nitrogen for RR21 is 48 kg per acre.[2] Half the nitrogen should be applied as a basal dressing at the time of sowing and the remainder broadcast as a top dressing at the time of the first irrigation (this application should be followed by immediate irrigation). The nitrogen is usually applied when used as a top dressing in the form of urea which is 46 per cent nitrogen. One bag is (in principle) 50kg (or half a quintal) and in the *rabi* season 1974–5 cost 105 rupees. Thus the required number of bags of urea to meet the recommendations for an acre would be $48/0.46 \times 1/50 = 2.09$ and the cost at 105 rupees per bag would be 219 rupees. The recommended doses might result in a total output of 17 quintals would give 2210 rupees. We discuss returns to fertilizer use below. Phosphorus and potassium are also part of the package. The recommended applications are 24 kg of phosphate (P_2O_5) and 12 kg of potash (K_2O) per acre. The phosphate, potash, and half the nitrogenous fertilizer should be applied as a basal dressing at the time of sowing.

For the previous *rabi* and *kharif* seasons and up to 15 November 1974 the supply of fertilizer had been rationed by the government at fixed official prices. A considerable open market, at higher prices, developed. The government price

[1] Throughout Chapters 7 and 8 we shall use the acre as our unit of area. We wish to make comparisons with results from research stations and the recommended prectices—these are given in terms of acres or hectares. A translation to *bighas* might be confusing to some since the factor converting a '*bigha*' to an acre varies across India. We have throughout this book taken 1 acre to be 6.4 *bighas*.

[2] In order to avoid switching back and forth between land-units we have converted many figures from hectares to acres. Thus some numbers which appear as 'round' when expressed per hectare (e.g. 120 kg, per hectare) look rather 'less round' when expressed per acre (e.g. 48 kg per acre).

of urea in *rabi* 1973–4, for example, was 55 rupees per 50 kg bag and the open market price was 90-100 rupees. Around the time of sowing, therefore, fertilizer was either rationed or had just ceased to be rationed. There were no suitable basal fertilizers available in the Seed Store for use at the time of sowing and though such fertilizer was available in the markets in nearby towns at that time, it was not always easy to obtain.

In December 1974, however, urea was freely available in the market at the new higher official price of 105 rupees per 50 kg bag and thus there were no real problems in obtaining fertilizer for use as a top dressing at the right time, provided a farmer had the cash, or could borrow it, and could arrange transport from nearby centres. Urea was available in limited quantities on credit from the Seed Store during December 1974. There were frequent claims, however, that bags from the Seed Store were (up to 10 per cent) underweight.

Weeding and the use of weedkillers are recommended practices and, in particular, weeding is recommended about a month after sowing. The recommended pesticides and herbicides would cost about 20 rupees an acre.

The main variation between the recommendations for RR21 and the other high-yielding varieties is in the date of sowing. For example, the growing season for Kalyansona in the Moradabad District is 135 days, 10 days longer than for RR21, and the recommended sowing date is 1 November (or even the last week in October). The recommended seed rate is 35 kg/acre, slightly lower than for RR21.

For the improved *desi* varieties, for example, K68 and C306, roughly half the doses of fertilizer are recommended. If they are grown unirrigated all the fertilizer should be applied as a basal dressing at the time of sowing (see Ludhiana, 1974, p. 7).

We now turn to previous findings from research studies on the effects of varying practices and varieties. We begin with the role of fertilizers since it was for the ability to respond without lodging to high doses of fertilizers that the new shorter-strawed varieties were developed. Work on comparing yields from the first Mexican varieties and the *desi* varieties at different levels of fertilizer began quickly. It was established (Singh and Sharma, 1968 and 1969) that at low doses the yields are similar (see Fig. 7.1) but at higher doses the Mexican varieties produce much higher output per acre. Comparisons of the first Mexican varieties and *desi* varieties were soon followed by an examination of fertilizer responses in the newer strains selected from the Mexican sample (see Fig. 7.2), and then by a similar exercise on the newer varieties which were developed after the initial selections (see Fig. 7.3).

Curves such as those shown in Figs. 7.1, 7.2, 7.3, and the research behind them, form the basis of fertilizer recommendations. It is not always clear whether fertilizer recommendations are intended to achieve the maximum profit (thus, under the assumptions that markets are perfect and there is no uncertainty, where the value of the marginal product of a unit of fertilizer equals its price) or maximum yield (marginal product equals zero). Agronomists at research stations often say that fertilizer is recommended up to the point where

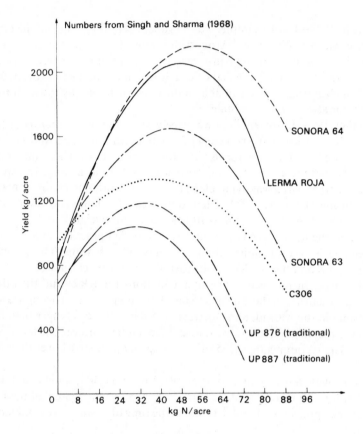

Fig. 7.1

Response of Original Mexican Varieties and Traditional (Desi) Varieties to Different Doses of Nitrogen.
Note: (i) The experiments were at U.P. Agricultural University, Pantnagar.
      (ii) The curves are quadratics fitted for each case.
      (iii) See § 7.1.2 for discussion.

its application yields 'insignificant' returns, yet when challenged as to whether this means marginal product equals zero suggest that they really had 'economic optimum' in mind. In the 1973 *Fertiliser Handbook* of the Fertiliser Association of India it is stated (p. 76), 'The results of the experiments are analysed to find out the most economical fertiliser recommendation under a given set of conditions'. Chapter 15 contain elaborations on methods of calculation although it seems to be *ex post facto* rationalization since the attempts to calculate economic optima using fitted functional forms from field trails, result (in most cases) in solutions *above* the actual recommendations. Agricultural economists on the other hand sometimes claim that the agronomists really do have maximum yield in mind and that the reason farmers apply less than the recommended amounts is that they recognize the difference between maximum yield and maximum profit and select the latter.

Examination of the response curves found in the research stations and the use

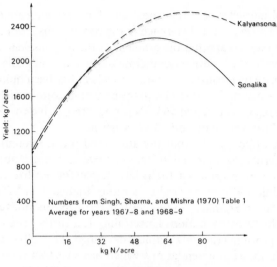

Fig. 7.2

Response of Selected Strains of Mexican Varieties to Different Doses of Nitrogen: Kalyansona, Sonalika

Note: (i) The curves are quadratics fitted for each case. The reported R^2 were 0.99 for Kalyansona and 0.94 for Sonalika.

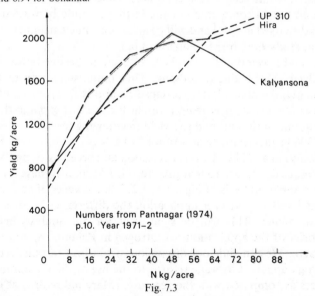

Fig. 7.3

Response of Recently Developed Varieties to Different Doses of Nitrogen: Hira, UP 310 (Kalyansona for Comparison)

Notes:
(i) The experiments were at U.P. Agricultural University (Pantnagar).
(ii) See § 7.1.2 for discussion.

of official market prices for wheat and fertilizer indicate that there does not seem to be a very great difference in the conclusions from the different objectives. The reasons are that the gradient of the response curve does not begin to drop off very much until a point close to the maximum has been reached, and that the price of fertilizer in relation to wheat has been quite low. For example Singh, Sharma, and Mishra (1970) found that maximum yield from Kalyansona and Sonalika was at 72 and 56 kg N per acre respectively whereas the 'economic optimum' rates were 68 and 53 kg N per acre.

It may, of course, be that the attempted profit maximizing choices of the farmers, as in the remark by the 'agricultural economist' above, are also correct but that the price farmers actually have to pay for fertilizer, taking into account adulteration and cost of credit, is rather higher than official prices and the (average and marginal) productivity of fertilizer on village plots rather lower than on the research station. Uncertainty is a further reason for applying less than the 'profit maximizing' choices described above. Risk aversion is generally ignored in the recommendations which are based on the results from experimental stations—the response curves relate output to input in given conditions and maximum profit is calculated assuming conditions of certainty. A clear indication that uncertainty is ignored is the recommendation that where a crop is unirrigated all fertilizer should be applied basally at the time of sowing. Risk aversion would lead a farmer to hold some top dressing back since if the rain were to fail to come much of the fertilizer would be wasted. Uncertainty has been discussed in § 3.4 and will be an important element in the discussion of our wheat study (see, in particular, § 8.6.3).

It can be seen that the yield curves begin to decline beyond a certain level of fertilizer. This is due to lodging. Thus diminishing returns to fertilizer set in suddenly, the plants lodge (collapse), and this sharp curvature of the response curve after an extensive region with little curvature explains the proximity of the 'economic optimum' and the yield maximizing level.

C306 begins to lodge at around 25 kg N per acre, Lerma Rojo at 40 kg and Kalyansona at 75 kg. Thus the selection and breeding of new varieties makes an enormous difference to marginal fertilizer responsiveness if one looks over the whole horizontal axis of Figs. 7.1, 7.2, 7.3. However, if one concentrates on the lower levels of fertilizer application the differences between the varieties are much smaller. This will be significant for our analysis below since a large majority of the applications of nitrogen in Palanpur were lower than 25 kg N per acre. We conclude our discussion of fertilizer responsiveness by indicating the high apparent average returns to the use of the recommended dose of fertilizers as compared with the zero use. (Marginal returns at input levels lower than the recommended dose would be higher). Singh, Sharma and Mishra (1970) suggest (for Pantnagar 1968) returns of the order of 400 per cent and the Fertiliser Association of India (1973, Chapter 15 p.269) returns for West U.P. (1968-70) of between 300 and 400 per cent. Thus the rarity of heavy doses in Palanpur requires discussion, and we shall examine the issues involved in some detail when we have presented our own estimates.

The importance of the date of sowing is illustrated in Table 7.1. The delaying of planting can cause very sharp losses. Shri Kumar of IFFCO Moradabad suggested, in his experience, that for our locality fifteen days' delay from 1 December could cause a 20 per cent loss in the yield from RR21 and this is illustrated in the above table. (And note that the maximum at 30 Nov. for the particular year 1971-2 for RR21 is not necessarily inconsistent with the recommendation of 10 Nov. for the date of sowing.)

Table 7.1 Grain yield (kg/acre) of different wheat varieties at different dates of sowing (1971-72)

Date of sowing	22 Oct.	10 Nov.	30 Nov.	20 Dec.	9 Jan.	29 Jan.	Mean
Kalyansona	1812	2261	1848	942	1014	580	1409
Sonalika (RR21)	1702	2070	2174	1644	1428	1101	1687
Hira	2029	2128	1812	978	755	528	1372

Source: Pantnagar (1974) p.2. Fertilizer (in kg/acre)
    N, 56; P_2O_5, 24; K_2O, 16.

The same table supports the advice to farmers that RR21 is a good variety for late sowing. This was of particular significance for *rabi* 1974-5 in Palanpur since many farmers planted late. One reason advanced was that in *rabi* 1973-4 there had been a late frost which caused severe damage to the crops. Some of the varieties, particularly *desi* varieties, which had been planted much earlier than the others (and late planted wheat) survived this frost with less damage since they were better developed and stronger. Thus the frost damaged most severely plots which had been planted in late October/early November. We were not convinced that this was the most important reason for late planting—see § 4.7.

The shorter growing season of some of the new varieties, (compare, for example, RR21 with 120-5 days and *desi* varieties of 140-50 days) provides new alternative crop rotations for farmers. It can become possible to fit in an extra crop, such as *moong* (a pulse), thus giving three crops in a year.

The nitrogen 'requirements' of late-sown wheat are lower than for the normal crop; Gill (1974, p.47) reports a study of Kalyansona in the Punjab in 1971-3 which showed that 'Contrary to the popular belief that the late sown crop needs relatively more nitrogen than the normal crop, the results of the study showed that the late crop of wheat sown in December and January needed nearly 20 per cent less nitrogen as compared with the crop sown in November'. By 'needed' here we are to understand economic optimum.

We mentioned above that the recommended seed rate for RR21 is 40 kg per acre and for Kalyansona around 35 kg per acre. It seems that small variations on the lower side of this level make little difference—Gill (1974, pp.39-40) reports a study at Ludhiana of Sonalika for 1968-70 where 'seed rates higher than 75 kg/hectare[3] did not affect the yield significantly'. Indeed in Ludhiana (1974) the recommended seed rates for RR21 and Kalyansona are 30-5 and

[3] 130 kg/acre.

25-30 kg per acre respectively (p.6). There seems to be a damaging effect of increasing the seed rate, however. Pantnagar (1974, p.3) report a study (in Pantnagar 1971-2) of Hira where the (very high) seed rate of 60 kg acre produced an output 5 per cent lower than a seed rate of 40 kg/acre.

Grain yield, however, is significantly affected by seed size. Gill (1974, p.42) reports that for Kalyansona in Ludhiana 1968-70, 'The average increase of bold [large] seed over small and unsorted bulk seed was 16.1% and 7.4% respectively'.

The central role of irrigation in the package can be seen from Table 7.2.

Table 7.2 Output of Kalyansona (kg/acre) without irrigation (1971-2)

Nitrogen level (kg/acre)	0	8	16	24
Output	325	414	472	499

Source : Pantnagar (1974) p.11.

This trial was at Pantnagar with sowing on 29 October and harvesting on 6 April. The responsiveness to nitrogen without irrigation was insignificant above 24 kg N per acre. Thus, without water, the average and marginal products of nitrogen are much lower, as is the level at which the marginal product becomes zero (see Fig. 7.3 and output levels in Table 7.1).

The effects of varying the frequency of irrigation are shown in Table 7.3.

Table 7.3 Effect of different irrigation treatments on wheat yield in Ludhiana (1972-3)

Irrigation treatment after sowing	Grain yield (kg/acre)
No irrigation	1084
3-week interval	1611
4-week interval	1496
5-week interval	1002

Source : Gill (1974) p.54 (Average over five varieties)

The yield figure is for an average of five new varieties(four dwarfs and one semi-dwarf), and all plots had a pre-sowing irrigation which is described as 'very essential'.

A high number of ploughings is recommended, both as a form of weed control and to provide a good seed bed. The Handbook of Agriculture (ICAR, 1969) suggests three or four ploughings for wheat prior to sowing and up to eight if the plot is fallow in the *kharif*.

This completes the substance of our review of the effects of varying the main inputs. We have concentrated on nitrogen since it is the responsiveness to high doses of nitrogen that have been treated as the hallmark of the new varieties. Plants, however, remove other nutrients from the soil and these have to be replaced if yields are to be maintained. The most important are phosphorus and potassium but the depletion of trace elements such as zinc may also cause declines in yields. This was thought to be an explanation for the decline in yields in the early 1970s in some parts of Ludhiana district of the Punjab (see Gill,

1974). However the appropriate balance of fertilizers, while important, takes us well beyond our technical competence. Further discussion is available, for example, in the Annual Reports of the Agricultural Universities at Ludhiana and Pantnagar.

We can summarize the conclusions from this review as follows. The recommended fertilizer doses for the new varieties are twice those for the traditional varieties and the yield for an average year under research station conditions would be from 50 – 100 per cent higher (depending on the varieties compared). The response of yield to fertilizer is approximately linear up to the point where the plant buckles or lodges. Average returns to fertilizer use seem to be around 300 – 400 per cent (and marginal returns are similar up to the point where lodging occurs) on the basis of research station findings. The returns and recommended doses are calculated for conditions of certainty. Yield is insensitive to seed rate over a broad range but is sensitive to the date of sowing. From four to six irrigations are recommended after sowing.

§ 7.1.3. Weeds, Diseases, and Pests

There are a variety of weedkillers available and the agricultural research stations report tests of their properties. They are not discussed here however since they are not used in Palanpur. Weeding, where it occurs, is done by hand. Shri Kumar estimates that the extra yield obtained by one weeding is, in our locality, on average around 15 per cent. Gill (1974, p. 64) reports a study (1973–4 season) where the outputs for an unweeded plot and a hand-weeded plot were 1240 and 1402 kg/acre respectively (the latter being 13 per cent higher).

Similarly, pesticides and chemicals to control diseases are not used in Palanpur. We confine our discussion therefore to descriptions of the main diseases and pests and the potential damage they can cause. The major diseases present in Palanpur, and they are the major diseases of West U.P. and the Punjab, are rusts and loose smut. The rusts are fungi and loose smut is a pathogen. Rusts are controlled, to the extent that this is possible, by selection of varieties that are rust resistant and by fungicides. The RR in RR21 stands for rust resistant. There are three types of rust: yellow, brown, and black.

Kalyansona and PV18 at the time of their release were resistant to yellow rust but somewhat susceptible to brown rust (Gill, 1974, p.67). However in *rabi* seasons 1970–1 and 1971–2 both varieties were heavily attacked by yellow rust. Sonalika-RR21 seems to have maintained its resistance to yellow rust. An increase in cloud cover can result in increased incidence of rust.

A major problem with the cultivation of just a few varieties in an area is that if these varieties become prone to certain diseases, such diseases can sweep through the area very quickly. With the older *desi* varieties one can suppose both that a certain amount of natural resistance developed and that the absence of variety control meant that there was a wide range of wheat seeds, providing some insurance against total loss. Thus control of disease in situations where farmers do not seem to use sprays to any large extent can be expected to be a continuing problem of the high-yielding varieties programme.

Losses due to rusts can be very large indeed, and they have caused problems for a long time. Kohli (1968) mentions outbreaks in 1827 and in 1839 and there were epidemics in 1946–7, 1952–3, and 1955–6. The attacks were so severe in these post-war years that in some districts yields were lower than the quantity of seed sown. Mehta (quoted on p.1 of ICAR, 1962) calculated, on a conservative basis, that 7–8 per cent of the Indian wheat crop was lost due to rust each year. Rust resistance is a major topic of research for wheat breeders (see ICAR, 1962).

In a field at Ludhiana during the *rabi* seasons of 1972–3 and 1973–4 fields without fungicide treatment were compared with those which had been frequently sprayed. The output loss due to rust was estimated to be 17.5 per cent for Kalyansona and 12 per cent for PV18 (Gill, 1974, p.68). In trials in areas especially susceptible to rust, increased yields of 31 per cent were observed for Kalyansona after spraying. Loose smut can be controlled by treatments of the seeds. Seeds treated with fungicides in a Ludhiana experiment (Gill, 1974, p. 72) gave 79 per cent germination with no loose smut as against 60 per cent germination, and 31 per cent of germinated plants affected, without treatment.

The most common pests are termites or white ants (which attack the seeds shortly after sowing), weevils, and aphids. Termites were present in several plots in Palanpur. Pest resistance plays only a minor role in wheat breeding (Kohli, 1968) but more intensive use of irrigation can create conditions favourable for pests.

Major uncertainties are, of course, introduced by the climate. The whole constellation of temperature, rainfall, cloud cover, frost, hail, and so on will affect yield. Over and above this, we have seen that uncertainties are introduced by diseases, particularly rust. We shall have more to say about uncertainty and decisions, below.

§ 7.2 Selection of Plots and Collection of Data

We describe in this section our method of selection of plots and the day-to-day procedures for the collection of data. The plots themselves and cultivators' practices are discussed in the next section.

We first obtained a map of the fields of the village from the *patwari* in Bilari. (Bilari is the nearby town which is the administrative headquarters for local government in the locality and the *patwari* is the village book/record keeper.) The fields on the *patwari's* map each had three digit numbers. We generated 100 three digit random numbers which formed the basis of our plot selection. We were interested only in those plots growing wheat.

The most straightforward procedure, were it possible, would have been to take into our sample those plots from our list of random numbers which were sown with wheat. However the *Patwari's* map was very out-of-date and did not accurately reflect the field divisions which had been chosen by farmers according to their convenience. The simple procedure served therefore as a guide rather than a rule. The rules for selection were as follows.

Rule 1 If *n* is one of the 100 random numbers, inspect plot *n*. If no wheat plot is largely contained within the boundaries of plot *n*, continue to the next random number.

Rule 2 If one wheat plot is largely contained within plot *n*, this wheat plot is included in the sample. If two or more plots are largely included within plot *n*, the largest area of which (expressed as a fraction of the total area) falls within the boundaries of plot *n*, is included in the sample.

The application of these simple rules generated forty-seven wheat plots from the 100 random numbers. The final sample actually used contained forty-seven plots but we gained one and lost one from the random sample. We lost one because it involved tenancy and the landlord refused, and forbade his tenant, to co-operate. We gained one because one farmer (Man Singh) was interested in our work, was experimenting with new types of seed, and was very keen to have an extra plot in the sample. Considerations of good public relations overrode a minor blemish to statistical procedure and having included an extra plot for him, we saw no great harm in including the observation in our analyses. We use the map reference numbers to identify our plots—the numbers have no other significance. The total acreage of the forty-seven plots was 34.8 acres giving an average size of 0.74 acres. As a proportion of the total area under wheat in *rabi* 1974-5 this is 30.1 per cent.

We should emphasize that it is the plot, not the farmer, which is our basic unit of observation and that some farmers had more than one plot in the sample. We are interested in our statistical analysis in relating the inputs on the plot to the output. The farmers themselves are discussed in the next sub-section and their beliefs about the productivity of inputs in § 8.5.

At the time of collection of the sample we carried out a quick informal check to see whether the sample was 'representative' as to the plots and cultivators of the village. This check, which proved positive, was confirmed when we later collected data on the cultivation patterns and land owned and leased-out. Two comparisons of the sample plots with the village as a whole follow. Nine out of forty-seven wheat plots were under tenancy in our sample and these nine constituted 23.2 per cent of the sample plot area. For the village as a whole 27.8 per cent of the wheat acreage is under tenancy. The 100 random numbers tried yielded forty-seven plots growing wheat. In the village as a whole 42 per cent of the cultivable area is under wheat in the *rabi* season.

Data on inputs were collected daily. Our research investigators, accompanied by ourselves when we were in the village, went round the fields once or twice a day and observed progress on the plots. The cultivators often notified us when activity had taken place or when it was about to take place—on most days from January to March there would be little activity on the wheat plots. All inputs were recorded within days or hours of their having occurred. Thus our method of collection was by word from the cultivator but there were frequent checks by direct observation.

We recorded the price of each input and where it was purchased, the types of fertilizer and seed, irrigation sources, implements, bullock hours, quantity and type of labour activity and the kind of labourer involved together with wages where relevant. The inputs were recorded separately for each day. The *kharif* 1974 crop, preceding the wheat, was noted. The soil type was judged by our research investigators. We then took samples of each type of soil and took them for analysis at Pantnagar Agricultural University. Data on the size of holding of the cultivator, his ownership of assets, and the make-up of his family were available from the cultivator questionnaire. The cultivators kindly kept the output from a plot separate at harvest and threshed it separately from other plots. Wheat, straw, and mustard (it was quite common to mix a little mustard with the wheat—see below) were weighed separately.

§ 7.3 Varieties and Practices on the Sample Plots

Cultivation practices for wheat in Palanpur show enormous variation between farmers. On one hand we have Man Singh, a young educated *Murao* farmer, who on one sample plot experimented with the new varieties Hira and 2009, applied fertilizer (purchased in the market) both at the time of sowing and as a top dressing, irrigated regularly using his own pumping set, and achieved an output of 13.50 quintals of wheat per acre. On the other hand, in contrast we have Ompal Singh, a middle-aged uneducated *Thakur* farmer, who used the (deteriorated) RR21 seed available from the Seed Store, used no fertilizer at the time of sowing, applied urea (bought on credit from the Seed Store) as a top dressing too late, and produced on his sample plot a yield of 3.95 quintals of wheat per acre. These two achieved the highest and lowest yields per acre on our sample plots. The average output of grain on the sample plots was 8.26 quintals per acre and the standard deviation was 2.46. Averages are taken over *plots* (not cultivators or by acreage) unless otherwise stated. In this section we shall describe the varieties chosen and practices used by farmers on our sample plots. We shall concentrate on the diversity but will identify those practices and groups of practices which were relatively common. We shall also find it useful in understanding some of our results to use the notions of good and bad practice and we shall explain what we mean by these terms. We discuss tenancy in the next section.

Of the forty-seven sample plots, twelve were cultivated by *Thakurs*, sixteen by *Muraos*, three by *Dhimars*, three by *Gadarias*, one by a *Dhobi*, four by *Telis*, seven by *Passis*, and one by a *Jatab*, Note, however, that some farmers contributed more than one plot: two *Thakur* farmers each contributed two plots, one *Murao* three plots, another *Murao* four plots, one *Passi* three plots, and another *Passi* two plots. Thus there were thirty-seven separate cultivators involved (thirty-one contributing just one plot and six more than one).

The average size of the cultivator's total holding for our sample plots was 6.25 acres. The largest was 16 acres and the smallest 0.27 acres. It is clear that sampling over plots rather than cultivators implies that the average size of holding for farmers of our sample plots is likely to be higher than for the farmers of the village as a whole. The average holding per household in the village is 3.57 acres, the maximum is 16 acres and the minimum zero.

By far the most common variety of seed on our wheat plots was RR21, being used in twenty-nine out of forty-seven cases. In sixteen of the twenty-nine cases of RR21 the source of the seed was the Seed Store. This seed is supplied on credit, the terms being that 125 per cent of the quantity of seed borrowed be returned in kind at harvest time. This has been the practice of the Seed Store for over twenty years and there has been no problem with recoupment of these seed loans (see Ansari, 1964, p. 6). As the dominant source of credit, the Seed Store is in a powerful position. It has attempted to supply recent varieties of wheat seed for some years. For example, in 1956 – 7 and 1957 – 8 Punjab 391 was supplied as well as the *desi* varieties of seed which were on offer. However since RR21 was first supplied in 1970 – 1 no new seed or varieties have been available from the Seed Store.

The credit method adopted, with the loan returned in kind, obviously involves severe problems with quality control. Farmers who have different varieties of wheat to thresh may not go to the trouble of keeping those varieties separate. The yield from mixed seed will be lower than the average for the varieties in the mixture (weighted by the proportions in the mixture) since different varieties come to maturity at different times, whereas the mixture will be harvested at one time. Further, farmers may try to return their worst quality grain in repayment of the loan and save the best for their own consumption or sale on the market. Careful quality inspection of returned seed would be required at the Seed Store and this does not occur.

The varieties of wheat seed on the sample plots are shown in Table 7.4. Note

Table 7.4. Types and sources of wheat seed used

Type	No. of Cases
RR21	29
1553	6
S308	1
Kalyansona	1
K 68	2
Hira	3
U.P. 310	1
U.P. 315	1
U.P. 215	1
2009	1
Hira/2009	1
Total	47

Sources of wheat seed used on sample plots	No. of Cases
Home produced	20
Seed Store	16
Bought in market	3
Obtained in Palanpur	5
Obtained from other villages	3
Total	47

that the sixteen cases where seed was purchased from the Seed Store involved RR21, which was all that was available at the Seed Store and thus was the obvious choice for someone who was short of cash for the purchase of seed and who had not kept back any from last year's crop (for twenty of the forty-seven cases the seed was home produced). One would expect such a circumstance to be associated with poverty but since some kind of organizational effort was required to go outside the Seed Store as a source (purchasing elsewhere or holding back a quantity from the previous year) laziness could be a second reason for selecting RR21. The correlation coefficient of the zero-one variable for RR21 (value 1 if RR21 is selected, 0 otherwise) for the plot with land holding per standard family member (*LOFA*, see § 5.7) for the cultivator of the plot is -0.29[4].

Doubtless both reasons have some force and they are not entirely independent, but given the correlation coefficient just quoted we regard the second as being of particular importance. We shall be taking the choice of RR21 as one measure of 'bad practice' and further reasons in support of this classification will emerge later in this and the next chapter.

The caste breakdown of the seed choices is interesting. Of the eighteen cases where RR21 was not chosen, four were *Thakur*, twelve *Murao*, and two *Passi*, whereas of the twenty-nine cases where RR21 was chosen, eight were *Thakur*, four *Murao*, three *Dhimar*, three *Gadaria*, four *Teli*, and five *Passi*. The *Muraos* dominate the non-RR21 choice (a little care is necessary, however, because seven of the twelve non-RR21 *Murao* choices were contributed by just two farmers).

The market price of wheat at the time of sowing was around 200 rupees per quintal or 2 rupees per kg. This is the price of ordinary sowing material such as RR21. Thus the cost for an acre at 40 kg per acre would be 80 rupees. If more pure or specialist seed is selected the cost is higher. For example the cost of 2009 was 8 rupees per kg in the Chandausi market. Most farmers would see R320 spent on seed for one acre as a very substantial amount of cash.

The sowing technique of many of the farmers was defective in several ways. The main fault was sowing too deep. The *desi* varieties of wheat should be sown at 4 inches, whereas the newer varieties usually require a depth of approximately 2 inches. In addition, the spacing of rows was often haphazard and too wide. Little attention was given to careful spacing along a row. The average seed rate was 39.4 kg/acre compared with the recommended quantity of 40 kg/acre for RR21 and 35 kg/acre for Kalyansona. We were advised by Shri Kumar that a little extra seed is required for late sowing. We saw in § 7.1.2, however, that output was insensitive to seed rate for variations of up to 20 per cent below recommended levels, that substantial increases above recommended levels can reduce output, and that recommended levels for RR21 elsewhere were below 40 kg/acre. There was not very much variation across the sample (the standard deviation of the rate was 4.2 kg/acre). A rough rule of thumb of 40 kg/acre

[4.]This is significant at the 5 per cent level. For a discussion of the correlation matrix and significance levels, see § 8.2.

seemed to be well-known to the cultivators. Given that the average rate was close to the maximum of the recommended rates across seed types, the general level is perhaps a little high.

The earliest date for a plot in the sample to be sown was 5 November and the latest 20 December. Most were planted at the end of November or the beginning of December. Twenty-five of the forty-seven plots were sown by the first of December. The recommended sowing date for RR21 is 10 November so that 1 December is three weeks late. And RR21 has a fairly short growing season of 120-5 days compared with, for example, Kalyansona at approximately 135 days. From our discussion in § 7.1.2 and Table 7.1 it seems that potential output falls sharply if sowing is delayed, particularly into December. We shall regard an early date of planting as an indication of 'good practice'. In our regression analysis we took the simple zero-one variable, 1 for planting before 1 December and 0 after. Correlations of this variable with others are examined in § 8.2.

In our detailed discussions with the farmers of their input choices (see § 8.5) we attempted to discover their reasons for planting late. Two reasons dominated. The first was that a late frost the previous year had damaged the crop. Secondly, some farmers remarked that the *kharif* harvest had been late due to late sowing because of poor summer rains. We took the second of these reasons more seriously (see § 4.7) although an energetic farmer should not have had too much difficulty in planting by 1 December. Indeed nearly half the sample managed it and the earliest was three-and-a-half weeks before that.

All the plots received some irrigation. *Including* the pre-irrigation (before sowing) the minimum number of irrigations was two, the maximum number was six, and the average 4.2. There was no pre-irrigation on eight plots but every plot had at least two irrigations after sowing. The distribution of the number of irrigations is given in Table 7.5a. Recall, see § 7.1.2, that the recommended number of irrigations (including pre-irrigation) for timely sowing is seven. However Shri Kumar suggested that, given the conditions of *rabi* 1974-5, four or five (including the pre-irrigation) were sufficient. Thus, as far as the number of irrigations goes, the average standard of practice in Palanpur is quite good. Methods of irrigation using pumping sets or Persian wheels are described in § 4.4.

The time taken to irrigate an acre varied a great deal. Where irrigation is by Persian wheel some bullocks will be faster than others and with either a Persian wheel or a pumping set the cultivator can decide how much water to put on. Our observations on irrigation at a given time could only be of a zero-one kind; either there was irrigation or there was not. We had no practical way in which the amount of water going on the field could be measured. The amount of time taken for a given technique (PW or PS) is a guide but only a very rough one. Bullocks vary in speed, pumps in efficiency, and channels in the extent to which water is wasted.

Table 7.5a Number of irrigations

Number of irrigations (including pre-irrigation)	Absolute frequency
2	4
3	8
4	15
5	15
6	5

Table 7.5b Source of irrigation actually used by sources available.

Source available	HPW	OPW	HPS	OPS
HPW	4			
OPW		6		
HPS			15	
OPS				10
HPW and HPS	4		4	
OPW and OPS		1		1
OPW and HPS		2		

Key : OPW　Own Persian Wheel
OPS　Own Pumping Set
HPW　Hired Persian Wheel (including landlord's)
HPS　Hired Pumping Set

Summary Statistics for Table 7.5b

Source of Irrigation Used		Source of Irrigation Available	
Persian Wheel Hired	8	Persian Wheel Hired	4
Persian Wheel Owned	7	Persian Wheel Owned	6
Pumping Set Hired	21	Pumping Set Hired	15
Pumping Set Owned	11	Pumping Set Owned	10
		PW Hired and PS Hired	8
		PW Owned and PS Owned	2
		PW Owned and PS Hired	2

Note : Source of irrigation used is for the first one after sowing. The figures for source used for the second after sowing are the same except that we have one more case of PS Hired and one less of PW Hired.

Table 7.5b indicates that where there is a choice the favoured method (by a narrow majority) is irrigation by pumping set. The cost would be approximately 30 rupees for an acre where irrigation is by hired pumping set together with the time of two people for five hours. Where irrigation is by hired Persian wheel the cost would be approximately 5 rupees for the hire of the wheel. Its use would require two people and a pair of bullocks for, say, thirty hours. The difference is 25 rupees less twenty-five hours of two people and two bullocks. The labour for irrigation is usually family and frequently the cultivator and a child. The market wage for one adult for an eight-hour day is approximately 4 rupees. Counting a child as half an adult the labour cost of the extra twenty-five hours would be approximately 18 rupees, leaving only 7 rupees for twenty-five hours of bullock power. The market for bullock services in the village is very limited but prices quoted in our discussions in August 1977 (see Chapter 10) were 10–20 rupees per acre for ploughing—roughly equivalent to a pair for eight hours.

Elsewhere where bullocks are hired, mention is made of 15 rupees for a pair for an eight hour day. Bullocks would be hired out only with a driver. Given that the family and bullocks would be used at a time when other demands were not high the above prices are on the high side, but it seems clear that the implicit price of 1 rupee an hour for a bullock-pair, man, and child required for a Persian wheel to become competitive with a pumping set is low. This calculation appears to be endorsed by the decisions of the cultivators who, on the whole, go for the pumping set where possible. The correlations of the number of irrigations with other variables are given in § 8.2. We shall regard a high number of irrigations as an indication of 'good practice'.

Fertilizer as a top dressing was more common than fertilizer at the time of sowing. One reason for this was that fertilizer was rather difficult to come by during November and early December even in the market. Restrictions on fertilizer purchase were relaxed only on 15th November 1974. Urea was delivered in a lorry to the Seed Store on 12th December but no phosphates, potash, or mixtures suitable for use at the time of sowing. For most farmers it was in any case already too late for use at sowing. It may also be the case that they believe the urea to be more profitable, possibly because one can see results fairly quickly after application. Such a belief is rather short-sighted, since the impoverishment of the soil by the depletion of particular nutrients can have a sharp effect on yields—see §7.1.2. We had no way of measuring quantities of different constituents for basal fertilizers and thus were not in a position to estimate the marginal productivity of phosphate and potash separately.

Of the forty-seven plots, twenty-three received fertilizer at the time of sowing (plus one green manuring) and thirty-nine at least one top dressing (and six of these plots received two top dressings). In all cases except one (when calcium nitrate was used) the top dressing was urea. For fifteen of the twenty-three cases of fertilizer used at the time of sowing some kind of mixture involving N, P, and K was used. As we have just noted it was impossible to obtain measurements on the breakdown by constitutent and we therefore employed a simple zero-one variable, where 1 indicated the presence of fertilizer at sowing Of the eight remaining cases seven were diammonium phosphate and one urea. For top dressings the weight of fertilizer applied can be usefully incorporated in the analysis since the fertilizer is homogeneous—urea.

The sources of the basal fertilizers at the time of sowing were entirely outside the village: for twenty-one of the twenty-three cases it was bought in the market and in two cases obtained from the Block in Chandausi. The source for the top dressing was in seventeen cases the Seed Store, in eighteen cases the market, in two cases other villages, and two cases the Block at Chandausi. After 12 December, as noted above, the Seed Store could supply urea. This was at the same price as in the market (105 rupees for a 50 kg bag) and was available on credit although both the fertilizer and the credit were rationed (see § 2.A.2 and §4.3). A journey to town was also saved. However, because of the rationing at the Seed Store and because bags purchased there were often underweight, many farmers bought their fertilizer in the market.

The average quantity of fertilizer used per acre as a top dressing (including the eight who applied none) was 31.8 kg/acre with a maximum of 76.0 kg/acre. Urea is 46 per cent nitrogen so that the average in N/acre is 14.6 kg and the maximum 35.0 kg.

The average quantity of fertilizer used per acre at the time of sowing (including the twenty-four plots which received none) was 18.8 kg/acre. We have noted that we do not have the break down by consituent but if, say, half were urea, then the average total quantity of urea applied would be $0.5 \times 18.8 + 31.8 = 41.2$ kg/acre, equivalent to 19.0 kg N/acre. This may be compared with recommended (see §7.1.2) applications of 48 kg N/acre.

On average, then, the Palanpur sample plots received doses of nitrogen well under half those recommended. Further, more than half of the plots received no phosphorus or potassium. But this conceals a very wide variation. Some plots received no fertilizer at all (for example plot 109) whereas plot 266, of size 0.64 acre, received 50 kg of an NPK mixture at the time of sowing and 45 kg urea as a top dressing. If half of the 50 kg were urea, that would give 70 kg of urea or $70/0.64 = 109.4$ kg urea/acre or 50.3 kg N/acre—just above the recommended dose of nitrogen. (This particular plot was sown very late—19 December—and the farmer said that he had in mind some sort of compensation. Note, however, that we saw in § 7.1.2. that the productivity of fertilizer is reduced by late planting).

We shall be taking the use of fertilizer at the time of sowing as another component of 'good practice'. It should be noted that it involved both ready cash and the effort of going to town to collect it. Higher doses of urea as a top dressing will be taken as indicating 'better practice'. An application of urea should be, and generally was, followed by an irrigation. Thus one might expect the number of applications of urea as a top dressing to be correlated with the number of irrigations (there was indeed a significant correlation—see § 8.2). Of the thirty-nine who applied a top dressing, six applied it twice.

Most of the plots (thirty-five out of forty-seven) were sown with mustard mixed with wheat. This is a common practice and is frowned upon by agricultural advisers. There seems to be two main motives for mixing. The first is that the wheat protects the mustard from certain wind-transported diseases and pests. The second is that mixing spreads risk—if one crop fails the other may not, and indeed would produce higher output in the absence of the crop that failed. The reason it is considered bad practice by many agriculturalists is that the mustard competes with the wheat for nutrients and water and in value terms wheat is more responsive to fertilizers than mustard—thus, in this sense, fertilizer absorbed by mustard is wasted. The total quantity of mustard involved is quite small—the average yield (across all plots) was only 0.42 quintals/acre compared with an average for wheat of 8.26 quintals/acre. The market price of mustard was approximately 200 rupees/quintal in June 1975, compared with wheat at approximately 130 rupees/quintal.

The most popular *kharif* crop in summer 1974 to precede the wheat on the sample plots was *bajra*. The frequencies of the different *kharif* crops are shown in Table 7.6 There is no simple presumption that a fallow *kharif* season will imply higher output. If fertilizer is applied to a *kharif* crop it may have benefits for the *rabi*. Further, a fallow period may be negatively correlated with the enthusiasm, organizing ability, or health of the farmer. A zero-one variable for whether of not a plot was left fallow is, however, included in the analysis to be presented later.

Table 7.6 *Kharif* crops preceding wheat

Crop	Number of Cases
Bajra	17
Maize	10
Fallow	9
Paddy	3
Ground-nut	3
Jowar	2
Cheri	1
Green manuring	1
Sorghum	1

Note : In two of the 17 cases *bajra* was mixed with ground-nut and in a further two with *urd*. For one of the ground-nut cases the plot was partly fallow.

The soil was classified by our research investigators into five types for the wheat plots: loam 1, loam 2, sandy loam 1, sandy loam 2, and sandy. The number of examples of the five types in the above order were 1, 5, 23, 14, and 4. The types were coded 1, 2, 3, 4, 5, and the code used as an explanatory variable for output per acre. It is clear both that the classification of the soil was rather unprofessional from the point of view of a soil scientist and that the simple code used to embody potential productivity is crude. More careful analysis of soil type was beyond the scope of the study. Note that the great majority of plots were classified either as sandy loam 1 or sandy loam 2. The choice between sandy loam 1 and sandy loam 2 here was often difficult and we did not have the facilities for accurate measurement. A few errors would destroy the value of the variable and there are likely to be several.

We saw in § 7.1.2 that several ploughings are encouraged both as a preparation of a good seed-bed and as a weed control. The number of ploughings on the sample plots ranged from two to nine with an average of 5.06. The frequency of each number from two to nine is given in Table 7.7. We shall be using the number of ploughings as an explanatory variable for output per acre and shall associate a higher number of ploughings with 'better practice'.

It takes approximately eight hours to plough an acre. The draught animals involved are either bullocks or buffaloes. To avoid repetition we shall speak of bullocks. These animals are very seldom rented but are occasionally exchanged. The exchange might be organized as follows. For example, suppose two brothers own a pair of bullocks each. They may decide to plough a field belonging to one of them together and then do the same for the other's field later. Alternatively two brothers might own one bullock each, and each might lend his to the other to form a pair on condition that the other reciprocates.

Table 7.7 Number of ploughings

Number of ploughings	Number of cases
2	1
3	9
4	10
5	7
6	11
7	5
8	3
9	1

Weeding was not a popular activity in Palanpur, notwithstanding Shri Kumar's estimates (§ 7.1.3) that one weeding could save 15 per cent of the crop. At an output of 8 quintals an acre and a price of 130 rupees a quintal 15 per cent would be worth 156 rupees. The price of weeding was 2 rupees/*bigha* or approximately 13 rupees an acre. Only eleven plots were weeded. It may be that Shri Kumar's estimates of the benefits of weeding are rather high—he may have had in mind doses of fertilizer higher than those prevailing in Palanpur.

No pesticides, herbicides, or fungicides were used on any plot.

The harvesting is carried out manually. The worker crouches and uses a small hand scythe. The wheat is tied into bundles, stacked, and then transported the same day to the threshing point. Output is transported either by bullock cart or on the head. The wheat is threshed by driving bullocks round and round over the wheat. As with Persian wheels, it is often children who drive the bullocks. Often three or four bullocks would be involved. Bullocks are occasionally exchanged for threshing as they are for ploughing. Finally, the grain is winnowed in the wind using a basket. We collected data on inputs and hours right through to the end of the winnowing process.

Much of the labour for harvesting is hired (see Table 7.8) and the payment is always one-twentieth of the amount harvested. The hired labourers generally work as a team which moves around from plot to plot and village to village. The wheat harvested by a labourer is kept separate. The employer then selects which one of each twenty bundles goes to the hired labourer—an incentive to keep the bundles of equal size.

The number of hours in pre-harvest, harvest, and post-harvest activities are given for each plot in Table 7.8 together with a breakdown between hired and family labour. It can be seen that the proportion of time spent on pre-harvest, harvest, and post-harvest activities varies a great deal. However pre-harvest hours invariably exceed harvest hours and the factor of proportionality (pre-harvest: harvest varies from roughly 1½ to 7. Hired labour is relatively greater in harvesting than either pre- or post-harvest activity. Post-harvest hours generally exceed the harvest hours—with the former ranging from roughly double the latter to equality.

We concentrated on the pre-harvest activities as a possible explanatory variable for output. The post-harvest activity will depend upon the quantity of wheat harvested rather than be an explanation of that quantity. It is true, of

Table 7.8 Labour on sample plots
Labour in Standard Hours per Acre

Plot No.	Cultivator No.	Output/Acre	Size Plot in Acres	Pre-Harvest			Harvest			Post-Harvest		
				F	H	T	F	H	T	F	H	T
194	125	6.98	1.26	102.3	6.4	108.7	19.0	39.7	58.7	106.4	10.3	116.7
164	106	8.81	0.98	97.0	61.2	158.2	0	73.5	73.5	50.0	56.1	106.1
197	113	7.16	0.25	84.0	36.0	120.0	0	48.0	48.0	92.0	84.0	176.0
074	114	3.95	0.48	202.0	43.8	245.8	0	52.1	52.1	128.1	12.5	140.6
342	304	9.57	0.94	103.2	0	103.2	67.6	0	67.6	127.7	0	127.7
338	112	10.87	0.31	206.4	32.3	238.7	0	64.5	64.5	154.8	0	154.8
625	116	10.03	0.63	117.5	33.3	150.8	0	55.6	55.6	82.5	68.3	150.8
052	118	10.30	0.94	68.0	95.8	163.8	0	76.6	76.6	54.3	43.6	97.9
366	118	9.13	0.80	52.5	47.5	100.0	11.2	56.3	67.5	57.5	40.0	97.5
358	117	4.96	0.31	106.5	12.9	119.4	29.1	29.0	58.1	64.5	64.5	129.0
379	111	10.42	0.50	366.0	12.0	378.0	12.0	48.0	60.0	92.0	62.0	154.0
377	111	11.87	0.50	348.0	56.0	404.0	14.0	56.0	70.0	96.0	64.0	160.0
412	103	7.07	1.25	253.4	40.0	293.4	0	64.0	64.0	69.6	9.6	79.2
088	303	8.72	1.09	100.9	0	100.9	68.8	0	68.8	124.8	0	124.8
422	606	8.96	0.94	90.4	0	90.4	33.5	38.3	71.8	96.8	0	96.8
502	401	6.45	0.31	474.2	0	474.2	67.7	0	67.7	161.3	0	161.3
064	406	5.32	0.47	229.8	12.8	242.6	38.3	0	38.3	136.2	0	136.2
391	410	9.02	0.28	350.0	64.3	414.3	0	64.3	64.3	110.7	0	110.7
208	605	7.95	0.63	164.3	0	164.3	11.9	55.6	67.5	85.7	0	85.7
224	611	8.06	0.31	332.3	16.1	348.4	96.8	0	96.8	174.2	0	174.2
599	610	6.41	0.80	137.5	10.0	147.5	30.0	30.0	60.0	100.6	0	100.6
554	707	7.35	1.36	128.7	0	128.7	50.1	0	50.1	82.4	0	82.4
591	204	5.79	1.09	133.9	66.1	200.0	0	58.3	58.3	38.6	38.5	77.1
058	219	12.41	0.50	244.0	10.0	254.0	32.0	64.0	96.0	122.0	0	122.0
512	219	12.10	0.80	156.3	10.0	166.3	30.0	40.0	70.0	120.0	0	120.0
266	219	8.89	0.63	227.0	9.5	236.5	66.7	0	66.7	125.4	0	125.4
500	227	12.08	1.20	155.8	4.2	160.0	22.5	48.8	71.3	80.8	0	80.8
157	227	11.80	0.95	196.9	6.3	203.2	17.9	48.4	66.3	88.4	0	88.4
360	227	13.50	0.60	198.3	5.0	203.3	80.0	26.7	106.7	96.7	0	96.7
475	227	8.89	0.64	123.4	0	123.4	56.3	25.0	81.3	118.7	0	118.7
215	201	10.55	0.55	278.2	60.0	338.2	54.6	0	54.6	63.7	63.6	127.3
229	202	9.21	0.63	306.3	54.0	360.3	57.1	0	57.1	66.7	58.7	125.4
137	206	10.16	0.45	60.0	171.1	231.1	17.8	53.3	71.1	64.5	64.4	128.9
134	206	11.73	0.85	57.6	131.8	189.4	16.5	49.4	65.9	51.7	51.8	103.5
462	217	6.57	0.70	87.1	0	87.1	64.3	0	64.3	138.6	0	138.6
477	217	9.12	0.47	172.4	10.6	183.0	38.3	25.5	63.8	100.0	0	100.0
318	503	4.80	1.25	283.2	11.2	294.4	67.2	0	67.2	93.6	4.8	98.4
130	301	5.45	1.56	162.8	42.3	205.1	76.9	0	76.9	142.6	0	142.6
361	612	7.09	0.39	156.4	0	156.4	53.9	0	53.9	174.4	0	174.4
312	702	6.55	0.63	123.8	34.9	158.7	25.4	38.1	63.5	52.4	52.4	104.8
156	702	4.91	0.63	93.7	49.2	142.9	25.4	38.1	63.5	60.3	60.3	120.6
301	702	4.96	0.94	109.6	37.2	146.8	17.0	42.6	59.6	40.5	52.1	92.6
400	704	6.81	0.47	229.8	8.5	238.3	51.1	0	51.1	191.5	0	191.5
042	704	4.55	0.55	95.4	9.1	104.5	43.6	0	43.6	143.6	0	143.6
350	226	8.99	1.72	159.9	9.3	169.2	32.6	46.5	79.1	79.9	0	79.9
252	210	6.09	0.47	183.0	117.0	300.0	68.1	51.1	119.2	46.8	46.8	93.6
109	803	5.32	0.47	183.0	0	183.0	83.0	0	83.0	95.7	0	95.7

Key : F = Family   H = Hired   T = Total

Note: In calculating standard hours men are weighted one, women one and children ½.

course, that poor harvesting, threshing, or winnowing can lose grain. We shall return to the question of the role of labour hours in explaining output in § 8.1.

We have now summarized the main features of cultivation practice on our sample plots. The direct inputs which we regard here (and in § 7.1.2) as being positively associated with 'good practice' are: the use of fertilizer at the time of sowing, the quantity of fertilizer as a top dressing, the number of ploughings, the number of irrigations, an irrigation within thirty days of sowing, weeding, and timely sowing. We suggest that the use of seed-type RR21 should be associated with 'bad practice'. Judging from these indicators and comparisons with recommended levels (see § 7.1) the average standard of wheat cultivation in Palanpur is not good. Less than half the plots received basal fertilizers, the average quantity of nitrogen applied was less than half the recommended dose, there was weeding on less than 25 per cent of the plots, and almost half of the plots were sown more than three weeks late (as compared to the recommended date). None of the cultivators treated their seeds and no pesticides or fungicides were used. The stronger points were the fairly high average number of irrigations and ploughings.

The poor average standard of cultivation conceals a great diversity. Thus, some farmers applied no fertilizers at all whereas others applied doses quite close to those recommended. Some irrigated only once after sowing, others as much as five times, and so on. Nonetheless, even the highest yield of 13.5 quintals per acre was substantially less than the levels of around 20 quintals per acre to be expected from research stations (see Table 7.1 and Figures 7.1, 7.2, and 7.3). In § 8.1 we shall discuss the determinants behind the choices of farmers when we present correlation matrices involving inputs, yield, and characteristics of cultivators. We turn now to an isssue which has been contentious both in theory and for policy, the relation between tenancy and input choice.

§ 7.4 Tenancy

There were nine cases of tenancy amongst the forty-seven cases in the sample. One tenanted plot could not be included because the landlord refused to co-operate and forbade his tenant to do so. Information on tenanted plots is summarized in Table 7.9, together with some figures allowing comparisons with non-tenanted plots. The average size of the tenanted plots was 0.89 acre compared with 0.74 acre for the whole sample.

The tenants tend to be of lower caste than the landlord. Our caste numbers correspond, roughly, to a hierarchy with lower numbers being higher status. The only two cases where the caste number of the landlord is higher than that of the tenant both involved Muslim landlords: for plot 554 the tenant was a *Passi* and plot 130 a *Dhimar*.

The tenancy arrangement was in each case share-cropping together with cost sharing, with the output and the costs split 50-50 (see § 5.2). One needs to pay attention to the details of the rule, however. The tenant is expected to do the harvesting. Much of the harvesting in the village is carried out by hired labour,

Table 7.9 Tenanted Plots

Plot no.	Cultivated no.	Plot size	Landlord	Source irrig.	Output/acre in quintals per acre	Seed source	Seed type	Total labour/acre (hours/acre)	Non irrigation hours/acre	No. of ploughings	Quantity (kg/acre) fertilizer as top dressing	No. of irrig.	Sowing before 1 Dec. (1 yes 0 No)	Actual date
342	304	0.94	115	HPS	9.57	HP	RR21	103.2	64.9	5	53.2	4	1	(22 Nov)
88	303	1.09	104	HPS	8.72	Village	RR21	100.9	63.3	5	45.9	4	0	(05 Dec)
422	606	0.94	401	HPS	8.96	SS	RR21	90.4	77.6	6	25.5	2	1	(10 Nov)
224	611	0.31	224	LPW	8.06	SS	RR21	348.4	135.5	8	38.7	4	0	(08 Dec)
599	610	0.80	224	HPS	6.41	SS	RR21	147.5	100.0	7	37.5	4	0	(20 Dec)
554	707	1.36	903	HPS	7.35	HP	Hira	128.7	42.0	3	36.8	3	0	(09 Dec)
130	301	1.56	503	HPS	5.45	SS	RR21	205.1	91.6	7	0	3	0	(19 Dec)
42	704	0.55	703	HPS	4.55	SS	RR21	104.5	65.4	4	32.7	3	1	(23 Nov)
109	803	0.47	701	HPS	5.32	SS	RR21	183.0	80.9	4	0	4	0	(02 Dec)
Average for tenants		0.89			7.15			156.9	80.1	5.4	30.0	3.6	0.33	
Averages for whole sample		0.74			8.26			207.0	92.6	5.1	31.8	4.2	0.53	
Averages non-tenant		0.70			8.52			218.9	95.5	5.0	32.2	4.3	0.58	

Notes : 1. Notation (i) Seed source HP = home produce; Village = purchased inside village; SS = Seed Store.
    (ii) Source irrigation (= first irrigation after sowing) HPS = hired pumping set; LPW = landlord Persian wheel.
2. Total labour/acre is in standard hours counting men as one, women as one, and children as half. The figures are for pre-harvest labour inputs only.
3. The plot reference numbers are not significant except as identifiers.
4. The number for cultivators indicate the caste in the first digit : 1 Thakur, 2 Murao, 3 Dhimar, 4 Gadaria, 5 Dhobi, 6 Teli, 7 Passi, 8 Jatab, 9 Others.

the payment being in the form of 5 per cent of the output. The hired harvester takes away from the field one sheaf for every twenty he harvests (one must be careful to take account of this in measuring yield - see p. 260) For only two of the tenanted plots (599 and 422, see Table 7.8) some harvesting was by hired labour (in each case roughly half the harvest labour). The amount paid to the hired harvesters would be subtracted from the tenant's share.

When irrigation is involved the landlord would split the cost of hiring a pumping set 50-50. Where the irrigation is by Persian wheel, however, the tenant is expected to drive the wheel with his own bullocks with no compensation by the landlord. There is an incentive to use the hired pumping set where a boring is nearby and eight out of the nine tenants did so. The remaining one used the landlord's Persian wheel with no charge imposed by the landlord. There were no cases in our sample of a Persian wheel being hired other than from the landlord, but in general if hiring is from a third party charges are split 50-50.

The tenant is expected to provide the seed without assistance from the landlord and it is notable that seven out of nine tenants selected RR21 on credit in kind from the Seed Store (of the remaining two one used Hira seed which had been kept back from the previous year, and the other RR21 purchased in the village).

Where fertilizer is applied cost is shared on a 50-50 basis but the landlord's agreement to any purchase has to be obtained. None of the tenanted plots had fertilizer applied at the time of sowing although plot 422 had green manuring. Two (plots 130 and 109) received no top dressing of urea. In the sample as a whole twenty-three plots received fertilizer at the time of sowing (and all such plots received a top dressing) and eight received no top dressing (and all such plots received no fertilizer at the time of sowing).

One must also take account of the timing of payments in a cost-sharing arrangement. It is often the case that the tenant must find the cash for fertilizer, for example, at the time of purchase and the landlord will repay him at the time of harvest. Thus, as we saw in Chapter 5, leasing-out can sometimes be a response to the liquidity problems facing a land-owner. The magnitude of the cash requirements involved for the four inputs just mentioned can be judged from the following. For the sample plots the average cost of fertilizer as a top dressing was R74 per acre, for fertilizer at the time of sowing R87 per acre, and for seed R 85 per acre (these averages are obtained by dividing total cost by acreage on which fertilizer or seed is applied). The cost of pre-irrigation by hired pumping set would around R 30 per acre and (including pre-irrigation) the average number of irrigations was approximately four. These costs may be compared with an average wheat revenue per acre (using a price of R 130 per quintal) of R 1074 and an average income per year for a household of R 7020. It can be seen that the liquidity problems would not be trivial. The fact that the landlord does not accept a half share of the burden of credit is a significant feature of the agreement.

The total number of hours per acre put into the plot before the harvest (counting men and women as one and children as half) averaged 156.9 for the tenanted plots and 218.9 for the non-tenanted plots. However this gives a misleading impression of the level of effective effort put into the plot, since the tenants (with one exception) used pumping sets for irrigation as opposed to the much more laborious Persian wheel. If we subtract hours worked on irrigation the figures give an average of 80.1 hours per acre for the tenanted plots and 95.5 hours per acre for the non-tenanted. This last diference is largely accounted for by the fact that none of the tenanted plots was weeded, whereas eleven out of the thirty-eight non-tenanted plots were. Weeding contributes 9.6 hours to the 95.5 hours for the non-tenanted plots.

From Table 7.9 we see that the average yield on tenanted plots, 7.15 quintals per acre, was rather lower than that on owner-cultivated plots, 8.52 quintals per acre. We shall be discussing the statistical significance of this and other differences between tenanted and owner-cultivated plots in § 8.2.

We have seen from the above discussions that the particular features of the tenancy agreement seem to have had a clear effect on the decisions of tenants. Thus the difficulty of obtaining fertilizer at the time of sowing and the absence of credit for it, together with the onus being on the tenant to provide the cash, led to no tenants applying fertilizer at the time of sowing, whereas twenty-three out of thirty-eight non-tenanted plots received such fertilizer. On the other hand, fertilizer for use as a top dressing was available on credit from the Seed Store and was applied by eight out of the nine tenants (and thirty-one out of the thirty-eight non-tenants). The absence of cost sharing for the labour and bullock time involved in the use of Persian wheels was associated with eight out of nine tenants using pumping sets (for which the cost of hiring is shared). Similarly the absence of cost sharing for seed resulted in eight out of nine tenants using RR21 which was available on credit from the Seed Store. And finally, weeding, an obvious case where labour—the cost of which is not shared—can be varied at the margin, is totally absent for tenanted plots although it occurs on more than 25 per cent of the non-tenanted ones.

The links between the incentive structure of the agreement and the inputs associated with tenanted plots might appear to suggest that notwithstanding agreements and supervision the tenant applies inputs at levels markedly different from the owner-cultivator. One must caution, however, that the size of sample is small and we have not yet examined whether the features of tenanted plots discussed are significantly different in the statistical sense from those of owner-cultivated plots. This last issue is taken up in the next chapter (see, in particular, § 8.2).

§ 7.5 Concluding Remarks

We first presented in this chapter a description of the high-yielding varieties of wheat and the work on research stations which lies behind the recommended package of practices. This was followed by a discussion of cultivation on our sample wheat plots and the introduction of the notion of 'good practice'. We pointed to the substantial variation between farmers and to the poor average standard of cultivation. Finally, we compared input levels on tenanted and owner-cultivated plots. We turn now to an econometric investigation of the determinant of output per acre on our sample plots.

8

WHEAT: Productivity and Expectations

§ 8.0 Introduction

This chapter is concerned first with the estimation of the relationship between on the one hand, output per acre on our sample wheat plots and, on the other, the levels of inputs and some characteristics of cultivators; and then with the interpretation of the results of that estimation. We shall be paying special attention to the estimated value marginal productivities of various inputs compared both with the costs of those inputs and with the views of cultivators as to the effects on yield of varying input levels. In § 8.1 we set out our choice of model and explanatory variables. The correlation matrix of our selected variables is presented in § 8.2. We shall be particularly interested in two features of that matrix. First, the relationships amongst the 'good practice' and associated variables introduced in the preceding chapter and, secondly, an analysis of variance for variables associated with tenancy.

Our main regression results are presented in § 8.3. The comparisons of estimated productivities with prices are contained in § 8.4. Cultivators' views on productivities are compared with our estimates in § 8.5 and we attempt to use our knowledge of plots and cultivators to understand residuals which are left 'unexplained' in the regressions. We draw some conclusions for economic theories of input choice in § 8.6, paying particular attention to choice under uncertainty. We speculate on possible practical improvements in cultivation technique in § 8.7. Concluding remarks are presented in § 8.8. There is an appendix on alternative functional forms.

§ 8.1 The Model and the Variables

We wish to understand the variations across plots in the yield per acre of wheat. We shall be using the techniques of regression, with output per acre as the variable to be explained, and the inputs employed together with certain measurable characteristics of cultivators as explanatory variables. Our task in this section is to explain our selection of the models we use in the regressions.

A standard approach to the analysis of production is to present the output of a farm or firm as a function of the three classical factors of production : labour, land, and capital. The detail embodied in our data permits our analysis to be rather more subtle. Thus, for example, instead of using a variable 'labour' we employ measures of the specific tasks performed by labour which constitute the direct inputs into production—the number of ploughings, the number of irrigations, whether or not the plot was weeded, and so on. This more detailed approach involves certain problems in defining tasks and we return to this issue below.

We are not here concerned with the output of the farm as a whole but with the output from a particular plot. One would expect two identical plots with identical inputs and identical cultivators to produce identical outputs. Thus it is reasonable to suppose that one plot of twice the size of another would, if identically treated, produce twice the output. Hence, we choose output per acre of the plot as the variable to be explained. The difference between the production function appropriate for a plot with a single crop and detailed input information and that appropriate for a farm with aggregated input information was discussed in § 3.3 and 6.1, as was the relation between output per acre and size of farm.

The examination of output per acre as a function of input per acre embodies the assumption of constant returns to scale. We examine the assumption statistically in the appendix to this chapter. We have two major choices in the selection of the equation to be estimated. We have to choose which of the many possible explanatory variables to include and secondly the manner in which the selected variables enter the relationship, that is, the functional form of the equation. In practice there is a trade-off between the degree of complexity one can allow in the two choices. One can concentrate on including detail of several types of explanatory variable, or devote one's energies and computer time to investigating complex functional forms. We decided to push the balance of our compromise into the investigation of more detail in the explanatory variables rather than functional forms. We did, however, investigate alternative functional forms and a brief discussion of these is presented here (further discussion is contained in the appendix to this chapter). We then examine the selection of explanatory variables. Finally in this section we discuss some problems with the measurement of the variable to be explained and briefly the stochastic specification, particularly as regards the residuals and the notion of 'good practice'.

We began our investigations with certain central agricultural variables in mind: fertilizers, irrigation, the number of ploughings, and the date of sowing. These are the variables which experience and research would suggest as the most important. There are important questions as to how, if at all, the timing of the inputs should be included, and we have omitted from our preliminary list the seed rate, weeding activities, soil type, and other potentially important agricultural variables. We return to these issues shortly but for the moment we wish to discuss functional forms.

Agriculturalists and agricultural economists have experimented with several functional forms to model output response curves for fertilizer and other inputs, and some of these are discussed in the appendix to this chapter. In this study, however, only three of these functional forms have been used: the linear, the quadratic, and log-linear. These are presented as equations (1), (2), (3):

$$y = a_0 + \sum_{i=1}^{n} a_i x_i \tag{1}$$

$$y = a_0 + \sum_{i=1}^{n} a_i x_i \sum_{i \leq j} b_{ij} x_i x_j \tag{2}$$

$$\log_e y = c_0 + \sum_{i=1}^{n} c_i \log x_i \tag{3}$$

WHEAT: Productivity and Expectations 253

where y is output per acre and x_i is the quantity per acre of the ith input.

We can think of (1) and (2) as linear and quadratic approximations respectively to a general production function

$$y = f(\mathbf{x}) \tag{4}$$

where $\mathbf{x}$ is the vector with ith component x_i. The linear approximation has the obvious advantage of simplicity. The quadratic allows one to consider diminishing or increasing returns to factors (as does the log-linear form) and further the notion of complements or substitutes. We shall describe i and j as complements (substitutes) if $\partial^2 F / \partial x_i \partial x_j$, or b_{ij} in (2), is positive (negative). This definition is not the same as the Hicksian one (which is in terms of the signs of the second derivatives with respect to input prices of the cost function, rather than of the production function). The linear form has the disadvantage that it does not allow calculation of the 'optimum' input level, in the sense of that level where the value of marginal product is equal to price.

In the event we concentrated on the linear and (to a lesser extent) the log-linear forms. Our reasons were that the linear form (1) gave results marginally better (see below) than the log-linear form (3) and the extra degree of approximation provided by (2) seemed to add rather little. The accuracy of an approximation clearly depends upon the range over which the approximation applies. The diminishing returns to fertilizer, for example, seem to set in at levels rather higher than those adopted by the cultivators on our sample plots. It is not surprising, therefore, that a linear approximation should turn out to be adequate. We concluded that, since the simple linear approximation was as good as any of the more complicated forms, we should concentrate our energies and computer time on looking in more detail at the inputs themselves. We return briefly to some points of detail on the functional form when we have completed this discussion. In the presentation of results we concentrate on the linear case, but present the log-linear as an alternative. Some quadratic results are given in the appendix.

Our criteria for model selection were as follows. We took into account the explained sum of squares and the plausibility of coefficients. For nested hypotheses we can carry out formal F-tests—see below. However the theory and practice of model selection in econometrics for non-nested hypotheses is not yet well developed. Accordingly we were fairly informal in comparing such models. A good survey of the state of knowledge and the problems, together with a comparison of some of the procedures in a Monte Carlo experiment, is contained in Pesaran (1974). For other recent discussions of model selection see Hausman (1978) and Pesaran and Deaton (1978).

There is a sizeable agricultural and agricultural economics literature on production functions for crops using irrigation water—see, for example, Carruthers (1968), Moore (1961), Wiesner (1970). Most of this discussion is in terms of the responsiveness of output per acre to variations in the quantity of water applied in feet or centimetres per acre. Since our measure of the intensity of irrigation is very crude—we have merely the number of times water was applied—we make no attempt to summarize this literature. We turn now to the problems of including the detailed information on inputs in our production relation.

There were two major aggregation problems in the treatment of inputs. The first is the aggregation of inputs, such as water and fertilizer, which occur at different points of time. The second concerns the aggregation of the tasks performed by labour. One could, in principle, treat inputs which occur at different dates, or at different distances in time from the date of sowing, as different inputs. It is clear, however, that scope for such a treatment is limited since we have only forty-seven observations and we must therefore keep the number of explanatory variables down to less than forty-seven; and it is desirable to keep the number of variables well below that figure. Moreover while the timing of some inputs is important, it is unlikely that fertilizer applied thirty-five days after sowing is sufficiently different from fertilizer applied thirty days after sowing to warrant treating them as different variables. Of course fertilizer applied a day before harvesting would be another matter but, understandably, there was no need in the sample to take account of such extreme eventualities.

We decided, in the end, to allow timing to enter in three ways: the date of sowing, the date of the first irrigation, and in the distinction between fertilizer at the time of sowing and fertilizer as a top dressing. Precise variables are defined below.

The aggregation problems raised by the tasks performed by labour are less severe but should not be dismissed. The number of different relevant tasks performed by labour are few in number relative to the number of dates. Further, most of the tasks are sufficiently distinct in nature, for example, weeding and irrigating, both to justify treating them separately in the production process and to make the activity easily identifiable. And it is, after all, the tasks themselves and the standard of their performance which influences production rather than the number of hours the tasks happened to take. There are problems, however, associated with measuring standard of performance. One should not use output to define standard tasks and then use standard tasks to explain output. We avoided these problems by assuming that each category of task, such as ploughing, irrigation, and weeding, is homogeneous, and using the number of ploughings, for example, as a variable. The number of hours becomes at best a proxy for quality of performance of tasks and we did not think it a particularly good proxy for our cultivators. Some would choose to work more slowly than others but we saw no special reason to connect this with quality of performance. We did not therefore think it appropriate to form a labour aggregate as an input. Since, however, many researchers have treated labour as a distinct input in this kind of analysis (see, for example, Hopper, 1965) we decided for comparison purposes and as a test of the argument just expounded, to try a labour aggregate as a separate explanatory variable.

The variables considered in our analysis of output per acre on the sample plots are set out in Table 8.1(a). This list is long and all the factors embodied in the variables have some claim to be taken seriously as possible explanations of

Table 8.1(a) Full List of Explanatory Variables for Output/Acre on Sample Plots (for notation for yield see Note (i)).

FRSWDUM	1 if fertilizer at time of sowing, 0 if not.
FERTACRE	Fertilizer as top dressing in kg of urea per acre.
FERT 25	*FERTACRE* + 25 (similarly *FERT* 35 etc.)
PLGHINGS	Number of ploughings.
SWNGDUM	1 if sown before 1 Dec., 0 if not.
SEEDACRE	Seed quantity in kg/acre.
IRIGNMBER	Number of irrigations.
CULT	Area cultivated by household.
LANDO	Size of cultivator's holding.
CULT/F3	Area cultivated per adult male engaged in agriculture.
LANDO/F3	Size of holding per adult male engaged in agriculture.
LOFA	Size of holding per standard family member (M = 1, W = 0.8, C = 0.5).
LABACRE	Labour per acre in standard hours (M = 1, W = 1, C = ½)
SOILTYPE	Soil type, ranked 1, 2, ..., 5. Number 1 supposed to be best.
SEEDRR21	1 if seed type RR21, 0 if not.
IRG 30	1 if irrigated in first 30 days after sowing, 0 if not.
KHARDUMY	1 if plot fallow in *kharif,* 0 if not.
WEEDDUMY	1 if weeded, 0 if not.
TENANCY	1 if plot under tenancy, 0 if not.
CASTE1	1 if Caste 1 (*Thakur*), 0 if not.
CASTE2	1 if Caste 2 (*Murao*), 0 if not.

A constant term was included. Output/acre 'corrected' is *CORWTACR* and uncorrected *WHEATACR,* see p. 260 for discussion of the distinction.

Table 8.1(b) Explanatory Variables for Main Model
FRSWDUM
FERTACRE
PLGHINGS
SWNGDUM
IRIGNMBR*
A constant term was included.

*This was eventually dropped from the main model owing to unsatisfactory results and further discussion of the 'main' model will refer to the first four variables only unless otherwise stated.

Notes : (i) The dependent variable is CORWTACR—yield in quintals per acre. This has been corrected from measured yield *WHEATACR* to take account of kind payment to harvesters (see end of §8.1)

(ii) *LN* preceding a variable name denotes the logarithm to the base *e*.

variation in output per acre. However the claims of some of them are stronger than those of others and it is necessary to be selective to keep our analysis of functional forms manageable (see below). We decided, therefore, to select certain variables of prime agricultural importance to form a main model. These are set out in Table 8.1(b) and are: the zero-one variable for whether fertilizer was applied at the time of sowing, the quantity of fertilizer (urea) applied as a top dressing, the number of ploughings, the zero-one variable for whether the plot was sown before 1 December, and the number of irrigations.

We ruled out from consideration for the main model those variables, such as caste of cultivator and whether the plot was under tenancy, which could not be considered as direct agricultural inputs. One reason for this is that in our discussion of residuals (see § 8.5 below) we wished to use our knowledge of the characteristics of farmers, and to include just some of those characteristics might cloud that discussion. Other variables were excluded from the main model on the grounds that they were rather poorly measured—for example, soil type. The variable seed per acre was excluded because we had thought that its variance and its effects were too small. We shall return to the variables referring to whether there was irrigation in the first thirty days, whether there was weeding, and the seed type when we have presented the results.

Results are presented, together with correlation matrices, in the next section, but we shall anticipate just one of these results since it is important for our discussion of the main model. All of the five variables (presented above) in that model performed well, in terms of signs, magnitudes, and standard errors of estimated coefficients, except for the number of irrigations. Possible reasons for this are discussed in the next section but its performance was sufficiently bad that we eventually decided to drop it from the main model.

Many of the variables in the list in Table 8.1 are obvious candidates in the explanation of variations in output per acre across plots and most have been introduced above. We shall confine our remarks on the discussions of explanatory variables to those that are less obvious or which presented particular measurement problems. The zero-one variable for fertilizer at the time of sowing (one if fertilizer used, zero otherwise) was adopted because we were unable to measure the quantities of the constituents. We did have data on the total quantity of fertilizer applied at the time of sowing but experiments at an early stage of our analysis with using this aggregate quantity showed less success, in terms of R^2 than the simple zero-one variable.. The variable which takes the value one if the plot was sown before 1 December, and zero otherwise, is clearly a very simple way to model the effects of a date of sowing. Our advice (see discussion around Table 7.1) was that delay into December resulted in sharp losses and 1 December seemed, therefore, the natural divide for a simple approach; and it turned out to be fairly successful (see § 8.3).

The size of holding per standard family member ($LOFA$) is intended to model wealth per 'equivalent' unit in the household. It was explained in § 5.7. The rationale for using wealth per standard family member is to allow examination of the notion that the very poor may take great care with the cultivation of their staple food—wheat—and that this care may be reflected in higher out put per acre for given input levels. Alternatively some have argued (see Griffin, 1974) that access to information is biased in favour of the more wealthy (as it is suggested are many other facilities) and one might, under this hypothesis and if one were to interpret wealth relative to size of family, expect higher outputs per acre for given input levels for more wealthy households. Note that these are just two examples of many possible effects associated with wealth.

Recall that Caste 1 is the *Thakur* and Caste 2 the *Murao* caste. They represent the two highest castes in the village hierarchy. If there is a caste bias in the provision of advice on the use of inputs one would again expect higher outputs per acre from given input levels for these higher castes (remember that while wealth is correlated with caste the correlation is far from perfect). The *Muraos*, as traditional cultivators, might be expected to do particularly well.

Our variable to describe the effects of tenancy is zero-one (one if the plot is under tenancy, zero otherwise). Note that this procedure omits any special details of the tenancy arrangement which might affect the behaviour of cultivators. This is not a serious loss for Palanpur where the contracts are fairly uniform, as described in § 5.2 and§ 7.4. We shall be particularly interested in the correlation between the zero-one tenancy variable and those variables describing input intensities on our sample plots. This will be statistically equivalent to an analysis of variance which examines the question whether input levels are significantly lower on tenanted than owner-cultivated plots. Thus we shall be testing the 'so-called Marshallian' view described in § 3.2 and discussed with respect to the sample plots in § 7.4.

When the zero-one tenancy variable is included in the regression equations along with the input variables we have an analysis of covariance; that is, we look at variations in output associated with tenancy for given measured inputs. In this sense we examine the notion that, notwithstanding the landlord's supervision, tenants apply their inputs less carefully. This might happen since there is no sharing in any costs associated with care yet the tenant receives only half of any extra output.

The inclusion of a zero-one variable to capture the effects of tenancy in the regression equations implies that these effects can be captured by a simple shift in the production function rather than a change in all the coefficients. In the linear or quadratic models this means that all marginal productivities are assumed constant across tenanted and non-tenanted plots. Such a procedure cannot capture the Marshallian idea that tenants operate on a part of the production function where marginal productivities are higher. We shall, however, as has just been described, be examining the Marshallian, view directly when we compare input levels on tenanted and owner-cultivated plots. Note that the log-linear form of the production function does allow marginal productivities to differ across plots.

There are methods, using a linear model, which will allow marginal products to differ for tenants and others. One could split the sample into two, those plots under tenancy and those not. One might test the hypothesis (using a Chow test) that the two sub-samples came from the same distribution. Alternatively one can incorporate tenancy through dummy variables which shift coefficients rather than the constant term : one could write the effect of the input level x as $(\alpha_1 + \alpha_2 z)x$ where z is one for tenancy and zero otherwise and α_1 and α_2 are to be estimated. Given the comparatively small number of observations on tenanted plots and that we are already directly examining the Marshallian view by looking at input levels, we decided not to adopt these alternative methods.

The inclusion of the cultivator holding (*LANDO*) as a variable represents an attempt to investigate the idea that there may be special management problems associated with large land holdings. There is a choice here between land cultivated and land owned but we selected land owned since the form of tenancy adopted in the village implies that the land-owner has management and supervision tasks whether or not he cultivates himself. These tasks are less onerous if he leased the land out, however; indeed this was part of our explanation in Chapter 5 for the quantity of land leased-out. As an alternative we also tried cultivator holding per male engaged in agriculture (*LANDO/F3*). We made this choice on the grounds of our *a priori* judgements. We have, however, included land cultivated (*CULT*) and *CULT/F3* in our correlation matrices. *LANDO* and *LANDO/F3* are carried through the regression analysis. In addition to the 'management effect' just described *LANDO* may embody some of the advantages of privileged access to advice which we attempt to capture in *LOFA* (see above). A higher value for *CULT* may indicate a stronger 'commitment to agriculture' (see § 6.7).

The soil-type was included as a discrete variable—taking numbers 1 to 5 with 1 for the best land and 5 for the worst. We have seen, however, in § 7.3 that most plots in our sample (thirty-seven out of forty-seven) were classified as 3 or 4, that is, sandy-loam 1 or sandy-loam 2. Given that our soil type classification was informal from the viewpoint of the soil scientist the quality difference between plots classified as sandy-loam 1 and sandy-loam 2 in terms of productivity for wheat may in some cases be negligible or even the reverse of the classification. A few instances of such mis-classification, which could easily arise, might destroy the effectiveness of soil type as an explanatory variable.

One experiment we tried was to take account of the interaction between the application of fertilizer and the date of sowing. We saw in § 7.1.2 that fertilizer is less productive if applied to late-sown wheat. We therefore included a variable which was the product of fertilizer per acre and the zero-one date of sowing variable. The results were not successful because, we suppose, it proved too highly correlated with the date of sowing variable (correlation coefficient of 0.76) and we do not discuss it further here. An option which we might have tried, but did not, would have been to include the product variable instead of the sowing date variable.

It is important that a wheat plot be irrigated regularly and the number of irrigations has been included as an explanatory variable. We saw in § 7.1.2 that the recommended date for the first irrigation was three weeks after sowing and that this irrigation was regarded as particularly important. Accordingly we included a zero-one variable, with one if irrigation occurred within the first thirty days and zero otherwise.

Yet another zero-one variable was for seed type : the variable takes the value one if the plot was sown with RR21 and zero otherwise. We saw in Table 7.4 that there were twenty-nine cases of RR21 in the sample of forty-seven and we remarked that this seed may have deteriorated in the preceding four years (it was brought to the village 'new' in 1970–1), and we had in mind that the coefficient on this zero-one variable would be negative.

Pre-harvest labour hours per acre (counting men and women as one and children as half) was included and we have already presented our views on the use of this variable. We should point out that some of the labour hours have in a sense already been included in the other activity variables such as irrigation and ploughing. Recall, however, that our argument was that if labour hours are to have any role at all here it must be in the care in which tasks are executed. We should also record here that the number of labour hours is importantly affected by choice of irrigation method : Persian wheel or pumping set. The final zero-one variable used was for weeding—one if weeding occurred and zero otherwise.

Before discussing one or two further details of functional forms we should make two general points about the variables we have introduced. First, we do not regard all the variables as having equal *a priori* plausibility. We have already isolated variables for our main model for example. We have argued that some variables, such as soil type, may be badly measured. And we have suggested that others such as labour per acre are unlikely to have an effect but have been included for comparison with other studies. Thus we shall be presenting results with only certain subsets of the variables included.

Second, the high number of zero-one classifications involved has pointed us towards analyses in terms of regressions which include zero-one variables, or analyses of covariance, rather than towards splitting the sample into sub-samples according to the particular classification. We have only forty-seven observations and dividing the sample by more than one zero-one variable would result in too few observations in the sub-samples. Note that the coefficient on the zero-one variable in the linear model tells us the additive shift (here the extra output per acre) which results when the variable takes the value one, over and above that which pertains when the value is zero.

Having presented our variables we return to a few points of detail on functional forms. We have already stated that the three which would be tried were the linear, quadratic, and the log-linear (see equations (1), (2), (3)).The experiments with functional form were conducted on the main model. This has five explanatory variables if the number of irrigations is included. In our experiments with the quadratic formulations we did want to include the number of irrigations since we had in mind that the interactions between fertilizer and irrigation might account for the insignificance of the number of irrigations as an explanatory variable. A full quadratic treatment where a model of the form of equation (2) had been used would then have involved twenty-five right-hand-side variables plus a constant term. We regarded this as too many for a data set of forty-seven observations and decided to concentrate on just a few of the interaction terms—such as that between fertilizer and irrigation—which were of particular interest and plausibility for the specific model, see § 8.3.

In the log-linear case we must take account of the fact that eight of the cultivators applied no fertilizer on the sample plots. The logarithm of zero is $-\infty$, a value inconvenient for regressions. We tried two approaches. The first was to drop these cultivators from the sample—leaving only thirty-nine observations. The second was to include as an explanatory variable log $(f + a)$ where f is fertilizer per acre and 'a' is a constant, and then search over 'a' to find the best fit. The region of possible 'a's selected was based on the amount of nitrogen that wheat extracts from the soil. A rough idea of the output that is available without fertilizer can then give us an indication of the amount of nitrogen available in the soil. The results of this search are described in the appendix.

We did not take the logarithms of the zero-one variables in the log-linear regressions. A log-linear equation including one continuous explanatory variable x, a zero-one variable z, and variable to be explained y would be

$$\log_e y = a + bz + c\log_e x \tag{5}$$

If we revert to the multiplicative form by taking anti-logarithms this becomes

$$y = Ae^{bz}x^c \tag{6}$$

where $A = e^a$. If z takes the value zero, e^{bz} is one, and if z takes the value one, e^{bz} is e^b. The coefficient on z in the log-linear form therefore gives us a multiplicative shift in the production function.

The measurement of output per acre presents some complications. First, we decided to exclude the by-product, straw, from the variable to be explained. We doubt that this exclusion is misleading because the output of straw is highly correlated with the output of wheat. And if we were to include the output of straw we should have to meet the problem of the relative prices of straw and wheat. For most farmers the straw is not traded but used as cattle feed, and so their opportunity cost is not easy to measure precisely. Second, we ignored the output of mustard where this was mixed with wheat. The addition of mustard seed with the wheat seed seemed to be a fairly casual business where a few handfuls of the mustard seed were tossed in. Consequently we had no measurement of the quantity of seed involved. We can, and shall however, take the output of mustard into account when interpreting the residuals. There were twelve plots without any mustard. If the presence of mustard lowers the output of wheat then, *ceteris paribus,* these twelve plots would show positive residuals.

The last complication with the measurement of output is that the portion paid to the labour that is hired to harvest the crop never reaches the threshing floor of the cultivator, and thus was not measured. We do, however, have a way of correcting for this aspect. We know the proportion α of the harvest labour standard hours which is hired and we know also that the payment is one-twentieth of the quantity harvested. If we assume that the hired and family labour harvest at the same rate, the total output is $1/(1 - 0.05\alpha)$ times the output which is measured after threshing by the cultivator. We refer to this total as the corrected output, or, simply, output.

Finally in this section we turn to the stochastic specification. We are dealing with a cross-section so we have none of the problems of temporal interrelation of errors which plague many time-series analyses in economics. We make the standard assumptions on the errors which we require to assert that the estimators will be unbiased, consistent, and optimum (in the sense of minimum variance) and to test hypotheses about coefficients—we suppose that errors are mutually independent and identically normally distributed and independent of the regressors. It is clear that this set of assumptions can be correct for at most one of the functional forms which we try, but each time we run a regression we implicitly make that assumption for the functional form being considered.

Problems of bias and inconsistency arise if an included variable is correlated with the error term. This is a difficulty which will arise when we discuss the notion of good practice. If we assert that 'good-practice' cultivators both apply more inputs and have higher residuals (get more out of given input levels) then we have just this difficulty. Nowshirvani (1967) pointed to such a problem of inconsistency in the work of Hopper (1965). Nowshirvani argued that if a farmer is aware of the output that will follow from his inputs then, if we assume profit maximization, those farmers who get more out of given inputs (high residuals) will also apply more inputs to equate value marginal product with price.

To the extent that the variables included to capture the characteristics of cultivators measure all that there is to measure in the way of good practice, so that residuals are purely random and unknown to farmers, the problem is overcome. There may, of course, be correlation amongst explanatory variables in that farmers of a certain type apply more inputs or that those who use one input intensively use another intensively, but this is a problem of multicollinearity and does not produce the problems of inconsistency which arise from correlation between an explanatory variable and the error term. Nowshirvani argued that correlation amongst explanatory variables would be perfect if all farmers were identical, were well-informed, profit-maximized under constant returns to scale and certainty facing fixed prices, and residuals were purely random and unknown to the farmers. This does not follow if farmers are imperfectly informed, make mistakes, or have varying attitudes to risk.

The notion of good practice is of value in understanding what is going on but is a slightly slippery term. We wish to take it into account but if we go too far in trying to measure it we run the risk of explaining nothing by explaining too much, in the sense of attributing all of the residual to good or bad practice. It is clear that in agriculture (and other things) substantial residual randomness does occur and we do not wish to attribute everything to deterministic factors. Ideally we measure all such factors and the remainder of the variation is explicable in terms of differential impact of the random phenomena, weather, pests, diseases, and so on. The plots were sufficiently dispersed geographically for it to be reasonably supposed that sources of these random effects were mutually independent. While we hope we have done as well as we can in meeting the statistical difficulties we have mentioned we cannot pretend to have eliminated the problems. We shall have to bear them in mind when we come to interpret results and discuss residuals.

We declined to construct a measure of 'good practice' from variables such as fertilizer and irrigation using, say, factor analysis. The technique of factor analysis (and similarly principal components) is particularly appropriate where the measures or scores constructed as explanatory variables are not of great inherent interest. But we are directly interested in the coefficient on fertilizer, for example, and this would be lost in such a procedure.

§ 8.2 The Correlation Matrix ; 'Good Practice' and Tenancy

§ 8.2.0 Introduction
The correlation matrix for the variables in the linear model is presented in Table 8.2(a) and for the log-linear model in Table 8.2(b). In each case we also give means and standard deviations. From this information it is a straightforward matter, using standard formulae, to calculate all the statistics one would want in any single-variable regressions. We leave it to the reader to perform the calculations for such simple regressions as appropriate. We shall refer to the linear case (Table 8.2 (a)) unless otherwise stated.

As in § 5.8.1, we judge the significance of the correlation coefficients in Table 8.2 using the result that the statistic

$$t = \left\{ \frac{(n-2)r^2}{(1-r^2)} \right\}^{\frac{1}{2}} \tag{7}$$

where r is the correlation coefficient in a sample of size n from a bivariate normal distribution, is distributed in Student's t-distribution with $(n-2)$ degrees of freedom on the hypothesis that the population correlation coefficient is zero. The 5 per cent significance level for t with 45 degrees of freedom is 2.02 (see Kendall and Stuart, 1973, p.653) and thus for our sample we have a 5 per cent significance level for r of 0.288 (these levels are to three significant figures). Similarly the 10 per cent significance level for r is 0.243 and the 20 per cent level 0.191. Looking at significance from the other direction we find in Table 8.2 (a) that the explanatory variable with the highest correlation coefficient with the corrected wheat output per acre is 0.651 for the zero-one variable for fertilizer at the time of sowing. This correlation coefficient has a t-value of 33.1.

The significance of a simple correlation coefficient is equivalent to significance of the coefficient on the independent variable in a simple linear regression. Inspection of the row for corrected wheat per acre (*CORWTACR*) in Table 8.2 (a) shows that the following nine variables would give significant coefficients in simple linear regressions with corrected wheat per acre as dependent variable: the zero-one variable for fertilizer at the time of sowing, fertilizer as a top dressing per acre, the number of irrigations, the zero-one variable for whether seed type RR21 was used, the zero-one variable for Caste 2, area cultivated by household, the zero-one variable for irrigation in the first thirty days after sowing, the zero-one variable for weeding, and the quantity of seed per acre. The variables are listed in order corresponding to the absolute magnitude of the correlation coefficient. All the coefficients are positive except for those corresponding to seed per acre and RR21. The only direct input variable that requires explanation is seed per acre and we return to this in § 8.3. We should not expect all these coefficients to remain significant when we pass

Table 8.2(a) Linear

Variable	Mean	Standard Deviation	WHEATACR	CORWTACR	PLGHINGS*	FERTACRE	FRSWDUM*	SWNGDUM*	TENANCY	LANDO	SOILTYPE	IRIGNMBR*	IRG 30*	SEEDACRE	SEEDRR21	CASTEI	CASTE2	LABACRE	LANDO/F3	LOF A	WEEDDUMY*	KHARDUMY*	CULT/F3	CULT
WHEATACR	8.05	2.36	1.00	1.00	0.15	0.61	0.63	0.22	-0.20	0.28	-0.20	0.58	0.40	-0.31	-0.58	0.005	0.49	0.13	-0.19	-0.02	0.32	-0.09	-0.25	0.46
CORWTACR	8.26	2.46		1.00	0.14	0.61	0.65	0.23	-0.22	0.28	-0.36	0.59	0.42	-0.31	-0.58	0.05	0.48	0.13	-0.18	-0.01	0.34	-0.09	-0.24	0.46
PLGHINGS	5.06	1.67			1.00	-0.07	-0.19	0.06	0.11	0.05	-0.36	-0.18	0.09	-0.41	-0.05	-0.41	0.14	0.15	0.02	0.04	-0.02	0.11	0.04	0.05
FERTACRE	31.80	19.26				1.00	0.37	-0.03	-0.05	0.02	-0.14	0.54	0.27	0.09	-0.40	0.003	0.40	0.22	-0.32	-0.004	0.38	-0.24	-0.23	0.13
FRSWDUM	0.49	0.51					1.00	0.07	-0.48	0.37	0.03	0.71	0.50	-0.08	-0.54	0.21	0.46	0.19	0.04	0.19	0.46	-0.15	-0.13	0.45
SWNGDUM	0.53	0.50						1.00	-0.19	0.30	0.10	-0.11	0.06	-0.21	-0.21	-0.04	-0.05	-0.04	0.15	0.02	0.02	0.24	0.11	0.39
TENANCY	0.19	0.40							1.00	-0.52	0.01	-0.28	-0.24	-0.001	0.27	-0.28	-0.35	-0.26	-0.50	-0.43	-0.27	-0.10	0.13	-0.24
LANDO	6.25	4.47								1.00	-0.05	0.09	0.23	-0.27	-0.47	-0.03	-0.59	-0.14	0.64	0.67	-0.11	0.10	-0.11	0.65
SOILTYPE	3.32	0.86									1.00	-0.20	-0.08	0.16	0.09	-0.10	-0.06	-0.01	0.11	0.12	-0.09	0.20	0.17	-0.14
IRIGNMBR	4.19	1.12										1.00	0.54	-0.01	-0.42	0.38	0.20	0.24	-0.29	-0.11	0.50	-0.43	-0.28	0.28
IRG 30	0.57	0.50											1.00	-0.28	-0.32	0.21	0.16	0.08	-0.004	0.11	0.17	-0.02	-0.08	0.34
SEEDACRE	39.39	4.20												1.00	0.33	0.03	-0.06	0.23	-0.08	-0.08	0.01	-0.10	-0.12	-0.39
SEEDRR21	0.62	0.49													1.00	0.06	-0.54	0.03	-0.13	-0.29	-0.18	-0.06	0.17	-0.40
CASTEI	0.26	0.44														1.00	-0.42	-0.002	0.08	0.03	0.37	-0.16	0.10	0.004
CASTE2	0.34	0.48															1.00	0.04	0.20	0.45	0.03	-0.01	-0.33	0.37
LABACRE	207.03	95.27																1.00	-0.18	-0.11	0.44	-0.17	-0.19	-0.14
LANDO/F3	3.54	2.22																	1.00	0.77	-0.10	0.06	0.36	0.13
LOFA	1.07	0.87																		1.00	0.02	0.04	-0.03	0.03
WEEDDUMY	0.23	0.43																			1.00	-0.27	-0.10	-0.09
KHARDUMY	0.19	0.40																				1.00	-0.01	0.06
CULT/F3	3.81	1.71																						1.00	0.18
CULT	6.24	3.16																							1.00

No. of cases 47

Note: Asterisks denote 'good practice' variables—see § 8.2.1. RR21 is associated with 'bad practice'.

Table 8.2 (b) Logarithmic

Variable	Mean	Standard Deviation	LNWHEAT4CR	LNCORWTACR	LNPLGHINGS	LNFERT25	FRSWDUM	SWNGDUM	TENANCY	LNLANDO	LNSOILTYPE	LNIRIGNMBR	IRG 30	LNSEEDACRE	SEEDRR21	CASTE1	CASTE2	LNLAB4CRE	LNLANDO/F3	LOFA	WEEDDUMY	KHARDUMY	LNCULT/F3	LNCULT
LNWHEAT4CR	2.04	0.31	1.00																					
LNCORWTACR	2.06	0.31	1.00	1.00																				
LNPLGHINGS	1.57	0.35	0.16	0.15	1.00																			
LNFERT25	3.97	0.39	0.62	0.62	-0.09	1.00																		
FRSWDUM	0.49	0.51	0.62	0.65	-0.20	0.38	1.00																	
SWNGDUM	0.53	0.50	0.21	0.21	0.08	-0.01	-0.07	1.00																
TENANCY	0.19	0.40	-0.17	-0.20	0.12	-0.04	-0.48	-0.19	1.00															
LNLANDO	1.50	0.96	0.19	0.21	-0.05	-0.02	0.41	0.37	-0.72	1.00														
LNSOILTYPE	1.16	0.30	-0.20	-0.19	-0.38	-0.13	0.004	0.07	0.02	-0.08	1.00													
LNIRIGNMBR	1.39	0.30	0.53	0.54	-0.18	0.52	0.68	-0.16	-0.24	0.06	-0.19	1.00												
IRG 30	0.57	0.50	0.37	0.39	0.08	0.26	0.50	0.06	-0.24	0.22	-0.08	0.50	1.00											
LNSEEDACRE	3.67	0.10	-0.31	-0.31	-0.38	0.06	-0.11	-0.20	0.02	-0.16	0.22	-0.04	-0.30	1.00										
SEEDRR21	0.62	0.49	-0.56	-0.57	-0.07	-0.39	-0.54	-0.21	0.27	-0.37	0.12	-0.35	-0.32	0.36	1.00									
CASTE1	0.26	0.44	0.004	0.04	-0.43	0.06	0.21	-0.04	-0.28	0.10	-0.08	0.32	0.21	0.04	0.06	1.00								
CASTE2	0.34	0.48	0.46	0.45	0.15	0.37	0.46	-0.05	-0.35	0.48	-0.08	0.20	0.16	-0.10	-0.54	-0.42	1.00							
LNLAB4CRE	5.24	0.44	0.13	0.13	0.18	0.19	0.25	-0.08	-0.31	-0.04	-0.02	0.28	0.14	0.20	-0.01	-0.02	0.11	1.00						
LNLANDO/F3	1.03	0.79	-0.09	-0.07	-0.12	-0.23	0.21	0.23	-0.68	0.82	0.07	-0.14	0.03	-0.004	-0.14	0.17	0.25	-0.10	1.00					
LNLOFA	-0.26	0.91	-0.003	0.02	-0.03	-0.04	0.31	0.16	-0.67	0.83	0.04	-0.06	0.19	-0.04	-0.23	0.14	0.41	-0.001	0.88	1.00				
WEEDDUMY	0.23	0.43	0.33	0.34	-0.02	0.37	0.46	0.02	-0.27	0.03	-0.04	0.45	0.17	0.02	-0.18	0.37	0.03	0.42	0.03	0.12	1.00			
KHARDUMY	0.19	0.40	-0.10	-0.10	0.16	-0.25	-0.15	-0.24	-0.10	0.13	0.17	-0.46	-0.02	-0.09	-0.06	-0.16	-0.01	-0.13	0.05	0.09	-0.27	1.00		
LNCULT/F3	1.24	0.45	-0.19	-0.18	0.01	-0.21	-0.06	0.08	0.13	-0.16	0.15	-0.19	-0.01	-0.10	0.15	0.07	-0.27	-0.12	0.17	-0.05	-0.06	-0.10	1.00	
LNCULT	1.71	0.50	0.34	0.35	0.10	0.13	0.40	0.43	-0.19	0.49	-0.14	0.17	0.35	-0.40	-0.35	-0.01	0.28	0.16	-0.01	-0.05	0.16	-0.05	0.33	1.00

No. of cases 47

to multiple regression and we shall see that they do not. Further, we shall find that the simple correlations conceal effects which will emerge when we pass to multiple regressions (see § 8.3).

It is interesting to note that of the four alternative variables intended to capture effects associated with size of owned or cultivated holding (*CULT*, *CULT/F3*, *LANDO*, and *LANDO/F3*) only *CULT* was significant with a correlation coefficient with *CORWTACR* of 0.464 (although *LANDO* was quite close to significance with a correlation coefficient of 0.282). The result is consistent with our findings on the intensity of cultivation in § 6.7. In view of this finding it might have been appropriate to carry *CULT* rather than *LANDO* through the regression analysis. However, the decision had already been made and it is most unlikely that the opposite decision would have produced any important changes in our main results.

§ 8.2.1 'Good Practice'

The direct inputs which we identified in § 7.1.2 and § 7.3 as being connected with good practice were fertilizer at the time of sowing and as a top dressing, the number of ploughings, the number of irrigations, an irrigation within thirty days of sowing, timely sowing, and weeding. We also suggested that the use of seed type RR21 should be associated with bad practice. We find that all these variables are contained in the list of significant single-variable correlations, and in this (weak) sense the notion of good practice is confirmed. It also turns out that there are significant correlations amongst those variables which are connected with good practice (this statement does not follow automatically from the preceding sentence). The 'good practice' variables in Table 8.1 (a) are marked with an asterisk and we see that the higher inter-correlations amongst variables are connected with irrigation and fertilizer, which are themselves strongly correlated. It turned out that of these variables, the irrigation variables, RR21, and the weeding dummy do not retain their significant correlation with output per acre (*CORWTACR*) when we pass to multiple regression. We shall be discussing in the next section whether this indicates that the original simple correlation with output per acre may be misleading or whether there are problems with multi-collinearity. The number of ploughings and zero-one variable for early sowing on the other hand were less strongly correlated with other variables.

We see that Caste 2, the *Muraos* or cultivating caste, score well on fertilizers and avoiding RR21 but less significantly on the number of irrigations and ploughings. On the other hand Caste 1, the *Thakurs*, seem to do well when it comes to irrigation but not fertilizers or RR21 and seem particularly averse to ploughing. It may be that some *Thakurs* view ploughing as not a particularly seemly activity for a high caste (see Hopper (1965) for a report of an even stronger attitude in the 1950s in village Senapur, East U.P).

The land cultivated by the household is significantly positively correlated with output per acre and most of the measures of good practice, as well as with the Caste 2, or *Murao*, variable. The correlations with good practice disappear when we divide by the number of men engaged in agriculture (to produce the variable *CULT/F3*). The size of holding of the cultivator is negatively correlated with tenancy and we see effects opposite to those described for tenancy in the next sub-section.

We turn now to three variables, soil type, seed per acre, and whether the plot was fallow in the *kharif*, which are agricultural variables but not in our good practice list. We recorded previously our lack of confidence in our measurement of soil type. It is only weakly correlated with all the other variables, except for the number of ploughings where we find that the better soil seems to be ploughed more often. The number of ploughings seems to be negatively correlated with the seed rate. Cultivators may have in mind some form of compensation in the sense that they put more seed into a plot that is less well prepared. This would be sensible in terms of its effects on profit only if fewer ploughings implied a higher marginal productivity of seed–that ploughings and seed rate are complements in the sense described above (see the discussion following equation (4) above). The seed rate is not significantly correlated with the other explanatory variables. The dummy variable for whether the plot was fallow in the preceding *kharif* (one if it was, zero if not) is not significantly correlated with output per acre. We explained in § 7.3 that there was no presumption that there should be a positive correlation. Note the negative correlation with the number of irrigations.

The output of mustard has not been included in the measure of output from the plot, for reasons explained in § 8.1. Neither have we included mustard output per acre as an explanatory variable, as something which might compete for nutrients and water, in the regression analysis presented here. The output per acre of mustard was not significantly correlated (coefficient–0.003) with that of wheat. However there is a significant positive correlation (0.313) between early sowing and yield of mustard. The mustard ripens earlier and is usually harvested well before the wheat. Delays in sowing give, therefore, a greater proportionate reduction in growing season for mustard than for wheat, making mustard less attractive for later-sown plots. In a regression analysis which included yield of mustard as an explanatory variable, the sowing dummy became insignificant and we found a positive coefficient on the yield of mustard. The result does not accord with the notion that the coefficient on mustard yield should be negative because they compete for nutrients and water (although the competition no doubt exists). We decided to exclude the yield of mustard from a list of explanatory variables since we wished to retain the more 'direct' variable for the date of sowing.

Note that a discussion in terms of the correlation coefficients for the log-linear model–see Table 8.2(b)–would lead to much the same conclusions.

§ 8.2.2. Tenancy

We examine in this sub-section the correlations of the output and input variables with the zero-one variable for tenancy. Here we are testing hypotheses

WHEAT: Productivity and Expectations   267

about differences between cultivation practices on tenanted and owner-cultivated plots. The correlation coefficients between tenancy and the 'good practice' variables are (see Table 8.2 (a)) as follows:$FRSWDUM - 0.475$, $FERTACRE - 0.045$, $PLGHINGS + 0.112$, $IRIGNMBR - 0.280$, $IRG30 - 0.237$, $SWNGDUM - 0.194$, $WEEDDUMY - 0.269$ (for definitions of variables see Table 8.1). The correlation coefficient with output per acre is -0.220 and with labour per acre ($LABACRE$) -0.259.

The signs of all the correlation coefficients (with the exception of $PLGHINGS$) are those that would be expected from the so-called Marshallian theory. They indicate that tenants use less care or lower levels of inputs. However, only the first of the correlations, that for fertilizer at the time of sowing, is significant. And the correlation of the tenancy variable with yield itself is insignificant.

There is mild support, then, in this wheat study for the so-called Marshallian view but it is certainly not strong. Nine cases of tenancy is in any case too few to say much with confidence. Our findings here must be set against the more broadly based studies of § 5.3 and Chapter 6 in which the Marshallian view received no support at all.

§ 8.3 The Main Regressions

We present results for the linear model first. The explanatory variables under consideration were shown in Table 8.1(a). We selected agricultural variables of special interest to be included in a main model and these were given in Table 8.1(b). The number of irrigations performed badly as an explanatory variable (low F-values for the test of significance of the coefficient) wherever fertilizer is included and we decided to abandon it from the main model. We present first, in Table 8.3, the results from the main model in linear form.

As explained in § 5.8.1, when we introduced our first regression output and the SPSS format, our criterion for significance is in general the 5 per cent level, or $t = 2$, $F = 4$. However we shall occasionally use the less rigorous criterion $F = 1$. The interest in the level $F = 1$ derives from the result that the standard measure of the goodness-of-fit of the over-all equation $\bar{R}^2$ increases if a variable whose coefficient would have t-value greater than one if included, is actually included in the equation. Note that the criteria $t \geq 1$ and $F \geq 1$ are equivalent. The significance level associated with $F = 1$ is however, around 30 per cent which is weak when compared with the traditional 5 per cent.

We can see from Table 8.3 that the variable, seed per acre, would be significant if adjoined to the main model and that there are several other variables which would have F-values greater than one if included. We are presented with a problem which is common in regression analysis—that of selection of which variables to include in the model and which to discard. We decided to adopt the technique of step-wise regression with a cut-off value of F equal to one. Thus we go on including variables one by one, with that entered at each step being the one which provides the largest increase in $\bar{R}^2$. Equivalently we select the variable with highest F value of those excluded from the current equation. We

Table 8.3. The Main Model—Linear

Multiple R	0.83	Number of cases	47
R squared	0.69	Number of variables	4
Standard error	1.44	F-Value for equation	23.23
		Dependent variable	$CORWTACR$

Variables in the equation

Variable	B	Standard error of B	F
FRSWDUM	2.55	0.46	30.74
FERTACRE	0.056	0.01	22.32
PLGHINGS	0.37	0.13	8.35
SWNGDUM	0.94	0.42	5.00
Constant	2.83		

Variables not in the equation

Variable	B IN	F
TENANCY	0.50	0.63
LANDO	0.01	0.02
SOILTYPE	−0.28	1.11
IRIGNMBR	0.27	0.73
IRG 30	0.05	0.01
SEEDACRE	−0.12	5.08
SEEDRR21	−0.60	1.18
CASTE1	0.31	0.34
CASTE2	0.24	0.20
LABACRE	−0.003	1.55
LANDO/F3	−0.12	1.36
LOFA	−0.35	2.02
WEEDDUMY	−0.49	0.73
KHARDUMY	0.11	0.03

Notes :   (i) See notes to Table 5.7.
        (ii) For definition of variables see Table 8.1.

go on including variables until there is no variable, the introduction of which would increase $\bar{R}^2$.

There are certain commonly advanced and important criticisms of step-wise regression (see, for example, Kendall and Stuart, 1973, p. 349), the most frequent of which refers to 'path-dependence'. The problem is that the method of choosing the largest increase in $\bar{R}^2$ at each single step does not necessarily provide the largest $\bar{R}^2$ for the number of variables eventually selected. Similarly if one began with all the variables and discarded them on the basis of the smallest decrease in $\bar{R}^2$ until, say, there were k variables in the equation, one would not necessarily arrive at the same k-variables as would be produced by step-wise regression. However we hope that reality is not as perverse as the worst that one can conceive.

For our case the process of step-wise regression does indeed start by selecting the variables of our main model, with the exception of the number of irrigations. The number of variables eventually selected was eight. The stopping criterion was to halt when none of the excluded variables had F-value greater than one. The selection procedure does not guarantee the maximization of $\bar{R}^2$ and we have not computed regressions for all possible selections of eight variables to establish that $\bar{R}^2$ has been maximized subject to the constraint of using not more than eight explanatory variables. Nevertheless inspection of both the F-values of excluded variables at step 8, and of which variables they happen to be, leads us to be optimistic that we have in fact maximized $\bar{R}^2$

The regression of output per acre on the eight explanatory variables produced by this procedure is presented in Table 8.4. The results from estimating the main model in log-linear form where we take logarithms of all variables except those which are zero-one are given in Table 8.5. The variable for fertilizer as a top dressing was $\log_e (f + 25)$ where f is the quantity of fertilizer in kg per acre. The number 25 was selected after a search process described in § 8.1, the results of which are presented in the appendix. We adjoined further

Table 8.4. The Extended Model—Linear

Multiple R	0.88	Number of cases	47
R squared	0.77	Number of variables	8
Standard error	1.30	F-Value for equation	15.97
		Dependent variabele	*CORWTACR*

Variables in the equation

Variable	B	Standard error of B	F
FRSWDUM	1.85	0.52	12.67
FERTACRE	0.05	0.01	17.00
PLGHINGS	0.27	0.14	3.64
SWNGDUM	0.93	0.39	5.51
SEEDACRE	-0.12	0.05	5.24
LOFA	-0.71	0.27	6.89
CASTE1	1.08	0.63	2.93
CASTE2	1.63	0.72	5.13
Constant	8.64		

Variables not in the equation

Variable	B IN	F
TENANCY	0.62	0.83
LANDO	0.01	0.01
SOILTYPE	-0.04	0.02
IRIGNMBR	0.002	0.00
IRG30	-0.16	0.10
SEEDRR21	-0.26	0.21
LABACRE	-0.001	0.41
LANDO/F3	-0.02	0.01
WEEDDUMY	-0.46	0.61
KHARDUMY	0.08	0.02

Notes : (i) See notes to Table 5.7.
      (ii) For definitions of variables see Table 8.1.

Table 8.5. The Main Model—Logarithmic

Multiple R	0.83	Number of cases	47
R squared	0.69	Number of variables	4
Standard error	0.18	F-Value for equation	23.36
		Dependent variable	LNCORWT-ACR

Variables in the equation

Variable	B	Standard error of B	F
FRSWDUM	0.32	0.06	30.23
LNFERT25	0.36	0.07	23.45
LNPLGHINGS	0.25	0.08	9.85
SWNGDUM	0.10	0.05	3.52
Constant	0.04		

Variables not in the equation

Variable	B IN	F
TENANCY	0.07	0.79
LNLANDO	− 0.02	0.35
LNSOILTYPE	− 0.05	0.26
LNIRIGNMBR	0.08	0.34
IRG30	− 0.02	0.06
LNSEEDACRE	− 0.52	3.31
SEEDRR21	− 0.06	0.70
CASTE1	0.03	0.20
CASTE2	0.01	0.01
LNLABACRE	− 0.10	2.50
LNLANDO/F3	− 0.04	1.11
LNLOFA	− 0.06	3.29
WEEDDUMY	− 0.06	0.67
KHARDUMY	0.01	0.01

Notes : (i) See notes to Table 5.7.
     (ii) For definitions of variables see Table 8.1.

variables to the main model for the log-linear case following a similar procedure and adopting similar criteria to those just described for the linear case. We turn now to a discussion of the variables selected and of estimated coefficients.

We begin with the main model and the linear case—see Table 8.3. All four variables are significant at the 5 per cent level, as would be the variable seed per acre were it to be introduced. All coefficients of included variables have the signs one would expect. We shall be discussing the economics of the use of fertilizer and of ploughings in § 8.4 and 8.6, together with more detailed examination of the estimates themseves. Let us for the moment give some understanding of the magnitude of the coefficients. Output per acre is measured in quintals (100 kg) of wheat per acre, fertilizer per acre is measured in kg per acre, the number of ploughings is integer, and there are zero-one variables for fertilizer at the time of sowing and for the date of sowing. Recall (Table 8.2(a)) that the average output per acre was 8.26 quintals. Thus the estimated coefficients indicate that fertilizer at the time of sowing provides a 31 per cent increase in output (from the mean level); 1 kg of urea per acre provides 5.6 kg of wheat per acre; one extra ploughing gives 37 kg of wheat per acre; and timely sowing (before 1 December) provides an extra 94 kg per acre, or an 11 per cent increase from the mean.

A partial check on the plausibility of these coefficients is available from comparisons with the effects of varying input levels found at agricultural research stations and discussed in § 7.1.2. The responsiveness of the yield to different levels of nitrogen was illustrated in Figs. 7.1, 7.2, and 7.3. Recalling that urea is 46 per cent nitrogen we have one kg of nitrogen produces 5.6/0.46 or 12.17 kg of wheat. This is rather lower than the gradients shown in Figs. 7.2 and 7.3. The study by Singh, Sharma, and Mishra (1970), for example, finds an average return of 22.8 kg of wheat (Sonalika or RR21) from 1 kg of nitrogen. But they have provided 'appropriate' complementary levels of other inputs such as water, phosphates, potash, pesticides, and so on, all of which we suppose would be at levels rather higher than Palanpur. A higher level of a complementary input would be expected to raise the marginal and average productivity of nitrogen.

Our coefficient for timely sowing seems consistent with Table 7.1 and the surrounding discussion on the effects of the date of sowing on yield, where for example we reported Shri Kumar's estimate that fifteen days' delay in December could cause a 20 per cent drop in yield. We have an 11 per cent difference for the crude zero-one classification of after or before 1 December. We are not aware of a direct estimate of the productivity of an extra ploughing although there have been studies of the productivity of bullock hours (see, for example, Hopper, 1965).

The coefficients estimated for the main model with its four variables are reduced when we pass to the extended model (see Table 8.4) with its extra variables. The new estimates are that fertilizer at the time of sowing provides a 22 per cent increase in output; one extra kg of urea an extra 4.8 kg of wheat; an extra ploughing gives 27 kg of wheat; and timely sowing an extra 93 kg. We find in addition that an extra kilogramme of seed per acre results in a 12 kg drop in wheat output per acre. We suppose that yield corresponds to seed per acre roughly as depicted in Fig. 8.1. This sign of the coefficient is consistent with findings at research stations, given that we have seen (§ 7.3) that seed per acre in Palanpur is slightly on the high side when compared with recommended levels; but the magnitude seems rather large.

It should be noted that, since the linear model is only an approximation to a relation between inputs and output which is certainly not linear, the constant term as the intercept in this linear approximation has no additional special interpretation. However the sharp movement in the constant between Table 8.3 which presents the main model and Table 8.4 which presents the extended model calls for comment. The explanation seems to lie with SEEDACRE which has been included in the extended model with a negative coefficient. As we saw

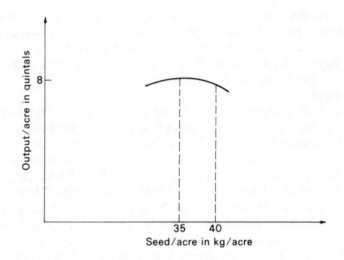

Fig. 8.1

above, § 7.3, the negative coefficient is not absurd but the true relationship is necessarily non-linear and, bearing in mind the relation sketched in Fig. 8.1, this probably explains the instability of the constant term.

The last three of the newly-included variables in Table 8.4 refer to characteristics of farmers. We see that Caste 2, the *Muraos* or traditional cultivators, do substantially better than other cultivators (roughly 20 per cent better than average non-*Muraos* with similar inputs) while members of the highest caste in the village, the *Thakur* caste, also do better than the average non-*Thakur*, with similar inputs. Finally we have an interesting relationship between output per acre and the size of holding per standard family member, *LOFA*. The average holding per standard family member for cultivators of our plots was 1.07 acres. The coefficient in the regression implies that a cultivator with an extra acre per standard family member would have, for given inputs, an output 9 per cent lower than average. The effect is not large but it is significant. Recall that in Chapter 5 *LOFA* played a significant role in explaining the quantity of land taken on lease in that poor families leased-in more land. We seem to have here a similar effect on output per acre for wheat. Note, however, that this was not an effect which emerged in our analysis of productivity for the farm as a whole in Chapter 6. It is possible that in this analysis the negative effect of *LOFA* on wheat yield is being negated by a positive effect for other crops. One might speculate that a family which is very poor would take particular care to cultivate a staple food crop rather carefully, possibly at the expense of inputs on other crops.

The difference between the 8-variable and 4-variable model is that the latter has four coefficients restricted to zero when compared with the former. We can test the linear hypothesis that the restrictions of the four coefficients to zero are correct by comparing the residual sum of squares for the two cases. If Σ_4^2 is the residual sum of squares for the 4-variable model and Σ_8^2 for the 8-variable model we have that

$$\phi = \frac{47-(8+1)}{4} \times \left(\frac{\Sigma_4^2 - \Sigma_8^2}{\Sigma_8^2} \right)$$

is distributed as F with degrees of freedom $(4, 47-(8+1))$ or $(4, 38)$. We find that in our case there is a value of 3.39 for ϕ, which compares with a 5 per cent significance level of 2.63 (see Kendall and Stuart, 1973, Appendix Table 7). The null hypothesis that the main (4-equation) model is appropriate would therefore be rejected at the 5 per cent level if tested against the 8-variable model.

We give now interpretations of coefficients for the main model in log-linear form (see Table 8.5) but now around the geometric rather than arithmetic means of variables (the anti-logarithm of the arithmetic mean of logarithms is the geometric mean). The estimated coefficients imply that fertilizer at the time of sowing gives a multiplicative factor on output of $e^{0.32} = 1.38$, or a 38 per cent increase. Similarly, timely sowing (before 1 December) provides $(e^{0.10} - 1) \times 100$ per cent = 11 per cent extra output. The elasticity of output with respect to the number of ploughings is 0.25, the geometric mean of output per acre is 7.88, the geometric mean of the number of ploughings is 4.79, and hence the productivity of an extra ploughing around the geometric means is $(7.88/4.79) \times 0.25 = 0.41$ quintals per acre.

Similarly we find that the geometric mean of $FERTACRE + 25$, is 64.3, and we have (see Table 8.5) that the marginal product of fertilizer is $0.36 \times 7.88/64.3$ or 0.044 quintals (4.4 kg) of wheat per kg of urea.

The extension of the main model, in the log-linear case, was less successful in terms of significance levels of coefficients and R^2 (see Table 8.6). The extra variables to enter were again seed per acre and holding per standard family member ($LOFA$), but the size of the cultivator holding and standard labour hours per acre replaced $CASTE2$ and $CASTE1$. Given the significance levels of coefficients, the simultaneous selection of holding per standard family member and the holding itself, and the sign of the coefficient of labour hours per acre this regression should be viewed with some circumspection. The test of the 4-variable model against the 8-variable model, analogous to that performed for the linear case, gives an F statistic of 2.38 compared with a 5 per cent significance level of 2.63 for degrees of freedom $(4, 38)$. The null hypothesis that the 4-variable model is correct would be accepted. We do not discuss the 8-variable model in the log-linear case any further.

§ 8.4 Prices and the Productivity of Inputs

In this sub-section we give simple comparisons of value marginal productivities and prices. It is a standard result in economic theory that, where agents act as if they face fixed prices for inputs and output, that is they behave competitively in both input and output markets, where there is no uncertainty, and they maximize the difference between the value of output and the cost of inputs, then the

Table 8.6. The Extended Model—Logarithmic

Multiple *R*	0.87	Number of cases	47
R squared	0.75	Number of variables	8
Standard error	0.17	*F*-Value for equation	14.43
		Dependent variable	*LNCORWTACR*

Variables in the equation

Variable	*B*	Standard error of *B*	*F*
FRSWDUM	0.34	0.07	26.16
LNFERT25	0.36	0.07	25.67
LNPLGHINGS	0.24	0.09	7.53
SWNGDUM	0.07	0.06	1.37
LNSEEDACRE	− 0.31	0.30	1.09
LNLOFA	− 0.11	0.05	4.22
LNLANDO	0.07	0.06	1.43
LNLABACRE	− 0.08	0.07	1.33
Constant	1.45		

Variables not in the equation

Variable	*B* IN	*F*
TENANCY	− 0.06	0.32
LNSOILTYPE	0.02	0.03
LNIRIGNMBR	− 0.01	0.01
IRG30	− 0.03	0.19
SEEDRR21	− 0.01	0.03
CASTE1	0.05	0.48
CASTE2	0.03	0.16
LNLANDO/F3	0.06	0.59
WEEDDUMY	0.003	0.002
KHARDUMY	0.01	0.01

Notes :   (i) See notes to Table 5.7.
          (ii) For definitions of variables see Table 8.1.

value of the marginal product of an input will be equal to its price. Thus comparison of value marginal productivities and prices provides a test of this simple theory. The relations between our estimates and more complex theories, particularly those involving uncertainty, are postponed to § 8.6, as is more detailed discussion of the estimates themselves.

We shall base our discussions on the results for the main model for both the linear and log-linear cases, respectively Tables 8.3 and 8.5. We take the linear case first, and there are three inputs for which we can make the appropriate comparisons: fertilizer as a top dressing, fertilizer at the time of sowing, and the number of ploughings. One must bear in mind that the estimated coefficients conceal variations across cultivators so that even if one found the value of marginal product equal to price, the equality need not hold for each, or any, farmer.

The marginal productivity of 1 kg of urea is 5.6 kg of wheat (see Table 8.3). A 50 kg bag of urea in November/December 1974 cost R105, thus the price of fertilizer as a top dressing was R2.1 per kg. The price of wheat in May 1975 was around R1.3 per kg – for further discussion of the price see § 8.6. We have then that an extra R2.1 of fertilizer yields R1.3 × 5.6 = R7.3 of wheat. Thus the ratio between value of marginal product and price is 3.5. This calculation takes no account of uncertainty as to the level and price of output or of interest and inflation and these are issues to which we return in § 8.6.

The results of our calculation seem quite close to those of Singh, Sharma, and Mishra (1970), who found average returns per rupee investment of fertilizer on four new varieties from R3.63 to R4.56 for optimum (profit maximizing) levels of nitrogen application as compared with zero application. They used a price of wheat of R0.76 per kg and a price of nitrogen (N) of R2.75 per kg giving a relative price of wheat to nitrogen of 0.276. This is very close to our own relative price of 1.3 × 0.46/2.1 = 0.285 (urea is 46 per cent N). Recall (§ 7.1.2 and § 8.3) that their estimate of the average yield response over the range 0 to 56 N per acre for Sonalika (RR21) was 22.8 kg of wheat from 1 kg of N, compared with our estimate of 12.17 kg of wheat from 1 kg of N around the mean of our sample (19.0 kg N per acre—see § 7.3). The reason that their result in terms of profitability is close to ours is that their measure of cost is (193 + 2.75 N) rupees, because they have included the cost of the phosphorus and potassium which were held constant as the level of nitrogen varied. The return to the nitrogen alone in their analysis would be R22.8 × 0.276 = R6.29 worth of wheat from R1 of nitrogen. We have already discussed (§ 8.3) the reason that their measured productivity is rather higher than ours.

The return to using fertilizer at the time of sowing was, according to the estimates in Table 8.3, 255 kg per acre of wheat. The average cost per acre of fertilizer at the time of sowing (where we average the total cost of basal fertilizer on sample plots over the acreage of the twenty-three plots where such fertilizer was used) was R87.4. The return per rupee spent on basal fertilizer is therefore R255 × 1.3/87.4 or R3.8. This estimate is rather crude, however, since the fertilizers used were different for different cultivators, as were the quantities, and no account of this was taken in the regression. Bearing this qualification in mind, however, it does seem that the returns to using basal fertilizers are a little higher than for top dressing, although both are high.

We see in Table 8.3 that the marginal productivity of a ploughing is 37 kg of wheat per acre or R48.1. It takes approximately an eight hour day with one team of bullocks to plough an acre. We have remarked in Chapter 4 that there was a minimal market for the services of bullocks in Palanpur. However where such markets did exist the prices mentioned were around 15 rupees per day (and this would include the owner as driver of the bullock team). This is the figure we used when discussing the cost of irrigation by Persian wheel (see § 7.3) and we shall retain it for use here. The return per rupee to an extra ploughing on the margin is then 48.1/15 = 3.2.

We can perform similar calculations for the log-linear model for small changes around the geometric means of variables. In the preceding sub-section we gave the following figures for the log-linear model: the marginal product of one kg of urea as 4.4 kg of wheat, fertilizer at the time of sowing providing a multiplicative factor of 1.38 compared with output with the same inputs except for no fertilizer at the time of sowing, and the marginal product of a ploughing as 41 kg of wheat.

In the case of the log-linear model one can provide estimates of the fertilizer level and number of ploughings which would maximize profit given prices of wheat, fertilizer, and ploughing and in the four cases: with or without fertilizer at the time of sowing, and with sowing before or after 1 December. The production function estimated from the regression in Table 8.5 is

$$y = \exp(-0.037 + 0.32\alpha_1 + 0.10\alpha_2)(f + 25)^{0.36} n^{0.25} \qquad (8)$$

where y is wheat output in quintals per acre, f is urea input in kg per acre, n is the number of ploughings, α_1 is one if fertilizer is applied at the time of sowing and zero if not, and α_2 is one if the plot is sown before 1 December and zero if not.

We prices p_y for output, p_f for fertilizer, and p_n for ploughings, we have profit maximizing levels of y, f, and n from

$$p_y dy/df = p_f, p_y dy/dn = p_n, y = A(f + 25)^{0.36} n^{0.25} \qquad (9)$$

where A is the exponential expression in (8). Solving equations (9) using $p_y = R130$ (recall that y is in quintals per acre), $p_f = R2.1$, $p_n = R15$, we have

$$y = 28.48 A^{2.56} \qquad (10)$$

The lowest value of A is for $\alpha_1 = \alpha_2 = 0$ when $A = e^{-0.037}$, and thus $A^{2.56} = e^{-0.095} = 0.91$, thus $y = 25.84$ quintals per acre. For the largest value of A, $\alpha_1 = \alpha_2 = 1$ and $A = e^{0.38} = 1.47$, and $y = 76.36$ quintals per acre. The corresponding values of f and n can be found from $f = 22.29y - 25$ and $n = 2.17y$.

The yield figures are quite ludicrously high and it is in any case obvious that a number of ploughings of 166 (in the case $\alpha_1 = \alpha_2 = 1$) is absurd. These calculations are yet another confirmation that, over the range of practices in our sample, the extent of diminishing returns is very small. If we extrapolate the fitted log-linear function outside this range we have to go to absurdly high levels of inputs to bring value marginal products into equality with prices. The lesson, of course, is that we should not so extrapolate.

We regard the calculations just performed as partial justification for concentrating on the linear model. In that case no attempt is made to capture curvature that does not seem to be there. Of course, in the linear case, there is no question of finding the level where value marginal products equal price since the value marginal products, given fixed prices, are constant.

§ 8.5 Discussion with Cultivators and the Residuals

We had lengthy discussions with the cultivators of the sample plots as to why they had taken the cultivation decisions that they had. In the course of these discussions we tried to ascertain their views on the likely consequences of alternative input levels. These sessions proved to be of general interest for our work and have been reported at length in § 4.7 where, however, we postponed extensive discussion of questions having particularly to do with wheat and the sample plots. We had, of course, greater contact with the farmers than these sessions as we met them frequently to record the activities on the sample plots and were also collecting data for our household survey. We begin this section by emphasizing and providing a little more detail concerning those parts of the discussion sessions which particularly had to do with our wheat study and then go on to link these discussions to the results, and particularly to the residuals, from the regressions reported in the preceding section. The questions which we asked were set out as Table 4.16 (p. 118)

We shall be paying particular attention here to the farmers' estimates of the productivity of various inputs and we shall be comparing them with our regression estimates reported in § 8.3. We should first emphasize, however, that just as there was great diversity in the practices on our sample plots reported in § 7.3 so there was substantial variation in attitudes, knowledge, and speculations amongst the cultivators of those plots. This must not be forgotten in any of the averages or general statements which may follow and is, of course, directly helpful in understanding the residuals. If we are to speak of an average we should say that farmers were fairly well aware of the productivity of inputs (although many were badly informed about sowing technique). They were, however, lacking in confidence in their estimates. This is, we presume, in part a result of their experience in the vagaries of agriculture and their comparative inexperience with the more intensive use of inputs such as fertilizer and irrigation.

The choice of seed type (Question 2–see Table 4.16 p.118) divides farmers into, broadly speaking, two groups : those who used RR21 and those who used other varieties. The arguments in favour of RR21 were in terms of the easy availability at the Seed Store, the automatic credit facilities, or that the seed had been kept back from previous years. Some, but not all, farmers referred to the decline in yield over the four or five years during which the RR21 had been available from the Seed Store. Of the farmers who referred to the decline only a few mentioned specific figures and these were around 30 or 40 per cent over four or five years (see below).

The standard unit which is used in discussions of output for quantities above 10 or 20 kg is *maunds* per *bigha*. One *maund* is 40 kg and there are 6.4 *bighas* per acre. Thus, for example, three *maunds* per *bigha* would be 7.68 quintals or 768 kg per acre. The average output of the sample plots, 8.26 quintals per acre, is 3.23 *maunds/bigha*. We shall follow the cultivators in our report on the discussion questionnaire and frequently work in terms of *maunds/bigha*. The decline in the yield of RR21 where it was quantified, was said to be from around four *maunds/bigha* to around three, over four or five years. Several farmers said that the seed that now went under the name of RR21 at the Seed Store was a mixture of various types.

Some farmers had been growing new varieties of seed other than RR21 for a few years and others had begun in the year of the study. The most common reason for adoption of the newer varieties, apart from dissatisfaction with the (experienced or observed) decline in the yield from RR21, was that other farmers had told them that the seed adopted was good. This word of mouth was mainly inside the village but there was some information from relatives or friends in other villages. Other farmers said that the seed type had been recommended to them by officers at the Block HQ in Chandausi.

Most of the cultivators thought that an extra irrigation over and above the number they planned to do would add nothing to output and some even suggested that it would do harm. There were a few who thought that an extra irrigation would provide more, but none estimated an increase in excess of 20 kg per *bigha* except for Ompal Singh, the farmer with the lowest output per *bigha* on our sample plots, who suggested an extra one maund or 40 kg per *bigha*. When the discussions took place (February 1975) most farmers had irrigated two or three times after sowing and were planning one or two more. They all thought that one fewer irrigation would cause a reduction in yield. The estimates of how much less varied from 5 kg/*bigha* to 20 kg/*bigha*, but most farmers were sufficiently unsure not to want to hazard a guess. Where farmers were prepared to estimate the effects on yield of both one more and one less they recognized that an extra irrigation would provide less than would be lost by omitting one. Those who hired-in the water source said that the problems of obtaining water at the right time were not great but some said that at certain times they had to wait two or three days for the services of a pumping set and had to ask several times. The economics of these decisions can be calculated using a price of R1.3 per kg for wheat (the price ruling in May 1975) and a cost of irrigating one *bigha* by pumping set of R 4 or 5 (see § 7.3).

The most common source of advice on the use of fertilizer was, as with the selection of seed type, other farmers. Few farmers knew what the recommended doses were and those who did thought that they were much too high (for our suggestions as to the reason, see below). A few of the farmers were of the view that soils became habituated to fertilizer and that once one started one would have to use more and more each year.

Many were prepared to speculate on the effect of using more fertilizer. The average dose of urea as a top dressing was 5 kg/*bigha*. There was a general consensus that doubling the dose would provide an extra ½ *maund/bigha*. The question on a downward movement seemed to be answered with less confidence, where it was answered at all, but some who used fertilizer at roughly the average level thought that using no fertilizer would lose around 1 *maund/bigha*. These estimates imply that an increase of 1 kg of urea produces 4 kg of wheat, and a decrease of 1 kg of urea loses 8 kg of wheat. These estimates seem broadly consistent with our estimated coefficient in the regression (see Table 8.3) where the implied productivity of an extra kg of urea is 5.6 kg of wheat. The economics of the answer can be judged using a price of wheat of R1.3 per kg and of urea R2.1 per kg.

The response of many farmers to the question why they did not apply more fertilizer if it was so profitable (we gave simple profit calculations based on their answer) was 'lack of finance'. There was also the view, already mentioned, amongst a few that the soil becomes habituated to fertilizer. Others replied that they would think some more about the calculations and would consider applying more next year.

The question of how extra production might be available with the application of more labour quickly became a question about weeding. We have already seen (§ 7.3) that only eleven of the forty-seven plots were weeded. Most farmers answered that they did not indulge in weeding because there were no weeds on their plots. Whilst it is true that the practice of ploughing several times is a fairly effective method of controlling weeds, and thereby conserving moisture and nutrients, the statement by many of the farmers that there were no weeds was manifestly false. It was the case, however, that we were unable to find a significant effect of weeding in our regression analysis and this may be because those plots which were weeded were those which were particularly badly affected by weeds. And a weedy plot may be associated with high doses of fertilizer since the fertilizer brings on weeds as well as the wheat. Given the above complexities it is perhaps unsurprising that we were unable to discover a significant effect of weeding. It may also be the case that the judgement of the farmers that the quantity of weeds on their plot was unimportant was justified but we should record that this judgement was shared neither by Shri Kumar of IFFCO nor by our two agricultural economist research assistants. We should also record that two cultivators estimated that the investment of R 2 per *bigha* in weeding (this was usually on a piece-rate basis) would provide a 10 per cent increase in output. This estimate is to be compared with Shri Kumar's of an increase of up to 15 per cent. An extra 10 per cent above the average is approximately 13 kg of wheat or R 16.9 per *bigha* (at a price of R 1.3 per kg), for an expenditure of R 2.

The residuals from the regression of Table 8.3 (the main model in linear form) are set out in Table 8.7. We include in that table the predicted value; actual yield is the sum of predicted and residual values. The number of the cultivator and the plot is also included. Recall that the first digit of the cultivator number indicates his caste. We include also a few brief remarks on our impressions from the discussion and from direct observation of the plot. We indicate those plots with a great deal, or no, mustard; where there was no fertilizer as a top dressing (and all such plots had no fertilizer at the time of sowing); and where there is tenancy.

In most cases the relations between the remarks, particulars of the plot, and residual are self-evident. We select a few plots and features for discussion.

Let us take the three negative residuals of largest absolute value and similarly the three positive. The three negative are for plot 197, cultivated by Jagdish Singh (*Thakur*), with a residual of − 2.53 quintals per acre; plot 591 cultivated by Madan Mohan (*Murao*), with − 2.51; and plot 42, cultivated by Laxmi (*Passi*) with − 2.56. Two of these are easily explained. Madan Mohan's wheat was weevilled and Laxmi's plot was attacked by white ants. We were a little surprised by Jagdish Singh's performance but we had noted that the seed bed was particularly badly prepared. His brother Ompal Singh and he live closely

TABLE 8.7. RESIDUALS

Plot No.	Cultivator No.	Name of Discussant	Predicted	Residual	Comment on Discussion and Plot.
194	125	Panchan Singh	5.06	1.92	Weeded.
164	106	Sri Singh (son-in-law)	7.36	1.45	Had strange ideas on fertilize $Desi$ wheat (K68).
197	113	Jagdish Singh	9.69	−2.53	Bad seed bed preparation.
74	114	Ompal Singh	5.70	$−1.75^x$	Badly informed on agricultur Badly timed irrigation.
342	304	Ramji Singh (landlord)	8.62	0.95^*	Landlord evasive.
338	112	Satya Pal Singh	11.10	−0.24	Rust and blight.
625	116	Beer Singh	9.57	0.46	Weeded.
52	118	Lock Pal (son)	9.69	0.61^x	Son seems well-
366	118	,, ,, ,,	7.91	1.22	informed.
358	117	Beer Singh (brother)	5.07	$−0.11^+$	See plot 625.
379	111	Poppu Singh (son)	9.12	1.30	Enthusiastic and educated so
377	111	,, ,, ,,	10.07	1.60	
412	103	Charan Singh	8.75	−1.67	Poor seed and land preparat
88	303	Ram Kumar	7.27	1.45*	No interview.
422	606	Hargian (landlord)	7.45	1.58*	Landlord
502	401	Hargian	8.93	−2.48	unenthusiastic.
64	406	Siya Ram	6.49	−1.17	Sick bullocks.
391	410	Omprakash	9.83	$−0.80^x$	Weeded with his own labour
208	605	Nasim	7.80	0.15	White ants.
224	611	Nisar (brother)	7.99	0.08*	Family leases-in a lot of land
599	610	Nisar	7.55	$−1.14^*$	and could not manage more.
554	707	Pitamber	6.01	1.34^{x*}	Unenthusiastic but did try H
591	204	Madan Mohan	8.30	−2.51	Weevilled wheat.
58	219	Sipahi (son)	12.08	0.33	Seemed enthusiastic
512	219	Sipahi (son)	12.07	0.02^x	and energetic (son).
266	219	Sipahi	10.88	$−1.99^x$	Rust.
500	227	Man Singh (son)	9.97	2.11^x	Educated, analytical,
157	227	Man Singh	10.34	1.46	and thoughtful—
360	227	Man Singh	10.81	2.69	see text.
475	227	Man Singh (brother)	9.20	−0.31	Loam I (Plot 360).
215	201	Bhajan Lal	8.74	1.81	Slight rust.
229	202	Gaidan Lal	8.66	0.55	Rust.
137	206	Kamlesh	11.49	$−1.33^x$	
134	206	Kamlesh	10.92	0.81^x	
462	217	Ram Div	6.39	0.18	$Desi$ wheat (K68).
477	217	Raj Kumar	9.07	0.05^x	
318	503	Sabbir	6.02	$−1.22^+$	White ants.
130	301	Sabbir (landlord)	5.45	0.00^+	Rust.
361	612	Sansad	7.08	0.61	
312	702	Bhagirata	7.14	$−0.59^+$	
156	702	,,	3.95	0.96^+	
301	702	,,	6.02	$−1.05^+$	
400	704	Laxmi	7.82	$−1.02^+$	Leases-in a lot of land.
42	704	,,	7.10	−2.56*	White ants.
350	226	Muma Lal	9.79	$−0.81^x$	Rich man.
252	210	Mohi Lal	7.43	−1.34	Rich man.
109	803	Dharmarir	4.32	0.99^+	

Notes :
(i) x No mustard   * Tenancy   + No fert
(ii) Where discussant differs from nominal cultivator relationship is shown in brackets.
(iii) Output in quintals/acre. Residuals from model as in Table 8.3 .

together, discuss a great deal, and Ompal Singh had the lowest output per acre on the sample plots, with a residual of − 1.75 and some peculiar ideas about the value of various practices. It may be that the family is not particularly good at farming.

The three largest positive residuals are plot 360, cultivated by Man Singh (*Murao*) with + 2.69; plot 500 cultivated by Baboo Ram (*Murao*) with + 2.11; and plot 125 cultivated by Panchan Singh (*Thakur*) with + 1.92. Man Singh is the son of Baboo Ram and is influential in the decisions on all the family plots. Plot 500 had been fallow in the *kharif* season and the seed had been purchased from Amar Pur Kashi, a nearby village with an energetic headman who had spent some time abroad and who tried to obtain good agricultural inputs for his village. Plot 360 was of the best soil class in the village, and the seed was a mixture of 2009 and Hira. The Hira was home produced but the 2009 had been bought in the market for the high price of R8 per kg and was probably rather good. And Man Singh was a young, energetic, and well-educated farmer (the only man in the village with a B.A.) who put much thought and care into his farming. Possibly Panchan Singh's weeding had some effect.

None of the three highest or the three lowest residuals involved tenancy. Mustard per acre does not seem to play a role in understanding residuals here—for example, of the twelve plots with no mustard six had a positive residual and six a negative (see also § 8.2).

We give two examples where we guessed, in advance of doing the regressions, the wrong sign for the residuals. Plot 137 was cultivated by Kamlesh, an energetic *Murao* who had acquired both a pumping set and a chaff-cutter and was something of a local entrepreneur. He had intensive inputs relative to the average with a predicted value of 11.49. However his output was 10.16, a residual of − 1.33. There were no mishaps such as rust or ants which were observable directly and we thought he would have a positive residual. It may be that his entrepreneurial activities diverted his attention from farming. Towards the lower end of the input spectrum we find Dharmarir, a *Jatab* who cultivated plot 109. The plot was under tenancy and both he and his son had work in the nearby town Chandausi. He did not seem particularly interested in agricultural questions during our discussion session and we thought he would have a negative residual. He had the lowest predicted value, 4.32, but an output of 5.31 and a residual of + 0.99 quintals per acre.

The lesson from these two cases is that we occasionally fell into the trap of being over-influenced by high input levels and thus predicting positive residuals. Apart from random factors, it is the care with which those inputs are used which one should look for in explaining the residuals. It is, however, reassuring that armed with the discussion sessions and direct observation of the plot, we were well-equipped to understand the majority of the residuals.[1]

---

[1]The reader should be reminded, although we hope it is obvious, that our discussions with cultivators and predictions of residuals took place a long time before we knew the outcome of the regression analysis.

§ 8.6 Some Observations on the Estimates and Discussion Sessions

§ 8.6.0 Introduction

The most striking feature of the estimates is their implications for the relationships between value marginal product and prices. We saw in § 8.4 that the ratios between the value marginal product and price for different inputs based on Table 8.3 were 3.5 for urea, 3.8 for fertilizer at the time of sowing, and 3.2 for ploughing. We shall investigate in this section possible reasons why these ratios are so high. We begin in § 8.6.1 by discussing whether we may have over- or under-estimated the value of the marginal product of an input. This involves looking at issues concerned with both price and quantity. We then, in § 8.6.2, discuss credit and in § 8.6.3 uncertainty. We shall be concluding that uncertainty and attitudes to risk provide the main explanation of the high ratios. In the final sub-section we address some more general theoretical issues.

There are a number of inputs for which the relation between marginal value product and price is not examined here: weeding, irrigation, seed type, and labour in general. We could not detect any effect of weeding and irrigation which was independent of the other main variables for our cross-section, although, of course, we believe them to be important. A similar comment applies to seed type and there is the further problem that the measure used in our regression is fairly crude (1 for RR21, 0 otherwise). We have explained our reasons for wishing to deal with labour through tasks performed rather than labour hours in § 8.1

§ 8.6.1 The Value of the Marginal Product

We must discuss both our estimates of the value of the marginal product of an input and the perceptions by cultivators of this value. It is perceptions of consequences and prices which will, in most models, govern input decisions. We begin with physical marginal product and go on to prices.

We saw in §8.5 that one cannot argue that in general the farmers were unaware of the productivity of their own inputs. We saw, for example, that the farmers were remarkably good at predicting the productivity of fertilizer as a top dressing, in the sense that their predictions accorded well with the results of our regressions. They may have been rather less well-informed on the effects of basal fertilizers. It seems that the general answer to the question why the discrepancy between the value of marginal products (as estimated) and prices is so large must lie in a different direction from any possible under-estimation by cultivators of productivity of inputs. Let us turn to possible errors in our estimations.

Apart from possible bias in our estimation technique, one reason that we may have over-estimated physical productivities would be that *rabi* 1974-5 was an above-average season. It was not a bad season and much better than *rabi* 1973-4 but for wheat in the Moradabad district it seems only a little above average—see Table 8.8.

Table 8.8 Wheat Yield and Prices in Moradabad District 1960-1 to 1974-5.

Rabi season	Area (acres)	Yield (quintals/ acre)	Price (rupees/ quintal)	Price × Yield (rupees/acre)
1960-1	65 586	3.50	38.2	133.7
1961-2	67 882	3.49	37.2	129.8
1962-3	65 907	2.88	42.8	123.3
1963-4	65 637	2.20	57.5	126.5
1964-5	61 069	3.65	66.9	244.2
1965-6	64 798	3.24	68.8	222.9
1966-7	71 802	4.01	125.6	503.7
1967-8	79 498	3.84	72.2	277.2
1968-9	79 700	4.96	79.5	394.3
1969-70	81 746	4.36	75.0	327.0
1970-1	89 394	5.91	74.0	437.3
1971-2	98 169	4.54	75.0	340.5
1972-3	95 308	3.95	85.0	335.8
1973-4	90 469	2.77	137.5	380.9
1974-5	91 058	4.62	120.3	555.8

Notes : (i) *Sources* : *Bulletin on Wheat Statistics in India,* Directorate of Economics and Statistics, Ministry of Agriculture, Government India 1972 plus private communication from Miss R. Anand of the Planning Commission, Government of India.

(ii) The price is the average of month-end May and June prices in the Chandausi market for 'white' wheat or May only when no trading was recorded in June. Prices for 1971, '72, and '73 were below the procurement price but of inferior quality. The prices for 1960-1, for example, would be for May 1961 for wheat planted in autumn 1960.

The average yield for the ten years 1965-6 to 1974-5 was 4.22 quintals per acre and for 1974-5 was 9.5 per cent above this level at 4.62 quintals per acre. We note here that the average yield for the sample plots was 8.26 quintals per acre. Thus yields in Palanpur are substantially above the average for Moradabad district. Much of the difference can, we suppose, be explained by the fact that all the sample plots were irrigated whereas the average for Moradabad district includes a substantial quantity of unirrigated land. We have no special reason to suppose that Palanpur land is of much higher quality than the average but this would provide another possible explanation. It may well be, however, that Palanpur cultivation is quite good when compared with the average for Moradabad district even though it is rather poor when compared with research station recommendations—see §7.3.

There may be some over-estimate of physical productivities because irrigation is positively correlated with fertilizer inputs. The number of irrigations is not, however, significantly correlated with the number of ploughings for which discrepancy between value marginal product and price is also high. And we attempted to capture complementarity between number of irrigations and fertilizer in our quadratic models (see the appendix to this chapter) without revealing a strong effect in our sample. Further, the consistency between our estimates and the farmers' own reinforces our view that any over-estimate of the physical effect of inputs in the production of wheat is not substantial.

We have ignored two quantities the inclusion of which would increase estimates of the value of marginal products: straw and mustard. On average each of these would add approximately 5 or 10 per cent to the value of output. We do not have direct estimates of marginal productivities of inputs which include these factors. We have also ignored two aspects which would reduce estimates of the value of marginal products: marketing costs and post-harvest activities. Again we should guess that adjustments to the value of output, and we suppose marginal products, would be of the order of 5 to 10 per cent for each of them. The broker's margin seems to be around R4 per quintal and the transport to the market by bullock cart (Palanpur is only seven miles from Chandausi) would not be very costly. Post-harvest labour time can be seen from Table 7.8. Average post-harvest hours per acre are around 100 or approximately twelve days of eight hours. At R4 per day this would give a valuation of approximately R50. The value of output per acre at R130 per quintal is around R1000. Most post-harvest labour is family labour and at a time when there is little else to do, so a price of R4 per day (roughly a market price earlier in the year) is, if anything, high rather than low.

We should suggest therefore that factors ignored in the valuation of output are not large when compared with the gap between value of marginal product of an input and its price and that the different considerations involved in these ignored factors are likely to (approximately)cancel out.

We turn now to the question of the appropriate price for wheat in the calculation of the value marginal products. The sequence of average weekly prices in the Chandausi market in March, April, and May 1975 is given in Table 8.9(a) and the average monthly prices for 1974–5 in Table 8.9(b). There was a government procurement price of R105 per quintal (announced in May 1975) but this was not relevant. Our farmers did not sell at this price and past experience would have suggested to them that they were likely to avoid being forced to sell at the government procurement price. There are anyway off-setting perks attached to selling at the lower government procurement price, such as subsidised fertilizer.

The price we chose, R130 per quintal, is the maximum price ruling in May (the average price in May was R123). Judging by the previous year's pattern our price of R130 per quintal would be about 10 per cent above the average for May/June (and the average month-end price of May and June was 120.3, see Table 8.8). Most of the farmers had harvested by the end of April and many of them had completed threshing and sowing by that date too. A lower bound for a farmer's valuation of his output at the time of harvest is, one can argue, given by the highest price he could have obtained.

Our further reason for choosing a price a little above the average for May/June is concerned with farmers' expectations. At the time fertilizer as a top dressing was being applied (December/January), the price of wheat was over R220 per quintal and at the time of ploughing and application of basal fertilizer the price was around R190 per quintal. When we were conducting the discussion sessions in February much of the initial uncertainty had passed (particularly the risk of frost in January) and it was clear that, barring accidents, the yield was not going to be too bad. Yet most of the farmers were predicting prices around R150. That too was the level being spoken of by the manager of the Seed Store. We should argue, therefore, that the price we have selected, R130 per quintal, cannot be construed as an over-estimate of the relevant output price in the computation of the ratio of the value of the marginal product of an input to its price.

Table 8.9 Wheat Prices in Chandausi Market 1974-5

(a) *Week*	*Rupees/quintal*	(b) *Month*	*Rupees/quintal*
March 1	205	March 1974	148
2	205	April	130
3	208	May	145
4	202	June	130
April 1	150	July	147
2	120	August	180
3	120	September	197
4	150	October	191
May 1	123	November	181
2	120	December	219
3	130	January 1975	228
4	125	February	225
5	118	March	205
		April	135
		May	123

Notes : (i) These prices are averaged over the month and certain types of wheat. The types correspond to Table 8.8 (see note (ii) to that table).
(ii) The figures were kindly provided by the Block Development Officer, Chandausi.

§ 8.6.2 Credit

Many farmers mentioned the absence of finance as an argument for not applying more fertilizer, and we are convinced that this is part of the explanation. It is only a part, however, and we are of the view that, in so far as this is a reason independent from uncertainty, it is quantitatively of less importance. While credit from the Seed Store was available at a rate of interest of 13 per cent, it was rationed. There were ways round the rationing, involving side-payments, but these of course increase the cost of credit. There was, however, a private credit market in the village at rates of interest of 2 or 3 per cent per month (see § 4.3). Thus the purchase of fertilizer financed by such a loan over nine months would involve an increase in the nominal cost of 20 or 30 per cent.[2] The cost of credit is not therefore sufficient by itself to explain the whole, or even the majority, of the discrepancy between prices and value marginal products.

The combination of the cost of credit and uncertainty may well be an important part of the story for in taking on a private loan one may run the risk of losing land. It is to uncertainty that we now turn.

[2] Note that since we are doing the calculation in money terms it is the nominal rate of interest that is relevant here. If the calculation were to be performed in real terms we should deflate the value of output for inflation and work with a real rate of interest; it would make little difference, see § 4.3.

§ 8.6.3 Uncertainty

It seems that the substance of the answer to the question of why the relation between value of marginal product and price is so high must lie in uncertainty and risk aversion. We can distinguish two types of uncertainty here: inter-temporal and cross-sectional. By the former we refer to the uncertainty associated with climatic conditions which would be common to all cultivators in a sufficiently small area. The cross-sectional variation refers to the highly localized problems which can afflict different farmers differently for given weather conditions. If all relevant deterministic factors are included in a regression equation, it is this uncertainty which is involved when we estimate the standard error in a cross-section equation. We should emphasize that the two contributions are not statistically independent – over-all weather conditions would affect cross-section dispersion.

The standard error estimated in the equation of Table 8.3 was 1.44 quintals per acre. If the distribution of errors were normal there would be a probability of 5 per cent of a given observation falling more than two standard errors from the regression line. Note that the largest absolute value of a residual was 2.89 (see Table 8.7). In so far as we have omitted certain systematic factors this is an over-estimate of the uncertainty—and in Table 8.4 with the 8 variable regression the estimated standard error was 1.30.

Some understanding of the inter-temporal uncertainty can be gained from a time series of price and yield per acre (see Table 8.8). We have not subjected these series to any sophisticated (or even unsophisticated) spectral analysis to try to estimate the magnitude of the uncertainty, but a pictorial impression can be gained from Figs. 8.2(a) and (b) which plot price and yield per acre against time for the Moradabad district of U.P. Note that our particular year 1974–5 was not a bad one in terms of yield. In Fig. 8.2(c) we plot price multiplied by yield per acre and it can be seen that yield per acre and value per acre move together. This is not surprising since price (depending upon national yield more than on the yield in a district) is not sufficiently negatively correlated with local output to offset output variations. The cross-section and the time series give some feel for the extent of uncertainty, but we should remember that the time series is aggregated over a whole district and thus would under-estimate substantially the uncertainty facing a particular farmer.

We shall now use the simple model of choice under uncertainty developed in § 3.4 in an attempt to understand how the gap between the value marginal productivity and price can be bridged by considerations of perceived risk and attitudes towards risk. Consider a farmer who is choosing a vector of inputs on a plot, $\mathbf{x}$ which he buys at fixed prices $\mathbf{p}$, where p_i is the price of input i. He wishes to choose $\mathbf{x}$ to maximize the expected utility of farm income

$$EU(Z + \theta f(\mathbf{x}) - \mathbf{p}.\mathbf{x}) \tag{11}$$

where Z is his income from other sources, $f(\ )$ is the production function on the plot, and θ is a random term capturing the uncertainty in yield on the particular

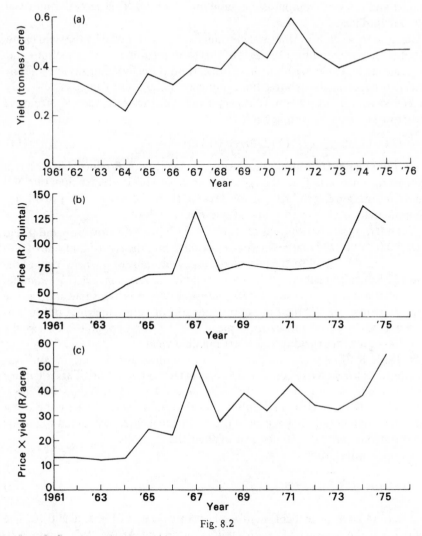

Fig. 8.2

plot and the uncertainty in price. We set the expectation of θ, $E\theta$, to one. We say that uncertainty is multiplicative; E denotes the expectation operator. In formulating the problem as in (11) we are working in terms of present values (the inputs occur some time before the output appears). Some interrelations between credit and uncertainty are discussed below.

Choosing **x** to maximize we have that, for each input i,

$$p_i E(U'(Y)) - \partial f / \partial x_i E(U'(Y))\theta) = 0 \tag{12}$$

where Y is total income, $Z + f(\mathbf{x}) - p\,\mathbf{x}$. Thus

$$\partial f / \partial x_i / p_i = E(U'(Y)) / E(U'(Y)\theta) \tag{13}$$

Hence in the case of multiplicative uncertainty the ratio between value marginal

product and price of an input is the same for all inputs. This accords quite well
with our findings.

The ratio between value marginal product and price is given by the right-hand
side of (13). We give some examples of this ratio for some utility functions and
distributions in Table 8.10 but there are certain things we can say in general.
First, if $U(\ )$ is concave (shows diminishing marginal utility) and θ is positively
correlated with Y, as we should expect given that the remainder of income is
likely to be connected with agriculture, then

$$E(U'(Y)\theta) \leqq EU'(Y)E(\theta) = EU'(Y) \tag{14}$$

Since $E\theta = 1$ and $U'(Y)$ is negatively correlated with θ (since $U'(\ )$ is a
decreasing function). Thus the right-hand side of (13) is greater than one and
the value marginal product will be greater than the price. We provided a
theoretical discussion of this type of question in § 3.4.

Secondly, if the distributions of θ and Y are bounded below by $\underline{\theta}$ and $\underline{Y}$ and
if $U'(\underline{Y})/U'(Y)$ is very large for $Y > \underline{Y}$, we have that the right-hand side of (13)
is approximately equal to $1/\underline{\theta}$ provided θ takes the value of $\underline{\theta}$ when Y takes the
value $\underline{Y}$. Roughly speaking, if the utility function is very concave (for example,
as in maxi-min), and the worst outcome for θ occurs in the same state as the
worst outcome for $\underline{Y}$, then the optimum ratio of value marginal product to
price will be close to the ratio of the mean θ to the worst possible θ, or here the
ratio of the average yield to the worst possible yield.

In Table 8.10, we use one particular distribution for income Y and two
distributions for θ. We select Y and θ to be perfectly correlated. This will make
for the highest possible ratio on the right-hand side of (13). We use two alternative discrete symmetric distributions for θ: a broad spread where the worst
outcome provides only 20 per cent of the mean and a narrower spread where the
worst outcome provides 40 per cent of the mean.

We use a utility function

$$U(Y) = (1/1 - \eta)Y^{1-\eta} \tag{15}$$

so that $U'(Y) = Y^{-\eta}$. In Table 8.10 we show three values of η: 2, 6, and 10. The
number η is the measure of relative risk aversion (see Arrow, 1970) and $\eta = 10$
would be considered highly risk-averse in many contexts (for a discussion of
values of η see Stern, 1977).

We can see that we need the broad spread and $\eta = 10$ before we can produce
values of the ratio between value marginal product and price close to what we
found. Note that the dispersion of θ is quite wide in this case as compared with
Fig. 8.2 (c) and our estimated standard error.

The following statistics assist in judging the dispersion of the distributions in
Table 8.10 relative to the circumstances faced by the farmers. The largest
absolute value of a residual (2.89, see Table 8.7) divided by the mean yield
(8.26) for the sample plots is 0.35 and the standard error of the equation in
Table 8.3 (1.44) divided by the mean yield is 0.17. The corresponding figures

for the narrow distribution (P^2) are 0.60 and 0.37 and for the broad distribution (P^1) are 0.80 and 0.49 (the latter figure in each case is the standard deviation of the distribution). The residuals and standard error from the cross-section understate,[3] however, the risk facing the particular farmer since these are estimated for a given year and the outcome for the year itself is random.

We suggested that an impression of inter-temporal randomness can be gained from Fig. 8.2 and Table 8.8. Over the ten years 1965 – 6 to 1974 – 5 the mean of price x yield (column 4 of Table 8.8) was R377.5 per acre. The largest deviation from the mean (1974–5) was (plus)R178.3 per acre and the standard deviation R95.5 per acre. The relevant ratios are thus 0.47 and 0.25. It should be noted that this calculation overstates the spread of inter-temporal risk since we have not taken account of inflation or of any time trend in output. The introduction of these two considerations would bring down deviations in later years.

From the picture of 'cross-section' and 'inter-temporal' risk conveyed by the above statistics it would appear that the broad distribution (P^2) does not understate the risk facing the farmer but it must not be forgotten that there is a possibility that the crop on a particular plot will fail completely.

A further consideration in judging the model of equation (11) and the calculations of Table 8.10, is whether the decision on the application of inputs should be applicable to the whole of income, thus whether Z should be suppressed. We argued in § 3.4, when we presented alternative models, that it was reasonable to suppose that other sources of income were not perfectly correlated with a given plot and therefore that one should not suppress Z.

We should suggest that the high degree of risk aversion which it appears one has to invoke in order to understand the ratio of value marginal product to price can easily be understood if one links poverty and the nature of the credit market to the uncertainty. The calculations based on the model of equation (11) have been in present value terms and thus interest has been recognized. The attendant risks of borrowing are, however, concealed in the aggregation of costs and benefits into money terms. The great, and understandable, fears of taking on a loan are that default consequent on crop failure may result in the loss of land, or in the case of the landless, the loss of such assets (for example, bullocks) that they have. If the loan were to exceed the assets (assuming that such a loan were available) the consequent penury would involve at best degradation and at worst starvation. Conservatism in such a context is hardly surprising.

It would seem to follow that if uncertainty is to be the explanation of the big gap between value marginal product and price, then the cultivators are both highly risk-averse and allow for a rather dispersed set of outcomes.

To summarize our discussion of the large gap between value marginal product and pice, we list what are, in our view, the three main reasons, in decreasing order of importance:

(i) uncertainty, risk aversion, and the consequences of default;

(ii) cost and availability of credit;

and (iii) the value of the marginal product was estimated in quite a good year.

[3] To the extent that residuals result from features of farmers that we failed to measure; the standard error overstates the uncertainties facing a particular farmer.

Table 8.10 The Ratio of Value of Marginal Product to Price

A.			Outcomes		
	1	2	3	4	5
Probability	0.125	0.25	0.25	0.25	0.125
P^1	0.2	0.6	1	1.4	1.8
$\theta = P^2$	0.4	0.7	1	1.3	1.6
Y	0.6	0.8	1	1.2	1.4
Y^{-2}	2.78	1.56	1	0.69	0.51
Y^{-6}	21.43	3.81	1	0.33	0.13
Y^{-10}	165.38	9.31	1	0.16	0.03

B.		$(EU'(Y))/(EU'(Y)\theta)$
η	P^1	P^2
2	1.66	1.24
6	2.65	1.89
10	3.99	2.28

It is shown in the text that the ratio of the value of marginal product to price, with multiplicative uncertainty, is $(EU'(Y))/E(U'(Y)\,\theta)$ where θ is the multiplicative random variable on output, Y is income, and $U(\ )$ is a utility function. We choose the special form of utility function where $U'(Y) = Y^{-\eta}$. See equations (11) – (15).

There are five outcomes: bad, fairly bad, average, fairly good, good, numbered 1—5 with probabilities as shown. The random variable θ has alternative distributions P^1 and P^2. The ratio of EU' to $EU'\theta$ is tabulated for $\eta = 2, 6, 10$ and P^1 and P^2. See text for discussion.

There is a substantial literature concerned with uncertainty in agriculture and the response of farmers to it and we shall not attempt a detailed comparison of our results and analysis with this literature. For references the reader may consult for example Roumasset, Boussard and Singh (1979) or recent issues of the American Journal of Agricultural Economics.

§ 8.6.4. Some General Isssues

We have two general lessons for the estimation of agricultural production functions, which are as follows. First, if tasks performed and direct inputs are sufficiently well specified, labour hours should not be included as a separate input and, if they are, we should not expect to find them a significant explanatory variable. Second, in a cross-section of plots in the field, as opposed to the agricultural research station, one should not necessarily assume substantial curvature in the production function. Diminishing returns will undoubtedly be a feature but, for fertilizer at least, they may set in rather suddenly and at higher levels of inputs than are observed in the fields of risk-averse farmers.

We turn now to some of the grander issues: whether agriculture in poor countries conforms to the competitive neo-classical model and whether the benefits of the 'Green Revolution' are slanted in favour of big farmers. We take the second issue first.

We found that efficiency in the use of inputs was negatively associated (see Table 8.4) with the size of holding per standard family unit (the coefficient on this variable is negative). This measure of wealth has its deficiencies but we suggest that it is not misleading in our village. It would appear therefore that any advantages associated with wealth are not manifested in the way in which inputs are used. On the contrary the greater the pressure of poverty the greater the care with the use of inputs.

There was no strong association of the size of holding per standard family member and the intensity of inputs—see the correlation matrix in Table 8.2. Thus the ideas advanced in, for example, Griffin (1974) of the bias of the 'Green Revolution' in favour of big farmers do not, if wealth is appropriately captured by our *LOFA* variable, receive confirmation in our wheat study. We do see, however, in the correlation matrix a positive association between the 'good practice' variables and both the size of holding cultivated and the zero-one variable for the *Murao* caste. Recall that the *Muraos* are second in the hierarchy and the traditional cultivators. The relation of the area cultivated to good practice is consistent with our finding in Chapter 6 that the intensity of fertilizer use for the farm as a whole is related to area cultivated—and recall that in that chapter land cultivated was more closely correlated with intensity than land owned and the relation of *LOFA* to intensity was insignificant.

The adoption of various newer varieties and intensive practices seemed to be particularly associated with the younger educated farmers. We expect that the connections with age and caste are not a long-run equilibrium. As other farmers see the success of certain practices they will probably be induced to follow suit. Pride is of some importance here. It is not an easy thing in Indian village life for an older man to follow a younger—particularly if the younger is of a lower caste. But for whatever reason, lack of awareness or lack of willingness, farmers are not in general adopting techniques which can be regarded as technically efficient.[4] We expect that as population growth in Palanpur manifests itself in teenage sons and daughters with their demand for land and need for dowries, such slack as is there will come under substantial pressure.

We are unable to confirm that neo-classical economics is alive and well and residing in Palanpur, at least in its simplest form. While there was a general awareness of the productivity of inputs it was far from universal. Further, there was a very substantial gap between value of marginal product and price. This we suggested was associated in part with the cost of credit but more importantly with uncertainty. We saw that it was possible to reconcile our results with expected utility maximization but we had to assume strong risk aversion and a broad perceived spectrum of possible outcomes. This uncertainty and the lower productivity of fertilizer in the field than on research stations make it rational for farmers to use much less than the recommended doses.[5] We are very sceptical of analyses (such as Hopper, 1965) of agriculture in poor countries which attempt to relate price and marginal product without the introduction of uncertainty.

---

[4] We have in mind here the notions of being on the production frontier or output maximizing for given cost.

[5] An indication that research stations ignore the uncertainty facing farmers when making their recommendations can be seen in the stipulation that all fertilizer on non-irrigated crops should be applied basally (see § 7.1).

§ 8.7 Some Practical Implications

We were often asked by Palanpur farmers whether we had any particular suggestions for them. It was occasionally embarrassing that we had very few that we could offer with any confidence. This rather brief section contains some. We did not, and do not, offer ourselves as agricultural advisers but the results of our analyses and regressions do seem to indicate one or two points.

We are not convinced that the majority of farmers are fully aware of the potentiality and importance of a mixture of fertilizers at the time of sowing. We found a very strong effect and as time goes by the continual use of nitrogenous fertilizer by itself will deplete the soil of phosphorus and potassium and make the use of these basal fertilizers still more important. One improvement that farmers could make at comparatively little cost is in their sowing technique (note that this is not a conclusion that follows from the regression analysis). They are still sowing too deep; the newer varieties should be sown at a depth of 2 inches rather than the 4 inches recommended for *desi* varieties. Insufficient care is taken with distances between rows and density along rows. It may be that this defective sowing technique is associated with the negative coefficient on the seed rate. We suspect too that more care with the quality of seed could have a substantial pay-off. One can observe directly that much of the sowing material is a mixture of varieties—this is bound to reduce yield since different varieties have different maturity periods.

Given the apparent importance of uncertainty in their decisions, farmers might find the use of pesticides and herbicides attractive if they were properly informed and considered it carefully. But the returns to pest control are likely to be higher where more farmers participate – there are positive externalities. Careful attention to seed could reduce the impact of loose smut—a pathogenic disease which was quite common. Either more weeding or more ploughings would seem advantageous but we cannot be confident about the former given our inability to find a significant effect.

We hesitate to suggest the application of more nitrogenous fertilizer, given the apparent awareness of its productivity, the uncertainty inherent in the activity, and the low level of basal fertilizers.

§ 8.8 Concluding Remarks

Although this has been a lengthy chapter we shall keep our concluding remarks brief. We have already summarized our theoretical and practical conclusions in the previous two sections.

The period of our study was one of agricultural change in Palanpur. Most farmers were using newer varieties of wheat but it would be misleading to say they had adopted the 'Green Revolution' or the 'high-yielding varieties package'. Fertilizer and water applications varied and the former at least were in general far below recommended levels. While varieties were new the particular sowing material used was often poor and the technique of sowing rather bad. This variation in practice provided substantial scope for the analysis of the determinants of output. It should be noted that whilst Palanpur practice may be poor compared with some ideal, yield of wheat is well above average for the Moradabad district.

Our regressions were fairly successful in that most variables suggested by common sense and previous agricultural research had significant coefficients of the right sign and sensible magnitudes. We stressed our preference for analysing production in terms of particular inputs rather than broad aggregates such as labour, and this seems to have been justified in the results. We found that the notion of 'good practice' was helpful in understanding results and there was a strong relation with land cultivated, the *Murao* caste, and the younger, educated farmers.

We found the discussion sessions particularly interesting. They indicated the wide variation in attitudes, energy, and awareness amongst farmers, as well as indicating that, in general, farmers were quite good at estimating the effects of varying practices. It may be that at a time of change they were particularly sensitive to such questions, whereas they would have found answers more difficult if practices had remained unchanged for a long period. The risk aversion which can be inferred from the high ratios of the value of the marginal product to the price of an input was supported in the farmers' statements.

The so-called Marshallian view of share tenancy received some weak support. But some of the clear and strong statements that are made about Indian agriculture were not supported at all by our wheat study: productivity per acre was positively (not negatively) associated with land cultivated, the newer practices and varieties were not adopted only or largely by the wealthy, and the simple neo-classical model with prices equal to marginal products could not be sustained. Finally, farmers were not doing the best that they could do given their resources. But one should not, and we did not, expect the world to be that simple.

Appendix to Chapter 8 Alternative Functional Forms

We shall begin by mentioning certain functional forms which are quite common in the literature but which we did not try and then, briefly, give our reasons for excluding them. We then describe certain tests that we did carry out on the functional forms which we adopted.

There are a number of forms, commonly used in the agricultural literature, for capturing the curvilinear response of yield to fertilizer. Examples are, where y is yield and x is fertilizer per acre:

$$y = a + b\sqrt{x} + cx \tag{A.1}$$

$$y^{-1} = a + b(x+c)^{-1} \tag{A.2}$$

$$y = y_0 + d(1 - 10^{-kx}) \tag{A.3}$$

Equation (A.3) enjoys the title of the Mitscherlich equation. Our reason or refraining from experimenting with these forms is that our experiments with the forms which we did try led us to the conclusion that over the range of inputs observed in our sample the non-linearities were not important. The non-linearities assume significance at higher input levels.

Much work on industrial and aggregate production functions in economics has been with constant elasticity of substitution or CES functions:

$$Y = (\alpha K^{-h} + \beta L^{-h})^{-1/h} \tag{A.4}$$

where Y is output, K is capital, and L labour. A reason this is rejected here is that for elasticities of substitution $\sigma(= 1/1 + h)$ less than or equal to one, output is zero if any single input is zero. This is clearly inappropriate for the case where fertilizer is an important input. One could attempt to accommodate the problem by replacing a variable which occasionally takes values of zero, K say, by $K + a$ where 'a' is a constant. One can then search for some optimum 'a' in the sense of minimizing unexplained sums of squares. Given our view that the data did not exhibit important non-linearities we did not embark on this procedure although we did adopt a similar procedure for the log-linear model which we shall now describe.

Given that there were some eight cultivators who applied no fertilizer we have a problem in estimating the log-linear form, as the logarithm of zero is $-\infty$, a value inconvenient for regressions. We tried two approaches. The first was to drop these cultivators from the sample – the results are not reported here. The second was to include as an explanatory variable $\log(f + a)$ where f is fertilizer per acre and 'a' a constant and then search over 'a' to find the best fit. The criterion is R^2. The region of search (a = 5 to 50 kg urea per acre) was based on the amount of nitrogen that wheat extracts from the soil. A rough idea of the output that can be obtained without fertilizer can then give us an indication of the amount of nitrogen available in the soil.

We searched over the grid a = 5 to 50 in steps of 5. The result is shown in Table 8.A.1. We perform a regression with the three variables of the main model and then ask which of the variables $\log(f + 5), \ldots, \log(f + 50)$ would have the highest F-value, and hence pro-

Table 8.A.1. Experiments with the Measurement of Fertilizers for the Logarithmic Form._____

Multiple R	0.72	Number of cases	47
R squared	0.52	Number of variables	3
Standard error	0.22	F-Value for equation	15.33
		Dependent variable	*CORWTACR*

Variables in the equation

Variable	B	Standard error of B	F
LNPLGHINGS	0.25	0.10	6.30
FRSWDUM	0.43	0.07	40.43
SWNGDUM	0.09	0.07	1.89
Constant	1.42		

Variables not in the equation

Variable	B IN	F
LNFERT 5	0.16	22.72
LNFERT 10	0.22	23.20
LNFERT 15	0.27	23.37
LNFERT 20	0.32	23.44
LNFERT 25	0.36	23.45
LNFERT 30	0.40	23.43
LNFERT 35	0.44	23.40
LNFERT 40	0.48	23.37
LNFERT 45	0.52	23.33
LNFERT 50	0.56	23.29

Notes : (i) See notes to Table 5.7.
(ii) Variables are defined in Table 8.1.

vide the highest R^2, if included. Given that the variables log $(f + a)$ for different 'a' are very highly correlated—for example, the lowest linear correlation is 0.970—it is not surprising that the difference in F-values is extremely small. However given this criterion, a = 25 kg of urea per acre is selected and this value of 'a' was used for the results for the log-linear model reported in § 8.3. This result agrees remarkably well with what one might expect from first principles. The 'IFFCO Plant Food Removal Guide'[6] states that 1.75 kg of nitrogen are removed from the soil per quintal of wheat grain and 0.50 per quintal of straw. Given that the straw to wheat ratio is, by weight, roughly 1.3 on our sample plots, one quintal of wheat would remove $1.75 + (1.3 \times 0.50) = 2.40$ kg of nitrogen. Suppose that without fertilizer the output per acre would be 5.5 quintals of wheat (the average over the eight plots that used no fertilizer was 5.47) then there must be available in an acre of soil 5.5×2.40 kg of nitrogen, which is equivalent to $5.5 \times 2.40/0.46 = 28.7$ kg of urea.

An alternative to using log $(f + 25)$ in the log-linear case is to drop the eight observations without fertilizer from the sample. We tried the regression using the main model and found an R^2 of 0.545. Given this drop in R^2 (from 0.690 with log $(f + 25)$) and that the eight observations form an important group in the sample, we preferred the 'log $(f + 25)$' procedure.

Although we argued above, § 8.1, that the appropriate specification for the relation between inputs and outputs should involve constant returns to scale, because plot size

[6] This is a plastic display similar to a slide-rule issued to farmers by IFFCO.

will not as such matter, this can be put to the test. There are various ways of examining the hypothesis of constant returns to scale—we choose a particularly simple one. We regress the logarithm of output of wheat (LNCORWH)on the logarithm of the acreage of the plot (*LNACR*) and ask whether the value one lies in the 95 per cent confidence interval of the coefficient. The result is presented in Table 8.A.2. The coefficient on *LNACR* was 1.02 and its standard error 0.10. Thus the hypothesis of constant returns embodied in the regressions of Chapter 8 cannot be rejected.

The results of our experiments on the inclusion of quadratic terms in the linear model are presented in Tables 8.A.3 and 8.A.4. We again based the experiment on the main model. However we included the number of irrigations in this case since one of the objectives in examining the quadratic form was to investigate whether the poor performance of the number of irrigations in the linear model was attributable to interactions with the level of fertilizer. We did not include any quadratic terms involving the zero-one variables (although we reported earlier that we could not find significant interaction between early sowing and fertilizer per acre as measured by the significance of the coefficient on the product of the two variables). We then have quadratic expressions in the three variables; the number of irrigations, the number of ploughings, and the level of fertilizer.

The *F*-test for the 12-coefficient model of Table 8.A.3 against the 5-coefficient main model of Table 8.3 (four variables plus the constant term) gives a statistic of 1.79 with (7, 35) degrees of freedom. The 5 per cent level for *F* with these degrees of freedom is 2.29 and thus we should (comfortably) accept the hypothesis that the main model was correct as against the quadratic model of Table 8.A.3.

An additional unsatisfactory feature of the quadratic model of Table 8.A.3 is the signs and significance of the coefficients. For example, the sign of the coefficient on the square of fertilizer per acre is positive whereas diminishing returns would require it to be negative, and five of the eleven coefficients on the included variables are insignificant. On the grounds of both the *F*-test and the significance of coefficients we are led to reject the quadratic model of Table 8.A.3.

We also tried an alternative 'pruned-down' version of the quadratic model where we removed the irrigation terms which had previously been dropped from the main model. This is presented in Table 8.A.4. The *F*-test for the 8-coefficient model of Table 8.A.4 against the 5-coefficient main model gives a statistic 0.94 compared with a 5 per cent level

Table 8.A.2. Testing for the Influence of Size of Plot.

Multiple R	0.84	Number of cases	47
R squared	0.71	Number of variables	1
Standard error	0.32	F-Value for equation	111.09
		Dependent variable	*LNCORWH*

Variables in the equation

Variable	B	Standard error of B	F
LNACR	1.02	0.10	111.09
Constant	2.07	0.01	30,464.19

Notes :   (i) See notes to Table 5.7.

(ii) *LNCORWH* is the natural logarithm of the total output from the plot.

(iii) *LNACR* is the natural logarithm of the area of the plot.

Table 8.A.3. A Quadratic Model

Multiple R	0.88	Number of cases	47
R squared	0.77	Number of variables	11
Standard error	1.35	F-Value for equation	10.71
		Dependent variable	*CORWTACR*

Variables in the equation

Variable	B	Standard error of B	F
PLGHFERT	− 0.001	0.01	0.01
PLGHINGS	0.64	1.34	0.23
IRIGNMBR	− 1.82	2.05	0.79
FERTACRE	0.23	0.09	5.95
SWNGDUM	0.93	0.44	4.45
FRSWDUM	2.61	0.63	17.07
PLGHIRIG	0.08	0.22	0.14
PLGHSQUR	− 0.05	0.08	0.40
IRIGSQUR	0.47	0.24	4.04
FERTSQUR	0.002	0.001	5.19
IRIGFERT	− 0.07	0.02	8.06
Constant	2.35		

Notes :　(i) See notes to Table 5.7
　　　　(ii) $PLGHFERT = (PLGHINGS) \times (FERTACRE)$
　　　　　　$PLGHIRIG = (PLGHINGS) \times IRIGNMBR$
　　　　　　$PLGHSQUR = (PLGHINGS)^2$
　　　　　　$IRIGSQUR = (IRIGNMBR)^2$
　　　　　　$FERTSQUR = (FERTACRE)^2$
　　　　　　$IRIGFERT = (IRIGNMBR) \times (FERTACRE)$

Table 8.A.4 A Quadratic Model (Pruned Version)

Multiple R	0.84	Number of cases	47
R squared	0.71	Number of variables	7
Standard error	1.44	F-Value for equation	13.61
		Dependent variable	*CORWTACR*

Variables in the equation

Variable	B	Standard error of B	F
PLGHFERT	0.003	0.01	0.19
PLGHINGS	1.39	0.89	2.43
FERTACRE	0.04	0.05	0.64
SWNGDUM	0.88	0.45	3.86
FRSWDUM	2.63	0.46	31.96
PLGHSQUR	− 0.10	0.07	1.97
FERTSQUR	− 0.0001	0.0004	0.08
Constant	0.66		

Notes: (i) See notes to Table 5.7.
　　　(ii) See notes to Table 8.A.3.

for F with (3, 39) degrees of freedom of 2.84 (see Kendall and Stuart, 1973, Appendix Table 7) so that again we should (comfortably) accept the null hypothesis that the main model is correct as against the model of Table 8.A.4.

One may suppose that the failure of the two experiments embodied in Table 8.A.3 and

8.A.4 is associated with the range of observations of our sample. While there is a considerable variation in practice amongst our cultivators (see § 7.3) the higher levels of cultivation intensity which occurred were not so high as to run into significant diminishing returns. And we saw in § 7.1.2 in our general discussion of agricultural practice and the level of inputs that, for fertilizers at least, diminishing returns set in suddenly and at high levels due to lodging. Lodging was not a problem on any of our sample plots.

Our inability to pick up interaction terms satisfactorily may be due to multicollinearity: the correlation coefficient between the product of the number of irrigations with fertilizer per acre and fertilizer per acre was 0.94, and between the product term and the number of irrigations 0.74.

Our experience with the fitting of quadratic models led us to abandon attempts to estimate more complex functional forms. The computational effort would have been considerable and there is reason to suppose that the extra explanatory power would have been negligible. We have not used the residuals to examine questions of non – linearities since we have used the direct formal tests described above.

9

Reflections on Economic Theory

§ 9.0 Introduction

The conclusions from our study are provided in Chapters 9 and 10. We begin, in this chapter, by reviewing various economic theories and hypotheses in the light of our experience of Palanpur. We shall suggest that certain of these theories, taken together, can explain much of what we found. On the other hand some important features are not easily explained and we shall point to possibilities for further theoretical research. We did not find that the village accorded with any single simple theory and we had to draw upon several models to explain its various features.

The next section provides a review of the structure of markets in Palanpur. We shall concentrate on the markets for labour, credit, fertilizer, irrigation, and outputs. Our conclusions on theories of the market for the services of land are postponed until § 9.3, where an issue of particular importance will be the interrelations between the various factor markets. We shall discuss in § 9.2 the behaviour of the agents in the village economy: their awareness of prices and productivities, their objectives, and their reaction to agricultural change.

In § 9.3 we shall be discussing certain aspects of tenancy in Palanpur. We shall appraise various theories of tenancy and since share tenancy is the dominant type of contract in Palanpur we shall pay particular attention to that form of tenure. Tenancy has featured prominently throughout this book and we have indicated our findings as they have occurred. We provide an over-all view of our results in this section. Uncertainty should be an important element of a discussion of many facets of agriculture and has entered at several points in our arguments. We shall devote § 9.4, however, exclusively to the ramifications of uncertainty for decisions and contracts. We shall concentrate, in particular, on the choice of the intensity of inputs.

In § 9.5 we shall draw together our conclusions from Palanpur for discussion of the relation between output per acre and size of holding in Indian agriculture. In Chapter 3 (§ 3.9) we drew attention to various claims which have been made concerning the 'Green Revolution', but we have not made this an explicit subject of study in our empirical work; certainly we have not devoted a particular section or chapter to it. Nonetheless, we have frequently made observations which bear on this issue and we provide a discussion of them in § 9.6. The concluding section will contain an over-all appraisal of the theoretical approach we have adopted and suggestions for further research.

§ 9.1 The Structure of Markets

The important markets in Palanpur were examined in Chapter 4. We should reiterate our statement at the beginning of that chapter that our use of the term 'market' is very general and all-embracing. We refer to the arrangements in force for the exchange of goods and factors or of the relevant services. We shall examine the theoretical implications of our findings for the different factor markets in the order followed in that chapter: labour, draught animals, credit, irrigation, and fertilizers. The linkages between these markets should be borne in mind throughout.

We begin, however, with a brief discussion of output markets. With the exception of one main output the market conditions faced by villagers of Palanpur can be described as 'perfect', in the usual sense that sellers behave as if they can sell as much as they like without affecting the price. The exception, to which we return shortly, is sugar. The part of the (non-sugar) crop which is marketed is, in general, sold in nearby towns, particularly Chandausi. That market is large in relation to the output of any farmer in Palanpur or even of Palanpur as a whole. It would be unreasonable for any farmer to believe that the amount which he sold would affect the price and there was no evidence that any farmer held such a belief. There would, of course, be uncertainty at the time of sowing about the price which would be ruling shortly after the time of harvest. Indeed there would be considerable uncertainty at a point in time after the harvest about the price which would be ruling next week. However that is a different question from whether or not a market is perfect and is one to which we return in § 9.4.

Where government procurement of crops is in operation and where the rules for procurement depend upon quantity produced, then the demand curve facing a producer would not be horizontal. There was a procurement scheme in operation for wheat in 1974–5 but this was irrelevant for Palanpur farmers since there were no very large producers in the village. And it was reasonable to suppose that the farmers did not view procurement as a serious problem.

Transport of produce to the market was cheap and straightforward—a few miles on a bullock cart. Thus no problems arose concerning monopoly of transport outlets. And there were no problems of limited opportunities for sales arising from a small number of purchasers.

The arrangements for selling sugar were described in § 4.5 and this detail will not be repeated here. Sugar was at that time a rather profitable crop and access to sales to the government mill, where prices were higher than the private market, was restricted. Of the alternative markets, the private mill involved just one purchaser but the *ghur* market could be described as perfect. As one might expect the restricted access to the government market gave rise to a certain amount of manipulation, with richer and more powerful farmers gaining priority, and there was some bad feeling.

There are now a variety of theories of the operation of labour markets in poor countries, and some of these were reviewed in § 3.3. We should conclude, however, that the simple and familiar supply and demand competitive model is not obviously inadequate as a description of the labour market in Palanpur. The wage rate is not rigid, there are large numbers of both buyers and sellers inside Palanpur, and there are opportunities for buying and selling labour outside the village too. This is not to say that anyone could be sure of buying or selling labour on a particular day.

The most prominent alternative in the recent literature to the standard supply and demand model is the so-called efficiency wage model. As explained in § 3.3 the idea is that productivity or the number of effective tasks performed by a worker depends upon his consumption which in turn depends upon his wage. In the model the employer chooses wages so that the cost per task performed is minimum. This can lead to a wage per day above that at which labourers offer themselves for work. We argued in Chapter 4 (§ 4.1) that the theory contributed little to an understanding of markets in Palanpur.

The particular feature of the village labour market which militated against the applicability of the efficiency wage theory was that labour hirings were on a day-to-day basis and there were very few long-term contracts. We have argued at length elsewhere (see Bliss and Stern, 1978) that if the theory provides an important explanation of wages we should expect to see long-term employment contracts.

A possible qualification to the assertion that the labour market is perfect lies in the existence of an understanding amongst sellers of labour and a similar one amongst the buyers concerning the appropriate price. Thus it may be considered rather improper for an employer to offer something above the current wage. Similarly, a labourer would not be popular amongst his fellow labourers if he undercut them. One must take care, however, in interpreting such an understanding as an imperfection and it was not clear in Palanpur whether disapproval from fellow labourers or employers could constitute a deterrent sufficiently powerful to prevent anyone from following his own wishes. Indeed in many markets which might be characterized as competitive a change in price would often come about, in response to the appearance of excess demand or supply, by one individual being the first to change his price. This individual might be the object of some disapproval but that would not necessarily tell us anything about the effectiveness of coalitions on one or other side of the market. Nevertheless we did retain the impression that the feeling of solidarity between suppliers of labour or demanders was of some consequence, at least in preventing wages from moving as much as they might otherwise have done.

The market for the services of draught animals in Palanpur is not distinguished by its perfection or imperfection but by its absence. We provided a number of speculations in § 4.2 as to why this might be so. It provides an important problem for further study and we shall return to the question when we make suggestions for further research at the end of this chapter. The absence of this market has considerable consequences for the land market and these will be discussed in § 9.3.

Credit is not, of course, a factor of production but it can be a major influence on the ability to purchase these factors. The major source of credit in Palanpur is the Co-operative Credit Union run from the Seed Store. It provides credit on given terms but borrowers cannot borrow as much as they like. Their limit is dependent upon land owned and the number of shares in the Union which have been purchased. Thus for many farmers the marginal source of credit is from private money-lenders. This credit did seem to be available, although the rates of interest were high—either 2 per cent or 3 per cent per month (nominal, compounded). It is important to emphasize that there is no single dominant money-lender in Palanpur. The lenders were a number of the more wealthy farmers. And one must remember too that many farmers might be able to find a member of their family who would help out.

Irrigation water seemed to be freely available at given rates. Most farmers who were involved in financial transactions for water hired pumping sets. There were several such sets in the village and owners were glad to rent them out. The only problems which arose were minor and concerned with obtaining the water at the desired time.

Fertilizer, too, could be bought at the time of our study in the market, at given prices, in any quantities likely to be desired by Palanpur farmers. This had not been so in immediately preceding years since there had been government rationing at regulated prices. Even in those years, however, there was a flourishing black market at prices which were well-known. Rationing was discontinued at the start of the *rabi* season of 1974–5 (there was some residual disruption of supplies of basal fertilizers for use at the time of sowing). Farmers without ready cash might be forced to borrow privately if they wished to purchase fertilizer.

We have found then that the output markets and several of the important factor markets might be described as perfect. But there are some very important qualifications and exceptions, an understanding of which is crucial to an explanation of cultivation and allocation decisions in Palanpur. We have seen that an increase in sales to the government sugar mill will involve the farmer in some trouble and expense, that the major source of credit is rationed, and that fertilizers had been rationed. The most important qualifications, however, concern the market for bullocks, which, being more or less absent, could hardly be described as perfect, and the market for the services of land. The land market is both very important and involves particular arrangements and we have, therefore, reserved a summary of our conclusions for theory to a separate section, § 9.3. Finally, the credit which any individual can obtain is limited by his circumstances.

The linkages between markets are also concentrated around land contracts. We mean by linkages here simultaneous contracts between two parties in more than one market: thus labour, land, credit, and irrigation contracts might be made simultaneously between tenant and landlord. The bargain, for example, might involve the tenant taking on land under share tenancy, agreeing to work on the plots cultivated by the landlord, and in return being provided with credit and irrigation facilities. Such simultaneous contracts were rare, outside land transactions, so we shall postpone further discussion until §9.3.

It should be noted that our definition of linkage is fairly narrow here. A particular feature of one market (for example, that for draught power) will have important and specific consequences for another (say, land). But it is always true in some way or other that markets are linked in this sense, and we therefore prefer to use the term in a narrower sense.

§ 9.2 The Behaviour of Agents

A model of the behaviour of an agent in an economy requires a specification of his relations with other participants in the economy, his information and beliefs concerning the world about him, and the objectives he wishes to pursue or the rules which he operates. We have already in the previous section described the relations amongst participants in the economy of Palanpur in so far as they affect the markets with which we are concerned. We begin this section with a discussion of the knowledge and beliefs of agents about their agricultural and economic environment.

Our evidence here is based on our frequent informal discussions with farmers during the *rabi* season of 1974–5 and, in particular, on the interviews with cultivators of the sample wheat plots which were presented in § 4.7 and 8.5. It will be recalled that we asked the cultivators about the markets where they purchased their inputs, the costs, and the effects on output of variations in levels of those inputs. The farmers were able to answer the questions about markets and costs without any difficulty and most of them were able to comment on the effects of changes in quantities of inputs applied. There was a striking correspondence between the consequences of changing these levels as stated by farmers and the marginal productivities which we estimated in our regression analysis. Thus, it seems, many farmers have a good idea as to the consequences of varying their input decisions. And it should be remembered that the techniques and inputs in question were relatively new to them.

On the other hand, several of the respondents were unwilling to speculate on the results of changes in their practice. 'I do not know, I have never tried' was, for example, quite a common answer to the question concerning the effects of one more irrigation, or a little extra fertilizer. Our claim that many farmers are aware of the consequences of alternative practices should not, therefore, be generalized to include all farmers.

There was a good knowledge as to where various inputs might be available. Thus even farmers who were using little or no fertilizer would know that it could be bought in the nearby town. The same was true of the new varieties of seed. It seemed, however, that there was a marked reluctance by some farmers to make the effort to search out these inputs. For example, such farmers might be short of ready cash and be unwilling or unable to borrow, they may be wary of running the risk of wasting their money if the crop were to fail, and some as we have noted may not believe these inputs to be profitable. We think that these reasons are important but retain the impression that for a few farmers at least the effort required to change their practices, search out the inputs, and gain information on their use made a significant contribution to their decision.

It appeared also that most farmers were not prepared to ignore the disutility of extra work in the fields. For example, weeding of wheat was comparatively rare although many farmers were prepared to grant that weeding would improve output. And some tenants claimed that landlords pressed them to do extra work on leased-in land, over and above the labour they were willing to apply.

It is clear then that farmers are well aware of the costs of inputs and, in particular, they count their own labour as a cost. Most of them are quite good at estimating the effects on output against which the costs of inputs are set. There remains the question of how these facets are put together in order to arrive at a decision.

We suggest that a model of the maximization of the value of output net of the costs of production, where one uses both cash and imputed values and costs, is, in general, inadequate as an explanation of the behaviour observed. We found in our analysis in Chapter 8 that the value of the marginal product was for the various inputs two to three times the price. We argued that this could not be explained by the cost of credit over the season for the inputs but could be understood in terms of risk aversion using a model of the maximization of expected utility. We return to this in our discussion of uncertainty in § 9.4, but we record here that we are suggesting that a maximization model, provided one selects an appropriate objective, can be successful in explaining the farmers' behaviour.

We must acknowledge, however, that there is great variation across farmers. There are many farmers who are alert to opportunities, who appraise the costs and benefits of their decisions, and appear to act as if they have clear objectives in mind. On the other hand there are also many cultivators who do not seek out opportunities, are not bothered with new techniques, and seem to plod along from day to day and year to year without a great deal in the way of analysis of their cultivation decisions.

These variations in attitudes amongst farmers can be seen clearly in the different adjustments one finds to technological change. Many farmers have sought out new varieties and some have tested them fairly carefully in their own fields. They have made an effort to irrigate at the appropriate time and with the right quantities of water and some have taken substantial loans to buy pumping sets. And many apply substantial quantities of fertilizer, both basal and as a top dressing. But other farmers seem happy to acquire their seed from the Seed Store even though they know it is of bad quality. They are not prepared to go to the nearby markets for higher quality, neither are they willing to use fertilizer unless it is provided for them by the Seed Store on easy credit. Some are not even prepared to apply fertilizer on those conditions. These differences in response are, we think, to an important extent associated with differences in attitudes to uncertainty. We should suggest also that they involve different levels of enthusiasm, entrepreneurship, and drive. It is of course difficult to distinguish between caution and indolence.

Whilst it is true that there are great variations in attitudes and responses one cannot leave these differences with merely the comment that some people are different from others. We shall explore the origins of these differences at a number of points in what follows. Thus in our discussion of uncertainty in § 9.4 we shall take account of differences in wealth. We shall be comparing owner-cultivators and tenants in § 9.3. And the differences in behaviour between large and small farmers will be a central topic in § 9.5. But there do remain big differences between reactions which it is hard to explain. Doubtless one must consider the combination of a number of factors: social, religious, psychological, and economic. We shall have something to say on this in the next chapter but we shall see that many big questions must remain unanswered.

§ 9.3 Tenancy

Our various investigations into tenancy have revealed a picture which is more or less consistent although there are some important gaps in it. We shall describe the over-all picture which emerges from our analyses in this section. We begin with the question of why tenancy exists at all. We shall then describe the features of tenancy contracts, their enforcement, and the nature of 'equilibrium' in Palanpur drawing contrasts and parallels with some of the theories of share tenancy which have recently been the subject of great attention in the literature. That literature (for a review see § 3.2) has been much concerned with the question of why share tenancy is chosen rather than other forms of contract. We shall be offering some speculations here but no definitive answers, and we shall speculate on reasons for the constancy of the rental share although we find it hard to provide clear insights. The section will be concluded with a comparison of our results from different chapters on the productivity of tenanted land as opposed to other land.

A neo-classical model with constant returns to scale and perfect markets for the services of all factors, and for outputs, cannot explain why it is that some factors are traded rather than others. The owner of land will obtain the same income from that land irrespective of whether he rents it out or buys in co-operating factor services. In Chapter 5 we explained the existence of tenancy through the existence of fixed, or imperfectly marketable, factors. Such factors were the services of draught animals and family labour. We introduced the concept of the desired cultivated area (*DCA*) and suggested that the land leased-in was an increasing function of the difference between *DCA* and land owned. This theory of the amount of land which will either be taken on lease or leased-out if land owned differs from *DCA* is, we believe, new in the literature. It bears a resemblance to capital stock adjustment theories of investment. The theory depends upon the notion that, in the short run, it is land cultivated which a household adjusts rather than the amount of family labour or the services of draught animals. This is based on the existence, for many families, of a reluctance to trade out family labour and on the absence of a market for the services of draught animals. We return to this last point in the concluding section of the chapter.

Tenancy in Palanpur is, almost entirely, share tenancy and the rental share is everywhere 50–50. We shall return to the reason for share tenancy and for that particular share but first we describe the nature of the share contracts which are ruling, and the associated equilibrium, in relation to recent theories.

Supervision and enforcement of contracts are central to the view of share tenancy presented by Cheung (see § 3.2). Competition amongst tenants is such that the income a tenant obtains from working the land cannot exceed that which he could get by selling the equivalent amount of labour in the local market. The cultivation intensity enforced is exactly that which would result from profit maximization by an entrepreneur hiring-in labour and complementary factors. Cheung describes arrangements in Taiwan where there are just a few large land-owners and many potential tenants and where the understanding between landlord and tenant is very detailed. The so-called Marshallian model, on the other hand, involves no obligations for the tenant concerning cultivation practice. The choice is the tenant's alone.

The arrangements for supervision and enforcement in Palanpur lie somewhere between the close control of the Cheung description and the free decision for the tenant in the so-called Marshallian model. The balance, however, lies nearer to Cheung. The crop to be cultivated is always agreed and there is cost sharing for purchased inputs. We showed in the Appendix to Chapter 3 that cost-sharing could be equivalent to the specification of cultivation levels. It is much more difficult to specify a level of care. But here it becomes important that many tenancy contracts are repeated from year to year and that certain tenants become known as better farmers. In § 3.2 we emphasized that Marshall himself argued that the landlord would have to supervise closely cultivation under share tenancy and recognized that this could result in the solution described by Cheung. That is why we have appended 'so-called' to Marshallian.

In our discussions with tenants and potential tenants it was rare to find someone who declared that he wished to take on more land under tenancy but was unable to find a landlord willing to give him extra. Similarly no landlord said that he wished to lease-out more land but could not find a tenant. In this sense there appears to be equilibrium.

Behind this apparent equality between supply and demand, however, stand some rationing processes. Under share tenancy without total enforcement of arrangements for the intensity of cultivation, landlords have an incentive to find as tenants better and more careful cultivators. Such prospective tenants receive therefore preferential treatment. They in turn have an incentive to build and keep their reputation as good cultivators.

A second form of rationing involves the ownership of draught animals. It was impossible in Palanpur to obtain land on lease without owning bullocks or he-buffaloes. A landlord would not be prepared to lease-out to a share tenant who was without such animals since the tenant would be unable to hire their use. Arrangements for borrowing bullocks from friends would not seem sufficiently reliable given that alternative tenants who do own draught animals are available.

Thus draught animals are an entrance ticket to tenancy. The availability of family labour is important too. Once a household has dropped out of the market for leasing and lost or sold its draught animals it would be very difficult to get back in. Given that such animals are subject to uncertain health and life-times it is not easy to borrow to purchase them. Similarly, if family members have left the village or found other employment it may not be easy to reverse the process quickly.

The 50–50 share seems to be accepted by all parties as the proper one. There are many landlords and many tenants and no single agent can dictate terms. There does not, however, seem to be any flexibility in rental share. There is a little flexibility over the items involved in cost-sharing but it is generally understood that the landlord shares in only the cash costs of fertilizer and ir-rigation. A tenant who accepted a higher rental share to the landlord would be regarded with disfavour by other tenants and a landlord who offered a lower rental share would be similarly regarded by other landlords. There would be similar, but less strong, disapproval if there were to be any deviation from that which was regarded as normal in other aspects of a contract.

The equilibrium we have described is not, therefore, the standard com-petitive equilibrium with each agent buying and selling as much as he wishes at prices which have adjusted to clear the market. Neither is there one dominant landlord choosing the rental share, the amount of land leased-out, and the cultivation intensity; nor is the tenant free to choose that intensity as he likes. Given the circumstances we have described an equilibrium with rationing would be a more accurate description than equilibrium.

It is clear that the share contracts we have described involve linkages between markets in the sense in which we have been using that term (see the end of § 9.1). The tenant takes on the land, a certain standard of cultivation is expected, and the level of co-operating inputs is understood. Where there is cost-sharing, and this is the general practice in Palanpur, credit is also involved. The tenant finances the purchase of fertilizer, for example, and the share of the landlord in the cost is paid at harvest time. In this sense the credit goes from tenant to landlord. A good credit position will therefore signal an attractive tenant. Note the contrast with, say, the position of Bhaduri (1973) where it is suggested that the landlord desires to keep the tenant in debt in order to main-tain economic power over him. But apart from the linkages implicit in the share contract there are not in general any other simultaneous contracts involved in the land market. Thus it would not usually be the case that a tenant would guarantee to work on the landlord's plot or that the landlord would advance the tenant a loan.

We have seen that certain features of the tenancy contract accord with standard theories and that the market is in a rationing equilibrium. Why is it that one institution is dominant, share tenancy, and that the rental share is fixed at 50-50?

We must confess to being unable to offer wholly convincing arguments as to why share tenancy is so dominant and why the share has stayed at the given level. We can say, however, that it is an institution which has come down through Moghul and British rule, that seems to be accepted as fair, and has some perceived advantages without any overwhelming disadvantages.

The main advantage is risk-sharing. Both land-owner and tenant see agriculture as a risky activity; some land-owners are unwilling to take on the risk of cultivating themselves and tenants are unwilling, in general, to run the risk of paying fixed rents. There is no obvious institution which provides an alternative to the risk-sharing provided by share tenancy. It is not the case that similar risk profiles are available from incurring risk by renting land at fixed rents and from hedging by working part-time for a fixed certain wage. In particular: wage employment does not provide a safe income; management is neither homogeneous nor marketed, so that the production function is not the same for each farmer and it does not show constant returns to scale; and men are not indifferent between being share tenants and being wage labourers (see § 3.2).

There is also the advantage to the landlord in modern U.P. legislation that share tenancy is not obviously illegal whereas fixed-rent tenancy is. The landlord, under share tenancy, can claim that the tenant is actually a labourer working under his instruction, for a share of the output. However, the villagers are not well informed about existing law and anyway have possible future legislation in mind as much as the current state of affairs.

It is harder to explain the absence of any change in the share during a period when the conditions of agriculture and the population have changed quite sharply. There are obvious advantages of simplicity in a 50–50 share but one should not overrate them. It is not very difficult to organize a 40–60 share, for example. On the other hand 50–50 might be seen to be a fair share of output in the particular sense that neither side gets more than the other. Moreover, the parties do not share output only but also costs, management, and risk. Where responsibility is more or less equally divided it is not a minor adjustment to depart from 50–50 split.

We regard it as likely that share tenancy will persist, for the reasons we have described, but it would be brave to argue that the conventional 50–50 share will withstand the population pressure which is likely to emerge over the next ten or twenty years.

Our final comments on tenancy concern cultivation practices and patterns on tenanted land as opposed to owner-cultivated land. We have examined this question in three different ways. In Chapter 5 (§ 5.3) we analysed output per acre for a household, and for a given crop (but, in particular, wheat) on tenanted and non-tenanted land. Our regression analysis in Chapter 6, where we studied the determination of the value of the output generated by a household, included the proportion of cultivated land under tenancy as an explanatory variable. Finally in Chapters 7 and 8 we looked at individual wheat plots and asked whether cultivation on tenanted plots was significantly different from owner-cultivated plots.

In Chapter 5 we found that the difference between yields for wheat on the two types of land was insignificant, when we compare output per acre for those households who have either tenanted or owner-cultivated land but not both; yet on the other hand when we make the comparison between output per acre on the two types of land for households cultivating both we find that the difference is significant, with yield on tenanted land being higher. In Chapter 6 the proportion of land under tenancy was never significant as an explanatory variable and in Chapter 7 and 8 we found that average output per acre on tenanted plots was lower than for non-tenanted plots but that the difference was insignificant. We asked also whether input levels were lower on tenanted plots and found significant differences only in the case of fertilizer at the time of sowing.

The questions posed when examining, on the one hand, yields for a crop on a plot, and on the other, the value of total output for a cultivator, are different. It is possible that variations in the intensity of the use of inputs will appear in the cropping pattern rather than in cultivation practices for a particular crop.

The general picture which emerges from our three studies is that tenancy does not make much difference to output per acre or to levels of inputs. One cannot conclude from a finding in one study of a small positive difference between yield for tenanted and non-tenanted plots (Chapter 5), in another no difference (Chapter 6), and a third a small negative difference (Chapter 7 and 8), that tenancy has an important influence on cultivation intensity. The evidence from Palanpur is contrary to the idea that tenancy provides an important disincentive to productivity.

It is interesting to speculate on the reasons why no disincentive effect has emerged. We have, it is true, emphasized supervision and cost-sharing but supervision cannot be complete for all the inputs not covered by cost-sharing. Why then does some residual difference in yield, for the two types of land, not persist? The explanation may be in some matter not considered by the theories we have looked at. For example, share tenancy involves the pooling of managerial and cultivating skills. Where one party is more highly skilled than the other his methods may predominate. There is the advantage of being able to discuss a problem with someone else who is seriously involved. It could be that where the tenant is observed closely by the landlord he performs better just because he is being observed. This type of consideration, which we believe may be important, shows what a complicated matter the theory of share tenancy can be.

§ 9.4 Uncertainty

Uncertainty is important in agriculture. It is of particular significance in a poor economy such as Palanpur as the consequence of a bad harvest is, for many, hunger. The ability to bear risk or to insure against it is small. It is not surprising, therefore, to find that a model which exhibits strong risk aversion seems to describe well the behaviour of the cultivators. We saw in § 8.4 that expected marginal products of inputs were two or three times the cost. This is obviously inconsistent with the maximization of the expectation of profit but is consistent with maximization of expected utility. However, we showed that the degree of risk aversion, measured by the elasticity of the marginal utility of income, would have to be strong to account fully for the factors of 2 or 3 described.

We suggested also that our finding that the ratio of expected marginal product to price was similar for a number of inputs was not inconsistent with the formulation of uncertainty commonly used in models of peasant agriculture, namely that stochastic terms enter the production function multiplicatively on output as a whole.

Whilst we argued that the cost of credit could not explain the differences we found between expected marginal product and price we should suggest that the interaction between credit and uncertainty is important. If the cost of defaulting on a loan is the loss of land one would be very wary of taking on the loan in the first place. Note, however, that this argument is concerned with the collateral for the loan rather than the interest rates charged.

There is, of course, nothing irrational about maximizing expected utility rather than expected profit. However, there are opportunities available to households for the reduction of risk, which are cheap but which they do not exploit. Here we should suggest that households are simply not acting rationally. We refer, in particular, to the use of insecticides and pesticides.

We have already argued in the previous section that uncertainty seems to be important in the determination of the kind of rental contract chosen. We suggested that it was an important part of the reason for selecting share tenancy rather than fixed rents.

There are some interesting questions concerning the connections between uncertainty and the topic of our next section, the relation between output per acre and size of holding. If uncertainty is an important determinant of decisions for a given farmer then differing attitudes to risk ought to tell us something about the differences in decisions between farmers. We argued in § 3.4 that one can deduce the way in which input intensity will vary across size of holding from hypotheses about the way in which attitudes to risk change in relation to income or wealth. We showed that, if it is assumed that absolute risk aversion declines with wealth, then the conclusion is that richer farmers will be prepared to apply more purchased inputs per acre than poorer farmers. On the other hand we saw that where income accrues only from the cultivation of land owned, and utility is defined as a function of income, then increasing relative risk aversion will imply that richer farmers will apply less purchased inputs per acre than smaller farmers. Our evidence suggested that the former model was preferable as a description of Palanpur since a regression of intensity of fertilizer use, on either land owned or land cultivated, shows a significant positive relation (§ 6.7).

§ 9.5 Productivity and Farm Size

We saw in Chapter 3 (§ 3.7) that there has been a lively discussion in the literature on Indian agriculture which seeks to explain an apparent negative relation between output per acre and size of farm. It is, therefore, a striking feature of our results (Chapter 6) that we found productivity to be invariant with respect to cultivated area. We must ask why our result has emerged.

First, however, we should recall that productivity per acre which is constant with farm size has been observed before for cross-sections of cultivators within a village (see Sen, 1975, Appendix C). Indeed it is for data bases which spread across districts or states that one finds the declining relationship. The discrepancy between intra-village samples and the others is interesting and a phenomenon which it is not easy to explain. But this is not our main concern here and we concentrate on whether the reasons which have been advanced for a declining relationship apply to Palanpur.

Sen has provided two arguments (see § 3.7). First, he suggests that on small family farms cultivators may push the application of labour beyond a point where the marginal product is equal to the market wage. They may do this rather than sell their labour outside if there are costs, subjective or otherwise, from selling labour. Second, he suggests that the reason larger farms have lower average land quality (a phenomenon noted by Khusro, 1973) is that population growth on more fertile land has been faster.

The former of these arguments has some qualified application to Palanpur. The qualification is that it is relevant only for certain castes and in particular *Thakurs* who regard selling their labour as demeaning. But the *Thakurs* do not provide a sufficiently high proportion of the households with little land for this consideration to have an important effect. Overall the absence of any very large holdings in Palanpur leads us to the conclusion that sharp qualitative differences, of the kind indicated by Sen, between the large capitalist farm and the small family farm are not relevant for our village. There is not a negative relation between land quality and size of holding in Palanpur.

A further argument, also from Khusro, has suggested that larger cultivated areas have a higher proportion of land leased-in. If tenants have lower output per acre then this might explain the negative relation. But we have seen in Palanpur that output per acre on tenanted land is not significantly different from that on owner-cultivated land.

We have seen that the major reasons advanced as to why one might observe output per acre which decreases with the size of cultivated holding do not apply to Palanpur; indeed we find output per acre to be unaffected by size of holding.

§ 9.6 The 'Green Revolution'

We have made clear (in § 3.9) our view that to speak simply of adopters and non-adopters of the new technology, or of the 'Green Revolution' as applying to one part of the community but not another, is to draw dichotomies which cannot be sustained by the experience of Palanpur. Farmers vary in their use of new seeds, chemical fertilizers, and irrigation; some apply more irrigation, where others apply more fertilizer, and nearly all of them use seeds which are not the traditional varieties. No farmer applies the full package of recommended inputs and the seeds used vary greatly in quality.

Risk aversion has been emphasized in § 9.4 and attitude to, and perception of, risk would be important in a decision to try different methods of cultivation. Distinct from, but related to, this aspect is the willingness to find out about and try out new methods. Here differences between farmers may be related to caste, wealth, and education but very substantial differences still remain after one has allowed for those variables.

We have avoided an undue separation of the effects of risk aversion and credit since the two are intimately tied together. The higher castes and the wealthy do find it easier to obtain credit but the fear of disaster and default discourages the poorer households, in particular, from taking on large loans. The interest rate itself does not appear to be the decisive discouragement since, were it not for uncertainty, the return to fertilizer application, for example, would more than support the interest cost.

What are the changes that irrigation, new seeds, and chemical fertilizers have brought to Palanpur? Our conclusions must be based on a comparison of the 1957–8 study with what we found in 1974–5 (see § 2.6). Output per acre is now much higher – see Table 2.17, p.32. The real hourly wage rate has not fallen greatly, notwithstanding a very large increase in population. Although we do not know about total hours bought and sold the stability of the wage rate in the face of the population increase leads us to suppose that these have increased substantially. And the big rise in irrigation and double-cropping would imply a large increase in work. The amount of land under tenancy has, we guess, changed little but it may have gone down slightly. Shares have not been altered and the practice of cost-sharing has been introduced together with the purchase of new inputs. Inequality in land-ownership appears to have decreased slightly (see Tables 2.9 and 2.15).

It is not easy to see how many of these changes have followed from the extension of irrigation,and the arrival of new seeds and chemical fertilizers, but we can offer some speculations. We place particular emphasis on irrigation and it must be noted that this by itself would have produced an increase in output, from double-cropping and increases in yield, and an increase in work requirements. We suggest that without these changes output per acre, the wage rate, and the demand for labour would be much lower than they now are. In this sense the benefits to land-owners, land cultivators, and wage labourers have been substantial.

What of the extravegant claims we reported in § 3.9? Many families in Palanpur are either hungry or live in fear of hunger. There is no sense in which Palanpur's 'food problem has been solved for good' (p.85 above). On the other hand, neither have small farmers been prevented or discouraged from participating in new methods; nor have they been forced to sell their land and work as hired labourers; nor have they been prevented from taking land on lease, and the shares required for leasing such land have not increased.

§ 9.7 Concluding Remarks

We have seen that much of the workings of the agricultural economy of Palanpur can be understood using standard methods and theories. It might be regarded as encouraging that this is so and it is something which, as theorists, we were not unhappy to find. But it is also encouraging from the point of view of theorists that there are important problems which are imperfectly understood. And we hope to have contributed some theoretical insights during the course of analysis.

There are a number of areas which we should suggest are important, and potentially fruitful for further research. We should like, for example, to be able to present a formal analysis of why it is that some markets emerge rather than others. For example, why is it that there is an insignificant market for the services of draught animals in Palanpur, and in many other villages, whereas such markets apparently exist elsewhere? Why is it that the 50-50 division in share tenancy remains so resilient?

We should suggest further that there remains great scope for analysing the all-pervasive role of uncertainty and information in agriculture. Why is it that farmers simultaneously display strong risk aversion while refraining from simple actions, such as the use of pesticides, which can reduce uncertainty? How far can one model the choice of cropping patterns as a response to uncertainty? This last question is one on which we have data for Palanpur, which are as yet unexploited, and which we hope to study in the future. But this is a matter for our further research.

10

A revisit and some speculations on the future

§ 10.0 Introduction

The present chapter will be concerned with various matters which in one way or another post-date the period of the studies with which Chapters 4 to 8 were concerned. In August 1977 the research team paid a short visit to the village during which events that took place since June 1975 were recounted to us, in particular the manner in which the Emergency[1] had affected the villagers, and some changes since we left the village were noted. The 1977 visit to the village and what we learnt from it are reported in § 10.1. There was not time within the space of this brief visit to conduct important new investigations but there were a few questions, which had come to light from our study of the research material that we had taken away with us, that we are anxious to have resolved. To this end we conducted some informal interviews with fifteen farmers. These interviews are described and some of the more interesting findings noted in § 10.2. In § 10.3, we try to say something on an important but difficult question which has been put to us a number of times by people interested in our studies: what conclusions for policy can be drawn from the work that we have undertaken? It was not our primary concern to arrive at policy conclusions but our findings do, at certain points, bear on policy and in this section we try to draw together such implications for policy as seem to be clearly suggested. Finally, § 10.4 is concerned with a vital question, which has to do with policy in a way as well: what does the future hold for the village of Palanpur? Of course we cannot pretend to know but it is a very interesting line of enquiry and our studies do have some bearing on it. Thus we have been rash enough to offer some views on this issue to conclude this second of our concluding chapters.

§ 10.1 The Village Revisited

The research team spent five days in Palanpur in August 1977. This was a very brief visit but, because we were already well acquainted with the village and the villagers, our time was very productive and we are able to learn a lot even in such a short time. This was the first time that we had seen the village during the heart of the *kharif* season. We saw the tail-end of the 1974 *kharif* when we first came to the village and we collected data from the farmers concerning the yields from that season, but now we could observe for the first time a variety of standing crops. Our return to the village apparently gave pleasure to its inhabitants—we had always said that we would return one day. As before we

[1] In June 1975 the then Prime Minister of India, Mrs Indira Gandhi, took special powers and arrested a large number of people. Formal amendments to the constitution eventually resulted, bestowing great power on the Prime Minister. The state of affairs is often referred to as 'the Emergency'. Mrs. Gandhi called a general election for March 1977 in which her party was decisively defeated. Among the policies which were adopted under the Emergency was an aggressive family planning drive under which men were pressured into accepting sterilization.

were made to feel greatly welcome.

The events that people related to us were naturally the most dramatic ones. One of the primary school teachers died in an accident on the railway line. In November 1976, two men from Palanpur died in a *dacoit* attack. The *dacoits* raided their house at night and there was an exchange of gunfire as a result of which these men incurred fatal wounds. As was remarked in Chapter 1 (§ 1.1), the Moradabad District has seen a lot of violent crime in the past but this was a dramatic example which was related to us more than once. The men who died were drinkers and gamblers noted for keeping violent company.

At the time of our visit electricity was coming to the village. A cable had been connected from the line that supplies the railway signal box and the station, and households were deciding whether to connect to the supply. A few households had it in mind to do so but this was only for domestic use, electric lights, and ceiling fans.

Another change which had come to the village since we were last there was that Palanpur now had its own market. During the period of our stay in the village in 1974–5 much less was bought or sold there. There was the shop, which mostly sold local medicines and a few supplies, and there was the dispensary. In addition there was some exchange between village households. None of these provided a good outlet for village produce and to sell or buy most things the villagers had to journey at least as far as Chandausi. Now an informal but busy market was operating every Monday. It took place on the strip of land between the railway station and the tea-shop and we saw it in operation. The sellers mostly squatted on the ground with whatever they had to sell in front of them.On offer there were: potatoes, onions, some grains, lentils, chillies, *biddies*, haircuts, and so on. The market was quite active in the sense that there were many people milling around and inspecting the goods.

As far as the villagers were concerned, the Emergency meant family planning and that meant sterilization. They were very afraid of compulsory sterilization and took evasive action whenever it was necessary. Farmers simply hid in the sugar cane whenever an official came to the village, which they were able to do since the official would normally arrive by rail and his arrival would quickly be notified to the villagers. Despite these attempts to evade sterilization, there were several carried out on inhabitants of the village. The number 10 was mentioned to us. Very likely these were men in one or other kind of government employment who did not have the option simply to run away. Under the Emergency government agencies were given quotas of sterilizations to fulfil, and the consequence was that government employees were frequently faced with promotion blocks or threats to their jobs unless they agreed to be sterilized.

The goverment's family planning policy during this period was exceedingly unpopular and it was the major cause of a shift away from what had previously been the established voting pattern of the village. Up until the Emergency the village had voted Congress with the exception of a minority of *Jan Sangh* supporters. As was quite typical in U.P., the dominant political power structure in the area was a coalition of Congress land-owners and officials, mostly

Thakurs, and in the past these had no difficulty in delivering the local vote, including the Palanpur vote, to the Congress candidate. With the election called by Mrs Gandhi for March 1977 all this changed and the votes of the village went overwhelmingly to the Opposition. As might be expected, all kinds of reasons were given for this change in the established voting pattern but everyone agreed that the chief reason was the detestation felt by the villagers for the policy of compulsory sterilization. Mrs Gandhi retained her popularity with some *Jatabs*–she had taken some pains to attract support from the lowest groups.

The list of changes could be extended to include some further minor ones. Some housebuilding that we had seen started had now been completed (this was in the *Thakur* quarter); and quite a number of trees had been cut down close to the grazing area beside the village. These changes, small in themselves, illustrate an important point. An Indian village seems on first acquaintance to be timeless and unchanging. In particular, mud and dust have a way of making everything appear to be very old and a great deal of what is going on looks as though it has, and in many cases it may have, been going on for centuries. But there is another side to that picture. Things do change, usually slowly, but nevertheless importantly and a revisit to a village after an interval of two years serves to underline this point. The market is so quaint and colourful that one might be forgiven for supposing that it was established long ago and hallowed by tradition. The newly constructed *pucca* extension to a house is constructed by exactly the same methods and with the same materials that served for the other *pucca* houses in the village. Once the plaster is on it, and some painted decoration has been applied, and the usual overlay of dirt and dust has accumulated, one cannot easily distinguish the new from the old; yet one is less than two years old.

We shall return in § 10.4 to a consideration of the question of how amenable a rural village like Palanpur is to change and evolution. But it should already be clear that one could not characterize the village as an institution proof against change and development. Palanpur has seen a lot of changes in its agriculture and land-ownership since Independence and even a short interval of a couple of years provides instances of small but significant developments.

§ 10.2 Interviews

The questions which formed the basis for the interviews of the revisit of August 1977 were all ones that had arisen in our study of our data or from the presentation of some preliminary findings at seminars. The questions fell into two categories. In some cases we were merely wanting to confirm that a view which we had previously formed was correct by turning into a direct question what had been an impression or an observation. All our questions concerning caste and its role in the village fell into this category. In other cases we wanted to extend our knowledge a little by making the subject of explicit discussion what had previously not been so treated. The question on the respondent's decision concerning the amount of sugar cane he grew was of this second type. Naturally the distinction is not always clear-cut.

As with the discussions with the cultivators of sample wheat plots which were described in § 4.7 and § 8.5, so in this case, the list of questions was only a guide to our discussion which was generally informal and relaxed. If a question proved not to be successful we dropped it. The questions and the responses to them will be presented according to subject matter and not strictly in accord with the order in which we happened to ask them.

The impression of the operation of the caste system in Palanpur that we had brought away from the village was to all intents and purposes that which is contained in the description of caste relations of Chapter 2 (§ 2.1). However, this description caused surprise to some people, particularly our assertion that it was difficult to rank the different castes clearly and unambiguously. It was suggested to us that the problem of ranking castes might be solved by a close observation of the exchange of food (who will and does take food from whom?), by the practices of addressing someone from another caste (who calls whom by his name as opposed to some other title?), and by the roles played by the various castes on ceremonial occasions, such as weddings. Questions on these caste issues were included in our interviews and we asked each respondent to give his own ranking of the castes within the village. These discussions were very interesting and also reassuring, but there is no point to reporting them in detail because they confirmed the impressions which are already incorporated in Chapter 2. These refined indicators of caste ranking are not useful in Palanpur, and do not help us to a more precise caste ranking than that at which we had already arrived.

Another question which served the purpose of confirming what we had already thought was concerned with payments at marriage. We wanted to know whether the practice of paying dowries, which we knew to be the usual one in the village, was in fact universal. To this end we asked our respondents whether they (meaning their caste) paid dowries or bride prices. The dowry was, indeed, by far the most usual arrangement. However, some of our respondents had heard of bride prices. A Muslim, a *Teli*, told an interesting story.

In the nearby village of Bhoori, three years ago, there was a boy called Faryad. A girl came to the village to visit relatives and this boy fell in love with her and wanted to marry her. The girl's father, no doubt mindful of his bargaining position, demanded R 500 which were paid.

The strong opinion of our respondents was that land is very rarely sold to pay dowries.

Our other questions were concerned with agricultural matters. The following were asked to each respondent. In addition some other questions surrounding these areas were asked selectively according to whether additional discussion seemed likely to be useful.

1.　Are you growing sugar now; if not why not, and if yes, would you like to grow more and what stops you from growing more?
2.　Have you heard of bullocks being hired-out to do ploughing in this (other) village(s)? If yes, give details where known.

3.   How do landlords decide which land to lease-out?
4.   How easy is it to get a private loan for agricultural purposes, in particular the purchase of fertilizer?

These were important questions which were in our minds because our study of the data from the 1974–5 seasons had raised them. Thus, to take an example, our interest in question 4 arose because of the finding, reported in § 8.4, that marginal value products for some inputs, and notably fertilizer, were far in excess of the prices of those inputs.

We selected fifteen farmers for interview. We chose those we knew would make interesting respondents in the light of their personalities or situations. We took care to achieve a balance of caste and land-ownership in our 'sample' but the choice of the exact men to be interviewed was casual and not according to any principles that could be written down. Nevertheless, these farmers roughly represent a cross-section of the village.

Of our fifteen respondents all but two were growing sugar cane on at least part of their land. One of those who was not growing sugar had no land at all, and the other claimed that he was too short of capital to grow cane. Lack of capital was the most commonly mentioned reason for not increasing the area under cane. There were grumbles about the operation of the 'ticket' system whereby a farmer could gain access to the government mill. But most respondents seemed to think that one could get more tickets if one were willing to commit more resources to sugar cane. Several answers could be interpreted as a preference for diversification and not putting too many resources exclusively into this one crop. Others mentioned lack of credit which was not at first sight consistent with the majority view concerning the answer to question 4.

On the hiring of bullocks there was a marked lack of unanimity. The answers to the question of whether bullocks were hired in the village broke down as follows:

Yes	No	Rarely
7	6	2

where those who had never heard of the practice are counted as 'Nos'. However, the inconsistency is not as sharp as might appear, because even those who had heard of examples, or were involved in such transactions, agreed that the practice was unusual. Those who had heard of examples gave different prices and all were agreed that only small parcels of land could be ploughed in this manner, and that there was a difficulty in getting the timing right if one had to rely on someone else. This no doubt explains the sometimes added remark that farmers would not lease land to people who had to rely on the hire of bullocks.

In asking question 3 we were interested (see above, Chapter 5, p.130) to see how many respondents would volunteer the view that farmers tended to lease-out their worst land. Eight did so, but some others remarked that if a farmer were leasing-out all his land, as was one of our respondents, then tenants would get whatever he had. This question did not prove to be particularly interesting in terms of the discussion into which it led.

In contrast, the answers to question 4 were fascinating. On the question of whether it was possible to obtain a private loan for an agricultural purpose, the answers broke down as follows:

Possible	Possible but difficult	Possible only with security	Impossible
8	1	1	2

The remaining three answers could not be classified. Two respondents said that they did not borrow and 'were against it', thus by-passing the question. A farmer involved heavily in money-lending found the topic too embarrassing to discuss.

Of the eight respondents who thought that money could be borrowed for agricultural purposes, several had actually done so. The two who said it was impossible were both *Jatabs*. These are in a special category because the law prohibits loans to *Jatabs* (to protect them from exploitation) and the lender could not recover a loan at law.

The most interesting questions in these interview sessions were those concerning bullocks and credit. The absence of a market for the hire of the services of bullocks was mostly confirmed but asking people explicitly about the matter brought to our attention the existence of a marginal market in which small-scale demands can be catered for. The inadequacies of that market for those who might be tempted to rely on it exclusively were brought out clearly in our discussion.

The balance of opinion and experience seem to be on the side of the view that there is money to be borrowed from private sources when the Co-operative Union will lend no more. Of course this is not to say that a great deal more could be borrowed than is already being borrowed but it does seem inaccurate to think of the farmers of Palanpur as typically facing unyielding credit constraints. That they do not attempt to commit more resources to agriculture must then reflect an unwillingness to change established practices, undertake risk, or whatever.

§ 10.3 Implications for Policy

None of the points that we are going to discuss in this section will seem surprising to students of India and Indian agriculture. However, while the policy implications are not, taken one at a time, novel, we think it interesting to note which particular conclusions for policy seem to stand out from our studies.

We should begin by bringing the reader's attention to the great diversity of practice which our investigations have revealed. This can be seen particularly clearly in the case of the sample wheat plot study (see § 7.3). As we noted in Chapter 7, all our farmers were departing considerably from official 'best practices' for the growing of wheat and the same would be the case with other crops. But in the case of some farmers this departure was much more marked than was the case with others. As we remarked in the previous chapter, there are many reasons which might account for these differences between the manner in which different farmers organize their agriculture. Size of holding is quite likely an important reason, as it correlates with wealth, and there are no doubt many other reasons to do with economic status and social psychology. Nevertheless, we are not inclined to underrate the importance of ignorance. We have found clear evidence of ignorance in certain practices which were common on the sample wheat plots, such as planting the seeds too deep. Many farmers have not shown themselves willing to seek out knowledge from their fellow-villagers, although one could learn a lot from talking to and observing what the most successful farmers in the village do.

Because there is great scope for improvement, it is tempting to say that it would be a good idea if there were more effective extension services that would bring the knowledge of better practices to a wider range of farmers than have received that knowledge to date. We believe that such services have been under-manned, and in particular that not enough effort has gone into making them effective, but the problems should not be underestimated.

First, and obviously, the institution of caste is inimical to the free flow and exchange of ideas. Extension officers are going typically to be of higher caste for a long time to come and they are likely to feel satisfied with what they are doing if they help the higher-caste farmers in the villages to do better. If they feel that the lower castes are to some extent beyond help, they would not find it difficult to point to examples which supported that view. On the other side, the lower castes respond to the higher with deference and mistrust and they in turn could point to examples of behaviour which would fully justify their suspicion.

Second, these problems could be surmounted if there were sufficient hunger for the knowledge of better practices on the part of a wider range of farmers: but often it simply is not there. This is to a considerable extent a cultural matter. The ideal that what another farmer is doing in his field next to one's own, is something that one could do oneself if one knew how, and that therefore it would be a good idea to find out how to do what he is doing, is not one that can be assumed. Indeed it sits unhappily with old traditions of doing what one's forefathers have always done with resignation and fatalism. No doubt pride is importantly involved. Farmers can be proud and may not like to confess that they have a lot to learn. Then again, it may be that only some people qualify as models and a man who would readily copy his brother will not do the same where it is a farmer of another caste. Finally, people may fear change; they see it yield good results, but who knows what risks are attendant upon it which may not be obvious?

These are familiar reasons for supposing that the problem of agricultural extension in village India is a formidable one. However, we are not inclined to dismiss the task as hopeless and there is no real evidence that it is. Substantial and serious agricultural extension giving real attention to the problems of small-scale and poorly educated farmers has hardly begun in the Moradabad District, at least in and around Palanpur. No doubt the resources are scarce at this time but if they could be found there is plenty of scope for their application.

Nevertheless, something else is needed in parallel and here we should point to the important influence which education seems to play. The returns to education are often denigrated. However, it is striking in Palanpur that nearly all the farmers who have been in the forefront of experiment and advance have received much more education than is usual for the village. We do not think that this is particularly because they have learnt a great deal about agriculture from their training. But more generally it seems to us that education can open up people's minds to new possibilities. In so doing it can undermine tradition and fatalism.

Again, it is not trivial to get education to the whole of a socially backward village. We have seen above § 2.A.2, that the participation of the various castes of Palanpur even in the Primary School was very uneven. And the Secondary High School drew its students almost exclusively from the high castes. Yet this problem seems to be essential. Without changes in cultural awareness we doubt whether reforms to advice and extension services will enable them to reach everyone.

Since we have stressed the importance of uncertainty at several points, it makes sense now to look at what implications it has for policy. We are not inclined to suggest that there is much to be gained from crop insurance. In principle it has something to offer but the administrative problems and the problems of 'moral hazard' are enormous. Better would be to improve the provision of credit on the lines of that already advanced by the Co-operative Credit Union through the Seed Store. As we have argued, it is not that credit is unavailable elsewhere, but rather that risk aversion deters farmers from undertaking to borrow from the other sources. The great popularity of the Seed Store credit is not to be wholly explained by its cost. Its attraction also lies in the possibility open to the farmer to roll over the loan if his harvest is poor, and that he does not need to put his land at risk. This is critical and we should speculate that the high 'take-up' of Seed Store credit is to be explained by the lower risk of forced sale of land that attaches to its use.

Next we should draw the reader's attention to the obvious implication of our finding, that there is great scope, at a relatively low cost, to improve the quality of seed used by the farmers of Palanpur. Clearly many farmers for some time to come are going to use as seed whatever the Seed Store provides, this partly for convenience and partly because of the credit terms that can be used where the Seed Store is the source. In this case it is unfortunate that the seed dispensed by the Seed Store is of such poor quality.

Finally we note that our findings have some implications for the question of the consequences of land reform. Land reform has often been advocated as a means to achieving a more equitable distribution of income and economic power. But an even stronger claim for it has sometimes been advanced, namely that it would simultaneously achieve an increase in total output bcause productivity per acre is higher on small than on large farms. In this case, so it is argued, there is no conflict between productivity and equity; a redistribution of land from large holders to small holders would improve both at one stroke.

It is notable that the results of our investigations reported in Chapter 6 fail to lend support to this view. We have not found a significant relation between farm size and output per acre; our findings are not inconsistent with constant returns to scale. Hence, for Palanpur at least, we would tentatively suggest that land reform should be evaluated on the basis of what it has to offer by way of improved distribution of income. There it does in principle have much to offer for, as we have noted, the distribution of land holdings in the village is quite uneven. It is true that the distribution of income is less uneven, but this is only what one would expect, for the distribution of wealth is usually more uneven than the distribution of income. In one way at least the distribution of land (as a proxy for wealth) is a better measure of the distribution of welfare than is income, because households with no land, or only a small holding, are insecure and have to sweat and labour to obtain their income more than do households with plenty of land.

It would be naive to suppose that the case for land reform is completed by the demonstration that it could, if put into effect, improve the distribution of income. There are considerable and obvious administrative problems, which even the land reforms which India has already attempted have served to highlight. Attempts to take away land from large holders would meet with steadfast resistance, through manipulation of the law, through corruption, and possibly in the limit through fighting to resist this change. It would, therefore, require a single-minded commitment from the authorities and the allocation of large resources in terms of the time of administrators and others. Whether such a policy would be a good idea is a large question involving grand political issues which a small-scale village study can hardly hope to resolve.

Another argument for land reform is that it tends to remove the need for tenancy, which would be a good idea were tenancy inefficient. This is the theoretical side to the 'land-to-the-tiller' argument. Our study has not provided impressive support for the inefficiencies inherent in share-cropping tenancy and we should wish to separate land redistribution, which in principle is a valuable policy, from the prohibition of tenancy *per se* which seems to us likely to be counter-productive. Indeed it is an implication of the account of tenancy which we gave in Chapter 5 that it serves a useful function where markets other than the market for leased-in land do not function well.

An important implication of the concentration of land-ownership is for innovation. While sometimes large land holdings can encourage farmers to take agriculture seriously and undertake efficient large-scale farming, the opposite response seems just as possible. A large land holding can be the basis merely for a comfortable and easy life, sitting back and letting the rents from a traditional method of cultivation roll in. Within the somewhat narrow range of cases in Palanpur one observes among the large land-owners examples which approximate to both types of response.

None of our conclusions for policy is a panacea and some of them would demand great effort and the employment of scarce personnel if they were to be implemented. However, we shall argue in the next section that there are going to be forces in favour of change in the village in the future, largely as a result of population growth, and in this case policies which would help farmers to adapt to their need for greater productivity may show a better response in the future than one might expect on today's experience.

§ 10.4 The Village in the Future

The present rate of population growth in Palanpur is quite rapid and there is no reason to think that it will fall in the very near future. If it did, that would itself be a substantial change. It seems that population pressure has not been an overwhelming problem in the past: the village has managed to adapt by undertaking some relatively simple alterations in practice, notably by moving over to double-cropping. The changeover to double-cropping, which followed upon the introduction of increased irrigation into the village, is itself a strong example of how the village can adapt, rapidly and decisively when an opportunity presents itself. Continued population growth will call for further adaptation; the question is: what form will that adaptation take next?

We do not rule out the possibility that the rate of population growth will come down. Birth rates in many Third World countries have recently fallen despite confident predictions that this could not happen until the next century. The villagers' detestation of sterilization which manifested itself during the Emergency is not evidence of a rejection of contraception as such.

However, we think that a slow-down in the rate of increase of the population is likely not to be the only adjustment because there are others available. The two major possibilities are improvements in agricultural practices and migration to employment outside the village.

To take the latter possibility first, we doubt that there will be great scope for Palanpur to solve its population problems by migration. The difficulty is for the migrants to obtain jobs. Without claiming a detailed knowledge of employment opportunities outside the village, we note that the villagers seem to have done quite well in obtaining jobs in towns within reach of the village. This may be because the proximity to the railway line makes it easier for them to commute than it would be for the inhabitants of other villages. But note also that many of the employees in these outside jobs are young men intending to return to agriculture when they marry and settle down. We suppose that employment at a distance is less attractive. With population pressure it may become unavoidable. Not all villagers in U.P. are going to be able to solve their population problems by means of out-migration because employment outside agriculture is not going to increase fast enough to make that possible. So there is going to have to be an absorption of labour into agriculture and that raises the next question: what can that labour do and how can it be fed?

The two questions are connected but somewhat separate. Any improvement in agricultural practices and in the intensity of cultivation will help to feed the growing labour force. Such improvements will in some cases require the application of more labour while in other cases they will not. To take two examples, the use of better seed requires little extra labour (probably none at all if the Seed Store were to provide it).On the other hand, switching over to higher-value crops, for example rice in place of *bajra,* involves an increased application of labour. We should expect this last example to be rather important in the future if population pressure continues to be a critical factor. The village's over-all cropping pattern may be varied and it reflects the decisions of the farmers in the light of their circumstances, needs, and resources. As the latter change, particularly under pressure from population growth, so will the farmers' choices of cropping patterns.In the light of past experience there is no reason at all to suppose that this type of adaptation will not take place.

What is certain is that the future will demand various adaptations from the households of Palanpur. We should expect that most will adapt but some will certainly do so slowly. This uneven adaptation may be an important source of inequality as measured in Palanpur and for this reason one might expect an increase in inequality in the future. Another reason for expecting the same outcome is that population growth will probably make labour less productive at the margin, and land more productive, than is presently the case. This will tend to push the distribution of income more in the direction of the distribution of land-ownership, which distribution is more unequal than the present distribution of income. The tendency could be overcome by technical progress of the land-augmenting variety. Palanpur has seen a lot of that type of technical progress in the past, notably through the introduction of double-cropping. At a guess there will be less in the future, but that is a guess that could easily be proved false.

We should expect the trend towards improved education to continue and perhaps to percolate down to more castes. Population pressure is likely to make more households interested in getting jobs outside the village and for such jobs an education is an important entry ticket. It will be interesting to see whether more girls start to participate in secondary education. There were three girls in the Secondary High School in 1974-5 but these were all from one household, the *ex-zamindar's* household at Chandorra village, and as such represent only a particular decision of one head of household.

Eventually, unless agriculture is to see much more technical progress than presently seems likely, and still assuming that out-migration is going to be limited by a lack of job opportunities, there will have to be a fall in the birth rate if there is not to be fall in the living standards of the population. Generally we believe that when the time comes at which the villagers want this they will achieve it, and that time may not be very far away. The lack of family planning in the village today reflects, we suggest, the fact that the villagers have not been unhappy with the family sizes that they have achieved.

These speculations about the future of Palanpur are an appropriate point at which to bring our argument to a close. In so doing we remark that the task of predicting the future of the village, which is inherently extremely difficult whatever information one has to hand, would be easier if we knew more about the village as we found it in 1974-5. Despite the fact we have offered lengthy and detailed description and analysis of many aspects of the village there remain considerable gaps. Three in particular stand out.

The choice of cropping pattern seems to us to be a very important decision. Our data bear on it and we have remarked on its likely role at more than one point. But it deserves more analysis than we have so far been able to give it and we hope to make it the subject of future research using our present data base. Secondly, we were disqualified by virtue of the short-term nature of our project, and also on account of the demands on our resources from the collection of the data which we did assemble, from investigating long-term decisions, how they are taken, and the comparison between beliefs about outcomes and the actual outcomes. Among these is the demographic decision, the choice of family size. We know much less about migration than we should ideally know and not enough about farmers' perceptions concerning opportunities for their sons outside the village now and in the future. Finally, there is room for more research on tenancy than we were able to undertake. We believe that a close study of cultivation patterns on tenanted and untenanted plots would be fruitful, as would cross-section and time-series analyses of the detail of tenancy contracts, but these would imply the collection of data that we were not able to assemble.

However, every study must draw its boundaries somewhere. People have sometimes remarked to us: 'How can a study based on one village teach us anything?' The remark is pertinent only if it were supposed that we are proposing generalizations for village India. We do not presume to do that. If what we have done seems interesting then it will have to be tested out elsewhere; taken alone it could only be suggestive. Nevertheless, we think that it is usefully suggestive. The intensive study of one village is an important testing ground for theories of rural development.

Glossary

Note: The Glossary gives meanings of Hindi words employed in the text, of abbreviations, and of some technical terms. As English has distinctly different sounds from Hindi, the rendering of Hindi words in the Roman script gives a poor idea of how they should be sounded. We have, however, adopted local usage even when an alternative spelling might give a better idea of how the word is pronounced. Definitions of regression variables may be found in Tables 5.5 (p.152), Table 6.3 (p.179), and Table 8.1 (p.255).

ADO	Assistant Development Officer. An official responsible for carrying out various duties under the Block Development Officer, including allocation of seed and fertilizer within the Block.
AERC	Agricultural Economic Research Centre of the University of Delhi.
Arher	A ten-month crop, known in English as the pigeon pea or red gram. It is eaten as *dal* (lentil). It is grown alone or in combination with *bajra*.
Bajra	A *kharif* crop, a millet which grows well in sandy soils. The grain is made into flour.
Bania	The name of a caste, whose occupation is merchant or shopkeeper: hence, a shopkeeper.
Bargujar	A sub-caste of *Thakurs*. There was one household in Palanpur belonging to this sub-caste.
BDO	Block Development Officer, the Official charged with the administration of government economic policies: distribution of seeds and fertilizers, and so on, at the Block level.
Bhathagar	A sub-caste of the *Passis*.
Bhumidar	A tenant who owns land in his own right and can sell it if he wishes. Under the *zamindari* abolition acts, tenants of the *zamindars* became *sirdars*, tenants of the state, but they could convert to *bhumidhari* status on payment of ten times land revenue.
Biddies	Simple cigarettes made from tobacco rolled in a leaf.
Bigha	A local unit of land area. In the past the size of a *bigha* varied with the quality of the land and this is still the case where land ceilings are concerned. However, even today, a *bigha* may represent more land in one region than it does in another. In Palanpur there are 6.4 *bighas* to one acre.
Block	An administrative sub-division of a District, at one time intended to contain roughly 100,000 persons.
Brahmin	One of the highest of the Hindu caste divisions. The *Brahmins* are priests and teachers and often cooks in city houses.
Cane Development Society	The organization responsible for the collection and processing of sugarcane. To have his cane accepted by the mill, the farmer must have had an allocation of an area on which the cane grown will be accepted at the mill.
Chamar	A sub-group of the untouchables. The *Chamars* are leather workers and rank very low, higher only than the Sweepers. In Palanpur the *Chamars* have adopted the name *Jatab* which is a rather more prestigious title.
Chapatis	Bread made from a round lump of unleavened flour rolled out into the shape of a pancake.

Collector	Magistrate and head of the civil service in a District.
Congress	The party that was in power in India during the time of the study, under the leadership of the then Prime Minister Mrs. Indira Gandhi.
Co-operative Union Seed Store.	The full title of the organization which operated from the Seed Store in Palanpur. For a description of its activities, see p.40.
Dacoit	Robber or bandit.
Desi	Country, hence local or traditional.
Development Officer (Block)	see BDO.
Dhimar	A service group in Hindu society. The *Dhimars* are water carriers.
Dhobi	A service group in Hindu society. The *Dhobis* are washermen; hence *Dhobi* also means washerman. The Palanpur *Dhobis* are Muslim.
District Co-operative Bank	A government bank which lends money to farmers for agricultural purposes.
Gadaria	A service group in Hindu society. The *Gadarias* are shepherds or goatherds.
Ghur	A mixture of sugar and molasses, produced by boiling sugar cane juice in an open pan until it is reduced to a brown treacly residue.
Gini Coefficient	A numerical representation of inequality in, for example, the distribution of income. The coefficient is 1.0 for complete equality and 0 for 'complete inequality'. For the mathematical formula for the coefficient, see p.207.
Gram	A *rabi* crop, it provides a source of vegetable protein and increases soil fertility, as it fixes nitrogen. It is often grown intermixed with other crops, such as wheat.
Haldia	Grower of turmeric, a spice frequently employed in Indian cooking.
Harijan	Mahatma Gandhi's name for the untouchables; it means 'people of God'.
HYVP	The High-Yielding Varieties Programme, see p.225.
IBRD	International Bank for Reconstruction and Development.
IDS	Institute of Development Studies of the University of Sussex, England.
IFFCO	Indian Farmers' Fertilizer Co-operative Ltd.
ISI	Indian Statistical Institute.
Jan Sangh	An aggressively Hindu political party; merged with the Janata party since 1977.
Jatab	The main body of *Harijans* or untouchables in Palanpur use this title to describe themselves. See also *Chamar*. It can be spelt *Jatav*.
Jowar	A *kharif* crop. It provides an edible grain, and plentiful fodder.
Khatheria	A *Thakur* sub-caste.
Kharif	The summer crop, see p.26
Khasta	A plot of land.
Krishna	One of the human incarnations of the Hindu deity *Vishnu*.
Kshatriyas	The second ranking in the Hindu four-tier arrangement of people. The *Kshatriyas* are warriors and in their own eyes they stand above all other castes.

Kucca	Rough or unmade, the opposite of *pucca*.
Lahi	Early mustard.
Lakh	A Hindi measure of quantity. One *lakh* is 100,000 units.
LDB	The Land Development Bank, see p.107.
Mali	A caste in a village close to Palanpur, normally gardeners.
Maund	A traditional unit of weight, 40 kg.
Menna	A caste in a village close to Palanpur.
Moghuls	The name for the last of the Muslim rulers of India. They ruled North and Central India from the sixteenth century until defeated by the Marakta in Central India and other rajas in the Provinces.
Moong	A pulse grown after the *rabi* harvest and before the *kharif* sowing, also during the *kharif* season.
Murao	A sub-group of the *Sudras*. They are vegetable growers and among the *Sudras* they are of high status.
Paisa (e)	A unit of monetary value. One hundred *paise* equal one *rupee*.
Panchayat	Hindi word meaning, roughly, committee of arbitrators. The village *panchayat* would settle intra-village disputes; a caste *panchayat* would settle disputes within a caste.
Parsees	Zorastur's followers who escaped from Persia, mostly to be found in Western India, numbering about 100,000.
Passi	One of the low-status groups of Palanpur. They were once migrants from East U.P. On their history and their ranking among the Palanpur castes, see p.37.
Patwari	Village Official: accountant and land record keeper.
Pucca	Of a house or building, constructed of brick not mud. Hence, by extension, 'cooked' not 'raw', well-made, proper, or correct.
Purabi	The name given to its caste grouping by one of the Palanpur households. Apparently it is a sub-division of the *Passis*.
Rabi	Winter crop or, see p.26.
Raj	Literally, rule, hence sometimes the government of India by the British.
Raja	Ruler
RBS College, Agra	Raja Balwant Singh College (ex B.R. College), Agra.
RR21	A variety of wheat, the RR stands for rust resistant. For a description of the characteristics of the variety, see § 7.1.1.
Rupee	The basic unit of currency in India. At the time of the study, one pound sterling was worth about 18.5 *rupees*.
Scheduled Castes	The groups mentioned in the Constitution of India as meriting particular favour in view of their oppressed position. The untouchable groups are included, but also tribals.
Seed Store	The Co-operative Union Seed Store, located in Palanpur, including all the activities run from that building, provision of seed, fertilizer, credit, and so on.
Sirdar	Tenant of the State. See under *Bhumidhar*.
SOAS	School of Oriental and African Studies, University of London, England.
SPSS	*Statistical Package for the Social Sciences,* University of Pittsburgh. Regression package employed in analysing the data.
Sudra	A member of the fourth tier in the Hindu ranking of people. The *Sudras* are labourers and service groups of various kinds.

Tehsil	Administrative area, a sub-division of the District.
Teli	A sub-group of the *Sudras,* they are oil-pressers. The Palanpur *Telis* are Muslims.
Thakur	A high caste. The *Thakurs* are *Kshatriyas,* traditionally warriors. The same people are known as *Rajputs* in other parts of India.
Tomor	A *Thakur* sub-caste.
UNDP	United Nations Development Programmes.
UNRISD	United Nations Research Institute for Social Development. The Global 2 Project sponsored by that institute included studies of the impact of high-yielding varieties of food grains.
U.P.	*Uttar Pradesh,* the United Provinces, the name of the North Indian State formed from the old provinces of Agra and Oudh.
Urd	A *kharif* crop, a pulse, whole black beans.
Yadav	The name of a caste in a village close to Palanpur, very likely a similar group to the *Rajputs* (*Kshatriyas*).
Zamindar	An hereditary agent who held land, paid revenue to the government of the Moghuls and later the British, and acted as an intermediary between the authorities and the cultivators of the soil.

References

Anand, S. (1978) 'Inequality and poverty in Malaysia: measurement and decomposition', mimeo, D. Phil., Oxford University.

Ansari, Nasim (1964) *Continuous Village Surveys*, No. 41, Palanpur: Moradabad: U.P.. Agricultural Economics Research Centre, University of Delhi, India.

Arrow, K.J. (1970) *Essays in the Theory of Risk-bearing*, Markham, Chicago; North-Holland, London.

Atkinson, A.B. (1970) 'On the measurement of inequality', *Journal of Economic Theory*, Vol. 2., pp. 244 – 63.

Baden-Powell, B.H. (1892) *The Land Systems of British India*, Vols. 1 & 2 Clarendon Press, Oxford.

Bardhan, P.K. (1973) 'Size, productivity and returns to scale in Indian agriculture', *Journal of Political Economy*, Nov. – Dec., pp. 1370 – 86.

_____ (1976) 'Variations in extent and forms of agricultural tenancy', *Economic and Political Weekly*, 18 September 1976, pp. 1541 – 7.

____ (1977) 'Variations in forms of tenancy in a peasant economy', *Journal of Development Economics*, June, pp. 105 – 18.

_____ and Rudra, A. (1977) 'On the interlinkage of land labour and credit relations in agriculture: an analysis of village survey data in East India', Mimeo, University of California, Berkeley.

____ and Srinivasan, T.N. (1971) 'Crop sharing tenancy in agriculture: a theoretical and empirical analysis', *American Economic Review*, March, Vol. 61, pp. 48 – 64.

Bell, C.L.G. (1975) 'Technological change, output and distribution in a land scarce agricultural economy', D.Phil., University of Sussex.

_____ (1977) 'Alternative theories of share-cropping: some tests using evidence from North-East India', *Journal of Development Studies*, Vol. 13, No. 4, July, pp. 317 – 46.

____ and Zusman, P. (1976) 'A bargaining theoretic approach to cropsharing contracts', *American Economic Review*, Sept., Vol. 66, pp. 578 – 88.

_____ (1977) 'Sharecropping equilibria with diverse tenants', Development Research Centre of the IBRD, June.

_____ (1978) 'Contracts for sharing output, cost and risk: a bargaining theoretic approach', Development Research Centre of the IBRD, mimeo, September.

Bhaduri, A. (1973) 'Agricultural backwardness under semi-feudalism', *Economic Journal*, March, Vol. 83, pp. 120 – 37.

Bhagwati, J.N. and Chakravarty, S. (1969) 'Contributions to Indian economic analysis: a survey', *American Economic Review*, Sept., Supplement, pp. 1 – 73.

Bharadwaj, K. (1974) *Production Conditions in Indian Agriculture*, Cambridge University Press.

Bhattacharjee, J.P. (1947) 'Cost of production and size of farms in West Bengal', *Indian Journal of Agricultural Economics*, Vol. 2, No. 2.

Bliss, C.J. and Stern, N.H. (1978) 'Productivity, wages and nutrition: Part I, the theory' and 'Part II, some observations', *Journal of Development Economics*, Vol. 5, No. 4, December, pp. 331 – 62 and 363 – 98.

Bulletin on Wheat Statistics in India, Directorate of Economics and Statistics, Ministry of Agriculture, Government of India, 1972.

Carruthers, I.D. (1968) 'Irrigation development planning: aspects of Pakistan experience', *Agrarian Development Studies*, Report No. 2, Economics Department, Wye College, Ashford, Kent.

Chaudhari, A.K. and Sirohi, A.S. (1973) 'Allocation of fertilizers amongst crops and regions in U.P.', *Indian Journal of Agricultural Economics*, Vol. 28, No. 3, July – Sept, pp. 46 – 60.

Chayanov, A.V. (1966) *The Theory of Peasant Economy*, Richard D. Irwin, Inc., Homewood, Illinois.

Chennareddy, V. (1967) 'Production efficiency in South Indian agriculture', *Journal of Farm Economics*, Vol. 49, No.4, November, pp. 816 – 20.

Cheung, S.N.S. (1969) *The Theory of Share Tenancy*, University of Chicago Press.

Cohn, B.S. (1959) 'Madophur revisited', *Economic Weekly*, Special Issue, July.

Debreu, G. (1957) *The Theory of Value; An Axiomatic Analysis of Economic Equilibrium*, Wiley, New York.

Etienne, G. (1968) *Studies in Indian Agriculture: The Art of the Possible*, University of California Press.

FAO – WHO (1973) *Energy and Protein Requirements*, Report of a joint FAO – WHO *Ad Hoc* Expert Committee, FAO, Rome.

Fertiliser Handbook (1973) Fertiliser Association of India, New Delhi.

Gill, K.S. (1974) *Research on wheat and triticale in the Punjab*, Department of Plant Breeding, Punjab Agricultural University, Ludhiana.

Griffin, K.B. (1974) *The Political Economy of Agrarian Change*, Macmillan, London.

Hammond, P.J (1977) 'The irrelevancy of share contracts', University of Essex Discussion Paper.

Hausman, J.A. (1978) 'Specification tests in econometrics', *Econometrica*, Vol. 46, No. 6, November, pp. 1251 – 72.

_____ and Wise, D.A. (1976) 'Evaluation of results from truncated samples: the New Jersey income maintenance experiment', *Annals of Economic and Social Measurement*, 6, pp. 421 – 45.

Higgs, H. (1894) 'Metayage in ancient France', *Economic Journal*, Vol. IV, pp. 1 – 13.

Hirschman, A. (1958) *The Strategy of Economic Development*, Yale University Press, New Haven.

Hoel, P.G. (1954) *Introduction to Mathematical Statistics*, Wiley, New York.

Hopper, W.D. (1965) 'Allocation efficiency in "traditional Indian agriculture"', *Journal of Farm Economics*, Vol. 47, August, pp. 611 – 24.

ICAR (1962) *Rust Resistance*, Indian Council for Agricultural Research, New Delhi.

_____ (1968) *Wheat Varieties in India*, Indian Council for Agricultural Research, New Delhi.

_____ (1969) *Handbook of Agriculture*, Indian Council for Agricultural Research, New Delhi.

Junankar, P.N. (1976) 'Land tenure and Indian agricultural productivity', *Journal of Development Studies*, October, pp. 42 – 60.

Kendall, M.G. and Stuart, A. (1969) *The Advanced Theory of Statistics*, 3rd edn., Vol. 1 (1969), Vol. 2 (1973), and Vol. 3 (1976), Griffin, London.

Khusro, A.M. (1972) 'Agriculture as business', *The Illustrated Weekly of India*, 13 February.

_____ (1973) *The Economics of Land Reform and Farm Size in India*, Macmillan (India).

Kohli, S.P. (1968) *Wheat Varieties in India*, Indian Council for Agricultural Research, New Delhi.

Koopmans, T.C. (1957) *Three Essays on the State of Economic Science*, McGraw-Hill.

Kutcher, G.D. and Scandizzo, P.L. (1976) 'A partial analysis of share tenancy relationships in North-East Brazil, *Journal of Development Economics*, 3, pp. 343 – 54.

Ladejinsky, W. (1977) *Agrarian Reform as Unfinished Business, The selected Papers of Wolf Ladejinsky (edited by L.J. Walinsky)*, Oxford University Press.

Leibenstein, H. (1957) *Economic Backwardness and Economic Growth*, Wiley. .

Lewis, W.A. (1955) *The Theory of Economic Growth*, George Allen and Unwin, London.

Lipton, M. (1968) 'The theory of the optimizing peasant', *Journal of Development Studies*, Vol. 4, No. 3, April, pp. 327 – 51.

Ludhiana (1974) *Package of Practices for* Rabi *Crops of Punjab*, Punjab Agricultural University, Ludhiana.

Marriot, McKim (1965) *Caste Ranking and Community Structure in Five Regions of India and Pakistan*, Poona.

Marshall, A. (1959) *Principles of Economics*, 8th edn., Macmillan, London.

Mirrlees, J.A. (1976) 'A pure theory of under-developed economies', in L. Reynolds (ed.), *Agriculture in Development Theory*, Yale University Press.

Moore, C.V. (1961) 'A general analytical frame-work for estimating the production function for crops using irrigation water', *Journal of Farm Economics*, Vol. 43, No. 4, pp. 876 – 80.

Muellbauer, J. (1974) 'Inequality measures, prices and household composition', *Review of Economic Studies*, XLI (4), No. 128, pp. 493 – 504.

Myrdal G. (1968) *Asian Drama: An Enquiry into the Poverty of Nations*, Allen Lane, Vol. 3.

Neale, Walter C. (1962) *Economic change in rural India: Land tenures and land reform in Uttar Pradesh 1800 – 1955*, Yale Studies in Economy (12), New Haven.

Newbery, D.M.G. (1977) 'Risk sharing, share-cropping and uncertain labour markets', *Review of Economic Studies*, Vol. XLIV (3), No. 138, pp. 585 – 94.

Nowshirvani, V.F. (1967) 'Allocation efficiency in traditional Indian agriculture: a comment', *Journal of Farm Economics*, Vol. 49, No.1, pp. 218 – 21.

Nurkse, R. (1953) *Problems of Capital Formation in Underdeveloped Countries*, Basil Blackwell, Oxford.

Pantnagar (1974). *Annual Report 1971 – 2: Research in Progress*, Experiment Station, G.B. Pant University of Agriculture and Technology, Pantnagar, U.P.

Pesaran, M.H. (1974) 'On the general problem of model selection', *Review of Economic Studies*, Vol. XLI (2), No.126, pp.153-72.

_____ and Deaton, A.S. (1978) 'Testing non-linear regression models', *Econometrica*, Vol. 46, No. 3, May, pp. 677 – 94.

Rao, C.H.H. (1971) 'Uncertainty, entrepreneurship and sharecropping in India', *Journal of Political Economy*, Vol.79, pp.578-95.

Randhawa, M.S. (1974) *Green Revolution*, Vikas Publishing House, Delhi.

Reid, J (1973) 'Sharecropping as an understandable market response: the post-bellum South', *Journal of Economic History*, 33, March, pp.106 – 30.

_____ (1974) 'Sharecropping in history and theory', mimeo, Department of Economics, University of Pennsylvania, June

_____ (1976) 'Sharecropping and agricultural uncertainty', *Economic Development and Cultural Change*, 24 (3) April, pp.549 – 76.

Roumasset, J.A., Boussard J-M, and Singh, I.J. (eds) (1979) *Risk, Uncertainty and Agricultural Development* S.E.A.R.C.A. and Agricultural Development Council, Laguna/New York

Rudra, A (1968) 'Farm size and yield per acre' *Economic and Political Weekly*, Vol. 3, Special Number, July,pp.1041 – 4.

_____ (1968a) 'More on returns to scale in Indian agriculture', *Economic and Political Weekly*, Review of Agricultural, October, pp. A 33 – 8.

Sahota, G.S. (1968) 'Efficiency of resource allocation in Indian agriculture', *American Journal of Agricultural Economics*, Vol. 50, No. 3, pp. 584 – 605.

Sayana, V.V. (1949) *Sharing and Fixed Tenancy Systems*, Business Week Press, Madras.

Scheffe, H. (1959) *The Analysis of Variance*, Wiley, New York.

Schultz, T.W. (1964) *Transforming Traditional Agriculture*, Yale University Press.

Sen, A.K. (1962) 'An aspect of Indian agriculture' *Economic Weekly*, annual number, vol. 14.

_____ (1964) 'Size of holdings and productivity', *Economic Weekly*, annual number, vol. 16.

_____ (1975) *Employment, Technology and Development*, Oxford University Press.

Singh, Roshan (1973) *The Social and Economic Implication of the Large Scale Introduction of High-Yielding Varieties in Food Grains (Wheat) in Muzzaffarnagar (U.P.)*, Raja Balwant Singh College, Agra, India.

Singh, I.J. and Sharma, K.C. (1968) 'Response of some Mexican Red and Indian Amber wheats to nitrogen', *Indian Journal of Agricultural Economics*, Vol. 23, No. 4, October – December, pp. 86 – 93.

_____ (1969) 'Production functions and economic optima in fertilizer use for some dwarf and tall varieties of wheat', *Research Bulletin* No. 5, U.P. Agricultural University, Pantnagar, Feb.

_____ and Mishra, J.P. (1970) 'Production functions for the new dwarf wheats', *Indian Journal of Agricultural Economics*, Vol. 25, No.1, January – March, pp. 74 – 8.

Srinivasan, T.N. (1972) *'Farm size and productivity: implications of choice under uncertainty'*, Sankhya (Indian Journal of Statistics, Series B), Vol. 34, Part 4, pp. 409 – 20.

_____ (1979) 'Agricultural backwardness under semi-feudalism', *Economic Journal*, Vol. 95, June, pp. 416 – 19.

Stern, N.H. (1977) 'The marginal valuation of income', in M.J. Artis and A.R. Nobay (eds.), *Studies in Modern Economic Analysis*, Basil Blackwell, Oxford.

Stiglitz, J.E. (1969) 'Rural – urban migration, surplus labour, and the relationship between urban and rural wages', *Eastern African Economic Review*, vol. 1, pp. 1 – 28.

_____ (1974) 'Incentives and risk sharing in sharecropping', *Review of Economic Studies*, Vol. XLI (2), No. 126, pp. 219 – 56.

_____ (1976) 'The efficiency wage hypothesis, surplus labour and the distribution of income in L.D.C.s', *Oxford Economic Papers*, Vol. 28, No. 2, June, pp. 185 – 207.

Todaro M.P. (1976) *Internal Migration in Developing Countries: A Review of Theory, Evidence, Methodology and Research Priorities,* International Labour Office, Geneva.

Weeks, J. (1970 – 1) 'Uncertainty, risk and wealth and income distribution in peasant agriculture', *Journal of Development Studies*, Vol. 7, pp. 28 – 36.

Wiesner C.J. (1970) *Climate, Irrigation and Agriculture*, Angus & Robertson, Sydney.

Wiser, William and Charlotte (1971) *Behind Mud Walls*, University of California Press.

Yap, Lorene Y.L. (1977) 'The attraction of cities: a review of the migration literature', *Journal of Development Economics*, Vol. 4, No. 3, September, pp. 239 – 64.

Zellner, A., Kmenta, J., and Dreze, J. (1966) 'Specification and estimation of Cobb – Douglas production function models', *Econometrica*, 34, October 1976, pp. 784 – 95.

Author Index

Subject Index